Penguin Masterstudies

Economics

David Spurl..g is a freelance lecturer
wide variety of institutions – rangin
university extramural department – bu
was at Birmingham Polytechnic.

His earlier career included actuarial w
passenger development work and cos
tical work in several areas, including f
market and surveys of the single he
departments.

His interests include politics; he stoo
constituency and he has been a borou
He has written several textbooks on
including *Discover Business Calculati*
Road Haulage Operators and *Test You*
(C.P.C.) (1985), *Penguin Passnotes: Ec*
GCSE, 1988), *Discover Business a*
Book-keeping and Accounts (1988) an
nomics: A Book of Revision Tests (198

D1347656

Penguin Masterstudies
Advisory Editors:
Stephen Coote and Bryan Loughrey

Economics

David Spurling, BSc, DGA, FCIT, M Inst TA, Cert Ed

Penguin Books

PENGUIN BOOKS

Published by the Penguin Group
27 Wrights Lane, London W8 5TZ, England
Viking Penguin Inc., 40 West 23rd Street, New York, New York 10010, USA
Penguin Books Australia Ltd, Ringwood, Victoria, Australia
Penguin Books Canada Ltd, 2801 John Street, Markham, Ontario, Canada L3R 1B4
Penguin Books (NZ) Ltd, 182–190 Wairau Road, Auckland 10, New Zealand

Penguin Books Ltd, Registered Offices: Harmondsworth, Middlesex, England

First published 1988

Made and printed in Great Britain by
Richard Clay Ltd, Bungay, Suffolk
Filmset in Monophoto Times

Contents

Acknowledgements

Many thanks for help received are due to Christopher Huhne for permission to reprint his article from the *Guardian*. I should also like to thank Andrew Varley and Christine Roach for their assistance in checking the material, any errors in which are, however, my responsibility. I am grateful to Vivienne Heuerman and Margaret Chipsham for their typing.

1. Introduction

1. What is the science of economics?

There are a number of different definitions of economics, such as the *'science of scarcity'* and the *'science of wealth'*, but perhaps a more useful definition is that it deals with *the allocation of scarce resources*. With some other sciences, such as mathematics, a series of propositions will usually lead to definite conclusions, but this is not the case in economics. It is sometimes defined as one of the *social sciences* because it deals with the ways in which human beings obtain resources, the ways in which they make decisions about production and the ways in which products are distributed to consumers. Because individuals differ in their behaviour and are not necessarily predictable, and because ideas and behaviour change, there is often room for disagreement. Even where economists agree on what is wrong, they may not necessarily be in agreement on how to remedy the situation. For example, many economists regard inflation as undesirable, but they recommend a host of different potential remedies. Perhaps the best-known types of remedies at the present time in the United Kingdom are: (i) *Keynesian*, loosely following the ideas of *Lord Keynes*; (ii) *monetarist*, tending to regard the money supply as the most important element of a solution. There is, however, a wide range of other opinions and in recent years there has been increasing interest in Marxist economics.

Economics may be subdivided into *microeconomics*, which deals with the theory of individuals and individual firms, and *macroeconomics*, which deals with ideas at the level of government, for example inflation, international trade, balance of payments, money and banking, etc.

2. Economic problems

(a) *Scarcity*

Perhaps the major economic problem is that of *scarcity*. If scarcity did not exist, economic problems would not exist. Air is not generally regarded as a scarce resource, but as a *free good* – a good whose supply is unlimited. Therefore, the allocation of air so that everyone's needs are

1

satisfied is not usually regarded as an economic problem. However, there may be conditions, such as under the sea or under the ground, where air has to be specially supplied and, therefore, paid for. In many countries the water supply may also be taken for granted, though in the drought-stricken areas of the world, particularly in Africa, the absence of water is a major problem.

While in a modern developed society we tend to think of money as being the main scarce resource, a little thought will show that most of the time we are concerned with what money will buy – the collection of goods and services which we can obtain through the use of money. Since most of us have less money than we would like, we have to consider how to get the most satisfaction from it. However, money is not the only scarce resource; time is another, although in many cases there may be a *substitution* between money and time (see Chapter 4).

(b) *Exchange*

In a modern developed society we normally use *money as a medium of exchange*. This occurs once we move into a society of *specialization* and are no longer producing all goods for ourselves. While it would be possible to exchange goods directly for other goods, by barter, it would make life much more difficult. Bartering does, however, still take place in areas such as international trade, particularly where exchange rates do not perform their underlying function. It also can be seen in this country in the transfer of council houses, for example.

The way in which wages, salaries and other incomes are paid is part of the subject of economics. Exchange, therefore, is one of the fundamental problems of economics.

(c) *Choice*

Another basic problem in economics is that of *choice*.

(i) Since most resources are scarce, individuals have to *choose between using one resource and using another*. In modern economies the choice is often one of choosing to spend one's money on one resource or another. *In many cases the key choices are those made at the margin.* For example, we do not usually choose between having either food or entertainment as a whole, but between having slightly more food and slightly less entertainment or slightly less food and slightly more entertainment.

(ii) We also make a number of choices when deciding upon the *type of occupation* we wish to pursue to give us our income. In near-full or full employment there may be a wide range of choice open to most individuals; in a recession there may be very little choice, even at quite low wages.

(iii) *Firms have to choose what they wish to produce and also to consider the quantities of the factors of production (land, labour and capital) they will need to use.* In a capitalist society a great deal of this choice will take place through the *price system*: firms choose whether to spend money on machines or on labour depending upon relative prices. Choices in the private sector will largely be made by the managers of the firms. Similarly, consumers may wish to buy more of a particular good or service if its price is reduced.

(iv) It is not only individuals that have to make choices; it also applies to *society as a whole*. While the range of goods and services is considerable in countries such as Sweden or the United Kingdom, the range of goods and services in some poor countries may be extremely limited.

(v) *One of the constant assumptions in economics is that people require more and more goods and services.* Some economists have criticized this assumption, and there seems to be some evidence that some individuals adopt so-called '*satisficing behaviour*'. This means that they require a certain amount of goods and services and make no effort to go beyond this level. However, many other people do not conform to this pattern and require more and more goods and services. The luxuries of one era have often become the so-called 'conventional necessities' of the following era.

(vi) Economists often assume that choices are made *rationally* (i.e. that all the information that is available is fully utilized) and this is one of the underlying assumptions of much of both microeconomic and macroeconomic theory. However, advertising may persuade us to buy goods or services which we do not need or, in some cases, may be positively harmful to us. There is a considerable degree of evidence, particularly in the transport industry, that consumers are not always rational; for example, the average motorist underestimates the cost of a journey in his car.

(vii) Choices usually have to be made by individuals or by society as a whole with incomplete or *imperfect information*. An individual, for example, who wishes to purchase some washing powder is unlikely to have *perfect information* as to the price charged by every single shop or supermarket in his locality and, in addition, he or she may not know whether a supermarket's own brand of washing powder is as good as a more famous brand. Furthermore, individuals do not have perfect information about their wants in the future because *the future is uncertain.*

3. Types of economic systems

(a) *Pure capitalist economies*

Under a *pure capitalist system*, few of which actually exist, decisions about what to supply and what is to be demanded are solely determined by the *price mechanism*. This means that if the price of a particular good rises, firms become more anxious to supply it and, therefore, either expand their existing production in that market or enter that market. Similarly, if wages rise in one sector and not in another, people tend to move to that occupation from another in so far as this is possible.

(b) *Planned economies*

In a *planned economy*, examples of which exist in Eastern Europe, *most of the major decisions about how to allocate resources are taken by the central authorities*. The government makes most of the decisions about how production should be organized, the level of wages to be paid and the prices to be paid by consumers. Nevertheless, even in a planned economy there are usually some decisions which are taken within the price mechanism. As with the pure capitalist economy, there are, in fact, few examples, if any, of a pure planned society.

Centralized control may help to overcome some of the problems of capitalist society, particularly *unemployment*, but some economists suggest that it tends to be inefficient because it might over-emphasize the quantity of production at the expense of quality and might ignore what customers actually require.

Centralized control may be able to alleviate some of the economic problems by *reducing the inequality of incomes*; in a truly capitalist society the poor may not be able to buy the items essential to life, while the very rich have spare money to spend on luxuries and relatively trivial items.

Perhaps one of the basic problems of a command system (i.e. a centrally planned economy) is that in a modern society *planning requires a considerable degree of information about the quantity and quality of inputs*. For example, an economist needs to take account not only of the total quantity of oil that might be available to the economy but also the particular type, since in many cases one type will not be a complete substitute for another. Therefore, the type of information that an economist requires in a command system is not merely a total inventory of input and output, but also a knowledge of which goods or services can be regarded as substitutes for others. The central planners also need to know the input mixture of relevant outputs. For some industries, with relatively few inputs and a homogeneous output, this may not pose any great problems. In other cases, where there is a great variety of inputs and a great variety of outputs (such as the oil industry, where there are many derivatives), the data may be far more complex. The use of computers with large memories (the price of which is falling rapidly) is of great assistance to central planning authorities.

Unless the central planners are completely dictatorial about the needs of consumers, they have to determine how consumers' needs may be met. This may mean using past data or some *value judgements* (see p. 10) or it may be done through the party system. It is difficult to obtain accurate information about the Eastern European economies, but many of the complaints seem to be about the quality of consumer products. There are particular problems when targets are given to factory managers solely in quantity terms. If this is done, the managers may be concerned only with the quantities produced and not with the quality of the product. While, as we mention later in the book, large-scale organizations may have some advantages, there can be disadvantages too, and these apply to centrally planned economies. For example, if there are insufficient inputs, this can have a large-scale impact upon the total economy. There are also particular problems in agriculture where, almost by definition, output can rarely be completely certain.

A centrally planned economy, like any other economy, has to determine its priorities between current consumption and building up the stock of capital goods. It might be thought that in many areas it is easier for a centrally planned system to do this – to decide to build up heavy engineering for the future, for example. A problem arises, however, in the flexibility or otherwise of the system. For instance, do the central planners take account of the changes in working practices which may be known to be feasible by the factory managers? How can they take account of the changes in demand from consumers? In many Eastern European countries there is still some scope for very small firms, of perhaps up to ten workers, which can cater for changing demands in society because they are more flexible.

A centrally planned economy which functions well should manage to avoid the widespread unemployment which has been a major problem in the Western economies. However, it is very difficult to obtain accurate data about this.

(c) *Mixed economies*

The most common method of allocating resources in Western society is through the *mixed economy*. The mixed economy has grown for a number of reasons. One is the influence of the economist *J. M. Keynes*, who published his influential *General Theory of Employment, Interest and Money* in 1936. He showed that there is no reason to believe that the free working of the price mechanism will result in full employment. As unemployment was rightly considered to be one of the major problems of the 1930s, his analysis has been adopted consciously or unconsciously by most Western governments from 1945 onwards. However, there has recently been some reaction away from this Keynesian influence. The Thatcher and Reagan administrations have imposed tight monetary targets. The Keynesian influence was most clearly seen in the UK between 1945 and 1951 when the Labour government brought many key industries under public control for reasons of economies of scale and (more importantly) because it was felt that only the government could provide a suitable method of control of these industries. This policy helped create a general consensus in favour of direct public control. However, it should not be thought that it is only the Labour party which has taken the initiative regarding public control: one of the earliest nationalized industries, London Transport, was brought under public control by a Conservative government.

The tendency, in both the public and the private sectors, to have larger firms and, in some cases, larger sizes of plant, has meant that it has been easier for the government, if it wishes, to have a strong influence over the private sector. The increasing importance of research and development, which the government has often influenced, has also tended to make for more planned control. The rapid increase in expenditure on defence means that the government has influenced the nature of many industries, including the shipbuilding and aviation industries, even where there is no formal public ownership.

4. Reasons for government intervention in the economy

(a) *To achieve economic objectives*

Governments since the war have regarded as being within their scope many economic objectives which would not previously have been considered so. Successive British governments, si..ce the publication of the

Beveridge Report in 1942, have regarded *full employment* as being a major objective. Most governments as well have assumed that *economic growth* is a desirable objective and that government policy should influence this.

(b) *The divergence between private and social costs*

Firms may, for example, find it cheaper to send undiluted pollution into the clouds, rivers or seas rather than install processes which yield less waste. This may not, however, be in the best interests of society. This problem could be overcome by making the polluter pay the *social cost*. While this might be possible, most governments have resorted to legislation instead to try to prevent some of the problems.

Social costs may be defined as the total costs to the community of a project and include both *private costs* (those which are borne by the producer or consumer) and *external costs* (those not borne by the producer or consumer). Pollution is the most commonly cited example of an external cost. However, unemployment is another external cost that could result from a particular project.

It might pay a firm to pursue a project of increased mechanization at a cost of increased unemployment. Part of this cost is borne by the firm in the form of a fall in the demand for its product, because workers who have become unemployed have less money with which to make purchases. The external part of the social cost of unemployment is a loss of potential production for society, resulting in a wastage of labour. (Labour cannot be stored: potential production by a person lost while he is unemployed cannot be made good.) The persistence of unemployment is linked to many social problems. Where governments have tended to intervene because of the divergence between private and social costs, they have generally done so to move the economy towards fuller employment. Some economists, particularly monetarists, have criticized these moves.

See Chapter 22 for a fuller discussion of the divergence between private and social costs.

(c) *To provide collective goods*

Collective goods are goods which generally cannot be paid for directly by individuals and must, therefore, be provided by the government. Examples of these are the defence of the country, which has to be provided collectively rather than individually, and, to some extent, services such as the police force, open spaces, and navigational aids. These may be regarded as *pure* or *semi-pure collective goods*. The road system is sometimes regarded as an example of a collective good although there would seem to be no reason why road pricing should not be introduced to reflect social costs. This has, to some extent, occurred in Singapore; in Hong Kong road pricing has now been abandoned, for political rather than economic reasons.

(d) *To provide merit goods*

Merit goods include health and education. It is felt that these commodities should be available to individuals irrespective of their income. An increasingly large proportion of the economy's resources has tended to be channelled into these fields, and most of this has been within the public sector.

5. Indicative planning

There has also been, from time to time, particularly in France and West Germany, and to a lesser extent in the United Kingdom, an interest in *indicative planning*, whereby governments try to anticipate what bottlenecks are likely to occur and what steps are required to remedy them. It is particularly noticeable in the case of training, where successive governments in the United Kingdom have tried to improve the quality of skilled labour available. Indicative planning has also been used to forecast surpluses.

6. The price mechanism

This is widely used in Western-style economies, but it would be a mistake to think that the Western economies rely exclusively on the price mechanism. The advantages of the price system are that the *prices act as signals to both producers and consumers*. For example, rises in the price of inputs indicate to producers that they may well need to use other inputs instead. An increase in the price of oil will probably lead producers to try to find long-term fuel substitutes, especially if it is thought that the increase in price is permanent. Conversely, a decrease in price, as in the price of computers in the early 1980s, will tend to mean that more of the item is used in production. Similarly, an increase in consumer demand will tend to raise prices, while a decrease will tend to lower prices.

(a) *Problems of the price mechanism*

Information may well be incomplete. If people are unaware of how quickly non-renewable resources, such as fossil fuels, are being used up, there could be a great danger of future generations having insufficient fuel. A major problem in many countries is the overworking of land: planting year in, year out, and not allowing the soil time to replenish its goodness. There is also the possibility that firms and other organizations may have time horizons which are too short and that they are not concerned about the effects of shortages in the future.

(b) *The price system frequently does not take into account costs which are external to the firm*

These are costs which are caused by the firm but which do not add to the firm's production costs: *the price mechanism tends to undervalue externalities*, and will lead to a greater production of goods causing unfavourable side-effects. This, however, is not an inherent problem of the price mechanism: there is no economic reason why, through the use of taxation and/or subsidies, externalities should not be charged to the firm.

7. Consumer sovereignty

The concept of *consumer sovereignty* implies that resources are allocated according to consumers' preferences, rather than according to the state's preferences. It may be argued that if there is any state intervention (i.e. if the price mechanism is not allowed to work completely freely) resources will not always be allocated according to consumer's preferences. However, *the degree to which consumers are 'sovereign' in a pure capitalist economy depends upon their ability to pay*. Individuals with low incomes may not have the ability to buy the items they wish to purchase. It may be that consumers with low incomes will have their wants satisfied only if there is some state intervention. For example, consumers may only be able to afford medical attention when they want it if the state provides a health service.

8. Opportunity cost

This is one of the most important terms in economics. It means *the next best alternative that has been foregone.* While *opportunity costs* are often quoted in terms of money, opportunity costs may also be in terms of time taken. For example, when considering whether to walk to a nearby park or to take the car or a bus, we are tending to estimate the relative cost and time. The importance of the term 'opportunity cost' can hardly be overstated. What might seem to be one of the newer branches of economics, namely cost benefit analysis (see Chapter 22), is mainly an analysis of opportunity costs to the country as a whole rather than just to individuals and to firms.

9. Economics and scientific method

We said in the opening paragraph that economics is one of the social sciences. What is meant, in this context, by the term 'science'?

(i) *Positive economics* is claimed to be a 'scientific' approach. If we make the assertion, for example, that inflation is related to money supply, we are making a statement which can be either proved or refuted by evidence. Positive economics itself deals only with what might be called 'positive' questions – those which do not rely on value judgements.

(ii) Another branch of economics, sometimes called *normative economics*, deals with *value judgements.* The statement 'The government should restrict inflation even if it leads to higher unemployment' is an example of a value judgement, because it is made on the basis of individual beliefs and cannot be scientifically tested.

Positive economics tries to evaluate theories by seeing whether the hypotheses successfully predict the results. This has been useful in evaluating empirical evidence, but may have led economists to concentrate too much on areas of economics which are easily quantifiable. There is the point that even a great deal of the 'evidence' itself may have been subject to bias. Also, there may be far too many variables to include them all in the data which is used as 'evidence'.

Within macroeconomics and even within microeconomics, a number of value judgements, even if only weak ones, are often found under the guise of positive economics. For example, the assumption that more goods and services are more desirable than fewer goods and services may be thought to be a positive statement, but it cannot be proved on any positive basis and relies on a value judgement only.

10. Economic reasoning

(i) Economists often use *deductive reasoning*, that is going from the general to the particular. In microeconomics the well-known model of perfect competition is an example of deductive reasoning since it uses a series of assumptions. The theory of monopoly uses another series of assumptions, including the assumption of profit maximization.

(ii) Economists sometimes use *inductive reasoning*, that is going from the particular to the general. For example, we might observe a few people buying a particular good and assume that their demand behaviour is typical of the population as a whole. From these observations we might formulate a general theory of demand.

(iii) To some extent, *introspective reasoning* – asking what one would do in particular circumstances – may be regarded as part of the inductive method. Applied economists may frequently use this, particularly when dealing, for example, with the likely market for new consumer durables, when no empirical data is likely to be available. For example, the author of this book had to use this method, to some extent, when considering the likely demand for colour televisions before they were in common use.

11. Wealth

We referred earlier in the chapter to the concept of economics as *the science of wealth*. While in ordinary everyday language we often use the word 'wealth' to denote the amount of money an individual has, in economics we generally consider the total amount of *resources*, whether goods or services, which an individual or a nation has. This is, to some extent, independent of money. For example, if, other things being equal, all prices and incomes were to be doubled throughout the economy, in *money terms* the wealth would have doubled, but in *real terms* we would be neither better nor worse off as a result.

Many economists are concerned with seeing how wealth is created. A great deal of wealth is created through the use of capital – that is, we forgo some portion of current income in order to derive greater income at a later stage. Some economists are also interested in the distribution of wealth (see Chapter 23).

*

QUESTION

'Since the price mechanism acts as an efficient indicator of the allocation of scarce resources, there is no reason for the government to intervene in economic decisions.' Discuss.

The price mechanism acts as an efficient indicator for the allocation of scarce resources if the assumptions of perfect competition prevail. These assumptions include perfect knowledge on the part of buyers and sellers, as well as the mobility of factors. In a modern Western society, it is comparatively rare for all these assumptions to hold and therefore we would expect the government to intervene, at least to prevent abuse of monopoly power.

The government may also intervene if there are externalities, for example pollution or noise, which are all by-products of production and affect consumers and non-consumers of the product or service alike. While the government could use the price mechanism, for example through the use of taxes or subsidies, to alter this, in many cases the government may decide that this is impractical and may impose direct legislation, such as the Clean Air Acts.

While textbooks often stress the long-term equilibrium, it may take a long while for this to occur. For example, in agriculture and in some other markets there is often instability of outputs and prices. The government may, therefore, intervene in order to stabilize prices and output. This can take a number of different forms, such as the EEC's Common Agricultural Policy or the former deficiency payments system (see Chapter 26).

The price system is not normally used for the allocation of public goods such as the provision of open spaces. It would be possible to devise a system of questionnaires, etc., to indicate how much people might be willing to pay for the provision of such goods, but this would be extremely cumbersome. For some services, such as the provision of roads, a direct form of pricing, as in Singapore, might be desirable. There seems to be no reason why the government could not have a system of road pricing, reflecting not only private costs but social costs.

The government might also feel that some goods are merit goods and that, therefore, they should be made available to everyone, regardless of income. Such items include housing and health.

For some services, such as education, especially for the very young, there is no way in which consumers can pay directly. Unless parents have perfect information and adequate resources, there will probably be some form of government intervention to make sure that children receive education, although this does not necessarily justify the state provision of education.

Other goods, such as cigarettes and alcohol, might be regarded as de-merit goods and, therefore, the government might impose high taxation on these to discourage consumption.

The income distribution may be thought to be unfair and the government may therefore wish to redistribute income through a system of taxes and subsidies.

At the macroeconomic level, particularly since the time of Keynes's book *The General Theory*, governments have often assumed responsibility for objectives such as full employment. There is no reason to assume that the price mechanism will result in full employment. While not all monetarists would agree with this (believing that the price mechanism if left alone, *will* lead to full employment), they would argue that the control of inflation is an important government objective and that the government should take steps to restrict money supply if necessary. The government has nearly always intervened in the price mechanism to prevent balance of payments problems. In theory, a freely floating exchange rate might overcome these problems, but few governments have allowed completely free floating. Although the pound has floated since 1972, the government has often intervened either to hold down the rate or to raise it.

MULTIPLE-CHOICE QUESTIONS

1. In the United Kingdom, a waiting list for council houses will occur if:
(*a*) council rents are fixed at the equilibrium level;
(*b*) rents are fixed below the equilibrium level;
(*c*) rents are fixed above the equilibrium level.
Answer – (*b*)

2. Which of the following are examples of social costs?

(A) As a result of the building of a reservoir, birdwatchers are able to observe a greater variety of wildfowl than before.

(B) As a result of the reservoir being built, farmers downstream receive less water and fertile soil from the river.

(C) As a result of a motorway being built in west London, householders have increased noise from traffic.

   (*a*) B only.

   (*b*) B and C only.

   (*c*) All.

   (*d*) None.

Answer – (*b*)

3. In most countries, car-owners underestimate the true costs of running a car. If this is true, what are the consequences?

   (*a*) More cars are bought than if there were perfect information.

   (*b*) Fewer cars are bought than if there were perfect information.

   (*c*) There is no effect on the demand for cars.

   (*d*) It is impossible to say without further information.

Answer – (*a*)

4. In which of the following ways might government intervene to reduce the effect of externalities?

(A) Through legislation.

(B) Through making the polluter pay.

(C) Through subsidizing the person who receives the disbenefit from externalities.

   (*a*) All.

   (*b*) None.

   (*c*) A only.

   (*d*) A and B only.

Answer – (*a*)

5. In a pure capitalist economy, which of the following will not generally be true?

   (*a*) There will always be full employment.

   (*b*) Producers will wish to find out what consumers want.

   (*c*) The demand for labour will reflect consumers' preferences for goods or services.

Answer – (*a*)

6. What will be the opportunity cost to society of the construction of the Channel Tunnel?

(*a*) The money spent by the British and French governments on the tunnel.

(*b*) The total money spent by private contractors to build the tunnel.

(*c*) The total sum spent by both government and private contractors to build the tunnel.

(*d*) The goods and services that would otherwise have been produced if the Channel Tunnel had not been constructed.

Answer – (*d*)

7. What is meant by the term 'free good'?
   (*a*) A good for which no price is paid as, for example, free public transport for old-age pensioners.
   (*b*) A good which is unlimited in availability, e.g. air.
   (*c*) A good for which there is no demand.
   (*d*) A good for which the marginal costs are zero.

Answer – (*b*)

8. Which of the following statements depends on a value judgement?
   (*a*) The government has placed too much stress on inflation at the expense of other objectives.
   (*b*) The abolition of many exchange controls has increased the volatility of sterling.
   (*c*) Import controls cannot entirely eradicate balance-of-payments deficits.
   (*d*) The Phillips curve shows that inflation and unemployment are correlated.

Answer – (*a*)

9. If, as a result of a bypass being built around a town, less noise and pollution occur to the residents of a city, would this be regarded as:
   (*a*) a social cost;
   (*b*) a social benefit;
   (*c*) a private cost;
   (*d*) a private benefit?

Answer – (*b*)

10. What is meant by the term 'wealth' in economics?
    (*a*) The total of all money held by private individuals.
    (*b*) The total amount of money which firms, the public sector and the consumer have.
    (*c*) The total stock of capital goods at historic prices.

(*d*) The total stock of capital goods at current prices.
Answer – (*d*)

11–13. For these questions, the possible answers are as follows:
   (*a*) if both statements are correct and the second is a correct explanation of the first;
   (*b*) if both statements are correct, but the second is not a correct explanation of the first;
   (*c*) if the first statement is correct and the second statement is incorrect;
   (*d*) if the second statement is correct and the first is incorrect;
   (*e*) if both statements are incorrect.

Assertion	Reason
11. The economist usually assumes that consumers wish to maximize their own satisfaction *Answer* – (*b*)	Firms are assumed to maximize profits.
12. In a free economy, the price mechanism uses consumers' preferences to determine the types of services and goods which will be produced. *Answer* – (*c*)	Consumers will always choose what is best for themselves.
13. A modern capitalist economy tends to make widespread use of extensive specialization. *Answer* – (*a*)	An increased volume of capital equipment tends to lead to economies of scale.

DATA RESPONSE

There is considerable evidence to show that most motorists vastly underestimate the real costs of motoring. It seems unlikely that in transport we will ever get an *optimal allocation of resources*, since if people underestimate the cost of motoring, there will be greater use of cars and less use of public transport. Some economists have argued that we could move further towards an optimal allocation of resources if the perceived cost of motoring were raised, for example through increasing the price of petrol while perhaps lowering the cost of the vehicle excise duty (more commonly referred to, though erroneously, as the road fund tax). Public transport operators who assume that motorists know the actual cost of motoring will overestimate the demand for public transport. Public transport operators can either try to make motorists aware of the true cost of motoring or adopt a fares policy (such as travel cards) which lowers the perceived cost of public transport.

(*a*) Explain the term in *italic* type.
(*b*) Explain how the divergence between perceived and actual costs affects the allocation of resources.
(*c*) What other markets are there where there is a wide divergence between actual and perceived costs?

SELF-EXAMINATION QUESTIONS

1. What is meant by a command system? What defects is a command system likely to have?

2. Why are there few, if any, examples, of a pure capitalist system?

3. What is meant by 'the mixed economy'? Does it combine the advantages of both the capitalist and the command systems or does it merely combine the worst aspects of both capitalist and command systems?

4. What does the price system do in a modern economy? In what ways could greater use of the price system overcome many of the disadvantages of a mixed economy? Why is the price system not used in this way?

5. What is meant by a subsistence or traditional economy? Are there any advantages of such a system compared with others?

6. How far is it true that experimentation is not possible in economics, unlike in the physical sciences?

7. What is meant by the term 'merit goods'? Are these likely to be under-provided or over-provided by the price mechanism?

8. What is meant by the term 'opportunity cost'? Some economists have suggested that this concept is the key to most understanding of micro-economics. How far is this true?

9. In what ways do modern governments influence the distribution of income?

10. Economics is sometimes defined as 'the science of scarcity' and sometimes as the 'science of wealth'. How is it possible to reconcile these two definitions?

11. What are the comparative merits of deductive and inductive methods of reasoning in economics?

12. What is meant by the statement 'Economics is a social science'? In what ways, if any, do the methods in social sciences differ from those in physical sciences?

13. How far will modern computer methods mean that it is possible to obtain more predictions following from economic theory?

14. What is meant by the term 'economic laws'? How far is such a phrase useful?

15. What do we mean in economics by the terms 'social cost' and 'private costs'? Why is the difference important?

16. Many economists have assumed that consumers are rational, by which they mean that consumers will maximize their satisfaction from the resources, including money and time, which are available to them. How far is this assumption reasonable in a modern developed country? Explain with reference to the large volume of persuasive advertising in such an economy.

17. Explain what is meant by 'positive economics' and 'normative economics'. Is it possible in practice to have a system of economics which is purely positive? Why is the distinction between the two important?

18. What is meant by saying that wealth must be capable of being transferred from individuals or groups to other individuals or groups?

2. Factors of production: introduction

1. Description of the factors of production

Factors of production are the *resources* used in the production and distribution of goods and services. The main factors of production are *land*, *labour* and *capital*. A fourth factor, *entrepreneurship*, or enterprise, is sometimes distinguished. An entrepreneur is the owner/manager of a firm. The separation of ownership from control (or management) in many modern firms has meant that the entrepreneur is difficult to define in most large firms.

Payment must be made to the owners of any factors used to produce or distribute a particular good or service. *Rent* is paid to landowners, *wages* to labour, *interest* to capital and *profit* to entrepreneurs. Resources (or factors of production) may be categorized as either *renewable* resources or *non-renewable* resources. Renewable resources are those resources whose supply is replenishable: the use of a renewable resource now does not reduce its availability to the user or to other people in the future. Renewable resources include labour and solar power. The use, however, of a non-renewable resource does reduce its availability to the user or to someone else in the future. Most minerals, for example oil, are non-renewable.

2. Renewable resources

(a) *Labour*

As already mentioned, *labour* is a renewable resource: a person who, say, finds paid employment straight after leaving school at the age of eighteen, is able to offer his employer the same amount of labour-hours per week (i.e. the same supply of labour per week) at the age of thirty as at the age of eighteen; furthermore, a person who upon leaving school at eighteen could not find paid employment for a whole year and was, therefore, unemployed for a year cannot offer any more labour-hours at the age of thirty than a person who has been working since the age of eighteen. Thus we say that labour, as well as being a renewable resource, is also a resource which *cannot be stored*: any potential production lost because some labour is unemployed cannot be made good. Labour is discussed in greater detail in Chapter 4.

(b) *Water*

Water should be a renewable resource and, indeed in the Western world, the supply of so-called 'pure' water is being constantly replenished. However, in many parts of the world, particularly in the drought-stricken areas of Africa, the supply of drinking water, at least in the short run (perhaps for periods of a year or more) is not replenished at all. The World Bank Report on Urban Development stressed the importance of pure water for the health of the world's population. Yet, even in the West the water supply may not actually be pure because rain water may be polluted by pollution in the atmosphere.

Water is important not only for drinking and washing purposes, but also as a major input for industry. *Water power* is extremely important in countries such as Zambia and Sweden for generating hydroelectricity. It is likely to become increasingly important in other countries as the supply of other resources, such as oil, becomes scarcer and scarcer.

(c) *Fishing stocks*

Fishing stocks should also be renewable. However, while fish will usually replace themselves, over-fishing has depleted stocks in many parts of the world, including the North Sea: over-fishing tends to lead to lower catches in the long run. The price mechanism itself will not help to overcome this problem since, in the short run, fishermen will carry on fishing until *diminishing marginal returns* (see Chapter 3) make it not worth while. The individual fisherman will only consider his own costs and benefits and not the long-term costs and benefits to all producers.

There have been a number of agreements from time to time to try to prevent over-fishing. For example, the EEC has a Common Fisheries Policy and agreements have been established by the North East Atlantic Fisheries Commission. However, there are often problems of enforcement.

(d) *Soil*

Soil should also be a renewable resource. However, in many areas of the world agricultural land is over-farmed: the soil is not allowed to regain its goodness. As a result of *over-cropping*, along with bad irrigation, the erosion of the plant cover and over-pasturization (i.e. where herds of animals are too large for the land space), many new large-scale desert areas have been created.

The supply of land itself is, of course, limited and the supply of land suitable for agricultural purposes has, in Europe in recent years, been increased only by reclaiming land from the sea, as in the Zuider Zee, in the Netherlands. Generally, the supply of agricultural land in Western-style economies has been declining in recent years, as more and more land has been used for urban development. This is generally because the price of land for urban development, such as for roadbuilding and housing, is much higher than the price of land for agricultural purposes. Once land has been built upon it is difficult for agriculture to reclaim it if, in the future, more agricultural land is required. The irreversibility of factors of production cannot readily be taken into account in a pure price-mechanism system because of the short time horizon of producers. Land is discussed in more detail in Chapter 3.

(e) *Air*

Clean air should also be a renewable resource, but air pollution is now a serious and widespread problem. However, pollution is by no means new. For example, there are stories of serious problems of smog in Victorian times. There have been some attempts at improving the quality of the air, noticeably with the Clean Air Act 1956. However, air pollution caused by, for example, lead additives in petrol, continues to be a problem. This is the main reason for the different levels of excise duty on unleaded petrol announced in the 1988 Budget.

(f) *Solar power*

Solar power is a renewable resource which, like labour, cannot be stored: any solar power not used now cannot be made good in the future.

(g) *Other renewable resources*

Timber, theoretically, could be regarded as renewable as new trees can be planted when old trees are uprooted. However, forests are being destroyed and not being replaced, a process known as *deforestation* (see the next section).

3. Non-renewable resources

Non-renewable resources include most minerals, such as oil, iron ore and coal. As we have seen, in many cases fishing stocks, clean air, clean water, timber, etc., may also be regarded as non-renewable resources or, at the very least, will not be replenished for many years. For example, even if new forests were planted, it would take a whole generation before these trees could be used as fuel or for paper.

(a) *Fossil fuels*

Perhaps the most publicized non-renewable resources are the minerals *coal* and, especially, *oil* (commonly referred to as *fossil fuels*). There are difficulties in determining the total stocks of oil since oil can be obtained from a variety of sources, such as shale or the oceans, although these sources will not generally be explored until cheaper sources have been tapped.

Oil is the most important fuel used in Western-style economies today. The over-reliance upon oil was highlighted in 1973 when OPEC countries raised the price of oil. Oil-importing economies which have remained reliant upon supplies of oil (despite the quadrupling of the price of oil and subsequent price rises) have found that their economic growth has suffered as a result. If they continue to be reliant upon oil as deposits fall, their economic growth is likely to continue to suffer. We deal in Chapter 21 with the MIT survey called *Limits to Growth*, which looked, among other things, at over-reliance on certain resources.

(b) *Agricultural land*

The supply of land is limited to the size of the earth's surface. The supply of *agricultural land* is further limited to the area of cultivable land. The area of cultivable land is being constantly reduced by the process of *urbanization*. Land used for urban development cannot easily be reclaimed by agriculture. We can, therefore, describe agricultural land as a non-renewable resource. Land is generally referred to as a non-renewable resource because there is a fixed supply of land space and once it has been built upon it cannot easily be used for other purposes. However, the economist's definition of land includes solar power, etc., so it must not always be regarded as a non-renewable resource. Land is discussed in greater detail in Chapter 3.

(c) *Forests*

Deforestation not only affects the supply of timber, but can also affect the climate. Furthermore, deforestation can affect the supplies of clean water, since farmers farther downstream may find that they have either too much or too little water; deforestation has also been blamed for floods, particularly in the Indian subcontinent.

While many Western economists have examined the problems which could be caused by a future lack of oil supplies, the problem in many parts of Africa is not so much a possible lack of oil but a possible lack of wood: wood contributes over half the energy resources in parts of Africa; people, particularly women, may have to spend more and more time gathering basic fuel as wood becomes scarcer.

(d) *Electricity*

Electricity may also be regarded as a non-renewable resource because it is usually derived from minerals. However, electricity may also be derived from water power (hydroelectricity), in which case it is a renewable resource.

4. Energy efficiency

We need to consider the end use of energy – what the fuel is used for. Certain requirements, such as the operation of escalators, can only be carried out practically by one fuel, in this case electricity. However, space heating, for example, can be achieved by using any fuel from a wide range of possibilities, and it is important to ask whether or not fuel could be used more efficiently. If we had perfect certainty about the future relative prices of different energy sources, differences in relative prices would reflect differences in opportunity costs. Such certainty does not, however, exist. Thus, the price mechanism does not provide very good signals as to which fuels should be used, given likely shortages in the future.

A lot of energy is lost: there are large energy losses during the transmission of electricity and the transportation of fuels such as coal. We also waste vast quantities of fuel through inefficient conservation measures. The use of cavity and loft insulation in houses could reduce dramatically the amount of fuel used in domestic consumption.

Somewhat belatedly, the Department of Energy is trying to encourage firms to be more efficient in their use of energy. The concept of the rational consumer does not seem to have applied to the domestic, private or public commercial sectors. There have been suggestions, particularly from the *Friends of the Earth* and *Amery Lovins*, that we should use '*soft energy*' sources. These are defined as those energy sources which use renewable resources, for example solar, tidal and wind power. Although some people regard this as going backwards, it should be noted that some of the newest Japanese ships use auxiliary sails, as well as conventional methods of propulsion. A greater diversity of energy sources, with less reliance on one or two sources, reduces the problems arising from shocks to supply and price; for example, reliance on oil meant that economies such as ours were adversely affected by the OPEC price rises in 1973. Greater diversity would also mean that economies would be less vulnerable to strikes by small groups of workers. Local energy sources, such as solar heating, would lead to less energy being lost in transmission.

*

DATA RESPONSE

During the 1960s, energy consumption in most Western-style countries grew very rapidly and in Japan it grew by over 10 per cent per year. This was partly because of the relatively low cost of oil and partly because of an increased demand for electricity. The number of cars also grew very rapidly. As a result of the OPEC price rises in 1973, which increased oil prices in real terms very considerably, many people realized, perhaps for the first time, that there was an underlying problem of scarce resources. Too many people had assumed that a nation's wealth and energy use were virtually the same. In practice, some economies, such as North America, used far more energy per head than comparable economies, such as West Germany.

In spite of the OPEC price rises and the 'energy crisis', few governments have really taken any effective action to curb energy demand. One does not need to be entirely Malthusian to believe that we should try to conserve energy now, if only for the benefit of future generations. If the price mechanism worked perfectly, as some economists seem to believe it does, then at the very least we would invest much more in energy-saving methods, such as cavity-wall insulation and the lagging of hot-water tanks. The model of the so-called 'rational man' may mislead us into believing that this is the way in which consumers actually react. However, surveys from consumers' associations, etc., illustrate the ways in which we waste vast sums of energy each year. Even allowing for high interest rates, many of the easy conservation methods would more than pay for themselves.

In Britain, we do not even, as a community, use energy effectively, whereas in Sweden for example, spare heat from electricity is used to warm houses and to heat water. Perhaps we should try to use electricity only where it is required, such as to operate lifts, and not for purposes where there are simpler and cheaper sources of energy to provide the necessary power. For example, heat can be obtained from sources other than electricity. One school of thought suggests that we should use 'soft technology', which would use renewable resources such as solar energy, wind and wave power and, possibly, organic waste. This would help to reduce our uncertainty regarding resources which may be finite.

(a) Why does the author suggest that we are not always rational?
(b) Can the price mechanism allocate non-renewable resources effectively? Explain your answer.
(c) Does the economic theory of perfect markets help us to balance future and present needs? Explain your answer.

SELF-EXAMINATION QUESTIONS

1. What is meant by the term 'renewable resources'?

2. In the absence of government intervention, what is likely to happen to fishing stocks as improved fishing techniques develop?

3. What is meant by the term 'non-renewable resources'? Why has there been more interest in non-renewable resources in recent years?

4. How far can the price mechanism overcome the problems of allocation of non-renewable resources?

5. How far is it true to say that land is a non-renewable resource?

6. Why is it often suggested that firms have short time horizons when using non-renewable resources? How far is this suggestion correct?

7. In what ways might the government intervene in the pricing of non-renewable resources and what would be the effects of this intervention?

3. Factors of production: land

1. Introduction

According to the economist, land generally includes all the *free gifts* of nature which can yield potential incomes. Land, therefore, includes not only agricultural land but also land which might be used for building, extracting mineral supplies, mining and fishing, and wind, water and solar power and so on. Thus, land should not always be considered as a non-renewable resource. Economists have tended to lay emphasis upon the fixed supply of land. However, this assumption is not necessarily completely true. Fertile land, for example, can be eroded by over-use or through neglect. Similarly, it is possible to increase supplies of agricultural land through better irrigation, reclamation and so on. None the less, the supply of agricultural land space is limited, even though the fertility of the soil could, theoretically, be improved indefinitely.

Since land space cannot easily be increased (unlike both labour and capital), it is perhaps unsurprising that *land values tend to rise as the size of the population rises*. This tendency is more likely to be true of urban land values than of rural land values, since in many economies, such as the UK, it is possible to increase the fertility of rural land considerably. Generally, we might expect the most valuable rural land to be the most fertile land. However, the most valuable land of all tends to be that land which is in urban use and, generally, we find that rents in urban areas are very high.

2. Economic rent

Economic rent is the payment to a factor of production over and above that which is necessary to keep it in its present employment. If a factor of production, whether land, labour or capital, does not receive at least its *transfer earnings* (i.e. the minimum payment necessary to keep it in its present employment), the owner of the factor will move it to alternative employment. For example, if people receive low wages and have reasonable skills, they will look for other occupations. This might occur, for example, if the government restricted salaries in the public sector while salaries in the private sector were rising: people who were not dedicated to their job in the public sector or who had a reasonable amount of ability, or both, would tend to move into occupations in the private sector.

Normally we would expect a factor of production to be earning its owner at least the value of its transfer earnings. However, in some cases, factors may earn an *economic rent*. Thus, if a worker in the private sector is earning £200 per week and could only earn £150 per week in the public sector, we can assume that he is earning an economic rent of £50 per week (as long as he would be prepared to move to the public-sector occupation if the wages were above those paid in the private sector). Many high-wage earners, such as entertainers, might have, in their wages, a strong element of economic rent. For example, if someone earns £1,000 per week as an entertainer, but would be prepared to do the job for £200 per week, we can say that he earns an economic rent of £800 per week. Economic rent in terms of labour is discussed in more detail in Chapter 4.

(a) *The classical concept of economic rent*

The concept of economic rent was applied originally to land. Many classical economists (notably *David Ricardo*) realized that, though the original land cost nothing (it is a free gift of nature), landlords require some return for use of the land; a landlord receives payment for use of a factor of production when he has done nothing to earn this rent. While this may be true of agricultural land, it may not be true of urban land, where rent, in the ordinary sense of the word, is often payable partly for the use of the land space, but also partly for the use of buildings. Thus 'rents' payable, for example, by council-house tenants consist partly of 'profits' to the owner for use of the capital (house) which he owns.

(b) *The concept of economic rent applied to land*

The concept of economic rent is, of course, nowadays applied not only to land, but also to labour and capital. However, in this chapter we are concerned with economic rent in terms of land.

The concept of economic rent is merely an elaboration on the concept of opportunity cost. If a plot of agricultural land (which earns the landowner a rent of £30 per week) could be, instead, left uncultivated to be an area of natural beauty (for which he could earn a rent of £10 per week), the opportunity cost (assuming that the latter option is the next best

27

alternative forgone) of using the land for cultivation is £10 per week. The economic rent to be gained by the landowner as a result of cultivating the land (assuming that he would be both willing and able to transform the plot into a beauty spot if the rent payable for the land being used for this purpose were to rise above the level payable for it being using for cultivation) is £20 per week.

If a plot of land has, however, no alternative to its present use, we can say that it earns all economic rent. A plot of land will have no alternative use if there is no demand for the plot to be used for any purpose other than its present purpose. Thus, a plot of infertile land, which can only earn a rent as an area of natural beauty (and even then only a very low rent of, say, £10 per week), earns a low rent because the level of demand is very low (as represented by the curve D_1 in Figure 1). If, however, oil is discovered in the area, the demand for use of the resources of the plot of land may well rise. We can show this rise in demand in Fig. 1 by shifting the demand curve from D_1 to D_2. We can assume that, as a result of the rise in demand, the rent the landlord can charge, if he uses the land for oil exploration, is £80 per week. If the landlord does not allow the land to be used for oil exploration, the opportunity cost of his attitude can be valued at £80 per week; if he does allow oil exploration, the land earns him an economic rent of £70 per week.

We have drawn the supply curve as perfectly inelastic, since in the short run supply cannot be altered, although in the long run the quantity of oil extracted from the ground can be varied.

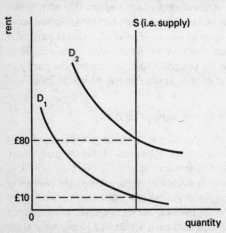

Figure 1. *Economic rent*

3. The law of diminishing returns

Economists devised the *law of diminishing returns* with land in mind. The law of diminishing returns, in terms of land, states that if we add successive amounts of another factor (i.e. either capital or labour), less and less *extra* output will eventually be yielded.

(i) The point beyond which a falling amount of extra output is yielded is called *the point of diminishing marginal returns*. The point of diminishing marginal returns is the point at which *marginal product* reaches its maximum. *Marginal product is defined as the extra output resulting from the employment of an extra unit of one factor of production*, holding all other factors constant. If the law of diminishing returns was not true, we could increase productivity on a small piece of land continuously. It should be noted that the law does not say that there may not be a time in which there are increasing marginal returns. For example, in previously virgin territory small increases in the amount of labour employed to reduce weeds may lead to increasing marginal returns. Similarly, in some cases, small amounts of fertilizers may more than proportionately increase the amount of crops grown.

(ii) Beyond the point of diminishing marginal returns, *total product (i.e. the total amount of output produced by the factors of production employèd) will probably continue to rise as successive units of labour or capital are added, but it will not rise by as much as it did when the previous unit was added*. Furthermore, there might indeed come a point where total product actually falls when an extra unit of labour or capital is added. The point at which total product reaches its maximum is known as *the point of diminishing total returns*. Total product might fall beyond a certain point because the addition, for example, of an extra worker to a given space of land may mean that workers start getting in each other's way.

(iii) *Average product* is the output produced per unit of the variable factor. The average product of labour is found by dividing total product by the number of workers employed. *The point of diminishing average returns is the point at which average product is at its maximum*. Beyond this point, output per worker (or output per unit of capital) declines.

(iv) From Figure 2b you will notice that *the point of diminishing average returns is the point at which average product equals marginal product*, i.e. $AP = MP$ when AP is at its maximum.

The average product curve slopes upwards as long as the marginal product curve is above it, whether marginal product is rising or falling. From this, we can say that average product will rise as long as an additional worker raises the average product of all workers, even if his contribution to output is less than the contribution of the worker employed immediately before him.

We show the typical concept of the law of diminishing returns and the relationship between average product and marginal product in the worked example illustrated in Table 1 and Figures 2a and 2b below.

Table 1. The law of diminishing returns

Quantity of labour	Total product (TP)	Average product (AP)	Marginal product (MP)
1	22	22	—
2	50	25	28
3	84	28	34
4	116	29	28
5	125	25	13
6	126	21	1
7	119	17	−7

We assume a fixed amount of land and capital. To this land and capital we add successive units of labour.

The figures chosen for the table allow us to show points of diminishing total returns, diminishing marginal returns and diminishing average returns. Marginal returns start to diminish after 3 units of labour are employed, average returns start to diminish after 4 units and total returns start to diminish after 6 units.

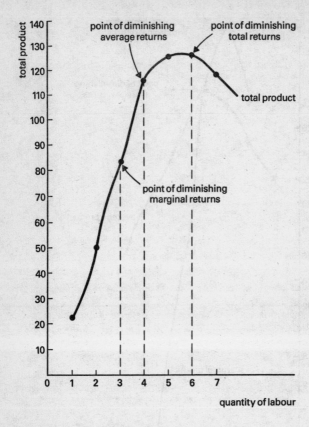

Figure 2a. *The law of diminishing returns: the total-product curve*

We have plotted the total-product curve from the information given in Table 1, showing both the point of diminishing marginal returns and the point of diminishing average returns. These points can be distinguished more clearly in Figure 2b.

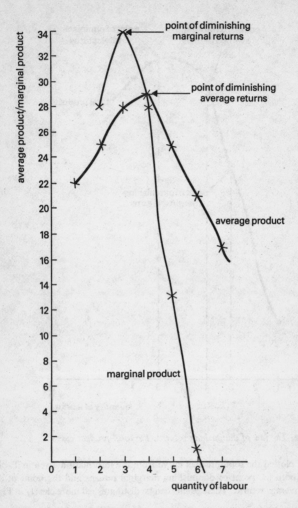

Figure 2b. *The law of diminishing returns: the marginal-product and average-product curves*

The law of diminishing returns has nowadays been applied widely to all factors of production. You should note that it refers to physical productivity and not to costs or profits. Similarly, it does not say what happens if we increase all factors of production at the same time, but only what happens if we increase one factor while holding all other factors constant, i.e. it does not rule out economies of scale. We discuss this concept in Chapter 9.

*

MULTIPLE CHOICE QUESTIONS

Questions 1–5 refer to the following information:

No. of workers	Total product
1	10
2	30
3	45
4	56
5	65
6	72
7	70

1. Which is the point of diminishing total returns?
   (*a*) Where 1 worker is employed.
   (*b*) Where 2 workers are employed.
   (*c*) Where 6 workers are employed.
   (*d*) Where 7 workers are employed.
Answer – (c)

2. Which is the point of diminishing average returns?
   (*a*) Where 1 worker is employed.
   (*b*) Where 2 workers are employed.
   (*c*) Where 3 workers are employed.
   (*d*) Where 4 workers are employed.
Answer – (c)

3. At which point are marginal returns at a maximum?
   (*a*) Where 1 worker is employed.
   (*b*) Where 2 workers are employed.
   (*c*) Where 3 workers are employed.
   (*d*) Where 6 workers are employed.
Answer – (b)

4. Which is the point of diminishing marginal returns?
   (*a*) Where 1 worker is employed.
   (*b*) Where 2 workers are employed.
   (*c*) Where 3 workers are employed.
   (*d*) Where 7 workers are employed.
Answer – (*b*)

5. At which point does average product equal marginal product?
   (*a*) Where 1 worker is employed.
   (*b*) Where 2 workers are employed.
   (*c*) Where 3 workers are employed.
   (*d*) At no point.
Answer – (*c*)

6. Average product equals marginal product:
   (*a*) at the point of diminishing total returns;
   (*b*) at the point of diminishing average returns;
   (*c*) at the point of diminishing marginal returns;
   (*d*) not necessarily at any of the above points.
Answer – (*b*)

7. The more elastic is supply:
   (*a*) the greater will be the economic rent for a given rise in demand;
   (*b*) the smaller will be the economic rent for a given rise in demand.
Answer – (*b*)

SELF-EXAMINATION QUESTIONS

1. If the owner of a plot of infertile land (the only use of which is as an area of natural beauty) discovers oil underneath its surface, explain how he should now use the plot of land if he is a profit-maximizer.

2. Explain the importance of the point of diminishing marginal returns to a profit-maximizing firm. To answer this question see also Chapter 7.

3. What does reaching the point at which average product equals marginal product indicate to a firm?

4. How might the supply of land be increased?

5. 'A landlord who receives a rent from someone for use of his land receives payment for doing nothing.' Discuss.

4. Factors of production: labour

1. Population

(a) Population trends

(i) *Trends in the total population.* When looking at the labour market it is helpful to look at the *total population* in the United Kingdom. This grew rapidly during Victorian times, but has grown less rapidly since. Many producers, as well as the government, will be interested in population changes – not only changes in the *size of the population*, but also in the *age structure*. We can find some forecasts for these in government publications such as *Economic Trends*.

Table 2. The size and age structure of the UK's population: trends and forecasts

	No. of people (in millions) in each age group				Total population (in millions)
	0–14	25–44	45–64	65+	
1941	11.1	19.5	10.9	4.3	44.8
1951	11.4	21.4	12.1	5.5	50.3
1961	12.4	20.8	13.4	6.2	52.8
1971	13.4	21.6	13.4	7.5	55.9
1984	11.0	24.5	12.6	8.4	56.5
1991*	10.9	24.7	12.2	8.9	56.8
2001*	11.8	23.6	13.6	8.7	57.7

* Forecast.
Source: Central Statistical Office, *Social Trends*, No. 16, HMSO, 1986.

(ii) One of the major trends in the United Kingdom has been the *downward trend in the death rate* since the 1875 Public Health Act. However, the death rate still varies between different regions and also between different classes.

(iii) *The birth rate has declined since the 1960s.*

(iv) *Flows of immigrants and emigrants* have not had a significant effect upon the UK's total population figures in recent years.

Table 3. Trends in the UK death rate by sex

	Rate per 1,000 of total population	Total number of deaths (in thousands)
1961		
males	12.6	322.0
females	11.4	309.8
1971		
males	12.2	328.5
females	11.1	316.5
1981		
males	12.0	329.1
females	11.4	328.8
1984		
males	11.7	321.1
females	11.2	323.8

Source: Central Statistical Office, *Social Trends*, No. 16, HMSO, 1986.

Table 4. Trends in the UK birth rate

	Births per 1,000 of total population	Total number of live births (in thousands)
1961	17.8	912
1971	16.0	870
1981	12.8	704
1984	12.8	702

Source: Central Statistical Office, *Social Trends*, No. 16, HMSO, 1986.

Table 5. The UK immigration and emigration flows (in thousands)

	Immigrants	Emigrants
1971	200	240
1981	153	233
1984	201	164

Source: Central Statistical Office, *Social Trends*, No. 16, HMSO, 1986.

2. The supply of labour

(a) *Definition of the working population*

The *working population* (or *labour force*) is defined as that part of the total population which consists of people of *working age* who are either employed or available for employment. In the United Kingdom, until 1986, conventionally men between the ages of 16 and 65 and women between the ages of 16 and 60 were considered to be of working age. In 1986, however, the European Court of Human Rights declared that having one retirement convention for men and another for women was illegal, so now women between the ages of 16 and 65 are considered to be of working age. Some people of working age may not make themselves available for employment straight away: they may remain in full-time education beyond the age of sixteen. Similarly, some people continue to work beyond the retirement age, while others retire early. Until the introduction of state pensions in 1909, most people, if they were able-bodied, worked until such time as they could afford to retire.

Table 6. Trends in the UK civilian-labour-force economic activity rates

	Activity rate in each age group (%)						Activity rate of total population aged 16+ (%)
Male age groups:	16–19	20–24	25–44	45–59	60–64	65+	
Female age groups:	16–19	20–24	25–44	45–54	55–59	60+	
1971							
males	69.4	87.7	95.4	94.8	82.9	19.2	80.5
females	65.0	60.2	52.4	62.0	50.9	12.4	43.9
1976							
males	70.5	85.9	95.7	94.9	80.4	14.5	78.9
females	68.2	64.8	60.0	66.5	54.3	10.3	46.8
1981							
males	72.4	85.1	95.7	93.0	69.3	10.3	76.5
females	70.4	68.8	61.7	68.0	53.4	8.3	47.6
1984							
males	72.9	84.6	94.4	89.1	56.7	8.2	74.2
females	68.7	69.0	65.1	69.1	51.1	7.6	48.4

Source: Central Statistical Office, *Social Trends*, No. 16, HMSO, 1986.

(b) *Factors affecting the supply of labour*

There are a number of commonly quoted factors which may affect the amount of time for which a particular individual is willing to devote his labour services to a particular firm or to the labour market as a whole.

Some of the most important factors which tend to affect the supply of labour are listed below. However, the extent to which each of these factors affect individuals' supply decisions are often difficult to determine.

(i) *Pay*. Actual pay may be difficult to determine. For example, some firms have their own pension schemes for their employees and many firms offer their employees various fringe benefits.

An individual may decide on a *reservation wage* and will not accept a job unless the wage offered at least matches this reservation wage. If the individual concerned can find no job where this reservation wage is offered, he will either revise his reservation wage or decide not to look for work, and so withdraw from the working population.

(ii) *Journey time to work*. The time taken to get to and from work may also influence the supply of labour. Not everyone is prepared to make long journeys to work. Those who are not prepared to commute long distances may decide to move nearer to the available work or may decide not to enter the labour force.

(iii) *Job satisfaction*. If a person does not consider that his job offers sufficient variety or if he finds his working environment unpleasant (perhaps because he does not get on well with his colleagues or manager), he may decide to leave and search for another job. In this case he will still be a member of the working population because he is looking for work. If he decides, however, not to look for another job after leaving, he ceases to be included in the working population.

(iv) *Training* is required for some jobs. This training may involve the individual undergoing full-time further or higher education and so he or she may not enter the labour force until later. Some training programmes imposed by professional associations or trade unions may involve on-the-job training, but may still involve individuals not working for one or two days per week, and attending lectures, etc., instead.

(v) *Future income*. Individuals are likely to be concerned about future earnings when deciding whether or not to enter the labour force. For example, an individual may decide to delay entering the labour force in order to continue his education because he feels that higher qualifications will lead to him obtaining higher incomes in the future.

Possible future earnings may be fairly easy to determine in occupations where wages are paid on an incremental scale, but it may be fairly difficult for other people to determine their likely future earnings.

(vi) *Imperfect information.* Some people may decide not to enter the labour force because they are not aware of the wages offered by all firms and because they are not aware of all existing vacancies. If they were, they might be willing to join the labour force.

(vii) *Prejudices.* Some people, particularly women, may decide not to look for work because of the prejudices of some employers and employees. If they do look for work, they may not consider some occupations because they are traditionally thought of as 'men's jobs'.

(c) *The income–leisure trade-off*

While the labour supply curve is usually shown as upward sloping, within an industry at any given time there are the possibilities of it being backward bending. The *backward-bending supply curve* shows that up to a certain point (point A in Figure 3), as the wage rate rises, an individual will want to work more hours. However, a rise in the wage rate means that an individual has to work fewer hours to obtain a given weekly income. Thus, beyond a certain wage rate, an individual will prefer to work fewer hours (i.e. have more hours of leisure) than to work more hours and receive a higher weekly wage.

This analysis is based upon the *income–leisure trade-off theory*, which assumes that individuals prefer leisure to work, but that most individuals

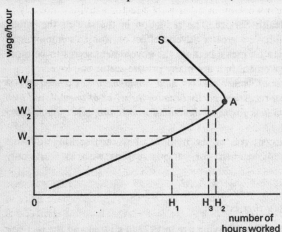

Figure 3. *The backward-bending supply curve*

have to devote some of their time to work rather than to leisure in order to obtain income. The theory assumes that people will work up to the point where they feel they have obtained sufficient income in any one week: they will trade off more leisure for less income than they could earn.

(d) *The employment of women*

One of the most dramatic changes in the working population in recent years has been the *rapid increase in the number of women employed.*

(i) This is partly because of the *increase in the mechanization of domestic activities*: housework is not as time-consuming now as it was in the past.

(ii) *The tendency towards smaller families* has also meant that women are now more likely to be willing to join the labour force.

(iii) Additionally, *the increase in the number of one-parent families has meant that more mothers have to look for work.*

(iv) Women's participation has also increased partly because of *changes in attitudes.* For example, up to about 1914, typing was usually regarded as a male occupation. The absence of men available for work during the two world wars meant that women necessarily took on a much wider range of tasks than in the past. This altered many of the atttitudes towards the employment of women. We can also see other changes, such as those brought about by legislation. For example, the 1944 Education Act allowed married women to become teachers in state schools for the first time. Similarly, there has been a vast increase in the number of women working in other public sector activities, notably in the National Health Service. The reduction in the size of the public sector could well have a greater adverse effect on women's employment opportunities than on men's because the government seems to be more keen to employ women than are many private-sector employers.

(v) *The number of women seeking paid employment has tended to rise during the current recession, partly because the wives of unemployed men are more likely to look for work than other women are, other things being equal.*

Despite the recent rise in the number of women seeking full-time employment, many women, for various reasons wish to work only part-time.

(e) *Higher and further education*

The raising of the school-leaving age in 1972 to sixteen and the increase in the number of people who stay in full-time education beyond the age

Table 7. The activity rate of women of working age (i.e. between 16 and 60) in 1984

Percentage in full-time employment	31.3
Percentage in part-time employment	23.1
Percentage in employment	54.5
Percentage self-employed	3.6
Total employment rate (percentage)	58.2
Percentage registered unemployed	7.1
Activity rate (percentage)	65.4

Source: Central Statistical Office, *Social Trends*, No. 16, HMSO, 1986.

of sixteen have tended to reduce the total size of the workforce, but should have increased the quality of the workforce.

Some students who enter higher or further education might do so partly in order to postpone the need to look for a job at a time of high unemployment, and to improve their chances of finding a job once they have completed their course.

There are vast differences between some of the different regions of the country in the proportion of people who stay at school beyond the age of sixteen. This may partly reflect income levels: poor parents cannot afford to support their children while they stay at school. However, this is not the only reason. For example, there may be different attitudes about education in different parts of the country.

(f) *Determination of the size of the working population*

The size of the working population may be difficult to determine because *some people remain in full-time education beyond the age of sixteen* and because *some people do not conform to the retirement conventions.*

It may also be difficult to determine the size of the working population because many people who are willing to work but who are unable to find employment are *not registered as unemployed either because they are ineligible for unemployment benefit or because they are unaware that they are entitled to receive unemployment benefit.*

The size of the potential workforce has grown in recent years, particularly as a result of the rise in the number of women seeking paid employment and because general improvements in health have meant that a greater proportion of the population is fit to work.

It should be noted, however, that the UK's working population may well diminish as a proportion of the total population. As life expectancy has increased, the proportion of the population in their seventies and eighties has increased substantially. This trend, of course, is not universal and you can, in fact, contrast this trend very sharply with the much larger proportion of young people in many Third World countries.

(g) *Determination of the quality of the working population*

The quality of the labour force is also very important. It is, however, difficult to quantify. Considerable data can be found in *Social Trends*, showing the increase in the number of people attaining specific GCE or CSE or GCSE grades. From census data we can also obtain estimates of the number of people obtaining professional qualifications. How far education should be regarded as improving vocational prospects is, of course, a matter of great controversy. There is, however, as can be seen from *Social Trends*, a strong correlation between levels of education and incomes, but there are problems in the interpretation of this. For example, it is sometimes suggested that education merely acts as a 'sifting' system: higher incomes merely reflect the value of people with greater potential ability rather than the value of education. More evidence can be found from standard textbooks, such as Blaug's *The Economics of Education*. In the United Kingdom, there have been several training Acts, including the 1964 Industrial Training Act, covering a large part of industry. The need for these Acts arose because some responsible firms, which implement good training programmes, frequently lost trained staff to other firms whose training programmes were less good.

3. The demand for labour

The demand for labour (as well as the demand for other factors of production) is a *derived demand*. Therefore, if the demand for a firm's product rises, then (other things being equal) there will be an increase in the demand for labour to produce it.

In basic economic theory, it is often suggested that a profit-maximizing firm will employ an extra worker only if this increases total profit. Therefore, *a profit-maximizing firm will only consider employing an extra* worker as long as this extra worker increases total revenue product without increasing total costs by as much.

(i) For a firm's total revenue product to rise as a result of the employment of an extra worker, total output must rise, other things being equal. *A firm will increase its demand for labour, therefore, if this extra worker increases total product, i.e. if marginal product is positive*, other things being equal.

The marginal product of labour is also known as the *marginal physical product of labour* (MPP_L). The MPP_L is assumed to be downward sloping because of the assumption of diminishing marginal returns (see Chapter 3).

Because of diminishing marginal returns, after a certain number, each extra worker employed will increase output by less than the previous extra worker employed.

(ii) If we assume that an extra worker will increase total product, we can say that *a profit-maximizing firm will only employ this extra worker if the increase in total output leads to a rise in total revenue*, other things being equal.

Total revenue will rise as total product rises if marginal revenue (MR) is positive. In perfect competition, each increase in output faces the same price per unit, i.e. MR is constant per unit of output, which implies that

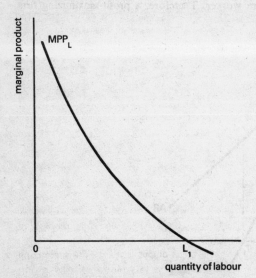

Figure 4. *The marginal physical product of labour*

MR is always positive. On the other hand, in imperfect competition, monopoly and oligopoly (which are more realistic conditions), the firm faces a downward-sloping average-revenue curve, i.e. the price per unit for its good or service falls with each increase in output. A downward-sloping average-revenue curve implies a downward-sloping marginal-revenue curve. There may, therefore, come a time when a rise in output leads to negative marginal revenue, i.e. a fall in total revenue.

The amount by which the employment of an extra worker adds to total revenue is known as the *marginal revenue product of labour* (MRP_L)

Thus, *marginal revenue product = marginal physical product × marginal revenue,* i.e. $MRP_L = MPP_L \times MR$.

Therefore, a *profit-maximizing firm will increase its demand for labour if the employment of an extra worker does not lead to a negative MRP_L,* other things being equal.

(iii) That the employment of an extra worker leads to an increase in the firm's total revenue product is a necessary but insufficient condition for a profit-maximizing firm to increase its demand for labour. *A firm will only increase its demand for labour if the employment of an extra worker increases total profit.* Total profit will rise only if the rise in total revenue product is greater than the rise in total costs resulting from the employment of an extra worker. Therefore, a profit-maximizing firm

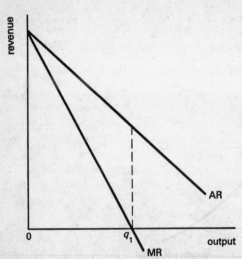

Figure 5. *Downward-sloping average-revenue and marginal-revenue curves*

will only increase its demand for labour if the rise in total revenue product exceeds the rise in its total wage bill. Another way of expressing the condition is to say that *a profit-maximizing firm will only increase its demand for labour if* $MRP_L > MC_L$.

Therefore, the *equilibrium demand and supply of labour is where* $MRP_L = MC_L$, i.e. *marginal revenue product of labour = marginal wage costs.*

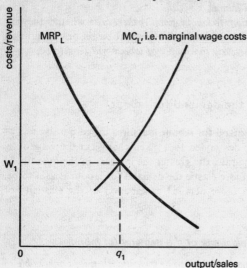

Figure 6. *The equilibrium supply of and demand for labour*

4. The elasticity of the supply of labour

The elasticity of the supply of labour measures the responsiveness of the supply of labour hours to a given change in the wage rate. Given an increase in the wage rate, the greater the increase in the quantity of labour supplied, the more elastic the supply of labour is said to be.

See Chapter 7 for a more detailed explanation of the elasticity of supply.

Factors affecting the elasticity of the supply of labour

(i) Generally, *the supply of unskilled labour is more elastic than the supply of skilled labour:* it is more difficult to increase the supply of skilled

45

labour than it is to increase the supply of unskilled labour because skilled labour has first to be trained.

(ii) *The higher the rate of unemployment, the more elastic the supply of labour will tend to be:* at times of full employment, a small rise in the wage rate will tend to produce a less than proportionate rise in activity rates.

(iii) *The supply of unionized labour tends to be more inelastic than the supply of non-unionized labour.*

(iv) *The more restrictions to labour mobility there are* – whether they are social ties, union-imposed restrictions, housing problems, or immigration laws, etc. – *the more inelastic the supply of labour will tend to be.*

5. The elasticity of the demand for labour

The elasticity of the demand for labour measures the responsiveness of the quantity of labour demanded to a given change in the wage rate. Given a fall in the wage rate, the greater the increase in the quantity of labour demanded, the more elastic the demand for labour is said to be.

See Chapter 6 for a more detailed explanation of the elasticity of demand.

Factors affecting the elasticity of the demand for labour

(i) *The demand for labour will tend to be inelastic when it is impossible to substitute one type of labour for another*, for example where there is a closed shop or where a specific skill is required.

(ii) *The demand for labour will tend to be inelastic when labour costs form only a small proportion of total costs.*

(iii) *The demand for labour from a firm will tend to be inelastic when the demand for the firm's products is inelastic.*

6. Why are there differences in wage levels?

(i) *Differences in profit levels.* Firms with high profits are more likely to be able to offer their workers higher wages than firms which are struggling to break even. Thus, part of the difference in wage levels can be explained by the existence of imperfect competition within industries and by the difference in the equilibrium prices (see Chapter 10) of the products of different industries.

(ii) *Some workers have acquired skills* as a result of undertaking a period of training during which time they had to forgo earnings. Thus, a school-leaver who goes to university for three years instead of to full-time work forgoes an income for this period in order to increase his skills. The student will expect higher wages in the future as reward for the acquisition of these skills. Other people, however, are unwilling to acquire these skills and, as a result, they will receive lower wages over their lifetime.

(iii) Craft unions are anxious to maintain the *differentials* of their members over unskilled workers, whereas general trade unions will try to close differentials between skilled and semi-skilled or unskilled workers. Therefore, *the more powerful the craft unions relative to the general unions, the greater differentials will tend to be*.

(iv) *Differences in elasticities in the supply of and demand for labour* also lead to differences in wage levels (see Sections 4 and 5 above).

(v) *Wages in some occupations, particularly in the non-commercial part of the public sector, cannot be determined by the workings of the price mechanism.* This is particularly true in the case of nurses. In such cases, public opinion might play a part in persuading governments to give such workers higher wages.

7. Economic rent

Some workers earn an *economic rent*, i.e. the wage or salary they receive is in excess of that which would keep them in their jobs.

It is often argued that people such as footballers, who presumably earn very high economic rents, are able to do so because they possess skills which very few people possess. However, their wages might be lower if their employers actually realized that economic rent was being earned. A tax levied on economic rent might reduce surpluses to workers who receive economic rent. However, the imposition of very high income tax on high incomes often merely leads to highly paid entertainers, for example, living abroad to avoid having to pay tax. Therefore, to be successful, a tax on economic rent has to exist internationally rather than just nationally.

In some cases, workers might earn an economic rent because of the existence of artificial barriers to entering a particular industry. For example, professional bodies might limit the number of members into the profession by insisting on unnecessarily difficult examinations, or trade unions might insist on unnecessarily long apprenticeships. Such barriers might be said to have existed until recently in the printing industry. Where economic rents are earned as the result of artificial barriers to entry, economic rent is more likely to be reduced by the removal of these barriers rather than by the imposition of taxation.

8. The mobility of labour

(a) *Occupational mobility*

(i) *A worker will be unable to move from one occupation to another if he does not possess the necessary skills.* The skills required for some jobs may, however, be skills insisted upon by trade unions or professional associations and not strictly necessary for doing the job competently.

(ii) *Occupational mobility may also be hampered by a lack of information of available vacancies.*

(b) *Geographical mobility*

(i) *People will be reluctant to move from one area of the country to another in search of work if they cannot be certain that there is a job available once they have moved.*

(ii) The existence of *social ties* to an area also tends to make labour fairly geographically immobile. Young people tend to be more geographically mobile than older people for such reasons.

(iii) Geographical mobility may be restricted, on an international scale, because of the existence of *immigration laws.*

(iv) House prices, particularly in the south-east of England, may deter people from moving.

Schemes to improve the geographical and occupational mobility of labour are discussed in greater detail in Chapter 24.

*

QUESTION

In the EEC there have been various moves towards equal pay for equal work. What is the economic significance of these moves?

If the economy worked on the basis of perfect competition, as described in many economic textbooks, there would almost certainly be equal pay for equal work. If factors of production are perfectly mobile in the economists' sense of the word, then workers would not work below the going rate, since they would be able to find employment elsewhere. Similarly, they could not be paid above the going rate for the job since employers could find alternative sources of labour. Firms would have no incentive to pay anything other than the market rate.

In practice, however, payments for work may differ, partly according to prejudices, such as prejudices towards people of different ages, sex or racial groups.

Many payments, particularly in the public sector and the larger commercial firms, may be made on an incremental basis, i.e. they rise year by year. While this may be partly justified on the grounds that recruitment and training of new labour is expensive, some of the differences in payments can hardly be justified on the grounds of productivity.

There are a number of problems in determining what equal work would constitute. On a production line, if one person is responsible for a particular task, it may be fairly easy to determine what his or her output is. Even here, however, some degree of quality control may be important to ensure that the total quantity produced is in fact of the same quality. However, even in this case there may be problems, since the machinery used may not be identical and, therefore, one worker may be able to produce more because of this. However, in many jobs, particularly those of management, personnel, accountancy, maintenance work, etc., the concept of equal work is much more difficult to apply. In practice, therefore, in order to see whether equal work is in fact being rewarded with equal pay, some measures such as job evaluation may be necessary.

MULTIPLE-CHOICE QUESTIONS

1. What characteristics are most common in a Western industrial society?
    (*a*) A high birth rate and a high death rate.
    (*b*) A low birth rate and a low death rate.
    (*c*) A low birth rate and a high death rate.
    (*d*) A high birth rate and a low death rate.
Answer – (*b*)

2. The economic activity rate for women in the labour market has tended to increase since 1945.
    (*a*) True.

    (*b*) False.

Answer – (*a*)

3. The UK's population has steadily declined this century.

    (*a*) True.

    (*b*) False.

Answer – (*b*)

4. There are more women than men in the UK.

    (*a*) True.

    (*b*) False.

Answer – (*a*)

5. Immigration is considerably in excess of emigration in the UK.

    (*a*) True.

    (*b*) False.

Answer – (*b*)

6. The number of people under eighteen years of age in the UK has declined rapidly.

    (*a*) True.

    (*b*) False.

Answer – (*b*)

7. The demand for labour is likely to be inelastic if:

    (*a*) the firm employs very specialized labour;

    (*b*) the firm has very high proportions of labour costs;

    (*c*) the firm is operating under conditions of almost perfect competition;

    (*d*) none of the above conditions apply.

Answer – (*a*)

8. People such as top entertainers are highly paid for which of the following reasons:

(A) their great skill means that they deserve high pay;

(B) there are relatively few people with the necessary skills;

(C) there is a considerable demand for such skills?

    (*a*) A and B only.

    (*b*) A and C only.

    (*c*) B and C only.

    (*d*) All.

Answer – (*c*)

DATA RESPONSE

1. In 1911 the total population of the United Kingdom was about 38 million. This had grown to 46 million by 1931 and to just under 56 million by 1980. It is not expected to grow significantly between 1980 and the year 2000 but may grow marginally to about 58 million. The number of births has dropped considerably from approximately 1,100,000 per annum between 1901 and 1911 to about 750,000 in 1980.

The number of children under five has remained reasonably constant (it was around $4\frac{1}{2}$ million between 1901 and 1971), but the number of people aged seventy-five or over has increased dramatically, from just over $\frac{1}{2}$ million in 1901 to $2\frac{1}{2}$ million in 1971.

There have also been quite sharp changes within the regional distribution of the population. Within Greater London, for example, the population dropped from 7.4 million in 1971 to 6.9 million in 1981, while in the remainder of the south-east there was a slight increase in the population. East Anglia by contrast gained over 10 per cent, while the increase in the number of people in the south-west was just under 10 per cent.

During this century there have been considerable increases in life expectancy, so that a male child born in 1980 could expect to live, on average, just over seventy years, while a female would be expected to live just over seventy-six years.

(a) What are the likely effects of the changing number of people in the over-75 group in the United Kingdom? What are the effects of the number of children under five years of age remaining reasonably constant?

(b) The author mentions changes in the regional distribution of population. What are some of the underlying causes of these changes?

2. The labour market is an imperfect one for a variety of reasons. To some extent, the supply and demand of labour consists of a series of non-competing markets, for example steeplejacks do not generally compete with other skilled workers and, in some cases, skilled workers do not compete directly with unskilled workers. Even within one industry, such as the transport industry, airline pilots are not competing with railway drivers.

There is often a lack of knowledge on the part of the suppliers of labour: it seems unlikely, for example, that manual workers will be aware of the prospects elsewhere. While job centres, professional executive registers and agencies may improve information, as do specialized journals and the local press, etc., information is by no means perfect and it is quite common to find examples of people doing virtually identical work for vastly different wages.

There are also immense problems for people wishing to move from one area to another. Moving house can be expensive and for council-house tenants it may be difficult, if not impossible, to move to another council house. The supply of rented accommodation has fallen rapidly and so cannot always be considered as an alternative.

In some cases there may be (legislation notwithstanding) prejudices on the part of employers or even sometimes by other people working within the industry. For example, many firms insist on specific age limits, e.g. twenty-eight to thirty-five, though there may be no real reason for this. There may be prejudices against people who have moved job often, though conversely firms often wish for people to have had a wide variety of experience. If people are very young they may find it difficult to obtain jobs due to their lack of work experience and this becomes a vicious circle for them.

There is often a considerable degree of stereotyping. For example, typists are usually expected to be female, although prior to 1914 it was considered the norm for the job to be done by men. The education system has often reinforced such stereotyping.

Economists often suggest that the wages will be determined at the point at which the marginal revenue product of labour equals the marginal wage cost. In practice, however, few firms actually know the productivity of additional workers. How, for example, do you judge the productivity of a footballer?

(a) Why might firms find it difficult to determine the marginal productivity of additional workers?

(b) Incremental schemes are often in use for office workers. What reasons does the above analysis suggest for these?

(c) What obstacles to labour mobility are there apart from those mentioned above?

SELF-EXAMINATION QUESTIONS

1. What effects does a rise in population have on the economy?

2. What factors have affected the size of the registered working population in the United Kingdom in recent years? What alternative measures

of working population are there, and in what ways, if any, might they be preferable?

3. What have been the main trends in occupational changes in recent years?

4. What factors have determined the numbers of women seeking paid employment? Are these trends likely to continue in the future? Explain your answer.

5. What factors determine the level of demand for labour?

6. How far does the concept of economic rent help to explain high wages in occupations such as entertainment and sport?

5. Factors of production: capital

1. Introduction

Up to the time of the Industrial Revolution most firms were small and the amount of finance available to them was limited to the amount the individual owner or partners could put into the firm. Only in a few industries were large firms common.

Since the eighteenth and nineteenth centuries in the United Kingdom there has been increasingly large-scale production. This trend would not have been possible without the ability to borrow capital. The introduction of *limited liability* in 1855 in the United Kingdom gave shareholders reduced risks. The use of limited companies (which we describe in Chapter 8) has meant that it is possible to obtain savings from large numbers of people, usually through financial institutions.

2. A definition of capital

The term *capital* refers to those goods which are used in the production of other goods or of services and so capital is regarded as a factor of production. Capital goods are goods which were themselves produced by other factors of production at some time in the past.

The economist uses the term 'capital' to denote physical goods, i.e. both durable goods and stocks of raw materials and semi-finished goods, whereas in everyday language 'capital' might also include money. Usually, the economist refers to capital as those assets which possess a monetary value, and which, in turn, will give future improvements to the economy's total wealth. For example, an office might purchase new machinery in the hope of increasing its productivity and, therefore, profits.

Economists normally distinguish between *fixed capital* (buildings, vehicles, machinery, etc.), and *working capital* (raw materials and semi-finished goods). The term '*social capital*' refers to an economy's total stock of capital. The term refers not only to fixed and working capital but also to that capital which is used to produce *non-commercial* goods and services, for example roads, education and libraries.

3. Sources of finance

The capital market in Western countries such as the United Kingdom includes the Stock Exchange, but the Stock Exchange is not the only element of it. For example, many firms, especially small, new ones, have no chance of obtaining money from the Stock Exchange, but may obtain money from friends or relatives as well as from *ploughing back* money into the company. Most small firms will tend to obtain the money to buy working capital from *bank loans* or *overdrafts*.

4. The supply of finance

The supply of finance from individuals to other individuals, firms or the government depends upon a number of factors, including those listed below.

(i) *The extent and effectiveness of the network of financial institutions of the country in question.* A country such as the UK which has a wide variety of financial institutions may give potential suppliers a greater choice than less sophisticated societies.

(ii) *The willingness of potential suppliers to sacrifice some current expenditure on consumption goods in order to have some resources available for investment or saving.* If an individual spends all of his money on consumption goods, he has no savings with which he can purchase shares or securities or with which he can make a deposit at a bank or building society.

An individual who chooses to save some of his money (instead of spending it all on current consumption) might decide to use it to purchase shares or securities in the hope of its yielding a dividend, or he might deposit it in a bank or building society to yield a rate of interest; either action will enable him to increase future consumption.

Whether savings are deposited in a financial institution or whether they are used to buy new shares or securities, they are available to companies to use to finance projects.

(iii) *Individuals will be more willing to save some of their money (rather than consume it all) if the expected reward is higher* (i.e. the expected *dividend* from shares or securities or the *interest rate* offered by banks or building societies), other things being equal.

We can assume that at times of high inflation (when interest rates are likely to be negative in real terms, as they were in the late 1970s) people are less willing to supply funds than they are at other times, other things being equal.

5. The demand for external finance

The level of a firm's demand for external finance may depend upon some of the factors listed below.

(i) *Liquidity problems.* A firm might require external finance because it has a temporary cashflow problem and cannot pay its workforce and other creditors.

(ii) *The need to replace existing fixed capital.* The purchasing of new machinery, offices, factories, etc., requires capital and there is no reason why the demand for capital should be met entirely from current assets.

Similarly, householders may require capital, particularly in order to purchase or to improve property. However, increasingly householders also borrow money to acquire consumer durables.

(iii) *The level of current interest rates.* We might assume that the higher the current real rates of interest, the less willing firms would be to borrow from financial institutions (as shown in Figure 7).

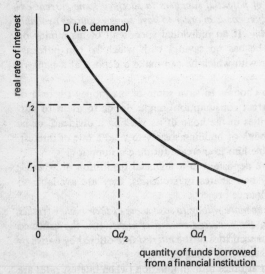

Figure 7. *The demand for external finance*

(iv) *The demand for external finance is connected to the decision to invest.* While the level of current interest rates is likely to be an important determinant, Keynes suggested that *expectations* are a more important determinant. For example, even if current real interest rates are low, a manager might expect real interest rates to fall to even lower levels and may, therefore, decide to postpone borrowing until they have done so. However, Keynes suggested that *expectations about future profits* are even more important than expectations about future interest rates. Thus, if a manager expects the demand for one of his firm's products to rise, he may decide to go ahead with an investment project (requiring external finance) straight away even if real interest rates are currently very high. A project which, for example, requires a firm to borrow £100,000 for a year, will require an interest payment of £10,000 if the interest rate is 10 per cent and of £8,000 if the interest rate is a couple of percentage points lower (8 per cent). The difference of £2,000 is not very significant within the context of the initial £100,000. Firms might formulate their expectations about future profits on the basis of past trends, as a result of market research, or completely irrationally (a possibility Keynes did not rule out).

6. Investment

Investment is defined by the economist as expenditure on capital goods, once expenditure on replacement capital has been allowed for. Therefore, the purchase of shares is not defined as investment, whereas the purchase of additional lorries by a road haulier is defined as investment.

(a) *The discounted-cashflow technique*

A profit-maximizing private firm or individual will only decide to invest if investment is expected to increase profits, i.e. if the benefits are expected to exceed the costs. In this sense the benefits are private benefits (i.e. revenue) and the costs are the costs of production plus any opportunity costs. Imagine, for example, a road haulier, with a one-year time horizon, who is deciding whether or not to purchase a new lorry priced at £10,000. We might assume that he expects that an additional lorry to his fleet will increase revenue over the following year by £20,000, but will require the hiring of a new driver at an annual salary of £8,000 and will increase other costs (for example, the cost of petrol, maintenance and vehicle excise duty) by £1,000 over the year. Therefore, his net benefit (before taking account of the initial outlay to purchase a new lorry of £10,000) will be £11,000 (i.e. £20,000 − £8,000 − £1,000). However, we must also take into account the opportunity cost of the investment before we can say whether or not it will be profitable for the road haulier to invest in a new lorry.

There is an opportunity cost of the investment by virtue of the fact that £1 next year is not worth as much as £1 today to an individual, even if there is zero inflation, because if you had £1 in hand today you could lend it at a rate of interest and have more than £1 next year. Therefore, the opportunity cost to a road haulier of spending the £10,000 he has in hand on a new lorry rather than lending it at the going interest rate of, say, 5 per cent equals £10,500, i.e. (1 + 5%) × £10,000. This is another way of saying that the road haulier regards £10,000 now to be worth £10,500 in one year's time (or £1 now to be worth £1.05 in one year's time). Now suppose that the road haulier did not have the £10,000 in his pocket and had to borrow £10,000 for a year to buy a new lorry; if he borrows this £10,000 rather than staying out of debt and not buying a new lorry, and if the rate of interest at which he borrows this £10,000 is 5 per cent, once again we can say that he values £1 now as being worth £1.05 in one year's time.

To calculate, therefore, whether it will be profitable for a road haulier to invest the £10,000 he has in pocket in a new lorry we use the discounted-cashflow (DCF) technique, which states that it is profitable to invest if the net benefit divided by the discount factor (i.e. 1 + the rate of interest) is greater than the initial outlay, i.e. if

$$I < \frac{b_1}{(1+i)^1} + \frac{b_2}{(1+i)^2} + \frac{b_3}{(1+i)^3} \cdots \frac{b_n}{(1+i)^n}$$

where I is the initial investment, b_n is the net benefit derived in the nth year and i is the rate of interest.

From the equation, it should be noted that £1 received in one year's time is viewed as being more valuable than £1 received in two years' time, etc. The equation has been calculated to n years, because an individual might expect an initial investment to produce net benefits not just in the first year, but in succeeding years as well (i.e. for as long as the capital good lasts).

(b) *DCF applied to government investment*

While private individuals and firms will probably only be interested in the private costs and benefits of investment, the government will be interested in the social costs and social benefits resulting from its investment decisions. Therefore, net benefit (b_n in the above equation) when applied to government investment will take account of the externalities (both harmful and favourable) likely to result from investment.

(c) *Problems with DCF*

(i) It should be noted that while DCF takes account of the importance of the expected rate of interest in the decision to invest, even if the expected net benefit divided by the discount factor is greater than the initial outlay, *a profit-maximizing firm is unlikely to invest if future sales are not expected to rise*.

(ii) Although the initial outlay is often known, *the rate of interest may vary considerably and unexpectedly in practice* and the opportunity costs fluctuate.

(iii) If DCF is applied to investment when the main benefits to be derived are favourable externalities, these *benefits may be difficult to calculate because of the difficulty of attaching financial values to them* (see Chapter 22).

(iv) *There are problems in trying to determine probable future revenue in an era of high inflation*. However, if both costs and benefits broadly rise in line with inflation there is no great problem.

*

QUESTION

What factors determine the supply of and demand for loanable funds?

Loanable funds are sources of finance made available for lending to individuals and institutions, and consist mainly of money which has been saved by either individuals or firms. These funds can be borrowed by individuals, firms or the government from various financial institutions.

One of the most emphasized determinants of the supply of and demand for loanable funds is the rate of interest. A high rate of interest will generally encourage a high supply of loanable funds and a low rate of interest will generally lead to a high demand for loanable funds.

However, the supply of loanable funds also depends partly upon the ability of individuals to save. This may, in turn, depend partly upon the preferences of individuals, i.e. whether they are '*improvident*' (prefer more consumption now rather than in the future) or '*thrifty*' (prefer more consumption in the future than now). Preferences to spend rather than to save may be partly due to the income of the individual (we might generally expect richer people to have a *higher propensity to save* than poorer people). The culture of the society might also affect people's decisions to save. The choice between current consumption and future consumption is discussed in greater detail in Chapter 12.

The supply of loanable funds also depends upon private-sector firms' savings. Whether firms save or spend depends partly on their overall profitability and upon whether they reinvest their profits or distribute them to their shareholders. In turn, this may depend partly upon the government's taxation policy.

Government's monetary policy, as well as its fiscal policy, affects the supply of loanable funds. In theory, a monetarist government will aim to have a balanced budget. A government which is pursuing a tight monetary policy might aim to reduce its borrowing and hence its demand for loanable funds. It might attempt to reduce its borrowing requirement by reducing its expenditure. Reduced government borrowing means, in effect, a fall in the government's demand for loanable funds, which forces interest rates to fall. This fall reduces the supply of loanable funds: the supply of loanable funds is reduced by virtue of a *contraction* along the loanable funds supply curve, as shown in Figure 8.

The government might, alternatively, decide to reduce its borrowing requirement by increasing taxation. A rise in taxation will lead to a decline in savings if people are forced to increase their *marginal propensity to consume*. If this is the case, the supply of loanable funds is reduced by *shifting* the supply curve (see Figure 9), leading to a rise in interest rates.

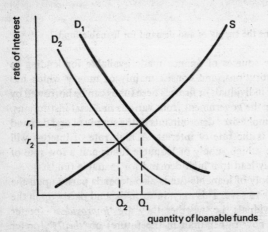

Figure 8. *The effect of the government reducing its borrowing requirement on the supply of loanable funds*

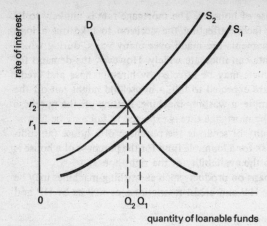

Figure 9. *The effect of higher taxation on the supply of loanable funds*

The demand for loanable funds is connected to the decision to invest. While interest rates will, thus, usually be important determinants of the level of demand for loanable funds, expectations are likely to be a more important determinant.

The demand for loanable funds comes from households, firms and governments. Firms may require loanable funds to build up fixed and working capital. They will tend to do this only if they expect demand for their products to grow; the amount of interest they have to pay on these funds will be of relatively minor significance in the decision to borrow. Similarly, firms may require funds for research and development. They will require funds for this reason only if they expect demand to expand. However, some investment is required to replace worn-out capital. Firms may choose to acquire a loan to pay for this investment only when interest rates are reasonably low.

Central and local governments may require loanable funds to finance capital investment in, for example, roads and the transport infrastructure. They may decide to invest in such capital in anticipation of a recession. Thus, they may wish to invest anti-cyclically. If the government expects a rise in the number of children in the total population, loanable funds may be required to finance the building of schools. Governments may also require loanable funds to overcome cashflow problems, because a great deal of government revenue comes late in the year, while government expenditure is more evenly spread over the whole year. The most important reason why households demand loanable funds is

61

probably the purchase of housing. The mortgage rate is unlikely to be the most important factor affecting the decision to take out a loan because mortgage payments are made over many years, during which time the mortgage rate can fluctuate widely. However, the demand for loans for some products may be affected by hire-purchase and credit rates. If these rates are expected to fall, a household might put off the purchase of, for example, a washing-machine. Putting off the purchase of a house because the mortgage rate is expected to fall may be unwise because of the difficulty of securing the purchase of a house (an individual's decision to ask for a loanable fund for the purchase of a house is very much subject to the availability of the right house).

The demand for loans on products such as washing-machines may be partly determined by HP and credit restrictions, as well as by HP and credit rates.

MULTIPLE-CHOICE QUESTIONS

1. Which of the following are defined as capital:
(A) a company car used only for private journeys;
(B) a private car used to deliver business leaflets to customers;
(C) roads, for use of which there is no direct charge made to motorists?
   (*a*) A only.
   (*b*) A and B only.
   (*c*) All.
   (*d*) B and C only.
   (*e*) B only.
Answer – (d)

2. Individuals will most probably lend more finance today, for a period of one month, if:
   (*a*) interest rates are currently at 10 per cent but are expected to fall to 8 per cent tomorrow;
   (*b*) interest rates are currently at 10 per cent but are expected to rise to 12 per cent tomorrow;
   (*c*) interest rates are currently at 10 per cent and are not expected to rise or fall in the foreseeable future;
   (*d*) interest rates are currently at 8 per cent and are not expected to rise or fall in the foreseeable future?
Answer – (a)

3. In which of the following circumstances is the level of current and

expected future interest rates most likely to affect the demand for external finance:

   (*a*) when external finance is required to meet cashflow problems;
   (*b*) when external finance is required to replace existing fixed capital;
   (*c*) when external finance is required to replace existing working capital?

Answer – (b)

Explanation. Investment in fixed capital is likely to be on a longer-term basis than investment in working capital and, therefore, more sensitive to changes in interest rates.

DATA RESPONSE

A great deal of capital is very specific and cannot readily be changed from one use to another. This is particularly true of oil refineries, specialized ships and so on. Some capital is also very geographically immobile. This is particularly true of social capital, such as canals and railway track. Because of this, such capital can only be used in one place and if it is not used for its specified purpose it is wasted. An example of extremely specific capital is the proposed Channel Tunnel. The opportunity cost of the Channel Tunnel once built would be virtually zero since it is difficult to think of any alternative uses for a thirty-mile-long tunnel.

The accumulation of capital usually requires postponing some present consumption in order to build up future living standards (see also Chapter 12). This might be done in a capitalist society through the use of financial institutions, which can take money from the household and other sectors and put it into the industrial sector; in a command economy it might be done only through the government.

While economists often stress capital as one factor of production, in practice there may be little difference between capital and labour. For example, to a large extent, a person who has received lengthy education, such as a don in a university, can be viewed in much the same way as capital, since consumption has been postponed in order to make capital investment (investment in human capital). A skilled workforce, in turn, will tend to lead to further accumulation of consumer goods.

   (*a*) The author suggests that consumption postponed makes capital available for investment to increase consumption in a future period. Is this always true? Explain your answer.

(*b*) In what ways can the use of educated people be regarded as comparable to the use of capital?

SELF-EXAMINATION QUESTIONS

1. Why is it often difficult to use the economist's concept of capital?

2. Which sources of finance are small firms most likely to use? Explain why.

3. What factors are likely to affect the supply of finance?

4. What factors are likely to affect the demand for external finance from: (*a*) individuals; (*b*) firms; (*c*) the government?

6. Demand

1. What is demand?

A *market demand curve* is used to show how much of a particular good or service consumers in the market wish to buy over a range of prices (other things being equal) at a particular time. It is a summation of *individual demand curves*, which show the demand for individual consumers.

2. Utility maximization

At this level it is usual to assume that *consumers aim to maximize their utility, i.e. satisfaction.* Since that which satisfies one person does not necessarily satisfy another, *it is difficult to measure utility.* Yet we can say that *a consumer's utility will be increased if he is able to purchase more goods or services: more is preferred to less.*

There is a constraint to how much utility a consumer can enjoy. This constraint is his level of income. *We would expect a consumer to buy as many goods and services as his level of income allows (subject to some savings).* The composition of goods and services a consumer decides to buy, given his level of income, depends upon which composition gives him greatest utility.

We would expect that, *as a consumer's level of income rises, he will demand more goods and services in order to maximize his utility.*

Similarly, *as the price of one good falls, real income rises: a consumer is able to buy more units of all goods and will buy more units of all normal goods.*

(a) *Diminishing marginal utility*

It is usually assumed that *as more of a particular good is consumed, total utility will rise but marginal utility will tend to fall.* This principle is easily applied to most foodstuffs: the third ice-cream (although increasing total satisfaction) may not increase total utility by as much as the second ice-cream.

The concept of diminishing marginal utility is a principle and not a

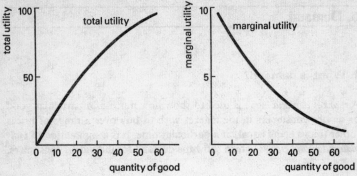

Figure 10. *Total and marginal utility*

law: there may be some exceptions, such as habit-forming drugs and similar substances.

The principle of diminishing marginal utility helps to explain the downward-sloping nature of the demand curve for most goods.

(b) *Marginal utility and demand*

A consumer will continue to buy more units of a good or service up to the point at which the marginal utility of the good or service equals the price, i.e. the point at which he could obtain the same utility by spending the same amount of money on another commodity. Were it not for diminishing marginal utility, an individual might well spend his money on just one product. It should be clear that an individual's total utility is maximized by spending his money on a basket of goods and services.

The principle of buying a particular commodity until the marginal utility derived from that commodity equals its price applies to all commodities. We can, therefore, readily show that there will be a position of consumer equilibrium if

$$\frac{\text{marginal utility of good A}}{\text{price of A}} = \frac{\text{marginal utility of good B}}{\text{price of B}} =$$

$$\frac{\text{marginal utility of any good}}{\text{price of that good}}.$$

A consumer's total utility will be maximized, subject to a budget constraint, by getting to a situation of consumer equilibrium. This is best shown by way of an example.

Table 8a

Quantity	Good A, price = £20			Good B, price = £30		
	Total utility	Marginal utility	MU/price	Total utility	Marginal utility	MU/price
1	60	60	3.0	72	72	2.4
2	115	55	2.75	141	69	2.3
3	165	50	2.5	207	66	2.2
4	209	44	2.2	267	60	2.0
5	249	40	2.0	321	54	1.8
6	285	36	1.8	369	48	1.6
7	319	34	1.7	414	45	1.5
8	351	32	1.6	450	36	1.2
9	382	31	1.55	480	30	1.0
10	412	30	1.5	504	24	0.8

We might imagine that a utility-maximizing individual has the utility schedules for two goods (A and B) as calculated in Table 8a above. We might also imagine that those two goods are the only two goods in the economy and that, given a level of income (i.e. a budget constraint), the individual will spend all of his income. In this example we will show how many units of good A and how many units of good B he will demand in differing circumstances.

(i) If the individual has a budget of £220, then, as a utility-maximizer, he will demand 5 units of good A plus 4 units of good B. Given the constraint of a budget of £220, it is this combination that gives him the greatest total utility, i.e. 249 + 267 = 516: no other combination will give him as much utility when he is subject to this constraint.

This combination fulfils the equilibrium condition of

$$\frac{MU_A}{\text{price A}} = \frac{MU_B}{\text{price B}},$$

subject to the budget constraint.

(ii) If the individual's budget rises to £270, then, as a utility maximizer, he will demand more units of good A and more units of good B, i.e. both goods are *normal* goods.

Given the constraint of £270, the individual will demand 6 units of good A (implying a total expenditure on A of £120) plus 5 units of good B (implying a total expenditure on B of £150).

This combination fulfils the equilibrium condition of

$$\frac{MU_A}{price\ A} = \frac{MU_B}{price\ B},$$

subject to the budget constraint.

(iii) How would a fall in the price of good A affect the individual's demand for both good A and good B? If the price of good A fell from £20 to £15 then we would replace the figures in the fourth column of Table 8a with the figures in Table 8b.

Table 8b

Quantity	Good A, price = £15 MU/price
1	4.0
2	3.67
3	3.33
4	2.93
5	2.67
6	2.4
7	2.27
8	2.13
9	2.07
10	2.0

Imagining that the price of B is still £30 and that the individual's budget is still £270, then, as a result of the fall in the price of A from £20 to £15, the individual will increase his demand for A from 6 units to 10 units (implying a rise in total expenditure on A from £120 to £150) and reduce his demand for good B from 5 units to 4 units (implying a total expenditure on B of £120). This action fulfils the equilibrium condition of

$$\frac{MU_A}{price\ A} = \frac{MU_B}{price\ B},$$

subject to the budget constraint.

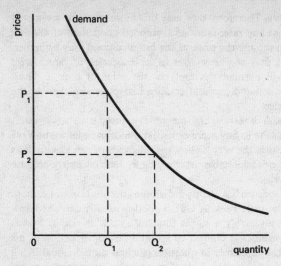

Figure 11. *Demand for a normal good*

This action also shows that good **A** is a normal good (i.e. more is demanded as its price falls) and that the elasticity of demand is elastic, i.e. total expenditure on A rises as the price falls, leading to a fall in the total expenditure on B.

3. The determinants of demand

We have already suggested that two of the most important determinants of an individual's demand for a particular good or service are income and price.

(a) *Price*

(i) Usually, *as the price of a commodity falls, a consumer demands more units of it*, whereas if the price increases less is demanded. This leads to the familiar downward-sloping demand curve, as shown in Figure 11.

(ii) There are, however, some exceptions to this general rule. Many consumers will not have, by any means, perfect knowledge of the goods or services which they are buying. They may, therefore, take *price as an indication of quality.* Therefore, they may buy more goods or services at higher prices or, at any rate, more of a branded good than of another similar good even though the price of the branded good may be higher.

(iii) Consumers may see *price rises as an indication of future price increases.* This will particularly apply to the price of houses. Thus, consumers might demand more after an initial price rise than at the original, lower price.

(iv) *'Veblen' goods or services* are sometimes referred to as *'snob goods'*. Consumers may desire to buy more expensive goods in order to show off their status or wealth: the very highest priced goods or services, such as Rolls-Royce cars or fashionable art, may be in demand partly because they are expensive.

(v) A *'Giffen' good* also has an upward-sloping demand curve, i.e. more is demanded as the price rises. A Giffen good is usually described as a necessity (almost invariably a staple foodstuff, such as rice or bread) upon which a consumer is obliged to spend a large proportion of his weekly income. The consumer in question (such as an individual living in a developing country) is described as having a very low weekly income. If the price of rice rises, the demand for it in such circumstances is also likely to rise because consumers will have to buy at least the same quantity of rice in order to survive, and this will leave them with so little money to buy other things that they feel they might as well spend the rest of their income on more rice.

(b) *The price of other goods*

(i) In the eyes of the consumer, one product may be a *substitute* for another. For example, margarine is often regarded as a close substitute for butter: *if the price of margarine falls, the demand for butter is likely to fall.*

(ii) The demand for some goods tends to rise as the demand for certain other goods rises. For example, if the demand for cars were to rise, the demand for petrol would also be expected to rise. If, therefore, *the price of cars were to fall (raising the demand for cars), we would expect the demand for petrol (which is said to be complementary to the demand for cars) to rise.*

(c) *Income*

As an individual's level of income rises we would expect a utility maximizer to buy more goods and services. Thus, assuming that the price of a particular commodity remains constant, a consumer can buy more units. If there is a rise in real income and no change in the price of a normal good, there will be a *shift* in the demand curve to the right.

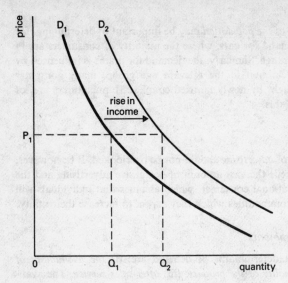

Figure 12. *A shift in demand resulting from a rise in income*

Inferior goods (of which Giffen goods are examples) are exceptions to this general rule: as an individual's income rises, he spends less on inferior goods. As people become richer they are likely to spend, for example, less on bus fares (being able, instead, to run a private car). Similarly, as people become richer they tend to spend less on margarine and more on butter. Manufacturers tend to be aware of this and have tried to alter the good so that it becomes a normal good: the introduction of so-called 'health margarines' might encourage people to buy more as income rises, no matter how much income rises.

(d) Existing stocks

Demand also depends, partly, upon the *existing stocks of goods*. For example, if a consumer already has a washing-machine, it is unlikely that he will want another one. Therefore, demand for some products may be in a *'saturation' market*, which means that the demand will mainly be a replacement one rather than a demand for new items. Again, manufacturers and producers will be aware of this and may try to introduce new or 'improved' products to alter the demand. Thus, demand partly depends upon whether the commodity is a durable or a non-durable.

(e) *Demography*

The age and size of the population may be important in determining, for example, the demand for cars, where the majority of consumers are in the 25 to 55 age range. Similarly, the demand for prams is influenced by the number of children in the relevant age group; many consumer durables are bought by newly married couples. Manufacturers are, of course, aware of this.

(f) *Advertising*

The importance of *advertising* should not be overlooked. It is, however, difficult to reconcile the vast amount of persuasive advertising and the concept of the rational consumer, which assumes that individuals will only buy those commodities which they expect to increase their utility.

(g) *Other determinants*

Other important determinants of demand are: (i) *the availability of credit;* (ii) *the quality of the product;* (iii) *after-sales service.* The availability of credit particularly affects the demand for consumer durables: a large percentage of television sets are bought on credit.

Movements along the demand curve and shifts of the demand curve

A change in the price of a commodity, other determinants being equal, will cause a movement along the demand curve, i.e. either an *extension along* or a *contraction along* the demand curve.

A change in one of the other determinants, other determinants (including price) being equal, will cause a shift of the demand curve either to the right or to the left. A shift to the right represents a rise in demand; a shift to the left represents a fall in demand (see Figure 12).

4. The elasticity of demand

The demand for some products is more responsive to a change in price than the demand for other products. In other words, a 10 per cent rise in the price of good A might lead to a 20 per cent fall in the quantity demanded, while the same 10 per cent rise in the price of good B might lead to a 5 per cent fall in the quantity demanded. Good A is said to be fairly price elastic and good B is said to be fairly price inelastic.

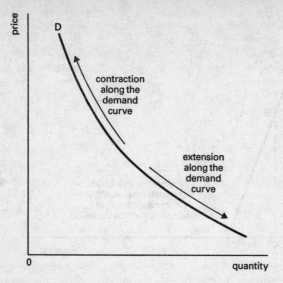

Figure 13. *Movements along the demand curve*

The formula for the price elasticity of demand is

$$\frac{\text{change in quantity demanded}}{\text{change in price}}, \text{ i.e. } \frac{\Delta Q}{\Delta P}.$$

Although with a downward sloping demand curve, any value for price elasticity is negative, economists usually disregard the minus sign. *The demand for a particular commodity is said to be price elastic if the absolute value of $\Delta Q/\Delta P$ is greater than one; it is said to be price inelastic if the absolute value of $\Delta Q/\Delta P$ is less than one.* In other words, *demand is said to be elastic if the total expenditure (which is the same thing as total revenue, i.e. unit price multiplied by the quantity demanded) falls as price rises*, while demand is said to be inelastic if total expenditure rises as price rises.

Where the elasticity of demand is equal to one in absolute terms, demand is said to have unit price elasticity: a rise in price will not alter total revenue.

It should be noted that on a downward-sloping linear demand curve (which has a constant slope) the price elasticity of demand varies from point to point: moving down such a curve the elasticity falls. The curve illustrated in Figure 15 has, for example, a price elasticity of 3 (i.e. elastic demand) when the price is £6, a price elasticity of 1 (i.e. unit elasticity)

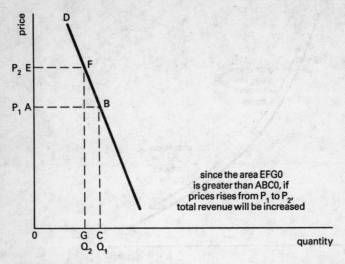

Figure 14a. *Price inelasticity of demand*

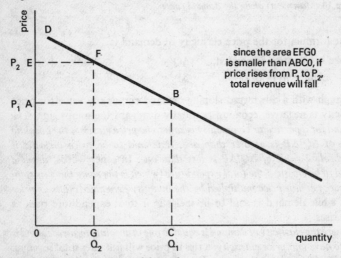

Figure 14b. *Price elasticity of demand*

when the price is £4 and a price elasticity of 0.33 (i.e. inelastic demand) when the price is £2. Thus, the price elasticity of demand is not the same thing as the slope of the demand curve.

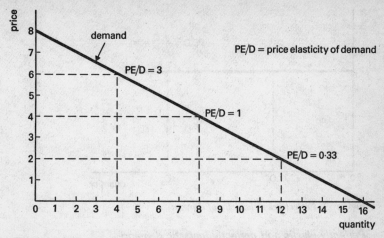

Figure 15. *How price elasticity changes over the length of a linear demand curve*

Given such a demand schedule, if the price is originally £6, a rise in price will reduce total revenue; if the price is originally £2, a rise in price (as long as it does not rise too much) will increase total revenue. It is worth producers' while, therefore, to keep raising their prices until the point along the demand curve is reached where demand is no longer inelastic.

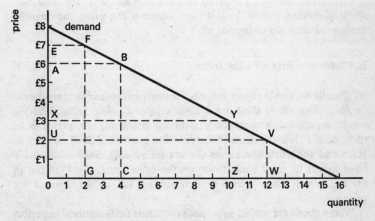

Figure 16. *The effect of a rise in price upon total revenue*

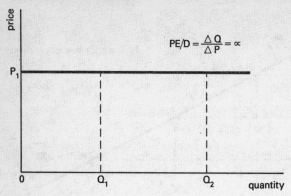

Figure 17. *Perfect price elasticity of demand*

Perfectly elastic and perfectly inelastic demand

On the other hand, both horizontal and vertical linear demand curves do have a constant price elasticity of demand.

A horizontal demand curve is used to illustrate *perfect elasticity (i.e. where the absolute value of elasticity is infinity).* It is clear from Figure 17 that any rise in price (however small) to a level above P_1, will lead to a complete loss of demand. This is because consumers switch to perfect substitutes. To put it another way, the quantity demanded will alter along the demand curve, but this will not cause any change in price.

Figure 18 illustrates a *perfectly inelastic demand curve: the price elasticity of demand is zero.* In this case, whatever the price, the quantity demanded does not change at all.

5. Determinants of elasticity

(i) Usually we would expect *the price elasticity of demand for a product to be fairly high where there are a large number of close substitutes.* We would expect the demand for a particular brand of, say, petrol to be more elastic than the demand for petrol in general: if Shell puts up its price and the other companies do not follow suit, Shell will quickly have to put its price back down; on the other hand, the 1974 rise in OPEC prices did not lead to a significant fall in the demand for oil.

Where goods are perfect substitutes for others (as is assumed in perfect competition), the demand curve for one firm's product is said to be

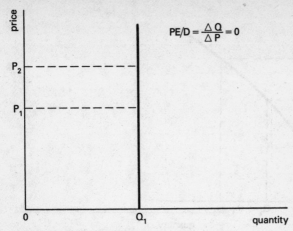

Figure 18. *Perfect price inelasticity of demand*

infinitely elastic and the demand curve is shown as a horizontal straight line: the product of one firm in the industry is said to be a perfect substitute for the product of another firm in the industry. If there are no substitutes at all and demand remains constant irrespective of price, it will be shown as a vertical straight line.

(ii) *The percentage of income spent on goods or services will also tend to determine the price elasticity of demand.* For example, the price of salt is only a very small part of personal expenditure and the demand for this therefore tends to be inelastic.

(iii) Economists often use the phrases *'necessities'* (*which by definition have inelastic demand*) *and 'luxuries'* (*which by definition have elastic demand*). However, it is probably best to avoid using these phrases in examinations: in a modern Western society there may be few commodities (apart from basic foodstuffs) which are necessary for survival, but many people would now regard a television set as a 'necessity', whereby a rise in price may lead to no significant fall in demand. A better phrase for such goods might be *'conventional necessities'*.

(iv) *Price elasticity of demand may change over time.* For example, if the price of British Rail season tickets rises, in the short run non-car-owners may have little choice but to pay the increase in price. In the longer run, however, if the season ticket is a large proportion of income, people can try to either change their job or move home or look for alternative modes of transport, including purchasing a car. People may also react more to sudden rather than gradual changes in price. For

77

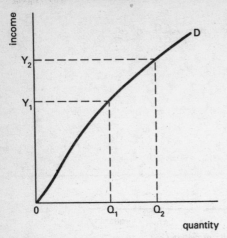

Figure 19. *The income elasticity of demand for a normal good*

example, a heavy increase in tax on petrol or cigarettes may have the immediate effect of reducing demand. However, once consumers get used to this price then the demand may revert back to its level of before the increase. If price increases are gradual, the demand curve may be fairly inelastic because people do not really notice.

6. The income elasticity of demand

The income elasticity of demand measures the responsiveness of demand to changes in income. It is positive for normal goods and negative for inferior goods.

The income elasticity is generally greater than one for 'luxuries' or superior goods and less than one for basic goods such as foodstuffs: as an individual's income rises he will spend a smaller proportion of his income on food and a greater proportion on, among other things, consumer durables. The income elasticity is represented by the following formula:

change in quantity demanded
_____
     change in income

or $\dfrac{\Delta Q}{\Delta Y}$,

where Y represents income.

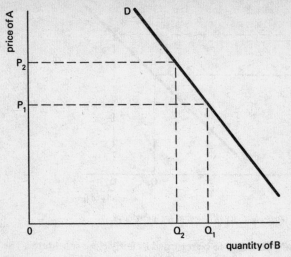

Figure 20. *The cross-elasticity of demand for complementary goods*

7. The cross-elasticity of demand

(a) *Complementary goods*

The cross-elasticity of demand measures the effect of a change in price of one good (for example, good A) upon the quantity demanded of another good (good B). The formula for the cross-elasticity of demand is

change in quantity demanded of **B**
―――――――――――――――――――
      change in price of A

or $\dfrac{\Delta Q_B}{\Delta P_A}$.

If a rise in the price of A leads to a fall in the demand for B (i.e. if there is a negative cross-elasticity), then the two goods are said to be complements. For example, as the price of bread rises the demand for butter may well fall. The higher the negative value of the cross-elasticity of demand, the more complementary are the two goods.

(b) *Substitutes*

If a rise in the price of A leads to a rise in the demand for B (i.e. if there is a positive cross-elasticity), then the two goods are said to be substitutes.

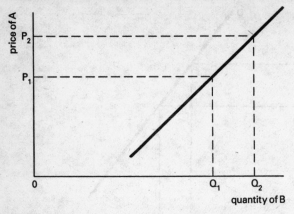

Figure 21. *The cross-elasticity of demand for substitutes*

Butter and margarine tend to be regarded as fairly close substitutes. The higher the positive value of the cross-elasticity of demand, the nearer the two goods are to being perfect substitutes. If the value of the cross-elasticity of demand is zero, then there is no relationship between the two goods being considered.

8. How do businessmen know what the demand curve looks like?

Businessmen may know from past experience what have been the effects of changes in price. For example, a bus operator should have data relating to changes in fares. A manufacturer may have data relating to sales of his particular products. However, since (as mentioned earlier in the chapter) a number of variables affect demand, it is unlikely that many (if any) businesses have perfect information. Usually most businesses will only have data relating to a small part of the total demand curve. The problem is even more acute (as we shall show in Chapter 10) in oligopoly, where the demand curve depends upon the reactions of other producers to any price changes which the oligopolist makes.

The problem of uncertainty in business is almost certainly greater on the demand than on the supply side. Because of this, businessmen may have their own market-research department to try to evaluate how consumers will react to changes in price or other variables; in some cases they may, before making a major launch or a new product, try to obtain some sample data.

*

1. What factors affect the demand for home computers?

The price of computers and the related products is important. For example, many people, when buying a home computer, also require a printer for output. The price of printers has fallen but not to the same extent as that of the home computer. Many home computers need a separate monitor, which could be the home television set. Whether people require a separate television depends partly upon home circumstances. Some home computers, however, have the monitor included in the price. The price of software must also be considered.

The price which people are prepared to pay for the computer may depend partly upon the purposes for which it is required. For example, people may be willing to pay less for a home computer designed solely for playing games but may be prepared to pay slightly more if they wish to teach themselves programming or to use it for educational or even for limited business purposes. The concept of price expectations may be important. Computer prices have been decreasing and some people may wait until the prices go down even further both in real and money terms.

The quality of the product may also be important. Perhaps, to be more precise, it is the perceived quality of the computer, since there is evidence to show that relatively few people have the necessary information to make a really informed choice.

Seasonal factors are also very important: a considerable proportion, perhaps almost three quarters of home computers, are bought in the September to December period in the United Kingdom.

The existing stock of computers may also be important. If people already have a computer they may decide to buy a more advanced one, but only recently has there been any large-scale development of a second-hand market whereby individuals can sell their old computer at a reasonable price before buying a new, more sophisticated computer.

The market for computers is likely to be extended by the demonstration effect: as more computers are bought so more people are exposed to their advantages (and their limitations).

The demand is likely to be influenced both by income and possibly by social class. These two are obviously correlated. Demographic aspects may also be important. For example, we might expect younger people to be more interested in buying computers than older people. At the present time, it seems that men are more likely to be willing to buy computers than women. The reasons for this are not very clear, although it may be related to social conditioning.

2. Why might the government need to consider the different types of elasticity of demand when imposing taxation on tobacco?

If the government were to consider further taxation on tobacco it might do so for two reasons: to reduce the health risks – in the United Kingdom, for example, it has been estimated that perhaps 100,000 people per year suffer premature death as a result of smoking – or to raise revenue. If the demand for cigarettes were very price elastic then a relatively small increase in tax would be sufficient to deter smoking quite considerably but the amount of revenue which the government would get, if levied on a percentage basis, would decline as a result of such a tax. If, however, as is likely over most ranges of price, the demand is inelastic, then raising the tax would have relatively little effect upon cigarette consumption and the government would raise revenue as a result of an increase in tax (see Figure 16, p. 75).

The government might also wish to consider the cross-elasticity of demand. For example, if it were to impose additional tax on cigarettes but not on pipe tobacco, then one would need to know whether or not they were close substitutes and this could be found by looking at the cross-elasticity. If they were close substitutes then raising tax on cigarettes but not on pipe tobacco would lead to lower revenue for the government as a result of the higher tax. If, however, they were not close substitutes then the government could proceed with the taxation. If, however, it was felt that, for other reasons, the government wished to encourage substitutes – for example, if research were to show that low tar brands were significantly less harmful than high tar brands – the government could tax high tar cigarettes at a higher rate in order to boost the substitution.

The government might also consider the income elasticity of demand. For example, if it were found, as is often claimed, that higher-income groups spend a smaller proportion of income on cigarettes than lower-income groups, then it might be felt that high duty on cigarettes was regressive, i.e. bore more heavily on the poor than the rich.

Measurement of the income elasticity of the demand for tobacco may also be helpful to a government formulating its public expenditure and income plans for, say, a five-year period: it could provide some indication of the revenue likely to be gained from taxation on tobacco if incomes were to rise during this period.

MULTIPLE-CHOICE QUESTIONS

1. A transport undertaking obtains the following price elasticity of demand for its services.

	Price elasticity of demand
(a) Business travel peak	0.3
(b) Business travel off peak	0.5
(c) Social travel peak	1.0
(d) Social travel off peak	1.5

In the light of this information, for which of the above circumstances would a small price reduction lead to an increase in sales and total revenue?
Answer – (d)

2. If a firm, from its market research, finds that the cross-elasticity of demand between products X and Y is +0.4 this means that an increase in the price of X by 10 per cent will lead to:
   (a) a more than proportionate increase in the sales of Y;
   (b) a less than proportionate increase in the sales of Y;
   (c) a decrease, but less than proportionate in the sales of Y;
   (d) a more than proportionate decrease in the sales of Y.
Answer – (b)

3. If, following an increase in price, the total revenue from the sales of a product is reduced, this implies that the price elasticity of demand for the product is:
   (a) elastic;
   (b) unitary;
   (c) inelastic;
   (d) completely inelastic.
Answer – (a)

4. If, following a general rise in incomes of 5 per cent, sales of a product rise by 5 per cent, other factors remaining equal, this implies that the income elasticity of demand for the product is;
   (a) +1;
   (b) −1;

   (*c*) 0;

   (*d*) completely income elastic.

Answer – (*a*)

5. Which of the following is most likely to cause the demand curve to shift to the right for computers?

   (*a*) A decrease in the price of computers.

   (*b*) An increase in the price of computers.

   (*c*) The demonstration effect, i.e. firms see other firms successfully using computers.

   (*d*) Articles in the press suggesting that the virtues of computers are over-rated.

Answer – (*c*)

6. Which of the following are most likely to cause a movement along the demand curve to the left?

   (*a*) An increase in the price of computers.

   (*b*) A decrease in the price of computers.

   (*c*) An increase in the price of wages paid to computer programmers.

   (*d*) A decrease in the wages paid to computer programmers.

Answer – (*a*)

7. Price elasticity of demand can be described as:

   (*a*) $\dfrac{\text{percentage change in price}}{\text{percentage change in demand}}$;

   (*b*) $\dfrac{\text{percentage change in price}}{\text{percentage change in income}}$;

   (*c*) $\dfrac{\text{percentage change in demand}}{\text{percentage change in income}}$;

   (*d*) $\dfrac{\text{percentage change in demand}}{\text{percentage change in price}}$.

Answer – (*d*)

8. If the price elasticity of demand is 0.5, a 10 per cent increase in price will lead to:

   (*a*) a decrease in demand of 5 per cent;

   (*b*) an increase in demand of 20 per cent;

   (*c*) a decrease in demand of 25 per cent;

   (*d*) an increase in demand of 5 per cent;

(*e*) an increase in demand of 10 per cent.
Answer – (*a*)

9. An increase in the price of petrol will most probably lead to:
  (*a*) a decrease in demand for cars;
  (*b*) an increase in the demand for cars;
  (*c*) the demand for cars remaining the same.
Answer – (*a*)

10. A reduction, such as that which occurred in the 1970s, in tariffs for goods sent between member states of the EEC will lead to which of the following:
(A) a decrease in exports from the United Kingdom to other members of the EEC;
(B) an increase in exports from the United Kingdom to other member states;
(C) an increase in imports from other member states of the EEC to the United Kingdom;
(D) a decrease in British imports from other EEC members?

  (*a*) A only.
  (*b*) A and D only.
  (*c*) B only.
  (*d*) B and C only.
Answer – (*d*)

11–14. The following factors might affect the price elasticity of demand:
  (*a*) the price of a substitute;
  (*b*) the price of complementary products or services;
  (*c*) the price as a proportion of total income;
  (*d*) advertising.
Which of the above factors is the main determinant of the price elasticity of demand for the following products?

11. Salt.
Answer – (*c*)

12. Computers, where the price remains constant, but the price of software decreases.
Answer – (*b*)

13. Margarine, when the EEC, in order to get rid of the so-called 'butter mountain', reduces the price of butter.
Answer – (*a*)

14. Beer, where the government has to raise the tax in order to conform to international regulations.
Answer – (a)

15–23. Among the main influences on demand are:
   (*a*) the price of the good or service;
   (*b*) the price of substitutes;
   (*c*) the price of complementary goods or services;
   (*d*) income;
   (*e*) taste;
   (*f*) the size of population;
   (*g*) income distribution;
   (*h*) the number of households.

15. If a household wins a bingo competition, this may affect its demand for a new washing-machine because — is altered.
Answer – (d)

16. An increase in the VAT on washing-machines may affect the demand for washing machines because — is altered.
Answer – (a)

17. A reduction in launderette prices may affect the demand for washing-machines because — is altered.
Answer – (b)

18. A reduction in the number of launderettes may affect the demand for washing-machines because — is altered.
Answer – (b)

19. An increase in the number of newly married couples may affect the demand for washing-machines because — is altered.
Answer – (h)

20. A baby boom may affect the demand for washing-machines because — is altered.
Answer – (f)

21. An increase in national insurance payments may affect the demand for washing-machines because — is altered.
Answer – (d)

22. An increase in the price of electricity for domestic, but not industrial, consumption may affect the demand for washing-machines because — is altered.
Answer – (c)

23. If the government raises the price of the television licence by 50 per cent this may affect the demand for television sets because — is altered.
Answer – (*c*)

*

DATA RESPONSE

1. The price elasticity of demand depends partly upon the *degree of substitutability* in the eyes of the consumer. This may, in turn, depend partly upon the degree of information available to the consumer. Usually this will be greater for goods or services purchased by firms rather than for households. *Persuasive advertising* may decrease the degree of substitutability in the eyes of the consumer. It is possible to find examples of this in the detergent industry and many others. There are likely to be a greater number of substitutes for brands of goods rather than for commodities as a whole and, therefore, the price elasticity of demand for one brand is likely to be more price elastic than for the entire market. The relevance of this should be obvious. For example, when, in September 1974, three of the major bread manufacturers put up their prices at the same time by the same amount, this led to relatively little loss of demand. However, if only one bread manufacturer had put up his price the loss of sales to that manufacturer might well have been considerable.

(*a*) Explain the terms in *italic* type.
(*b*) Does advertising always decrease substitutability in the eyes of the consumer? Explain your answer.
(*c*) What would you expect the effects on demand to be if:
　(i) one major oil company raised its prices while others did not;
　(ii) all major oil producers raised their prices at the same time?

2. The demand for shipbuilding is strongly *correlated* to the volume of world trade. It also depends upon the existing size of shipping fleets. If there is already excess capacity then, even if there is an upturn in world trade, there is unlikely to be an increase in orders for ships. Conversely, even if there were only a mild upturn in world trade but there were already difficulties in obtaining suitable ships, the demand for shipbuilding would tend to rise.

Shipbuilding is an example of the capital-goods industry and is very much an example of *derived demand*. Some economists and statisticians have, therefore, tried to predict future trading patterns, especially in oil, which accounts for a large percentage of the total demand for shipping.

The demand for shipbuilding also depends upon price, although this is fairly complicated since many countries *subsidize* their shipbuilding industries in order to increase employment in these industries.

The demand for shipbuilding may also depend upon the quality of the ship and the delivery dates. Delivery dates may be particularly important where the shipowner feels there are short-term opportunities. The demand for shipbuilding may also be reduced if canals, such as the Suez and Panama canals, are increased in size, enabling larger ships to have shorter routes and, thus, to be used more efficiently. The major cause of a decline in the number of ships ordered has been improved handling methods, which enable ships to be used much more intensely.

(*a*) Explain the terms in *italic* type.

(*b*) Why might the demand for ships be expected to decline in the future?

SELF-EXAMINATION QUESTIONS

1. Economists usually assume that if price decreases, demand will increase and vice versa. What exceptions, if any, are there to this rule?

2. Economists assume that the demand curve is generally downward sloping, partly because of diminishing marginal utility. Explain why there might be exceptions to the principle of diminishing marginal utility.

3. Diamonds are inessential to life whereas water is essential. Why then is water cheap but diamonds expensive? Explain in relation to the concept of marginal utility.

4. 'Economists overemphasize the importance of price when considering demand.' Discuss.

5. Why might car manufacturers be interested in the cross price elasticity of demand of: (*a*) other firm's products with their own; (*b*) different models of their own cars?

7. Supply

1. The industry's supply curve and the firm's supply curve

It is important to distinguish between the supply curve for the individual firm and the supply curve for the industry as a whole. Logically, *the supply curve for the industry can be found from a summation of all the individual producers' supply curves.*

Usually (as in Fig. 22), *the supply curve is drawn as upward sloping*, since the higher the unit price, the more profit-maximizing firms will wish to produce.

One of the underlying hypotheses in orthodox microeconomic theory is indeed that *firms aim at profit maximization*. To achieve this, they will

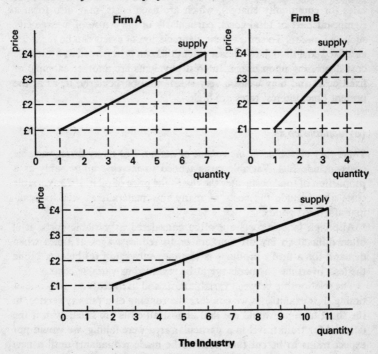

Figure 22. *How the industry's supply curve is calculated*

supply additional items until the marginal revenue equals marginal cost. Factors of production (i.e. land, labour and capital) are required by firms in order to be able to provide a supply of goods and services. As a firm employs more factors of production, its total costs (i.e. the rewards to these factors – rent, wages and profits) rise, requiring it to supply more units of its product: *a firm produces a supply of goods and services in order to cover its costs.*

2. A definition of costs

(a) *Fixed costs*

Fixed costs are those costs which occur whatever the level of output, and even if there is no output at all. Fixed costs include management and administration costs, which, in some service industries, are very high, while in some other industries they are relatively insignificant. Rents and rates (or community charge), which are fixed costs, may also form a significant part of total costs, particularly in the centre of a large city such as London. To some extent, depreciation of assets can be regarded as a fixed cost though to a lesser extent this can be regarded as a variable cost depending upon usage. Interest payments are another example of fixed costs and may well be very substantial particularly, if, as at the present time, interest rates are high.

(b) *Variable costs*

These vary according to the volume of output. For many firms, variable costs include fuel. Variable costs tended to increase appreciably as a proportion of total costs after the rise in the price of oil in 1973. Variable costs also include the costs of many raw materials as well as semi-manufactured goods.

Although labour costs are often considered as variable costs, it is often difficult to lay off workers or to reduce wages at times when demand for a firm's products is low (see subsection (c) below). None the less, overtime payments might be regarded as variable costs.

The relationship between variable costs and fixed costs is partly one of timing. For example, if we consider the running of a railway service, in the short term we would see that almost all costs are fixed: even if the demand for train travel in a particular area were falling, we would not expect trains to be cut (and staff to be made redundant) until a new timetable had been organized.

(c) *Labour costs*

As we have already suggested, *it is difficult to classify labour costs as being either fixed or variable:* much depends upon the terms of contract. For example, casual labour, which was common in the 1960s in the docks, can be hired or laid off according to demand and therefore casual-labour costs are variable costs. However, following legislation in the 1970s, most workers can only be laid off at the expense of relatively high redundancy payments (though the government usually meets part of this expense) and therefore most labour costs can be regarded as fixed.

The importance of high fixed labour costs is that any disruption, whether caused by strikes, accidents, poor management or whatever, will tend to lead to difficulties for the firm, since these costs will still have to be paid irrespective of whether there is output or not.

(d) *Total costs*

Total costs are fixed costs plus variable costs. Where high capital cost projects, such as the Channel Tunnel (which would have cost £3,800m at 1983 prices) are being considered, the importance of estimating demand accurately can hardly be overlooked. Especially so in the case of the Channel Tunnel, as the opportunity cost of the Channel Tunnel, once built, will be almost negligible, i.e. it is difficult to see what else such a project could be used for. Fixed costs have, in many industries, tended to increase as a proportion of the total, as firms have become more capital-intensive. Where this is the case, it becomes even more important to carry out sensible investment appraisal.

(e) *Marginal costs*

Another important cost which firms have to consider is marginal cost. *Marginal cost is defined as the change in cost resulting from a change in the number of factor inputs.* The marginal cost curve, above the point where average variable costs equal marginal costs, is the supply curve.

It is often convenient to divide marginal costs into short-run marginal costs and long-run marginal costs (see section 4 below).

(f) *Average costs*

These may be defined as total costs divided by the total number of units produced.

(g) *The relationship between average cost and marginal cost*

The marginal-cost curve will cross the average-cost curve at its lowest point. A little thought shows the logic of this fact. For example, if a firm had total costs of £1,000 and produced ten units the average cost is £100, and if the marginal cost of the eleventh unit was greater than £100, then the average cost would rise, while if the marginal cost was less than £100, the average cost would fall.

3. The principle of diminishing marginal returns

There is a limit to the amount of goods and services a firm can produce (or supply) given a certain amount of factors. We usually expect that as a firm increases the amount of factors it employs (for example, as it employs further workers), it will be able to increase its total output, i.e. there will be increasing total returns. However, we also usually expect that the rise in total output as more and more factors are employed will get smaller and smaller, i.e. diminishing marginal returns are usually assumed. This concept was introduced in Chapter 3.

Where the principle of diminishing returns applies this means that it becomes increasingly difficult (or costly) for a firm to increase the supply of goods and services: total product can only be increased by employing more and more factors of production; more factors of production can be employed only at the expense of higher total costs. In other words, *we would expect the supply curve to become increasingly steep.*

We might assume that a firm, if it wishes to increase its output, will attempt to do so by increasing the number of workers it employs and not by increasing the amount of capital or land it uses (these two factors we will assume are held constant).

This firm (assuming that it is *a profit-maximizer*) *will employ an extra worker only as long as total output is increased as a result, i.e. as long as marginal product is positive.* Assuming diminishing marginal returns, the value of marginal product becomes smaller and smaller as more and more workers are employed. Diminishing marginal returns are assumed in the model contained in Table 9.

Employing an extra worker involves additions to the firm's total costs. Using the figures in Table 9, if the firm wishes to employ an extra worker it must pay this worker a wage of £100. Thus, the firm's total costs rise by £100 as it employs one more worker.

Table 9. The costs and output schedules of a firm producing radios

Quantity of labour	Total product	Average product	Marginal product	Variable costs (£)	Fixed costs (£)	Total costs (£)	Average variable costs (£)	Average costs (£)	Marginal costs (£)
0	0	0	0	0	75	75	—	—	—
1	20	20	20	100	75	175	5.00	8.75	5.0
2	44	22	24	200	75	275	4.55	6.25	4.17
3	63	21	19	300	75	375	4.76	5.95	5.26
4	76	19	13	400	75	475	5.26	6.25	7.69
5	85	17	9	500	75	575	5.88	6.76	11.11
6	92	15⅓	7	600	75	675	6.52	7.34	14.29

$$\text{Average variable costs} = \frac{\text{total variable costs}}{\text{total product}}$$

$$\text{Average costs} = \frac{\text{total costs}}{\text{total product}}$$

$$\text{Marginal costs} = \frac{\text{change in total costs}}{\text{marginal product}}$$

(a) *Covering average variable costs*

For it to be worth while for the firm in our model (or any profit-maximizing firm) to start producing any output of radios (or, to put it another way, for it to be worth the firm employing any workers at all), it must cover its costs.

Given a cost schedule, *a profit-maximizing firm will not produce an output at which it does not cover at least its average variable costs.* In our model, the firm's average variable costs are the labour costs per unit of output. If the level of demand is such that the price it is able to charge is less than these costs, then there is no point in the firm being in business. In other words, if consumers are willing to pay only £4.17 for a radio, the firm could produce 44 radios (and be able to sell all of them) and cover its marginal costs, but it will not be able to cover its average variable costs (see Figure 24). There is no point in the firm beginning production at all until the going price is where marginal cost equals average variable cost, i.e. *the 'shutdown' price is where $MC = AVC$.* A profit-maximizing firm will supply nothing if the going price is less than average variable cost,

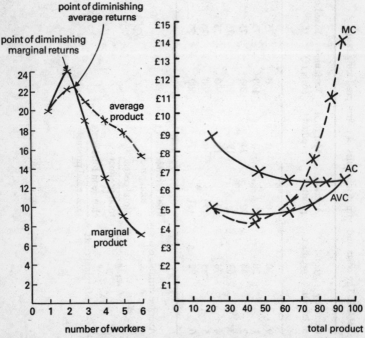

Figure 23. *The costs and output of a firm producing radios*

i.e. if P ⟨ AVC, supply = 0.

It should be noted that *the marginal cost curve always cuts the average variable cost curve where the average variable cost curve is at its lowest point,*

i.e. *MC = AVC, where AVC is at its minimum.*

(b) *Covering average costs*

Even if the firm is producing at a price greater than AVC, it may still not be breaking even, i.e. total costs may still be greater than total revenue.

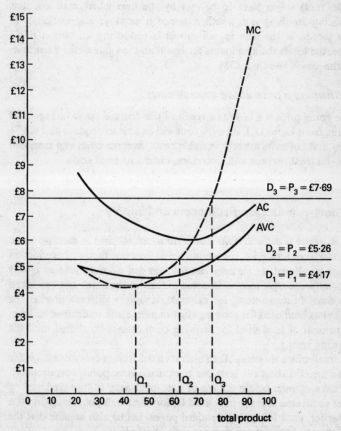

Figure 24. *Pricing and output of a firm producing radios*

If, for example, demand rises (in Figure 24) from D_1 to D_2, so that the going price of radios rises to £5.26, if the firm produces 63 radios it will be able to sell them all and will cover its marginal costs and its average variable costs. However, its total costs are higher than total revenue, i.e. average costs are greater than average revenue (which is the same thing as the demand curve unless there is price discrimination; see Chapter 10).

The 'break-even price' is the point where $P = AC = MC$.

It may be worth while for a profit-maximizing firm to supply an output when the price is below the 'break-even' point, because (as long as the price is covering AVC), the loss to the firm will be smaller than the costs of producing nothing, since the firm has fixed costs (for example, rent) which have to be met by the firm whether or not it is producing anything (i.e. whether or not it employs any workers). In other words, if the firm in our model is producing an output of 63 radios, the losses the firm incurs are less than the value of the fixed costs (i.e. the loss is less than £75).

(c) *Charging a price above average costs*

If the going price is £7.69 (as a result of the demand curve in Figure 24 shifting from D_2 to D_3), then the firm will be able to produce and sell 76 radios and cover its average variable costs, average costs and marginal costs. Its total revenue will, therefore, exceed its total costs.

4. Short-run and long-run costs and supply

The short run is defined as the period for which the firm in question has at least one fixed factor, i.e. the amount of at least one factor of production cannot be altered. *In the long run the firm can alter the amount of any factor of production it uses.* In some industries the short run can last a long time. In agriculture, for example, it is very difficult to alter the amount of land used for growing corn to meet a rise in demand in June: the amount of land used for growing corn cannot be altered until the following spring.

A small office may be able to alter its fixed factors every week, i.e. for such a firm the short run lasts one week; for a large public corporation it may take months before the use of new machinery is approved.

Let us assume that the only fixed factor of a small publishing firm is a typewriter, used for typing standard pages. Let us also assume that the short run for the firm lasts a week because it takes a week to order and deliver a new typewriter.

A typewriter might originally have cost £20 to buy and one page could be typed, using this machine, every hour. If the typist is paid £4.00 per hour the average cost of the first page typed using the machine is £24.00. The average cost falls with each additional page typed. Eventually, however, the fall in average costs as one more page is typed becomes almost insignificant: the difference in the average cost of typing the 100th page and the 101st page is negligible. We would even expect the average cost to start rising: as the typewriter becomes older the keys might start jamming, so that it takes the typist longer and longer to type one page.

From what we have said so far, we might expect the short-run average cost schedule to look something like $SRAC_1$, illustrated in Figure 25. The firm might decide, however, to replace the typewriter, before its average costs start rising, with a word-processor. By employing a word-processor the firm moves on to a new short-run average-cost-curve schedule ($SRAC_2$ in Figure 25). This word-processor might cost £500 but the typist might be able to type one page in half an hour.

The average cost of the first page typed using the word processor will be very high, but it will decline steeply, until the time when this word-processing machine starts to slow down, so that its average costs start to rise.

If the firm after a time replaces one word-processor with a more expensive but more productive one, it will move from short-run average-cost curve $SRAC_3$ to short-run average-cost curve $SRAC_4$ as illustrated

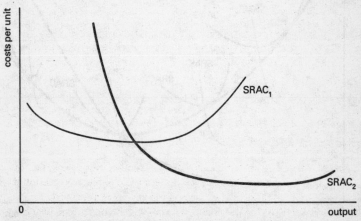

Figure 25. *The short-run average-cost curves of a small publishing firm*

in Figure 26, forming a long-run average-cost curve tangential to this series of short-run average cost curves.

Where long-run average costs are at a minimum, the optimum size of plant or, in our example, the optimum size of word-processor has been reached. The point corresponds to the minimum point of a short-run average cost curve. Through this point a short-run marginal cost curve and a long-run marginal cost curve will pass.

We would expect the long-run marginal cost curve (or supply curve) to be less steep, i.e. more elastic, than the short-run marginal cost curve (or supply curve) because in the long run output can be more easily altered because all factors are variable (see section 6).

5. Shifts in supply

(i) As we have shown in Figure 26, *as the scale of production is increased the supply curve (marginal cost curve) is shifted to the right, i.e. supply is increased.*

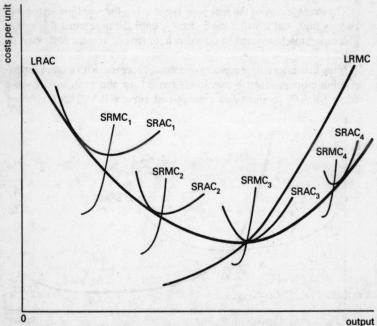

Figure 26. *The relationship between the long-run average-cost and short-run average-cost curves, and long-run and short-run marginal-cost curves*

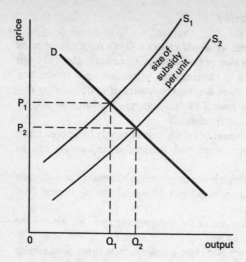

Figure 27. *The effect on supply of a subsidy to producers*

(ii) *The supply curve will also be shifted if there are other changes in the input mix.* For example, if transport costs are reduced (perhaps because of containerization) we would expect the supply curve to be shifted to the right. On the other hand, if the price of crude oil rises, we would expect firms' supply curves to be shifted to the left.

(iii) In some industries, such as agriculture, there may be a *subsidy to producers*. As a result, the supply curve will shift downwards (i.e. to the right), since the firms concerned will be able to produce a given amount of output more cheaply.

Conversely, if *taxes* are imposed, such as value added tax, then the supply curve will shift upwards (i.e. to the left).

(iv) The supply curve may also be altered for an industry or firm by *the imposition of tariffs or of non-tariff barriers to international trade.* The supply curve for many temperate agricultural foodstuffs within the E E C is influenced by tariffs, since tariffs are imposed on imports from outside the E E C to raise the price of these imports up to or above the E E C level in an attempt to reduce their supply.

(v) In the very long run we might expect there to be *improvements in technology* (such as have been brought about as a result of the 'chip revolution'). Such improvements in technology would be likely to change the whole nature of the supply curve, changing its elasticity and shifting it to the right.

6. The elasticity of supply

(i) As we have already said, *we would expect a firm's supply curve to be more elastic in the long run than in the short run,* since in the short run not all factors can be varied. In an extreme case, where factors of production are perfectly mobile and there are no economies of scale (and no diseconomies of scale) to be gained in the long run, the long-run supply curve would in fact be perfectly elastic.

In the *very long run* we would normally expect supply to be even more elastic than in the long run, since even the level of technology can be altered.

In the very short run (which is the time it takes to deliver the output to the market place) no factors at all can be varied, which implies that supply is perfectly inelastic.

(ii) *The more sellers there are in the industry, the more elastic will the industry supply curve tend to be.*

(iii) *If the firm or industry has spare capacity, then, other things being equal, supply will be more elastic than if it is operating at full capacity.*

7. Predicting the supply curve

It may be difficult to predict what the supply curve of a firm will look like. This applies even to a profit-maximizing firm.

(i) We would normally expect, for example, that when the going price falls below the average variable cost, a profit-maximizing firm will supply nothing. However, a firm may be reluctant to lose the goodwill of its customers and the laying off of workers may cause problems of industrial relations. *A firm may, therefore, continue to produce something if price falls below A V C (as long as it expects this fall to be only temporary) in the hope of maintaining consumer and worker loyalty* and, as a result, of increasing profits in the future.

Furthermore, many firms are multi-product firms and may lack detailed knowledge of each of their products. As a result, they may not be aware of times when the price of one of their products falls below A V C.

(ii) *The supply curve is difficult to predict for firms where there are long time-lags between the decision to produce and the final product,* especially if the technology is comparatively unknown. The production problem for such firms is thus that the good or service has to be produced for a considerable time before demand is known. For items such as airports and hydroelectricity and nuclear-power plants the timelags are extremely long. To overcome these problems, sophisticated market-research techniques are required.

(iii) *Prediction is also difficult when firms are not producing directly for the public.* Such firms might be producing for the government (dependent on government demand). The demand for such products will not necessarily depend on general market conditions: it may depend upon the ideology of the particular government (the demand for missiles will tend to fluctuate as different governments take office). Thus, *the uncertainty of demand adds to the production problems.* Some of the problems might be overcome through long-term contracts with the government or whoever is the potential buyer.

(iv) The problems of production are also that *firms need to take account of different factor prices as well as of changes in technology*, which means that there can be differences in the input mix. Changes in trade unions' and other people's attitudes may lead to a growth or decline in restrictive practices. These again can influence production. The growth of technical knowledge can also influence the firm's production plans.

(v) If externalities result from production, governments may intervene to restrict production. Thus, *government regulations can influence supply.*

*

QUESTION

What is the economic significance of the terms 'fixed costs' and 'variable costs'?

Fixed costs are those costs which do not vary with output. When setting up any project a firm will have to consider the cost of land, the rent payable or the interest payable on a loan for premises, as well as the likely variable costs, which, for example, might include labour and material costs. Before investing, if the firm wishes to make a profit, it will try to carry out some sort of market research to ensure that all costs, i.e. both fixed and variable, will be more than covered by revenue. Once, however, the firm is in operation, the minimum that it can charge and still stay in operation will be its variable costs and, in this respect, the fixed costs are irrelevant. The economist's claim that bygones are forever bygones is an important one here. For example, once the Channel Tunnel is built the original costs will be irrelevant to any pricing decisions. Of course, it is unlikely that a decision to build the Channel Tunnel would have been taken unless it was expected to be profitable. Once built, the opportunity cost of the Channel Tunnel will be virtually zero since it is difficult to imagine any alternative use for it.

101

In practice, the difference between fixed and variable costs will differ according to the time period being considered. For example, in the short term almost all costs, except material costs, will tend to be fixed: it is not generally possible to reduce the labour force without some minimum notice being given; other costs, such as rent, rates (or community charge), heating and lighting, exist whatever the level of output. However, in a slightly longer term, firms might be able to move from their premises and control the size of the workforce more easily.

MULTIPLE-CHOICE QUESTIONS

1. Which of the following would be fixed costs to a firm:
(A) a mortgage on premises at a fixed interest rate;
(B) a mortgage on premises which fluctuates according to the general trends in interest rates;
(C) a contract which allows the firm to hire a fluctuating number of vehicles at a fixed cost per vehicle;
(D) a number of freelance workers working for a firm where hours may fluctuate, but which has an arrangement that their wages per hour are fixed for a period of two years?
  (*a*) A only.
  (*b*) A and B only.
  (*c*) A, B and C only.
  (*d*) D only.
  (*e*) All.
Answer – (*b*)

Table 10. A firm's costs

Output	Variable costs	Total costs
0	0	100
1	20	120
2	35	135
3	45	145
4	55	155
5	70	170
6	90	190
7	120	220
8	170	270

Questions 2–4 refer to Table 10.

2. What are the firms's fixed costs?
  (*a*) 0.
  (*b*) 100.
  (*c*) 270.
  (*d*) It is impossible to tell from the given information.
Answer – (*b*)

3. At what level of output are average variable costs minimized?
  (*a*) 0.   (*f*) 5.
  (*b*) 1.   (*g*) 6.
  (*c*) 2.   (*h*) 7.
  (*d*) 3.   (*i*) 8.
  (*e*) 4.
Answer – (*e*)

4. At what level of output are average costs minimized?
  (*a*) 0.   (*f*) 5.
  (*b*) 1.   (*g*) 6.
  (*c*) 2.   (*h*) 7.
  (*d*) 3.   (*i*) 8.
  (*e*) 4.
Answer – (*h*)

5. Under what circumstances would a short-run supply curve for a good be inelastic?
(A) In the agricultural industry, where the good is perishable.
(B) In the agricultural industry, where the good can be easily stored and where there are large buffer stocks.
(C) In the manufacturing industry, where most people are highly skilled and there is a staff shortage and machinery is fully utilized.
(D) In the manufacturing industry, where labour is mainly unskilled and the industry is in a recession.
  (*a*) A only.
  (*b*) A and B only.
  (*c*) A and C only.
  (*d*) C and D only.
Answer – (*c*)

6–8. In the diagram overleaf, showing S_0, S_1 and S_2, explain how the following would affect the supply curve, given S_0 as the norm.

103

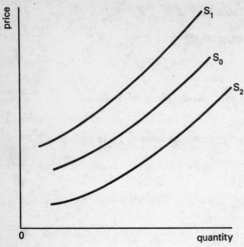

Figure 28

Product	Changes
6. Take-away food	Value added tax is imposed for the first time.
7. The road haulage industry	An increase in the price of Derv (this is the fuel used).
8. An office using modern equipment.	The price of computers falls and their productivity increases.

(*a*) Supply stays at S_0.
(*b*) Supply shifts to S_1.
(*c*) Supply shifts to S_2.

Answers – 6 – (*b*); 7 – (*b*); 8 – (*c*).

DATA RESPONSE

Quantity of labour	Output
1	150
2	200
3	280
4	350
5	400
6	420
7	430

Given that fixed costs total £2,500 and that wages (the only variable costs) are £5,000 per worker:

  (*a*) at which quantity of labour are average costs at their lowest;
  (*b*) at which quantity of labour is marginal cost at its lowest?

SELF-EXAMINATION QUESTIONS

1. Economists often suggest that firms' supply curves will be partially determined by the marginal physical productivity of factors, including labour. How is it possible to assess this when workers interact and when there is no direct physical measurement of the job, for example as with personnel officers or teachers?

2. How far do changing prices, as, for example, have occurred following the chip revolution, alter the supply curves of individual firms?

3. For some items, such as rare stamps, supply cannot be increased. Using appropriate diagrams show what happens if prices or demand increases.

4. What is the difference between fixed and variable costs? Explain how, in a manufacturing industry, these affect the supply curve.

5. Usually we assume that the higher the price, the more will be supplied. Under what circumstances might this not occur?

6. Explain how (*a*) a proportionate tax and (*b*) a proportionate subsidy would affect the supply curve.

7. Explain why the price elasticity of supply might be different in the short and the long term with reference to the electricity industry.

8. Explain how a decrease in the price of raw materials could affect the supply curve.

9. What will happen to the supply of timber in (*a*) the short run and (*b*) the long run, if timber prices increase?

10. What will happen to supplies of: (*a*) wheat; (*b*) fish; (*c*) shipping space; (*d*) houses; (*e*) cars, in (i) the short run and (ii) the long run, if prices rise considerably or if prices fall considerably?

11. Governments sometimes impose maximum prices, either as a result of prices and incomes policies or for social reasons. Explain, with the use of a diagram, how this might affect the supply curve. State the assumptions that you are making.

8. Private-sector organizations

1. The sole trader

(a) *Advantages*

(i) Sole traders have the advantage that they *can start with the minimum of formalities*.

(ii) The term 'sole trader' implies that he or she is the sole owner of the business and will usually *make most of the key decisions*. It does not, as some students seem to think, mean that there is only one person in the business: the sole trader can have employees.

(iii) Another advantage of the small firm (and, in particular, of the sole trader) is the *ability to make quick decisions*. This is particularly useful where there are frequent changes in prices or activities, e.g. in greengrocery and in road haulage. However, quick decision-making can be disadvantageous if it leads to impulsive decisions. In larger firms, with some degree of bureaucracy, decision-making may be slightly improved.

(b) *Problems*

(i) One of the problems for the sole trader, as for many very small businesses, is that *there is a considerable degree of legislation to be complied with in employing other people*. This, though, may be more of a problem which is perceived rather than actual: small businesses, including the sole trader, can receive information and advice about the social legislation from the Department of Trade and Industry's Small Firms' Advice Centres; commercial bankers also publish regular information, often in the form of booklets; increasingly, local authorities, concerned about loss of rates if small firms do not establish themselves, also offer advice on finance, premises and, in some cases, give grants to small businesses.

(ii) Another of the main problems for small businesses seems to be their *marketing and costing*. Sole traders can obtain advice from banks, accountants or solicitors before setting up in business, although there has been some criticism in magazines suggesting that some bank managers' knowledge may be limited.

106

While most traditional economists assume profit maximization, the *Bolton Committee 1971* (which carried out one of the few thorough appraisals of the small-business sector) suggested that one of the major objectives of many small businesses (including sole traders) is independence rather than profit maximization.

Some surveys seem to suggest that, in view of sole traders' *opportunity costs* (i.e. what they could earn elsewhere), they would be better off if they were employed by someone else, rather than trying to set up their own firm. However, during the recession many sole traders have set up partly because they have been made redundant.

In the retail trade, assistance with pricing may well be given by manufacturers or wholesalers who give a series of recommended prices. In the retail trade it is also often possible to observe the prices of competitors. However, in other industries, where prices are not necessarily published and information is less readily available, pricing may cause more of a problem. Many small firms use the mark-up principle, i.e. looking at average costs and adding on a percentage. While some economists have condemned the practice of marking up, they ignore the problems which many small firms have in obtaining adequate data about the price elasticity of demand.

As far as costing is concerned, not all small firms make allowances, for example, for the replacement of equipment. This is a growing criticism of small road-haulage firms.

(iii) Many small firms, particularly sole traders, use the owners' premises as offices. One possible limitation to this practice is *the need to obtain planning permission*, but this may not present any problems if the business does not create a nuisance for other people. The problem of obtaining suitable premises has not been helped by the increasing tendency towards larger shopping precincts (where the initial costs of rents are high) and the demolition of much of the older inner-city areas, which had presented opportunities for setting up small-scale businesses.

(iv) Another problem involved in setting up business is *the possible difficulty in obtaining finance*. Sole traders rely on personal finances, such as second mortgages. However, many financial institutions, including the commercial banks, are now more willing to help the very small firm.

(v) A major disadvantage is that the sole trader has *unlimited liability*.

(vi) There are also *problems involved in taking holidays or falling sick*: activities could be severely disrupted. Business will usually have to be brought to an end with the death of the owner.

2. Partnerships

Partnerships are governed by the *1890 Partnership Act*, and the legislation lays down a model partnership which can be used unless the partners agree otherwise. There must be a minimum of two and a maximum of twenty partners, generally.

(a) *The advantage of a partnership over a sole trader*

The major advantage of a partnership compared with a sole trader is that between them *they may have more skills and capital* than a sole trader. There is more possibility of scope for skilled, professional management and, in some cases, it is possible for people without the necessary capital but with skills to join those who have capital available.

(b) *Disadvantages*

(i) *Decision-making may take longer than with a sole trader* and, though the legal maximum is generally twenty partners, if there is any great overlap of functions, decision-making may well be very time-consuming.

(ii) One of the major disadvantages of partnerships (as of sole traders) is that the owners have *unlimited liability*.

(iii) *A partnership will be affected by the death of a partner*, since, at that stage, part of the capital may have to be sold. It may, therefore, be advisable for partners to take out life assurances on each other to overcome this problem.

(c) *Why form a partnership rather than a limited company?*

(i) It is generally *cheaper to set up a partnership than a limited company*.

(ii) In some professions there are *rules forbidding the formation of limited companies*: partnerships are often found in such professions.

(iii) Depending on current legislation, *partnerships may need less documentation (such as less detailed accounts) and may have tax advantages* (this is often the case in West Germany). Thus, there is a tendency for there to be less disclosure of information and reduced administration costs, which could lead to poor accounting.

(d) *Other features of partnerships*

(i) *Once people become partners they cannot be removed* unless there is prior agreement to the contrary.

(ii) *Partners share equally in capital and profits (or losses)* unless there is an agreement to the contrary.

(iii) *All partners are entitled to be part of the management.*

(e) *Sleeping partners*

While there is a small number of limited partnerships, under the *1907 Limited Partnership Act*, there can also be so-called '*sleeping partners*'. They have *limited liability*, but are not allowed to take part in the running of the business. Not all partners can be sleeping partners.
This form of ownership is very uncommon.

3. Limited companies

There are a number of formalities to be gone through before a limited company can be set up. These include obtaining *Articles of Association* (which govern the internal affairs of the company) and a *Memorandum of Association* (which gives details of the liability of members, the amount of share capital and so on, i.e. it governs the company's external affairs).

(a) *Limited liability*

Limited companies in the United Kingdom are divided into two types, namely *private companies* and *public companies*.

Both private companies and public companies have the advantage over sole traders and partnerships of *limited liability*. This advantage accrues to the owners (shareholders).

In the case of very small-scale private limited companies, this advantage of limited liability may not be as great as many textbooks suggest. For example, with a very small private limited company, when seeking premises, the directors may have to give personal guarantees, since the landlords will be only too aware of the problems if such a small firm was to go bankrupt. None the less, generally limited liability has been important. It means that, in the event of bankruptcy, the most that the shareholders will lose is the value of their shares. Limited liability has led to the growth of many firms where there is a separation between management and ownership.

(b) *Differences between private and public companies*

(i) Under the *1985 Companies Act*, both private and public companies have to have a minimum of two members but *public companies have to have a minimum of fifty thousand pounds capital.*

(ii) The most important difference is that *in a private limited company there are restrictions on the sales of shares* and generally shares can only be sold without advertisement. *In public companies, however, as the name implies, shares can be sold publicly*, with the company being quoted on the Stock Exchange: the Stock Exchange can be used as a source of finance; the public will subscribe for shares after they have seen a prospectus which gives an idea of the history of the company and its profit record. Some public companies go far beyond the minimum legislation and give a great deal of information which is helpful to prospective shareholders and, possibly, also to employees. Firms may also issue *rights issues*. These are shares which are sold to existing shareholders. One of the advantages of these is that the administration costs are likely to be lower than with other shares since the firm can contact its existing shareholders more cheaply than the general public and the proportion of take-up is likely to be higher. However, the disadvantage is that it probably limits the total capital available.

(c) *The divorce of ownership from control*

In both private and public limited companies *directors are in control*. Theoretically, members of the company, i.e. the shareholders, could elect a new board at annual general meetings. However, in the very large public companies, for example the newly privatized British Telecom (where the number of shareholders is over 2 million), it seems unlikely that they could really have effective control over the affairs. Members may, however, exercise some control if, for example, profits are too low or if another firm wishes to make a takeover bid or to merge.

In large public companies, there is likely to be *a divorce between management of the company and ownership*. This has had a number of important consequences:

(i) *it has led to management becoming more specialized*: people without capital have become part of a management structure;

(ii) according to some economists, *it has led to management pursuing its own objectives* – such as growth maximization (see Chapter 9) – subject to minimum profit levels being achieved.

4. Holding companies

Holding companies are companies which hold more than 50 per cent of the shares in another company. They can lead to *possible economies of scale*, which we discuss further in Chapter 9. They can, however, lead to abuse if a company builds up a pyramid of control over other companies with relatively little capital. This, however, has largely been prevented in the United Kingdom by the Company Acts.

5. Multinationals

Multinationals are companies which operate in more than one country. Unilever is a good example of a multinational company. The advantages of multinationals, from the shareholders' viewpoint, are that *there are possible economies of scale* and there may be *greater spreading of risks*. Several economists, however (notably J. K. Galbraith), have expressed reservations about their *lack of accountability*, either to shareholders or to the countries in which they operate. Developing countries may welcome multinationals, as long as they are not too dominant, since they provide training for workers and managers, and provide employment, but they may be worried about the outflow of dividends to overseas shareholders. They will, however, take account of the opportunity costs: if, for example, a multinational's product previously had to be imported, the balance of payments would be worse without the multinational producing the product in the developing country in question.

6. Workers' cooperatives

There have been workers' cooperatives for a considerable time but there has been a considerable increase in their number in recent years. By 1984 there were about seven hundred cooperatives affiliated to the *Industrial*

Co-ownership Movement (a federal body aiming to represent workers' cooperatives and to give advice to its members).

Some co-ownership firms are founded when the firm for which they are working goes bankrupt. This was the case with Meriden Cooperative, which took over a motorcycle factory. There are immense difficulties in such circumstances, since the morale of existing staff may already be low and the fact that the previous firm went bankrupt indicates that there are probably many problems. Others have been formed partly through the altruism of the previous owners. One of the largest cooperatives is Scott Bader, formed by a Quaker. The largest workers' cooperative is the John Lewis partnership which controls, among other organizations, Waitrose supermarkets.

Whereas public companies increasingly show a divorce between management and ownership, this is untrue of workers' cooperatives, where workers generally elect managers at the annual meetings and contribute towards the capital of the organization. Managers are often appointed for about a five-year period, in order to ensure that there is some continuity of management, but to avoid the problems of having managers appointed for life, which would partially defeat one of the objectives, i.e. that *all workers should be able to participate in decisions about their own firm.*

In many workers' cooperatives there is less difference in pay between the lowest and the highest paid workers than in most firms. The cooperatives claim that this reduces the problems caused by large differentials, but some economists have claimed that this makes it difficult to attract the appropriate level of top management.

Workers' cooperatives, like other cooperatives, are incorporated under the relevant partnership acts and there has to be a minimum of two members. Like limited companies, there is no maximum number, though some managers within workers' cooperatives would suggest that too large a number of workers would tend to make the firms more bureaucratic and would make it more difficult to conform to the original objectives. The members of a cooperative have limited liability.

7. Consumers' cooperatives

The best-known consumers' cooperatives in the United Kingdom are the Co-operative Retail Societies and the Co-operative Wholesale Society. These can be found in the high streets of most major towns and in many smaller towns and villages. They grew from the first cooperative store in Rochdale in 1844, when the aim was that they would buy food at wholesale prices and sell mainly to their own members.

The Co-operative Retail Societies still have a very large percentage of the total share of the food and other markets, though in recent years it has declined. The Co-operatives have had problems, partly because of apathy and partly because some Co-operative Retail Societies were too small to gain potential economies of scale.

Unlike private and public companies, where the number of votes depends upon the size of shareholding, in the Co-op the principle of '*one person, one vote*' applies.

The objectives are not profit maximization but to *provide goods and services to the consumers at reasonable prices* and to *pay fair wages to the workers*. The Co-operative Retail Societies used to redistribute any profits, often in the form of dividends, but this practice has now declined.

The Co-operative Retail Societies have, among themselves, set up the Co-operative Wholesale Society which, in some ways, is like other wholesalers. Profits from the Co-operative Wholesale Society are shared between retail societies. The Co-operative Wholesale Society is itself a fairly large manufacturer of many goods.

8. Non-profit-making private-sector organizations

In the United Kingdom these include the building societies and mutual insurance companies, where there are no shareholders. Mutual insurance companies can be very large. (Building societies can now become public limited companies, however.)

9. National Enterprise Board

One of the main roles of the *National Enterprise Board* was to encourage mergers of companies where it was thought there were potential economies of scale. It was set up to encourage industrial efficiency.

*

QUESTION

Why does separation of ownership from control often occur in modern Western European economies? What are the economic consequences of this?

One of the reasons for the separation is that in the larger public companies there are often too many owners (i.e. shareholders) for each one to be able to exert any significant control. British Telecom, for example, had, when it was privatized, over 2 million shareholders; while some managers and workers have shares, not all shareholders are managers or workers of British Telecom.

Often, especially with multinational companies, the owners may live in different countries from the workers and managers.

There are some advantages of this separation. For example, it has enabled people without capital to become managers if they are seen to have the necessary ability. Equally, companies do not have to depend upon people with both money and managerial ability, since the managerial ability can be brought in. From the firm's viewpoint, financing, especially of public companies, becomes easier, because there is a wide variety of methods of obtaining large-scale funds, including the issue of ordinary shares, preference shares and debentures, as well as overdrafts, loans and government finance, etc. These different types of finance will appeal to different types of investors and this money can be used to optimize production.

There are, however, a number of disadvantages. For example, shareholders may have a very narrow time horizon and be interested only in capital gains, in which case prospects for long-term research and development and future growth of the company may well be sacrificed for these aims. Also, shareholders may take little interest in the conditions of employees. Such criticisms have been levelled against the activities of some multinational companies operating in the Third World.

In other cases, there are suggestions that the separation of ownership from control has led to managers pursuing their own interests, perhaps salary maximization, rather than profit maximization. There is certain evidence that in some companies there is little correlation between profitability and managers' salaries.

The divorce of ownership from control may also lead to considerable economic power being in the hands of relatively few people. This is one of the criticisms which has been made particularly of some of the very large financial institutions. Some of the largest multinationals may well have a turnover which exceeds the gross national product of the smaller Third World countries. This gives them immense power which is not always properly used. J. K. Galbraith, in particular, has criticized some of the practices of some multinational companies.

While in theory shareholders can control the company, in practice the large numbers of shareholders in many companies and the inability to obtain information or to understand the relevant information can lead to problems. If the company performs badly, the only option of shareholders, in many cases, is to dispose of their shares. However, even in the cases where shareholders do seem to play a part in management, for example in football league clubs, there is no guarantee that they will exercise control in a sensible manner.

MULTIPLE-CHOICE QUESTIONS

The following are some of the major forms of private-sector business organizations:

(a) workers' cooperatives;
(b) consumers' cooperatives;
(c) public limited companies;
(d) private limited companies;
(e) partnerships.

To which of the above forms of organization do the following apply?
1. Each member has one vote. *Answer* – (b)
2. The organization will generally cease upon the death of one of its members. *Answer* – (e)
3. There are limits on the number of members, and at least one member has unlimited liability. *Answer* – (e)
4. The workers will generally elect the managers. *Answer* – (a)
5. Shares are issued but are not freely transferable. *Answer* – (d)
6. There is no limit to the number of shareholders and voting is based on the number of shares held. *Answer* – (c)

SELF-EXAMINATION QUESTIONS

1. What is meant by the term 'sole trader'? Why are sole traders more frequently found in some trades than in others?

2. What are the advantages of partnerships compared with sole traders? Are there any disadvantages?

3. Small firms will be helpful to the economy, as they create greater competition; the government should therefore discourage them. Discuss.

4. What are multinationals? Should developing countries welcome or try to refuse the growth of multinationals in their countries?

5. What are the advantages of multinationals from the point of view of (*a*) the shareholders and (*b*) the workers?

6. What are the advantages of holding companies?

7. In what ways do the consumer cooperatives differ from other organizations? How far in practice do their pricing and output policies differ from those of other organizations?

8. The National Enterprise Board was set up to encourage mergers of companies if there are potential economies of scale. Why might the price mechanism not be used to secure the same effects?

9. 'The sole trader has too many roles to play to be really efficient.' Discuss.

10. Why might it be difficult to find evidence of profit maximization, as defined by the economist, when looking at sole traders' accounts?

11. Some economists have suggested that multinationals are accountable neither to shareholders nor to the countries in which they operate. How far is this a valid criticism?

12. Why has there been increasing interest in workers' cooperatives in recent years? What are the disadvantages to workers in such organizations?

13. It is often said that in large-scale companies there is a divorce of control from ownership. How can this arise and what are the economic consequences?

14. The Bolton Committee 1971 suggested that independence might be a major factor for setting up small firms. How is this likely to be true today and what would be the economic consequences of such objectives?

15. The Co-operative Societies generally charge the same prices irrespective of the location of their shops. What are the economic consequences of this? Explain your answer with references to a small Co-operative Society located in a village with limited demand and to another Co-operative located in a high-rent area.

16. 'Multinationals should be welcomed by developing countries since they will pay higher wages than local firms and train more workers, but should be discouraged when profits do not go back to the country in which they are made.' Discuss.

9. The size of firms

1. Why do firms wish to grow?

Especially since the Second World War, the average size of firms has been growing. This phenomenon has been particularly apparent in the UK.

(i) *Some firms aim specifically to maximize their growth*, perhaps for *prestige purposes*.

(ii) Furthermore, business managers may wish their firms to grow where their *salaries are likely to grow accordingly*.

(iii) The growth of a firm may be necessary so that the firm can *specialize*, i.e. hire specialist workers (only large firms may be able to afford to hire specialist statisticians and accountants, etc.) and be able to afford specialist capital equipment.

(iv) As a result of specialization (the division of labour) and of the growth in the size of a firm, *economies of scale* are likely to be derived. For example, financial risks may be reduced (see section 4).

2. How do we define the size of the firm?

We might look at the size of a firm in terms of its *assets*, the size of its *turnover, the number of people employed* or *the volume of production* (*i.e. output*).

Each measure has different merits and may produce different results from the other measures. For example, an oil refinery may employ very few people, but a large amount of capital; conversely the Post Office has comparatively little capital, but a large number of employees.

Concentration figures

Figures relating to *output* are commonly used to measure the extent to which the size of firms is growing. From these figures, *concentration ratios* can be constructed which show how much of the total output, the three biggest, ten biggest or one hundred biggest, for example, firms in the economy or in a particular industry account for. If the largest firms

Table 11. The share of the hundred largest firms in manufacturing as measured by net output

Year	1909	1935	1948	1953	1958	1963	1970	1978
Share (%)	16	23	22	26	33	38	40	41

Source: *Census of Production*, HMSO.

(which are likely to be a changing group) account for a growing percentage of total output over time, this is an indication of the growing importance of large firms in the economy.

Table 11 shows the growing importance of large manufacturing firms in the economy by use of *aggregate concentration ratios* showing the share of the hundred largest manufacturing firms over time.

3. How do firms grow?

Internal growth (i.e. the growth of plant size) has not been significant in explaining the growth of firms during the twentieth century. *Almost all of the growth of firm size is explained by merger activity.* This suggests that consumption demand for firms' existing products has not risen over time; rather that firms have looked to increase their total sales by increasing the number of products they market.

Merger activity tends to take three forms: *vertical acquisitions; horizontal acquisitions; diversification.*

(a) *Vertical integration*

(i) A firm may grow by starting to manufacture a product it previously bought by taking over or merging with the firm which produces it. There are many examples of car manufacturers buying up component firms. This type of integration is referred to as *backward vertical integration*.

(ii) Firms may also go in for '*forward integration*', for example acquiring retailing outlets in an effort to reduce distribution costs. However, unless management has sufficient expertise, this will not necessarily reduce costs though it may reduce uncertainty. Many public houses are owned by breweries. Similarly, most garages are owned by oil companies.

As well as possibly reducing distribution costs, vertical integration may well help firms use by-products more effectively, although if the respective firms are physically adjacent these economies may still arise irrespective of ownership.

(b) *Horizontal integration*

Expansion may also be achieved through *horizontal integration*, whereby firms engaged in similar activities merge. For example, the merger between the National Provincial and the Westminster banks in the late 1960s coupled two firms which were providing the same type of services. There may be advantages in the retail and other industries, as with building societies, in having a large number of branches, and this may well result from horizontal integration.

(c) *Diversification*

A firm might grow by *diversifying into unrelated fields*, possibly through takeovers or mergers, thereby forming a *conglomerate*.

The importance of diversification as a factor in the growth of firm size can be illustrated as follows: the thousand largest firms on average supplied 6.6 markets (industrial groups) in 1958 and 7.7 in 1968, a rise in diversification of 15 per cent.

A firm will probably only diversify if it believes that it has sufficient management expertise to take over another firm in an entirely different field.

In some cases, diversification occurs because of '*asset stripping*', for example if the firm taken over has valuable land or factories which are under-utilized then some of this space could be used for more profitable purposes.

An example of a conglomerate in the United Kingdom is Unilever, which includes ice-cream, margarine and detergents among its products.

(d) *Research and development*

Firms may sometimes grow where, as a result of *research and development*, previous by-products become new products and are sold rather than wasted. This is true, to some extent, in the chemical industry.

119

4. Economies of scale

Most of the evidence about the economies of scale shows that, in manufacturing, there is greater potential for economies of scale at the level of the plant than at the level of the firm. Yet, as we have already suggested, firms have, on the whole, grown without any significant growth in plant size.

(a) *Internal economies of scale at the plant level*

As the size of a plant is increased there are *greater possibilities for hiring specialist workers* and possibilities for *better utilization of capital equipment*.

The theory of large numbers states that a larger plant will get better utilization than a smaller plant from similar equipment.

(b) *Internal economies of scale at the firm level*

(i) *Large firms are usually able to offer a wider variety of jobs than small firms* and can offer greater promotion opportunities. None the less, the Bolton Committee, 1971, still suggested that industrial relations are better in smaller than in larger firms.

(ii) *Managerial economies.* Generally, large firms are able to employ specialist marketing managers, accountants, etc.

(iii) *Technical economies.* Large firms are better able to afford expensive capital equipment than are small firms. Until recently, the use of computers was mainly confined to large firms, but the rapid decrease in prices has meant that this is no longer true.

(iv) *Financial economies.* The larger firm will often be able to borrow on more favourable terms than the smaller one: it will often be quoted lower interest rates than the smaller one.

A large firm might find that it can get cheaper loans than a small firm, for two main reasons:

1. *Administrative costs do not increase proportionately* and therefore a share rights issue for, say, £20m will not entail twenty times the administrative costs of that of a smaller firm borrowing £1m.

2. In many cases, *investors do not have perfect knowledge and therefore may be more inclined to lend money to a large firm rather than to a small one*, even if the small firm's financial record is better. Banks are inclined to lend to large firms at a lower rate of interest than to small firms because large firms can offer more collateral.

(v) *Marketing economies.* It is usually just as easy to market several products as one. For example, a salesman working for a large chocolate manufacturer is able to demonstrate several different types of chocolate bar to a retailer just as easily as a salesman working for a manufacturer who produces only one type of chocolate bar is able to demonstrate his one product.

The growth of firms in the bakery industry can be explained mainly in terms of marketing factors.

(vi) *Risk-bearing economies.* A larger firm may be able to spread its risks over a wider variety of products than a smaller firm, so that any fluctuations in demand are relatively small overall.

A large-scale driving school operating throughout the country will find that there are fluctuations in demand. These, however, will be relatively much smaller than for a sole trader who tries to run his own driving school. It is also easier for a large firm, say an oil company, to speculate as to the possibility of finding oil in a particular area. The company might spend a lot in investigation, but it knows that the likely returns are very large. A small firm, however, might be very unwilling to take the risk of even one major exploration, since, if it were unsuccessful, it could mean bankruptcy for the firm, even if there were the likelihood of large-scale profits eventually. Similarly, a larger-scale firm may be able to diversify into several different products, each of which will be potentially profitable. A smaller firm would be unwilling, generally, to go outside its existing field because of the risks involved.

(vii) Large firms can use their market powers to *buy materials in bulk*, and, thereby, obtain raw materials, components and fuel more cheaply than small firms. In some cases the advantages may not be the cheaper costs so much as the fact that large firms can often obtain components which are geared to their own specialist needs. For example, a large firm may be able to afford computer packages which are designed for that firm alone; a smaller firm would probably be able to afford computer packages, but these would be designed for the general industry and might not be entirely suitable for the particular firm.

(viii) *Volume economies.* Distribution costs may be lower for large firms, since, with a greater volume of traffic, it may be possible to run larger lorries. These are usually cheaper to operate per tonne than smaller lorries. Large firms may be able to have their own company trains, use containers, etc.

In the United Kingdon the largest lorry for most purposes is 38 tonnes. They have the advantage to the firm of not using as much fuel as two

19-tonne lorries and the costs of hiring drivers are lower; these lorries can still be purchased by fairly small firms.

(c) *External economies of scale.*

There may be certain advantages (or economies of scale) which are derived as a result of an industry being established in a particular locality. These are known as *economies of scale from localization* or *external economies of scale.*

There may, therefore, be advantages to a firm if it locates in an area where other firms in the industry are already established.

(i) For example, *local colleges may provide suitable courses for the training of employees.* In the north of England colleges provide courses relevant to the textile industry.

(ii) There is also the possibility of *specialist financial institutions* setting up in the area.

(iii) *Component manufacturers may be established nearby.*

(iv) *Distribution costs may be lower* if firms providing complementary services are available in the same area.

5. Limits to the growth of firms

(i) Perhaps the main constraint upon the growth of a firm in any one sector is *the level of effective demand.* There may still, however, be potential for a firm to diversify into new geographical areas or into the production of new goods and services: the market may be saturated in one country, but it may be possible to expand into another. Indeed, in recent years there has been the growth of the multinational firm.

(ii) There may be limitations imposed upon diversification. If a firm expands into another country, it may find *problems of marketing and communication.*

(iii) There may be *legislation* restricting merger and takeover activity and international laws restricting the activities of multi-nationals.

(iv) As firms grow and grow, there is the possibility of management and coordination problems (*dis-economies of scale,* see section 6).

6. Dis-economies of scale

There are a number of potential dis-economies of scale resulting from a firm growing too large.

(i) These potential dis-economies include the problems of *lateral communication*. For example, if a firm is organized on a departmental basis, it may be difficult for junior or middle management to coordinate decisions quickly with people from other departments: *the span of control should not be too great*.

(ii) Similarly, *the chain of command should not be too great*: a lengthy chain of command may prevent messages being relayed effectively and quickly downwards; there are likely to be even greater problems in communicating from the bottom to the top, such as when there are potential changes in demand of which the board is unaware.

7. Research on the economies of scale

There has been a considerable amount of academic research on the economies of scale, especially at the plant level. The findings of researchers such as *Professor Bain* suggest that, while some firms have grown through expansion of plant size, *most firms have grown by increasing the number of plants in their firm*. This would seem to suggest that firms themselves feel that economies of scale are more important at the firm's level rather than the plant level.

Problems of measuring the extent to which economies of scale exist

It is difficult to measure the extent to which a large firm in a particular 'industry' has advantages, in terms of economies of scale, over a smaller firm in the industry, since the large firm may in fact straddle more than one 'industry' as defined by the Standard Industrial Classification.

Furthermore, while a small firm may exist in the same industry as a large firm, it may not in fact be competing with the large firm, because it serves a different market or makes different products.

It should also be noted that at any one time we do not necessarily see a firm (whether large or small) at its optimal size.

Economists often use *survival data* as a guidance to the extent to which economies of scale exist. Survival data looks at the performance of a number of comparable size, over time, to see which firms survive.

*

QUESTION

What are the advantages and disadvantages of vertical integration?

Some firms feel that by having control over their suppliers, through common ownership, they can achieve better quality control and they may be able to plan to deal with any periods of shortages more effectively. However, other firms, notably Marks and Spencer, have often been able to obtain a high degree of quality control through negotiations and consultations with their suppliers, without the need for a takeover. There are disadvantages of vertical integration. For example, if the supply of components is greater than that required by the parent company (for example, a car manufacturer) it will have to dispose of this surplus. In some cases surpluses are sold to rival firms.

Where vertical integration means, for example, that a garage is tied to an oil company or a public house to a brewery, it is difficult for someone to set up a competing garage or public house unless he is also backed by a supplier. Furthermore, where a public house is owned by a brewery, customers' choice may be restricted to one type of beer since only the parent company's beer may be on sale.

Because of the disadvantages, some firms have adopted a policy of vertical disintegration, whereby they shed certain responsibilities and allow other firms to take these responsibilities over. This, in particular, applies to the distribution function which, in many cases, is best performed by hire-and-reward firms which carry goods for other people. Particularly in a recession, other firms may be willing to operate at little more than their variable costs, in order to maintain their own businesses.

Vertical disintegration sometimes releases land, which can then be used more efficiently and profitably for other purposes.

MULTIPLE-CHOICE QUESTIONS

1–2. The following may represent some economies of scale:
   (*a*) demand fluctuates proportionately less for larger organizations;
   (*b*) finance can often be obtained proportionately more cheaply by larger firms;
   (*c*) for many machines there is a minimum size of firm at which maximum efficiency can be obtained;
   (*d*) outside firms will often give discounts on large-scale orders;

(*e*) for a given volume of demand, marketing costs will be less for a large firm than a small firm;

(*f*) specialist component firms will tend to be set up when there is sufficient demand.

1. Which of the above are internal economies of scale?
Answers – (*a*), (*b*), (*c*), (*d*), (*e*)

2. Which of the above are external economies of scale?
Answer – (*f*)

3–6. The following are possible answers to the next five questions:
   (*a*) marketing economies of scale;
   (*b*) managerial economies of scale;
   (*c*) financial economies of scale;
   (*d*) risk-bearing economies of scale;
   (*e*) volume economies of scale;
   (*f*) economies in overheads;
   (*g*) external economies of scale.
What types of economies of scale do we find in the following examples?

3. It is proportionately cheaper to build a large oil tanker rather than several smaller ones.
Answer – (*e*)

4. A large firm, with a proven track record, will be able to borrow more cheaply than a small firm.
Answer – (*c*)

5. A sole trader will often have to be involved in a wide variety of tasks, whereas in a large organization he can specialize.
Answer – (*b*)

6. A large firm will be able to use a computerized system with a linked computer network at a low cost per employee, whereas a smaller firm will not be able to do this.
Answer – (*f*)

7. Some economists have suggested that in large bus companies, which have identical buses to those of smaller companies, the number of employees per bus is larger. Thus, the average costs of production are higher than for small companies. If this is applicable, which of the following must be true:
   (*a*) that there are dis-economies of scale;
   (*b*) that there are diminishing returns to labour;

    (*c*) that there are diminishing returns of capital;

    (*d*) that the main problem is lack of demand?

Answer – (*a*)

9–13. There are a variety of ways in which firms might grow, such as:

    (*a*) backward integration;

    (*b*) forward integration;

    (*c*) diversification;

    (*d*) horizontal integration.

The following are examples of which type of integration?

9. An insurance firm merges with another insurance firm in order to be able to advertise cost effectively.

Answer – (*d*)

10. Two building societies merge, since computerization costs will be lower than if they buy computers separately.

Answer – (*d*)

11. A brewery takes over a chain of public houses.

Answer – (*b*)

12. A chocolate manufacturer takes over a range of cocoa plantations.

Answer – (*a*)

13. A firm which is engaged in the manufacturing of detergents takes over a firm selling beer.

Answer – (*c*)

DATA RESPONSE

The World Bank report on small-scale enterprises suggested that there are many advantages in investing in small-scale enterprise, since investment costs per job are typically much lower than investment costs in larger firms. For example, it suggested that in India the typical cost of investment is only about 6–11 per cent of that of larger firms, presumably because smaller firms are less capital-intensive than larger ones. It suggested that small-scale enterprise is helpful for developing countries, not only for this reason, but also because it helps to encourage technological innovation, as well as contributing to competition. It gives the community stability and there are fewer unfavourable externalities than with larger factories. It also encourages firms to contract for sub-assembly work and parts.

    It suggested that the main problems for small firms are lack of access to institutional credit and government facilities, and inadequate infrastructure facilities.

The World Bank report suggested that two thirds of employment in the industrial sector of the developing world was in small-scale enterprises. The World Bank is likely to encourage smaller enterprises in the years to come.

(a) The World Bank report suggested that investment costs per job in small-scale enterprises are lower than in larger units in developing countries. Why might this be so? Do you think this is also true in developed countries? Explain your reasoning.

(b) How would you test the hypothesis that small enterprises lead to greater technological innovation?

(c) Why might smaller enterprises have less access to institutional credit than larger organizations?

SELF-EXAMINATION QUESTIONS

1. Why might it be easier to measure economies of scale at plant level rather than at the level of the firm?

2. Why is it difficult to compare firms which have diversified in different directions?

3. How far does demand limit economies of scale? Is the limitation of demand a reason for diversification?

4. How far does specialization of labour and equipment lead to potential economies of scale? What are the main dis-economies of scale?

5. How far do fashions in economies of scale, for example the moves towards 'Big is Beautiful' in the late 1960s and the converse of 'Small is Beautiful' in the early 1980s, account for the waves of mergers?

6. 'All dis-economies of scale arise from management problems.' Discuss.

7. Large firms sometimes complain about unfair competition from smaller firms since they do not have the same overheads. Is this a valid reason for restricting entry into an industry? Explain your answer.

8. How is it possible, if at all, to measure economies of scale in a conglomerate organization?

9. Why, if economies of scale are so important, do small firms exist in most sectors of industry?

10. In the transport industry small firms tend to exist in the part of the industry which caters for irregular services whereas in the regular market large firms predominate. Which underlying economic theories might explain this?

11. How far does the existence of economies of scale at plant level explain the increase in larger size firms?

12. How far, if at all, does the introduction of small computers with very large memories affect the optimum size of firms?

13. What conceptual problems arise in trying to analyse economies of scale within industries?

14. In some industries, such as road haulage, there seems to be little evidence about economies of scale. What might be the reasons for this?

15. One government report suggested that small firms might perform the 'seed-bed' function, i.e. eventually they would grow into larger firms. How far is this valid?

16. Firms may grow horizontally or vertically, or form conglomerates. What are the advantages and disadvantages to (*a*) the firm and (*b*) the community of these types of growth?

17. 'All obstacles to growth of firms are ultimately due to inefficiency of management.' Discuss this statement critically.

10. Pricing and output

1. Perfect competition

(a) *The assumptions of perfect competition*

(i) *Producers aim to maximize their profits.*

(ii) *Consumers aim to maximize their own utility* and thus have no undue preferences.

(iii) *Consumers regard the products which they buy as homogeneous,* i.e. they regard the product of one firm to be identical in character to that produced by another firm in the industry.

(iv) *There are a large number of independent actual and potential buyers and sellers.*

(v) *Firms are price takers,* i.e. they cannot influence the market price by increasing or decreasing their production.

(vi) *Both producers and consumers have perfect knowledge.* This rules out the possibility of any *product differentiation* that makes homogeneous products appear heterogeneous. It also implies that firms have sufficient knowledge of their costs and revenue to know when to enter and when to leave the industry.

(vii) *There are no barriers to entry into the industry.*

(viii) *Factors of production are mobile between alternative uses.*

(ix) *Productive processes are divisible.*

(b) *What is the importance of these assumptions?*

(i) If consumers regard products as homogeneous and have perfect knowledge, *they will not buy a product or service if its price is above the market price.* The assumption that there is a large number of independent buyers and sellers reinforces this, and, since each firm is only a small part of the total market, firms have to accept the market price. Each firm is faced by a *perfectly elastic demand* curve: if a firm raises its price above the industry's going price, it will sell no output. Therefore, *average revenue (i.e. demand) equals marginal revenue equals price.* Even if some firms try to collude, the large number of potential customers would make any collusion ineffective.

(ii) The assumption of free entry and exit to the industry and the assumption that factors of production are mobile *rule out any degree of monopoly power*.

(iii) In the perfect competition model, as in other models of the firm, profits are defined as total revenue minus total cost. The perfectly competitive firm will be in equilibrium if there is no reason for it to produce more or less. Another way of saying this is that *the equilibrium is marginal cost = marginal revenue*. For example, if a firm's lowest average cost for a product is 16p while all other firms in the industry have a lowest average cost of 15p, by charging a price where average cost equals marginal cost, the firm in question would be charging a higher price than the other firms. It would, therefore, sell nothing because the existence of perfect information and no product differentiation would mean that consumers would take their custom elsewhere. *The firm has a perfectly elastic demand curve*, the position of which is completely outside its control. Only by reducing its costs to the point where marginal cost equals average cost equals marginal revenue (namely 15p) is the firm going to sell any of its output. Thus, the firm has to reduce the marginal-cost schedule from MC_1 to MC_2 and the average-cost schedule from AC_1 to AC_2, in Figure 29a, in order to be in long-run equilibrium, which requires the firm to shift its supply curve to the right. It might be able to achieve this through improvements in technology (see Chapter 7).

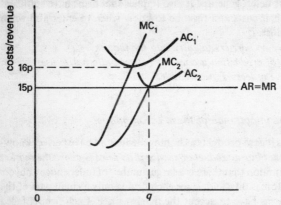

Figure 29a. *A perfectly competitive firm: having in the short run higher costs than other firms in the industry*

On the other hand, a firm might have a lowest average cost of 14p, while all other firms in the industry have a lowest average cost of 15p and might, therefore, charge a lower price than all other firms in the industry. In this case, the existence of perfect information and perfect mobility of factors of production means that labour, for example, in the firm in question sees that workers in other firms in the industry are receiving higher wages than they are and so they either demand higher wages or go to work for another firm. The only way the firm in question will be able to get people to work for it is to raise its wage so that it is in line with the wages paid by all the other firms in the industry, so raising its costs (from AC_1 to AC_2 and from MC_1 to MC_2 in Figure 29b). Thus, in the short run, the firm can charge a price of 15p per unit and make *super-normal profits*. These super-normal profits are eliminated in the long run. We return to the concept of super-normal profits on p. 132.

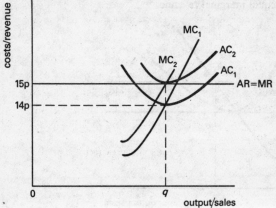

Figure 29b. *A perfectly competitive firm: originally having lower costs than other firms in the industry*

(c) *Short-run equilibrium in perfect competition*

It is important to note that the economist's definition of profit has little to do with the accountant's definition of profits. *The normal profit is one which will keep a firm in the industry. Super-normal or abnormal profits are defined as profits which are over and above these normal profits. Super-normal profits are defined as those profits made above average costs.* Part of a firm's average costs consists of payment to the entrepreneur, i.e. profit.

In the short run the perfectly competitive firm will continue in production as long as it covers its average variable costs. If there are perfectly competitive firms making super-normal profits, however, new firms (having perfect knowledge) may be attracted to enter the industry.

A firm will be able to make super-normal profits if the point at which its marginal costs are equal to average costs is lower than the going

131

price, i.e. if AC < P. Such a situation might arise because the firm has undertaken a programme of research and development which has enabled it to develop a process of production whereby its costs per unit are lower than those of other firms.

Since it has been assumed that perfectly competitive firms are profit maximizers, the firm in question will produce where marginal costs equal marginal revenue. In perfect competition, the marginal-revenue curve is the same as the demand curve, so the firm will produce at the point where the marginal-cost curve cuts the marginal-revenue curve or, in other words, where marginal cost cuts the average-revenue curve. Therefore, price will equal marginal revenue.

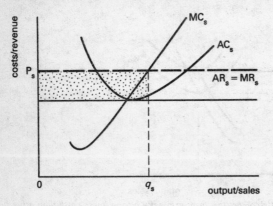

Figure 30a *A perfectly competitive firm: short-run equilibrium making super-normal profits*

The firm in question is producing an output where MC = MR (the equilibrium condition), but it is not fulfilling the condition for normal profits, i.e. the level of output at which MC = MR does not correspond to the point at which AC = P. Since AC is less than P at the output at which MC = MR, the firm in question makes super-normal profits, shown by the shaded area in Figure 30a.

(d) *Long-run equilibrium in perfect competition*

In the long run, any super-normal profits being made will be eliminated. This is because new firms will have been attracted to enter the industry. Existing firms are unable, as we assume, to prevent other firms entering the industry. The effect of new firms entering the industry will be for the industry's supply curve to shift rightwards. This reduces the industry's equilibrium price. New firms will continue to enter the industry while there are still super-normal profits being made (i.e. while equilibrium price is still above P_L in Figure 30b). Thus the industry's supply curve will continue to shift rightwards until S_L is reached. Since there is no consumer loyalty to one particular firm (no product differentiation), as the number of new firms entering the industry increases so the proportionate share of sales of the existing firms in the industry falls. Thus, the firm's demand curve shifts from AR_S towards AR_L in Figure 30b. The entering of new firms into the industry reduces the possibility of firms making super-normal profits. Thus, in the long run, super-normal profits cannot be made in perfect competition.

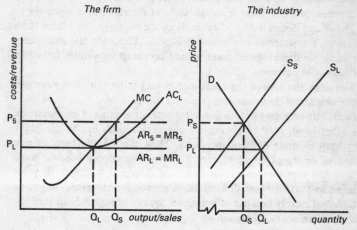

Figure 30b. *Long-run equilibrium in perfect competition*

If in the short run existing firms had been making less than normal profits (i.e. losses), firms will have been tempted to leave the industry. Such action shifts the industry's supply curve leftwards, raising the market price towards the level at which normal profits can be made.

Changes in prices are signals to firms to enter or leave the industry. Long-run equilibrium will occur when the firms in the industry are just making normal profits, so that firms wish neither to enter nor to leave the industry. Thus, *for long-run equilibrium, MC must equal MR* (the equilibrium for any profit-maximizing firm whatever the market structure) *and AC must equal price*. It should be noted that this concept, while widely quoted in examinations, may never be reached in practice.

(e) *The industry's demand curve*

It should be noted that the demand curve for the industry as a whole tends to be downward sloping because a rise in price within the industry somewhere or a price rise enforced by all firms in the industry will tend not to reduce demand for the industry's product completely: one industry tends not to be perfectly competitive with another industry.

2. Monopoly

(a) *What is a 'monopoly'?*

The economist's definition of *a monopolist is 'the sole producer of goods or services for which there is no substitute in the eyes of the consumer'.*

The Water Board is a good example of a monopoly, since there is no substitute for water at any reasonable price. There are few substitutes for water for drinking and washing and no cheap substitutes for water for industrial purposes.

The term 'the eyes of the consumer' is very important. For example, there are about two hundred varieties of potatoes. For most consumers, however, one potato is a substitute for another. Detergents, on the other hand, may be chemically almost identical, but to the buyer they may be quite different products. Thus, the manufacturer of one brand of detergent might be seen to have a monopoly because some people will buy that particular brand of detergent whatever its price relative to that of other detergents. A monopoly, therefore, might be established merely because of consumer loyalty brought about through the use of *product differentiation.*

(b) *Monopolistic pricing*

Monopolists are likely to be faced by a downward-sloping demand (average-revenue) curve.

Profit-maximizing monopolists (like any other profit-maximizing firm) will produce at the point where marginal cost equals marginal revenue, i.e. $MC = MR$.

Given an output Q_1 (which in Figure 31 is the output at which $MC = MR$), a monopolist will be able to sell all of this output as long as it charges a price no higher than the demand (AR) curve allows, i.e. P_1. By charging price P_1, the firm makes super-normal profits, since this price is above average cost.

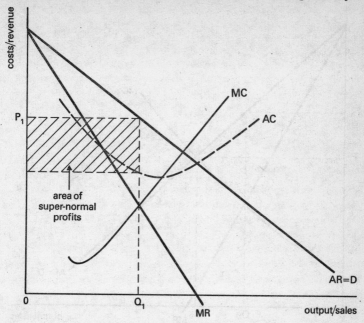

Figure 31. *Pricing and output in monopoly*

(c) *Pricing and output policy in perfect competiton and in monopoly compared*

Since in perfect competition each firm produces an output at the point where $MC = AR$ (since $AR = MR$), a perfectly competitive industry (faced with the cost and revenue schedules illustrated in Figure 32) will produce an output Q_C.

Furthermore, since perfectly competitive firms charge a price at the point where $MC = AR$ (given the same cost and revenue schedules), the perfectly competitive industry will charge price P_C.

If this same industry was monopolistic, the industry (or firm) would produce an output Q_M (i.e. where $MC = MR$) and would charge a price P_M (i.e. the highest price at which the industry will sell all of output Q_M).

From Figure 32 it is clear that profit-maximizing monopoly both produces a lower output and charges a higher price than profit-maximizing perfect competition, given the same cost and revenue conditions.

135

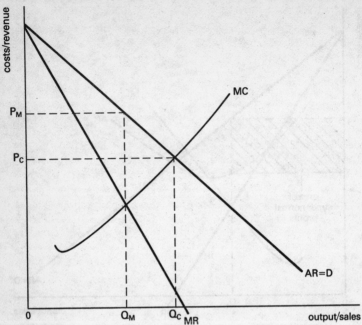

Figure 32. *Pricing and output policy in perfect competition and in monopoly compared*

(d) *Measuring monopoly power*

(i) In economics, we can try to measure the degree of monopoly by the use of *cross price elasticity*. For example, if we found that the price of a particular car, say the Mini, rose but this had no effect on demand for Rolls-Royce cars, we would say that Minis were no substitute for Rolls-Royces. On the other hand, if we saw that the increase in the price of Minis led to more people using rail transport, we would suggest that (under certain circumstances) Minis are a substitute for rail travel and vice versa. It is not often, however, that we can obtain data about cross price elasticity without research.

(ii) It might be possible to measure the degree of monopoly power through the use of *concentration ratios*. For example, we can find out the percentage of output of the three largest manufacturers in an industry. One problem here is that the published data may be out of date. Another is that if we look, for example, at the car industry, the manufacturer of small cars in the United Kingdom may compete more with foreign car

136

manufacturers than with large British manufacturers: foreign manufacturers are not included in the concentration data. Also, small cars tend to compete more with public transport, such as British Rail, than with the manufacturers of large cars, which are within the same industry. Another problem is that a firm could be a monopolist in certain parts of its industry but not in others. For example, the electricity boards in the United Kingdom have a virtual monopoly on the use of electricity for lighting. This has been vividly shown when there have been strikes or breakdowns in the electricity industry. On the other hand, for heating purposes the electricity industry has to compete with a number of other fuels, for example oil, gas and solid fuels.

(iii) Another possible method of trying to measure monopoly power is to *see which industries super-normal profits are made in.* We can see from the market models that in perfect competition it is not possible to make super-normal profits in the long run, whereas in monopoly it is. However, if the firm was inefficient it could still be a monopolist but not make super-normal profits because of its inefficiency. We would need to be able to define what the term 'normal profits' means anyway and we should note that there may be a difference between the economist's concept of profits and the accountant's, which makes 'super-normal profits' difficult to find.

(e) *Why do monopolies exist?*

Often firms have monopolistic positions because there are *barriers to entry into the industry.*

(i) One such barrier to entry might include *the initial cost of setting up a plant.* In many industries, such as the oil-refining industry, this cost is very high.

(ii) Another barrier to entry might concern *access to resources or outlets.* For example, a new petrol company may have difficulty trying to establish itself in the United Kingdom, where most garages are tied to the major oil firms, and a new brewery would find it difficult to obtain outlets, since most public houses are already tied to brewers. Similarly, there may be problems of obtaining certain supplies. For example, in the 1960s Jaguar Cars were not part of the then British Motor Corporation; when the British Motor Corporation bought up Pressed Steel, agreements had to be reached that Pressed Steel would supply Jaguar Cars with body pressings, otherwise great problems would have ensued for Jaguar. Where there have been problems of access to outlets, the Monopolies and Mergers Commission has sometimes intervened. For example, it recommended, in the case of beer, that tied houses might sell more than one brand.

(iii) *Patent rights* might also be a barrier to entry. For example, if a firm has patent rights over certain types of photocopying, it might be difficult for new firms to enter the photocopying industry.

The government has allowed copyrights and patent rights as it is felt that these are reasonable forms of monopoly, since the ownership of copyrights and patent rights reflects the ownership of ideas or processes developed as a result of research and development undertaken by firms at their own expense. They can, therefore, be regarded as some sort of payment or reward to entrepreneurs. However, the government might insist that there should not be any abuse of monopoly and, as a result, might insist that people can use ideas currently copyrighted under a franchising system.

For a long time only solicitors were allowed to carry out conveyancing (the system of transference of ownership of property). However, conveyancing is no longer confined to solicitors only.

(iv) Another barrier to entry is that of *brand differentiation,* such as exists in the detergent market, where the two major firms, Unilever and Procter and Gamble, have had a large share of the market through heavy advertising. The Monopolies Commission in this case has suggested that there should be less advertising of certain brands.

(v) *High research and development costs* might be a barrier to entry. This barrier could apply, for example, to the aircraft industry. One way of reducing the costs of research and development to the firm might be for the government itself to provide research and development. Alternatively, the government taking over the firm might have a similar effect.

(vi) *High tariffs*, effectively preventing imports, bar foreign firms from competing with British firms in the UK. However, this barrier to entry has been reduced, to some extent, by the UK's entry into the Common Market in 1973. Very high tariffs in the past applied, for example, to fertilizers.

3. Oligopoly

(a) *The assumptions of oligopoly*

(i) *A small number of firms account for a large percentage of the industry's output.* In a special case, as for a long while in the detergent industry (where there have been two main producers), there might be a *duopoly.*

(ii) *There is a high degree of interdependence*: one firm's decision depends on how it predicts its rivals will react.

(iii) *Firms may be price-setters*, whereby they can influence the market price by increasing or decreasing their output.

(iv) *There is imperfect knowledge on the part of both producers and consumers.* Thus, firms are *uncertain* how their rivals will react to their actions; there is the possibility of *product differentiation.*

(v) *There may be barriers to entry into the industry* imposed by high fixed costs of capital or by advertising.

(b) *The existence of oligopolies*

There are many examples of oligopoly within the United Kingdom. For example, the production of tyres, newspapers and some chemicals, as well as the car industry, can be regarded as oligopolistic.

(i) An oligopoly might exist because of high fixed costs requiring a firm in the industry to be very large in order to benefit fully from economies of scale. Such an oligopoly may be called a *natural oligopoly.*

(ii) *Countervailing power* helps explain the existence of some oligopolies, particularly duopolies. Countervailing power is where one firm is balanced by the power held by an opposing firm in the industry so that one firm is prevented from emerging as a monopolist and so that their marketing behaviour (for example, extensive advertising) acts as an effective barrier to other firms entering the industry.

(iii) *Monopoly legislation* may prevent an outright monopolist emerging in a particular industry.

(c) *Pricing and output in oligopoly*

In perfect competition, the demand curve for the individual firm is known and (given the assumptions about its costs) we can predict that the firm will produce at the point at which its marginal cost equals marginal revenue for profit maximization. This is also the point at which its marginal cost equals price. Therefore, if we know the cost conditions of the firm, we can make predictions of its output and prices.

In a monopoly where a single price is charged we can again make the assumption that, if the monopolist is profit-maximizing, he will produce at the point where marginal revenue equals marginal cost and (again knowing the demand curve, perhaps from market research or from past sales data) we can make a prediction about its pricing.

In oligopoly, however, the firm's demand curve and marginal revenue are difficult to determine, since they depend upon the reactions of other firms. Economists, therefore, have formulated a number of different ideas regarding the pricing and output decisions of oligopolistic firms.

(i) One of the earliest theories in oligopoly, in fact *duopoly*, dates from the 1830s. It was one in which *Cournot* assumed that sellers would profit-maximize. Using the assumption that other sellers would hold their own output constant, Cournot said that firms would arrive at an equilibrium position. This, however, was derived from a theory rather than from observation.

(ii) *Sweezy*, in the 1930s, tried to develop a theory from observations that oligopoly prices seemed to be more sticky than prices under other market conditions. Sweezy's assumptions led to the development of the so-called 'kinked' demand curve. The kinked-demand-curve theory assumes that a firm will not wish to raise its price, since it assumes that other firms will not follow. It will therefore assume that demand is fairly elastic and that if it raises its price its market share will fall by a greater amount (i.e. its total revenue falls). The kinked demand curve also assumes that if a firm lowers its price below its original point other firms will follow, so that the firm's share of the total market will not rise by as much as price falls. Thus, demand is assumed to be inelastic below the original price and a fall in price will reduce total revenue.

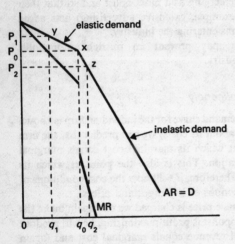

Figure 33. *The kinked demand curve*

The kinked demand curve implies that the prices of an oligopolistic firm's products will be fairly stable: a firm will wish neither to raise its prices (because rival firms will not follow) nor to lower its prices (because rival firms will follow). Indeed, Sweezy's assumptions were made at a time (in the 1930s) when most prices were more stable than at other times (for example, the late 1970s) so that it is not surprising that oligopolistic firms' prices were stable. The 1930s was a period of recession, in which most firms were likely to have spare capacity. Therefore, a firm which reduced its prices would be able to increase its output in anticipation of any increase in demand (if only a small increase in demand) resulting from the fall in price. However, firms were reluctant to reduce their prices, since their rivals would also have spare capacity and might have been able to undercut them.

The 1950s, too, was a period of stable prices. It was also one of near-full employment and most firms, even in industries where fixed costs were high, would have been able to produce at or near to the level where their average costs were at a minimum. Firms would, therefore, have had little incentive to reduce prices in the hope of increasing sales/output: an increase in output would have increased costs.

From the mid-1970s, however, there was high inflation and there was no reason to assume that oligopolistic firms would keep their prices stable. For example, in the aviation industry (an oligopolistic industry) prices rose in the mid-1970s largely as a result of a rise in oil prices. Thus, there is no reason to assume that Sweezy's assumptions will always hold. Where, however, Sweezy's assumptions do hold and competitive firms find it difficult to raise prices without suffering a decline in total revenue, there may be a strong incentive to collude (see section 4 below).

(iii) A more helpful general theory for oligopoly may be that of *the theory of games*. Here the assumption is that the firm will try to make predictions about what its rivals will do or how they will react to its own actions, whether in terms of changes in pricing or in terms of changes of output; unlike the kinked demand curve, it does not assume that in all cases a rise in the price charged by one firm will not be matched by other firms in the industry; instead, the theory-of-games approach assumes that, in some cases, there may be a *price leader*: if the leading firm raises its prices, other firms may follow because they view a price-cutting war as self-defeating.

Generally, we might expect the price leader to be the firm with the largest sales in the market, but this may not always be so. A very large firm with only a small share of the market might be in a strong position to dictate prices. If the other firms did not follow, it could afford to cut prices, probably using its fighting companies, and thus eliminate other firms from the market. (*Fighting companies* are set up under another name to reduce prices in the short run and thus eliminate the competition. When the competition disappears, the fighting company goes too.)

(d) *The importance of high output and sales in oligopoly*

Many oligopolies are industries in which fixed costs form a very large proportion of total costs. These high fixed costs act as a barrier to entry of firms and in many oligopolistic industries, such as the car industry and newspaper publishing, help to explain why there are very few firms established. In such industries a great deal of output is required before average costs reach their lowest point and it is often a major aim of such firms to produce (and sell) a vast quantity of their product. Given that it is very difficult for any such manufacturer to be able to reach the point of production at which average costs are at their lowest, we might assume that a car manufacturer produces an output at a point where average costs are still falling, implying that any reduction in demand will increase average costs (as shown in Figure 34).

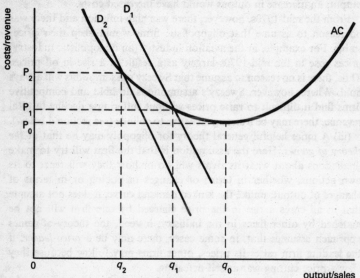

Figure 34. *How high average costs in many oligopolies affect pricing and output*

(e) *How might an oligopolistic firm increase the demand for its product?*

A profit-maximizing oligopolistic firm in an industry where there are high costs of production will be anxious to avoid a falling demand for its products, because a fall in demand will reduce revenue and will probably increase average costs, thereby reducing profits.

If the demand for an oligopolistic firm's products falls, it might attempt to raise its profits by pursuing one or more of the courses of action listed below.

(i) *Increasing the demand for its products.* An oligopolistic car manufacturer, for example, might attempt to increase the demand for its products by persuading the government to reduce the taxation on company cars or by differentiating its products from those of its rivals by involving itself in a 'knocking' campaign – comparing its cars with those of its rivals in terms of, for example, petrol consumption – by extending the range of warranties or guarantees offered, etc. See sub-section (f), below, for a fuller discussion of non-price competition in oligopoly.

(ii) *Indulging in price discrimination.* If the firm in question responds to a fall in demand for its products by raising its prices *per se*, it may well find that other firms in the industry do not raise their prices in response and that, as a result, its revenue (and profits) fall, even if there is some degree of product differentiation. Thus, while demand (as illustrated by either demand curve in Figure 34) might be inelastic as price falls, it might actually be elastic as price rises.

The firm might be able to avoid the dilemma of having revenue (and profits) falling as it raises its prices by indulging in some form of *price discrimination*. Price discrimination involves charging different prices in different markets for the same good, where this is not due to differences in costs between the different markets. Price discrimination tends to be practised if there are different price elasticities of demand in different markets. For example, a car manufacturer who wishes to increase his profits might consider raising his prices in general. If, however, he expects his rivals not to follow his lead, he might expect the demand for his cars in general to be elastic and for a price rise to reduce revenue. If, though, he believes that the demand for those models most likely to be bought as company cars is price inelastic as price rises, he may decide to raise the price of those models and leave the price of models most likely to be bought as private cars alone.

(iii) *Expanding into new markets* (which might be regarded as a form of non-price competition) might involve, for example, a manufacturer of small cars going upmarket to compete with the likes of Rolls-Royce. However, there are likely to be high costs of tooling up. Furthermore, the reactions of rivals must be considered: even if the firm finds a new market which is profitable in the short run, in the long run other firms in the industry might also expand into this market. Also, the firm will need to bear in mind the cross-elasticity of demand of its own cars. Will, for

143

example, expensive cars compete with the firm's existing models? Will customers tend to prefer, in any case, an established product or will there be conspicuous consumption (i.e. the desire to be forced to buy something), whereby a new product will sell because of the novelty aspect?

(f) *Non-price competition in oligopoly*

Because of the uncertainty faced by oligopolistic firms as to how their rivals will react to any price rise or fall they might initiate, oligopolistic firms are often reluctant to indulge in price competition, preferring instead to indulge in some form of *product differentiation*, i.e. non-price competition.

Thus, instead of involving themselves in a 'price-cutting war' with their rivals in order to increase their sales, oligopolistic firms might try to differentiate their products from those of their rivals, particularly through branding and/or advertising.

i. Why might it be desirable to avoid price competition in oligopoly?

Profit-maximizing oligopolistic firms will be particularly anxious to avoid 'price-cutting wars' since, if demand for their products proves to be inelastic as price falls, a fall in price will reduce revenue.

Furthermore, a 'price-cutting war' might not be beneficial to the consumer: if one firm in an oligopolistic industry were larger than the others and decided to undercut these other firms, they would be forced to follow in order to maintain their sales; this would reduce their revenue and might lead to liquidity problems for them; they might eventually be forced out of business. Where a 'price-cutting war' results in business failure (as happened in the area of public transport in the 1920s, when a number of large bus companies undercut the fares of small bus companies, forcing them out of business), this may not be in the interests of the consumer. Those firms left may not be the 'best', but merely those with the greatest financial resources. Price-cutting in some industries, particularly the air transport industry, might be dangerous because it might lead to a lack of maintenance and to inadequate investment.

If product differentiation shifts the firm's demand curve to the right, in oligopolies where fixed costs are high, the firm is more likely to be producing nearer the point of minimum average costs when it pursues product differentiation than when it does not.

ii. Advertising as a barrier to entry in oligopoly

The theory of perfect competition assumes that consumers have perfect information and that the products of all firms in the industry are homogeneous 'in the eyes of the consumer'. In reality, however, consumers do not have perfect information and as a result may be influenced in their decision to buy by the recommendations of another consumer or by the recommendations of the producer himself. In this way, advertising will tend to shift the demand curve for the products of the firm in question to the right.

Advertising as a means of increasing demand is likely to increase the costs of production and may, therefore, be a barrier to entry for new firms. As a result of advertising, it is possible that an oligopoly might be created or maintained. The detergent industry is a case in point. The detergent industry is not an industry where traditionally there are necessarily high fixed costs. However, concentrated advertising campaigns (together with branding) by the two main firms in the industry, Lever Brothers and Proctor and Gamble, have led to them creating a virtual duopoly. A new firm wishing to enter the industry, in order to be successful, would have to engage in an advertising campaign, which, in itself, can be said to represent a high fixed cost.

Lever Brothers and Proctor and Gamble have created a barrier to entry not by just producing and advertising one product each, but by producing and advertising several brands each. Assuming that there are just these two detergent manufacturers in the industry and that they each produce and advertise one brand of washing powder, a new firm entering the industry would expect (assuming that the new firm advertises as heavily, has an identical cost structure and charges an identical price to that of the existing two manufacturers and assuming random consumer choice) to obtain one third of the market. If, however, the two original manufacturers advertised not just one brand of washing powder each but five brands each (advertising each brand separately), a new firm producing and advertising just one brand would expect to obtain one eleventh of the total market. In order to capture one third of the market, it would (other things being equal) have to advertise not just one but five brands of washing powder.

In many ways, one brand of a detergent manufacturer's washing powder might well compete with another. However, one brand might be advertised as suitable for twin-tub washing-machines, another as suitable for automatic washing-machines and another as suitable for hand washing; alternatively one brand might be advertised as suitable for washing one type of material and another as suitable for washing another type of material. In this way, different brands of a basic product are produced to cater for different sections of the market. Product differentiation is, in many ways, akin to the concept of price discrimination.

4. Collusive oligopoly

Since individual oligopolistic firms cannot be certain how their rivals will react to their actions, they may wish to collude. Collusion reduces uncertainty: unless there is collusion, the demand curve is likely to be subjective. Firms which choose to collude might decide to collude on price but compete on quality or they might decide to compete on both price and quality.

(a) *Incentives for collusion*

(i) Oligopolistic firms are most likely to wish to collude *if they are in an industry in which demand for the industry's product is inelastic, but demand for individual brands is almost completely elastic* as one firm lowers its price. In such a situation, if one firm lowers the price (given interdependence) it will lose because all other firms in the industry will follow. There will be an incentive for all firms in the industry to get together and raise their prices, since this will raise their profits. If, on the other hand, one firm lowers its price and the others do not follow (i.e. if demand for an individual brand is inelastic as price rises), it will not wish to collude: it will be happy in competitive oligopoly.

Furthermore, if one firm raises its price and everyone follows (i.e. if demand for an individual brand is inelastic as price rises), profits for the industry and for the firm will rise and there will be no incentive for collusion. If this is the situation, it is unlikely that the product is homogeneous.

(ii) *The more alike cost structures are*, the more likely oligopolistic firms are to wish to collude. We can say that the more homogeneous the product and the more alike the firms' costs, the greater is the incentive to collude. This is because different cost conditions might lead a large firm to think it can eliminate rivals by predatory pricing behaviour, i.e. undercutting rivals, which will make it keen for competitive oligopoly. If, however, all firms had similar cost structures, it would not be easy to eliminate rivals.

(iii) The number of firms in the industry might affect the decision to collude. Generally, we might assume that *the smaller the number of firms, the more likely collusion is.*

(iv) How far firms are able to collude may depend, to some extent, on *government legislation* (see section 7 below).

Within many countries, including the United Kingdom, cartels will usually be illegal under monopoly legislation. However, in certain periods, particularly between the First and Second World War, cartels were sometimes encouraged, especially where there was over-capacity within an industry.

(b) *How might collusion be organized?*

Ironically, while firms have a strong incentive to collude where the demand for the product of the industry as a whole is generally fairly inelastic, there is also an incentive for one firm to go against any agreement secretly. Thus, if firms agree to raise their prices, it might be easy for one firm to undercut the other firms secretly, particularly if there is a large number of firms in the agreement.

Because of the problem of secret undercutting, the best way to collude may be on a geographical basis, whereby one firm sells only in, say, London, another sells only in the Midlands, etc.

Collusion often takes the form of a *cartel*, whereby a group of firms *formally* agrees to set prices and, often, output. The rules of a cartel are legally enforceable.

The aim of a cartel is usually to increase the profits of the firms concerned, since in the absence of agreed prices, any one firm may decide to reduce its prices, which might be profitable for the firm itself, but will reduce the profits of the industry as a whole.

Among the well-known cartels are OPEC and the International Air Transport Association (IATA). IATA tries to stipulate the levels of price to be charged for scheduled air services. However, the agreement has tended to collapse as individual firms reduce their fares for chartered flights and make it difficult to distinguish between chartered services and scheduled services.

5. Monopolistic competition

Edward Chamberlain was one of the main economists responsible for propounding the theory of monopolistic competition in the 1930s. He noticed that in many industries, including the retail industry, the traditional models of monopoly and perfect competition do not apply.

The assumptions of monopolistic competition

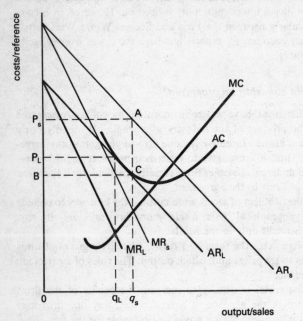

Figure 35. *Short-run and long-run equilibrium in monopolistic competition*

A monopolistic firm will make super-normal profits in the short-run (represented by the area $P_S ABC$) if the price (P_S) is above average costs (AC), i.e. if AC is below average revenue (AR$_S$).

If there are no barriers to entry, new firms will wish to enter the industry until super-normal profits are no longer being made, i.e. until the price equals AC.

The entry of new firms will reduce the demand for the output of the firm illustrated in the diagram, i.e. the average-revenue curve will be shifted to the left. Thus, marginal revenue will also be shifted to the left.

The entry of new firms does not effect the cost structure of the firm in question (other things being equal). Therefore the profit-maximizing output will be lower in the long run than in the short run (q_L compared to q_S) and the profit-maximizing price (i.e. equal to average revenue) will be lower in the long-run than in the short run (P_L compared to P_S).

(i) *Many firms* compete through a *differentiated product*. In the retail industry firms sell products which are usually slightly differentiated from their competitors' products.

(ii) Because of this product differentiation, the *demand curve for individual firms is downward sloping* rather than horizontal. In this respect, if a firm was able to lower prices, it would gain some but not all of its competitors' markets. If one firm raises its prices, it does not lose the whole of its market. The more highly differentiated the product, the less reason there will be for following other firms and the more inelastic will be the demand.

(iii) There are *no barriers to entry* (unlike in oligopoly, where high initial costs of setting up business may prove to be a barrier to some firms), *except those created as a result of branding and advertising*.

(iv) Because of the absence of barriers, it is possible that in the long run abnormal profits will be competed away.

(v) The short-run equilibrium is similar to monopoly equilibrium.

6. Non-price competition

(a) *Types of non-price competition*

(i) Non-price competition, which is practised in order to extend markets, might take the form, in the retailing industry for example, of shops giving *free deliveries* or carpet shops offering *free fitting*. Free deliveries may be regarded as somewhere in between price and non-price competition. These have become less common because the cost of sorting and transport has become high. For large items (such as furniture), however, firms may still deliver, thereby distinguishing themselves from other firms which do not deliver at all or only at a very high cost. Free delivery, as a form of non-price competition, does not only apply to firms at the retail level: metal stockholders might deliver to customers as a means of extending their market.

(ii) *Warranties* are sometimes offered as a form of non-price competition. However, in many ways these are a form of price competition.

(iii) The use of *credit* is a very important form of competition. For example, over 90 per cent of mail-order firms offer goods on credit. Also, a very large percentage of colour televisions are sold either on the basis of credit or are rented: some television retailers exist almost entirely in the rental or hire-purchase market.

(iv) Most banks tend to adopt the same opening hours as their rivals and offer similar services, but try to differentiate their products through the use of *various offers to young savers, students, etc.*

(v) The use of *qualified sales staff* and possibly *repairs and after-sales service* may also be regarded, to some extent, as a means of non-price competition.

(vi) *Expanding into new markets* may be regarded as a form of non-price competition. While traditionally many stores have tended to specialize, nowadays many stores are much more diversified. For example, Boots, formerly a specialist chemist, have moved into gardening and photographic equipment, and computers; Marks and Spencer have moved far more into the food market.

(vii) *Trading stamps.* The advantage of trading stamps from a retailer's point of view was that they were flexible, in the sense that they could use them to change prices without administrative costs, for example double stamps on a Thursday. In the last few years, however, there have been moves away from trading stamps and retailers have tended to concentrate on straight price competition.

(viii) *Advertising* is one of the two main forms of non-price competition. Advertising is usually assumed to increase demand, i.e. shift the demand curve to the right, and make the demand curve less elastic for individual firms. Usually, but not always, there may be a time lag before other firms in the industry retaliate.

In some cases, advertising will add to the firm's costs without necessarily adding to total revenue. This might well be said to be the case in the detergent industry, where more advertising tends not to increase demand for the firms concerned, but rather acts as a *barrier to new firms entering.* See also section 3 above.

(ix) The other main form of non-price competition is *branding*, whereby the design of a basic product is varied.

Branding might be used to help a firm expand into new markets. However, the more brands of a basic product a firm produces, the more advertising the firm is likely to have to undertake. See also section 3 above.

(b) *Resale price maintenance*

Resale price maintenance (R P M) is the practice whereby a manufacturer requires distributors selling the product not to undercut a minimum price. The practice was common until the *1964 Resale Prices Act* (see section 7 below).

RPM in markets makes non-price competition between distributors very important.

In some markets, the industry itself has agreed on prices, so that non-price competition is the only form of competition. For example, air fares on scheduled flights have been fixed by IATA, so that companies have had to compete in areas other than price – for example, offering improved standards of service, offering services to new foreign destinations or using Concorde on shuttle services.

7. Monopoly and restrictive practices legislation

(a) *1948 Monopolies and Restrictive Practices (Inquiry and Control) Act*

The first major piece of monopoly legislation was the *1948 Monopolies and Restrictive Practices (Inquiry and Control) Act.* This set up the *Monopolies and Restrictive Practices Commission, charged with discovering the nature and scope of the problems of restrictive practices and the practices of monopolies* by investigating the practices of industries referred to it by the Board of Trade. However, the Act did not apply to nationalized industries, transport, distribution, the professions or trade unions. *The Commission's powers were purely advisory*: it had no powers of coercion. Most of its work was in the field of restrictive practices: it looked at the practices of only two monopolized industries (which were defined by the Act as firms which had a third of an industry's output or firms which were acting in such a way as to prevent or restrict competition), namely industrial gases and matches.

As an effective policy tool the *1948 Act was a failure.* By 1956 the Commission had looked at only twenty-one cases and in not one of these cases were the Commission's recommendations effectively carried out. There seems to have been *no presumption made by the Act that monopoly or restrictive practices are either harmful or helpful to the economy.*

(b) *1956 Restrictive Trade Practices Act*

In 1955 the Commission published a general report, *Collective Discrimination – a Report on Exclusive Dealing, Aggregated Rebates and other Discriminatory Trade Practices.* This report led to the *1956 Restrictive Trade Practices Act.*

As a result of the 1956 Act *the problem of restrictive practices was treated separately from the problem of monopoly.*

The Monopolies and Restrictive Practices Commission was reconstituted under the 1956 Act and renamed the *Monopolies Commission.* The Commission was concerned almost exclusively with the practices of dominant firms. The 1956 Act set up the *Restrictive Practices Court* to investigate restrictive practices. The court was required to assume that agreements between two or more firms to restrict prices, quantities or qualities are against the public interest unless they could be shown to have other advantages, for example, in improving public safety. The collective enforcement of *resale price maintenance (R P M)* was, thus, deemed to be illegal unless it could be proved to be in the public interest. The 1956 Act was consolidated slightly by the *1976 Restrictive Practices Act.*

(c) *Resale Prices Act 1964*

Under the *Resale Prices Act 1964 all resale price agreements were assumed to be against the public interest,* unless it could be proved otherwise in the Restrictive Practices Court.

(d) *Monopolies and Mergers Act 1965*

The *Monopolies and Mergers Act 1965* widened the powers of the Monopolies Commission (which was renamed the *Monopolies and Mergers Commission* or *M M C*) so that it could investigate mergers as well as established monopolies. However, of seven hundred mergers between November 1973 and December 1977, only twenty-three were referred to the M M C.

(e) *Fair Trading Act 1973*

(i) The *Fair Trading Act 1973* replaced and *consolidated the 1948 and 1965 Acts.*

(ii) Under the 1973 Act, *firms are defined as monopolies if they supply 25 per cent or more of a total market.*

(iii) The Fair Trading Act *extended monopoly legislation to nationalized industries and can also examine restrictive labour practices.*

(iv) *The office of Director General of Fair Trading was established.* The Director General can investigate unfair trading and hold informal discussions.

(v) *Where the Director General finds areas of activity not in consumers' interests he may make recommendations to the relevant government minister or he may begin procedures which could lead to the banning of the practice.* If he takes the latter option, he consults the *Consumer Protection Advisory Committee (CPAC)*. CPAC has, for example, investigated the sale of new and used cars and of package holidays.

(f) *Competition Act 1980*

The *Competition Act 1980 extended the powers of the Office of Fair Trading,* which (under the 1980 Act) can now investigate the commercial activities of any firm, including nationalized industries and local authorities. If the Office of Fair Trading finds a practice to be in restraint of competition and the guilty firm does not abandon the practice, the practice is referred to the MMC for investigation.

(g) *Other legislation*

EEC Articles 85 and 86 deal with restrictive practices and monopolies. They *prohibit all restrictive practices.*

The *EEC also prohibits mergers which involve more than 200 million international units of account or 25 per cent of a national market.*

*

QUESTIONS

1. What are super-normal profits? When will they be maintained in the long run and when will they not be maintained in the long run?

Super-normal profits are defined as profits made over and above normal profits. The existence of super-normal profits encourages new firms to enter the industry in question. As new firms enter, super-normal profits are reduced until firms in the industry are only making normal profits, in which case new firms will no longer wish to enter the industry and no existing firms will wish to leave it.

In perfect competition, super-normal profits can only be made in the short run because there are no barriers to entry. The existence of super-normal profits in the short run will lead to new firms entering the industry. These new firms will shift the industry's supply curve to the right (without shifting the industry's demand curve) and will, as a result, reduce the market price. Because, under the assumptions of perfect competition, any new firm will have an equal share of the market, the demand curve of existing firms will be reduced and their super-normal profits reduced (eliminated in the long run). See Figure 30b, p. 133.

In models of oligopoly and monopoly (and to lesser extent in monopolistic competition), however, super-normal profits can continue to be made in the long run because of potential barriers to entry, including the barrier created as a result of product differentiation. We can find many examples of super-normal profits existing in the long run. For example, it has often been claimed that solicitors made super-normal profits on conveyancing when other firms were not free to enter the market. In fairness to solicitors, however, they often argued that because they made super-normal profits on conveyancing, they were able to cross-subsidize other services which they offered.

Even monopolies and oligopolies, however, might be deterred from making continual super-normal profits partly because outside firms might then make stronger efforts to enter the industry and partly because of concern that the government might intervene. For example, when the commercial banks made very large profits during a period of high interest rates, the government imposed a special windfall tax in the early 1980s. There are, however, a number of problems involved in trying to distinguish between normal profits and super-normal profits. Normal profits, for example, might reflect changes in interest rates and also the degree of risk involved. We would expect that private-sector firms would, over a long period, be making a higher rate of return for investors than if investors were investing in a safe form of savings such as National Savings or building-society accounts. However, interest rates fluctuate very widely and to show that, at one stage, profits or dividends are much higher than those paid on safe investments would not necessarily indicate that super-normal profits are being made. In some industries the degree of risk is very high, so we might expect that profits, in say the oil industry, which has a considerable degree of risk, to be higher than for a firm mainly engaged in selling ordinary clothes or food, where the degree of risk is much smaller. The larger profits would not necessarily indicate that super-normal profits were being made. For the small firm, accounting profits may well overstate profits in the economist's sense of the word since some of the profits will include computed costs, such as the entrepreneur's wages, which he would be able to obtain elsewhere. Similarly, in many firms, the opportunity costs of land and property are not shown by the figures in the accounts, and, therefore, tend to overstate profits compared to the economist's definition.

2. Why might the government be concerned about mergers between private-sector firms? What difficulties might the government have in assessing whether or not such mergers are in the public interest?

Successive governments in the United Kingdom have introduced legislation against possible abuses of monopoly power and have been particularly concerned about the effect of mergers upon the monopoly power of the firms involved.

When considering the effect of mergers, governments have to assess the potential economies of scale which could occur. In some cases, mergers have been positively encouraged as, for example, with the creation of British Leyland (now known as the Rover Group) from the companies of Leyland and the British Motor Corporation. The government, at the time, felt that the potential economies of scale would outweigh any possible disadvantages arising from monopoly power. Although there are relatively few car companies operating within the United Kingdom, the abuse of monopoly power is unlikely since there are large numbers of overseas firms in the market, notably from France, Germany and Japan. This means that a British firm would be unlikely to raise its prices or reduce its output in the manner assumed of a typical monopolist. Sometimes the government might be concerned about vertical integration if it meant that supplies of raw materials or components would not be available to rivals as a result of the merger. A case in point occurred when the former British Motor Corporation took over a steel firm, Pressed Steel. Concern was expressed that Jaguar, which was then an independent company, might not be able to receive adequate supplies from Pressed Steel. Assurances had to be given by the British Motor Corporation that body pressings would be supplied to Jaguar. However, the government would have to weigh up the possible abuses of the power against the advantages of continuity of supply and possible lower costs as a result of such vertical integration. Vertical integration could also possibly lead to more successful marketing of products.

In the banking sector, banks have sometimes merged horizontally, since fixed costs (such as setting up a computer system) can be spread over a wide number of outlets. Customers may also benefit, from being able to bank at a larger number of branches. Building societies have often merged for much the same reasons. However, the government has looked unfavourably upon certain potential mergers of banks, feeling that these might lead to an increase in monopoly power. There is also the fact that, while many mergers have been made in optimistic mood (claiming to lead to the reduction of costs, etc.), evidence has shown that these claimed advantages do not always occur. Governments might, therefore, wish to look at the potential efficiency, although some governments might take the view that the efficiency or otherwise of private-sector firms should not be a major concern of the state. So far, the assumption has been that mergers tend to increase monopoly power. In a few cases governments might wish to encourage smaller firms to merge ('defensive' mergers), which would perhaps enable them to compete more vigorously against larger firms, particularly overseas ones. For example, a government might look favourably upon mergers by small computer firms if they are likely to lead to lower deficits on the balance of trade of the information-technology industry. Feelings apparent here might also be that research and development, particularly in computers and ancillary equipment, is better done by large firms rather than small ones, although there is a great deal of conflicting evidence about this.

In some cases, governments might be concerned not so much about economic power, but about political power. For example, there are special provisions in the United Kingdom regarding newspaper mergers partly because of this. The same considerations might apply to other parts of the media industry, such as radio and television.

MULTIPLE-CHOICE QUESTIONS

1. Which of the following is true of the demand curve for the individual firm in perfect competition:

    (*a*) it is perfectly elastic;

    (*b*) it is perfectly inelastic;

    (*c*) it is positive, but lower than one;

    (*d*) it is negative?

Answer – (*a*)

2. Which of the following is generally true of the demand curve for an industry under conditions of perfect competition:

    (*a*) it is perfectly price elastic;

    (*b*) it is perfectly price inelastic;

    (*c*) it is positive;

    (*d*) it is negative?

Answer – (*d*)

3. Which of the following is not true of a firm operating under conditions of perfect competition in the long run:

    (*a*) price equals marginal cost;

(b) the marginal cost curve cuts the average cost curve where the average cost curve is at a minimum;

(c) the firm will be making only normal profits;

(d) the firm will be just covering average variable costs?

Answer – (d)

4. The following are assumptions of perfect competition, with one exception. Which is the exception?

(a) There are a large number of independent buyers and sellers.

(b) Consumers regard the product of one firm as a perfect substitute for the products of other firms.

(c) There is no undue discrimination on the part of the buyers or sellers.

(d) Individual firms will find it profitable to advertise.

Answer – (d)

5. In profit-maximizing perfect competition which of the following must be true:

(A) marginal revenue equals marginal costs;

(B) marginal revenue equals average revenue;

(C) normal profits are made in equilibrium?

(a) A only.

(b) A, B, and C are all true.

(c) B and C only are true.

(d) A and B only are true.

Answer – (b)

6. In perfect competition which of the following is true? The price elasticity of demand for the firm is:

(a) zero;

(b) minus one;

(c) plus one;

(d) minus infinity;

(e) plus infinity.

Answer – (d)

7. Which of the following might prevent perfect competition leading to the optimal allocation of resources:

(A) the existence of economies of scale;

(B) the divergence between private and social costs;

(C) the existence of collective goods?

(a) A only.

(b) A and B only.

(c) B and C only.

(d) All.

Answer – (d)

8. In the standard model of perfect competition, which of the following is true in the short run:

    (a) firms will continue to produce as long as marginal revenue is above zero;

    (b) firms will only continue to produce providing they are covering their average costs;

    (c) firms will continue to produce providing they are covering their variable costs;

    (d) firms will continue to produce providing they are covering their fixed costs?

Answer – (c)

9. In a monopoly, which of the following is not necessarily true:

    (a) the firm will be able to make more profits if it indulges in price discrimination, which reduces consumer surplus;

    (b) marginal revenue equals marginal cost is a condition for profit maximization;

    (c) price will always be higher and output lower than if there were perfect competition;

    (d) the demand curve is downward sloping?

Answer – (c). Explanation: A monopoly may have economies of scale which a perfectly competitive firm does not have.

10. A monopolist will maximize profits by fixing a price at which:

    (a) the total revenue is maximized;

    (b) marginal cost equals marginal revenue;

    (c) average revenue is maximized;

    (d) the price elasticity of demand equals one.

Answer – (b)

11. In an industry where there are significant economies of large-scale production, there is only one firm. If it is broken up by government intervention, which of the following will apply in the long run:

    (a) price will be higher and total output will be lower;

    (b) price will be lower and total output will be higher;

    (c) price will be lower and total output will be lower;

    (d) there is insufficient information as to whether price or quantity will be higher or lower?

Answer – (d)

12. In oligopoly, which of the following is true:
   (*a*) firms never compete on price;
   (*b*) firms always compete on price;
   (*c*) a firm's marginal revenue is determined solely by the firm;
   (*d*) a firm's marginal revenue depends upon the decision of other firms?

Answer – (*d*)

13. Oligopolies are more likely to collude if which of the following conditions exist:
(A) there is a small number, rather than a large number, of sellers;
(B) there are restrictions, rather than no restrictions, on entry;
(C) the firms have widely differing, rather than similar, cost structures;
(D) the firms are of similar, rather than vastly different size?
   (*a*) A only.
   (*b*) A and B only.
   (*c*) C only.
   (*d*) A, B and D only.
   (*e*) Another combination of the above factors.

Answer – (*d*)

14. Oligopolistic collusion is most likely to occur where the industry's demand is
   (*a*) price elastic;
   (*b*) price inelastic.

Answer – (*b*)

15. According to the kinked demand curve, if an oligopolist firm raises its prices:
   (*a*) other firms will follow;
   (*b*) other firms will not follow.

Answer – (*b*)

16. Which of the following are generally true of oligopoly:
(A) there are barriers to entry;
(B) there is often non-price competition;
(C) the firms recognize their interdependence?
   (*a*) A only.
   (*b*) B only.
   (*c*) C only.
   (*d*) B and C only.
   (*e*) All

Answer – (*e*)

17. There is no one general theory of oligopoly mainly because:
   (*a*) it is difficult to determine marginal costs in oligopoly;
   (*b*) it is difficult to determine marginal revenue in oligopoly;
   (*c*) it is difficult to determine fixed costs in oligopoly.
Answer – (*b*)

18. In monopolistic competition which of the following is true?
   (*a*) the firm has a downward-sloping demand curve;
   (*b*) the firm has a horizontal demand curve;
   (*c*) the products are regarded as homogeneous?
Answer – (*a*)

19. The practice of price discrimination involves a producer charging a higher price in one market than in another because:
   (*a*) costs differ from market to market;
   (*b*) the price elasticity of demand differs from market to market;
   (*c*) both costs and the price elasticity of demand differ from market to market.
Answer – (*b*)

20–24. The situations listed in the next five questions refer most closely to which of the market forms listed below in each case:
   (*a*) perfect competition;
   (*b*) monopolistic competition;
   (*c*) oligopoly;
   (*d*) monopsony;
   (*e*) monopoly?

20. British Rail is the main buyer of signalman's services.
Answer – (*d*)

21. A small number of car firms supply the United Kingdom market.
Answer – (*c*)

22. A very large number of shipping firms in the tramp-shipping market supply shipping space at very similar prices, particularly as the Baltic Exchange gives very adequate information.
Answer – (*a*)

23. A fairly large number of small firms supply computer software at slightly different prices.
Answer – (*b*)

24. The regional electricity boards supply electricity at different prices to different groups of consumers.
Answer – (*e*)

25. Countervailing power is likely to exist when:
    (*a*) a monopoly sells to a variety of small retailers;
    (*b*) a company sells its goods or services to a small number of large firms
    (*c*) a firm sells its goods or services to a small number of small firms.
Answer – (*b*)

26–30. For the next five questions, the possible answers are as follows:
    (*a*) both statements are true and the second is an explanation of the first;
    (*b*) both statements are true, but the second is not an explanation of the first;
    (*c*) the first statement is true, but the second statement is false;
    (*d*) the first statement is false, but the second statement is true;
    (*e*) both statements are false.
Decide which of the above answers applies to each of the five following pairs of statements.

First statement	*Second statement*
26. Monopolies will always charge less than firms operating under conditions of perfect competition. *Answer* – (*d*)	Monopolies usually have the advantages of economies of scale.
27. Monopolies will always charge more than firms operating under conditions of perfect competition. *Answer* – (*d*)	Monopolists can restrict market supply and, therefore, raise the price.
28. In oligopoly, there is often a considerable degree of non-price competition. *Answer* – (*a*)	Oligopolistic firms often wish to avoid price competition since they may fear that if other firms react it could lead to a price war.

29. There is no general theory of oligopoly.

There are problems of determining marginal revenue of oligopolies, since much will depend upon the reactions of other firms.

Answer – (*a*)

30. In oligopoly, firms will generally find it easier to collude if they have a reasonably identical cost structure.

If oligopolistic firms have quite different cost structures, low-cost firms would have a strong incentive not to collude, since they make larger profits than other firms, other things being equal.

Answer – (*a*)

DATA RESPONSE

1. The theoretical definition of a monopoly is a firm which is the sole producer of a good or service for which there is *no substitute in the eyes of the consumer*. In economic jargon, the *cross-elasticity of demand* for the product is zero. Perhaps the nearest to such a concept in the United Kingdom is the Water Board.

Often we need to have an empirical measure of monopoly power. We might look, for example, at the largest firms in an industry and see whether they form a large part of total output. We can obtain such statistics from the Census of Production. There are, however, a number of limitations to such methods. For example, the data itself may be out of date. Furthermore, producers from other fields may well compete. For example, while the Central Electricity Generating Board is responsible for most of the electricity supplied, it still faces competition from the oil, coal, and gas industries for central heating. However, for lighting purposes the regional electricity boards have considerable degrees of monopoly power. Sometimes a company could have a small percentage of the total market and yet have a very large share of the market in a particular region or for a specialized product. For example, some breweries might well have a small percentage of a total share and yet have a monopoly within a particular region. There may also be competition from imports, for example in the car industry, which will not show up in government statistics.

(*a*) Explain the terms in *italic* type.

(*b*) Why might the government wish to define a monopoly?

(*c*) How do you think the degree of monopoly power within a particular industry might best be measured? Explain your thinking.

2. While the kinked demand curve is often shown in textbooks, a theory-of-games approach, i.e. considering the reactions of rivals and the actions that can be taken in turn, may well be more helpful when considering individual industries. For example, if we look at the newspaper industry we can see that it, to some extent, subdivides into groups: the *Times*, *Telegraph*, *Independent* and *Guardian* compete for the so-called 'quality' end of the market; the *Sun*, *Mirror* and *Star* compete in the popular section of the newspaper market; the *Daily Express*, *Daily Mail* and *Today* compete in the middle market.

If, for example, the *Daily Telegraph* wished to try to raise its revenue, it might try lowering its price. This might extend sales (it might lead to a fall in the sales of the *Guardian*, *Independent* and *Times*) and raise its advertising revenue. However, the *Guardian*, *Independent* and *Times* might respond by lowering their prices. Alternatively, the *Daily Telegraph* might try to raise its revenue by raising its price. The effect upon revenue of this action will depend not only upon the cross-elasticity of demand but also upon the effects on advertising revenue. The *Daily Telegraph* might try to raise revenue by merging with another newspaper. However, the readership might not be loyal to a merged newspaper. The owners of the *Daily Telegraph* might be able to increase their revenue by launching a sister newspaper to the *Daily Telegraph*. The Express Group launched the *Daily Star* as a sister newspaper to the *Daily Express*. Non-price competition has been very noticeable within the newspaper industry in recent years, particularly in the popular and middle sections of the market, with the proliferation of bingo competitions. Even *The Times* has launched a 'Portfolio' competition, which is, in effect, a high-class form of bingo.

(*a*) The author suggests that a fall in the price of the *Daily Telegraph* might lead to a fall in the sales of the *Guardian*, *Independent* and *Times*. However, why might the sales of the *Guardian*, *Independent* and *Times* be little affected by a fall in price of the *Daily Telegraph* by even as much as, say, 5p?

(*b*) Why might a rise in the price of one newspaper: (i) lead to a rise in price of other newspapers; (ii) not lead to a rise in price of other newspapers? Explain, in particular, why a rise in the price of, say, the *Daily Telegraph* might or might not lead to a rise in the price of the *Guardian*, *Independent* and *Times*.

(c) Why did *The Times* introduce its 'Portfolio' competition? Why has neither the *Guardian* nor the *Independent* responded with such a competition, while the *Telegraph* has?

3.

Model 1a. Petroleum industry in competitive oligopoly

Firm A		Each of the other five firms*	
Price per litre	Quantity sold per day ('000 litres)	Price per litre	Quantity sold per day ('000 litres)
39p	101	39p	101
40p	100	40p	100
41p	0	40p	120

The original price is 40p. When firm A lowers the price to 39p, the other firms in the industry follow; when firm A raises its price to 41p, the other firms do not follow (they continue to charge 40p).

Model 1b. Petroleum industry in collusive oligopoly

Firm A		Each of the other five firms*	
Price per litre	Quantity sold per day ('000 litres)	Price per litre	Quantity sold per day ('000 litres)
39p	101	39p	101
40p	100	40p	100
41p	99	41p	99

If all firms in the industry decide to collude, when A raises its price from 40p to 41p, all other firms in the industry will also raise their prices to 41p.

* For the sake of this model we assume that there are six petroleum firms.

Model 2a. Newspapers in competitive oligopoly

Firm A		Each of the other two firms*	
Price per newspaper	Quantity sold per day ('000)	Price per newspaper	Quantity sold per day ('000)
24p	510	24p	550
25p	500	25p	500
26p	470	25p	510

The original price is 25p. When firm A lowers its price to 24p, both the other firms follow; when firm A raises its price to 26p, the other firms do not follow (they continue to charge 25p).

Model 2b. Newspapers in collusive oligopoly

Firm A		Each of the other two firms*	
Price per newspaper	Quantity sold per day ('000)	Price per newspaper	Quantity sold per day ('000)
24p	510	24p	510
25p	500	25p	500
26p	490	26p	490

If all firms in the industry decide to collude, when A raises its price from 25p to 26p, both the other firms in the industry will also raise their prices to 26p.

(a) For each of the above models, calculate the effect of collusion upon the industry's total revenue (bearing in mind our assumption that there are six firms in the petroleum industry and three firms in the newspaper industry) and upon the individual firms' total revenue compared to the situation under competitive oligopoly. Using these calculations, state in which of the two models (if any) there will be an incentive to collude. Explain why there is or is not an incentive to collude in terms of the price elasticity of demand for the product of the industry as a whole and the price elasticity of demand for the brands of the individual firms.

* For the sake of the model we assume that there are three newspaper firms.

(*b*) What can be said about the degree of product differentiation achieved by firm A in model 1 over its rivals' products? How might a petrol company attempt to differentiate its product from that of its rivals? (Bear in mind, for example, how the Shell Oil Company attempted to differentiate the brand of petrol known as Formula Shell from other brands of petrol.)

4. The market for shipping space, which can be regarded as a homogeneous product, is shared between tramp operators, who will carry goods wherever they feel there is sufficient demand to make a profit, and liner-conference operators, who operate fixed schedules to destinations irrespective (in the short term) of demand. It is usually asserted that tramp-shipping rates will be above those of liner rates if there is a sudden increase in demand, while, during a recession, tramp rates will fall to a rate which just covers variable costs. The conference operators claim that the stability of pricing and the regular timetable enables nations to carry out trading in a more successful manner than if they were faced with widespread fluctuations.

(*a*) Explain, using appropriate diagrams, the effects of changes in demand on tramp-shipping rates and why the above comments about relative prices may or may not be true.

(*b*) Under what circumstances would it pay all shipping lines to belong to a conference system? What factors might reduce the effectiveness of such a cartel?

SELF-EXAMINATION QUESTIONS

1. Since perfect competition occurs infrequently in a modern economy such as the United Kingdom, why is it important to study the concept of perfect competition?

2. What is meant by saying that, in perfect competition, the firm is a 'price-taker'? What would be the effect of an individual firm advertising in conditions of perfect competition? Why might it pay businesses to advertise collectively as, for example, with some agricultural products?

3. In perfect competition it is usually assumed that consumers have perfect knowledge. How far is this assumption likely to be valid in a modern society and how does advertising influence this?

4. Why are commercial buyers likely to have better information than the typical consumer? What are the economic consequences of this?

5. In conditions approximating to perfect competition, what will happen to wages and prices of materials if a small firm wishes to increase production and expand from, say, fifteen employees to one hundred?

6. In perfect competition, as with other models, marginal revenue equals marginal cost is a necessary condition for profit maximization. Explain why marginal revenue will equal average revenue and, hence, why average revenue equals marginal cost. What is the economic significance of this type of reasoning?

7. If perfect competition is desirable (as many economists suggest), how can there ever be wasteful competition? Illustrate your answer with reference to assets which are geographically immobile.

8. How can we decide whether an industry is competitive? Outline the main measures of monopoly power and show how these can be difficult to apply in practice.

9. What is the economist's definition of a monopoly? Which of the following, if any, might constitute a monopoly and why:
   (*a*) London Regional Transport;
   (*b*) the Electricity Board;
   (*c*) Rolls-Royce cars;
   (*d*) a diamond company;
   (*e*) British Rail;
   (*f*) the regional water boards?

10. In monopoly, average revenue is greater than marginal revenue and marginal revenue equals marginal cost. Therefore, average revenue is greater than marginal cost. This contrasts with perfect competition where average revenue equals marginal cost. What are the implications of this for government attitudes towards monopoly?

11. What is meant by a 'discriminating' monopoly? Explain what problems, if any, would occur if the following wished to charge a higher price for their goods or services:
   (*a*) a fishmonger;
   (*b*) a doctor;
   (*c*) theatre owners;
   (*d*) railways;
   (*e*) hairdressers;
   (*f*) light-bulb manufacturers.

167

12. What is meant by the term 'countervailing power'? Explain in relation to the large supermarkets purchasing from large manufacturers and in relation to the practices of oil producers and the oil companies.

13. Explain why economists differ as to whether monopoly or competition will lead to greater research and development.

14. Under what circumstances might the government be concerned about monopolies establishing very low prices? Hint: think of fighting companies.

15. What is meant by monopsony? Give an example. Explain the economic consequences of the existence of this monopsony.

16. In some towns there are limits on the number of licences given to taxi drivers. Explain, with the use of diagrams, the likely consequences of this on both supply and price.

17. It is often stated that the monopolist faces a downward-sloping demand curve, unlike a firm in perfect competition. Explain from this, why, if the monopolist charges one price and is profit maximizing, price will be greater than marginal cost.

18. Give examples of oligopoly in the United Kingdom. In what ways do such oligopolistic firms compete with each other?

19. Why is there no one general theory of oligopoly which is universally accepted? Explain, with reference to the problems of determining marginal revenue when oligopolies compete.

20. Under what conditions will oligopolistic firms find it easy and under what conditions will they find it difficult to collude? Explain your answer with reference to the size of firms and the attitude of governments.

21. What was resale price maintenance? What effects did this have on retail industry? What effect is it likely to have had on the number of retail outlets?

22. Under what circumstances might sellers in a market agree on a price? What would be the economic consequences of this? Why has the British government abolished collective price maintenance?

23. Why might governments be particularly concerned about newspaper mergers when the amount of financial assets might be relatively small compared with other firms?

24. Why is non-price competition often important in oligopoly?

25. What are the assumptions that P. Sweezy made regarding oligopolistic firms? How valid are these assumptions in the 1980s?

26. What is meant by the theory-of-games approach to oligopoly? To which oligopolies in modern society might this approach be applied?

27. What barriers to entry may occur in different industries? What actions, if any, can the government take to eliminate any such barriers?

28. Explain why, for perfumes and soaps, product differentiation may be common.

29. Why might price leadership avoid the problem of price rigidity or cut-throat competition in oligopoly? Why is price leadership not necessarily desirable?

30. The following are possible ways in which firms can either restrict competition or compete in order to achieve stability of price or output. Analyse the practices and explain why they may or may not be in the consumer's interest in the long term.

   (a) Some computer firms have threatened to prevent supplies of computers to retailers who reduce their prices below the recommended levels. The computer companies claim that higher prices enable all the retailers to carry out the levels of after-service which the computers need, as well as to give other services, such as adequate training and information to potential customers.

   (b) Where a monopoly is challenged by a new company it sometimes sets up a fighting company, i.e. a company which belongs to the main firm but seems as though it is independent. The fighting company then reduces its prices, even if this means making losses, so as to drive the new independent company out of business.

   (c) Car firms have agreed to charge different prices in different geographical areas. For example, car prices have often been higher in the United Kingdom than in other E E C countries. The differences are not wholly due to any difference in transport or taxation costs.

   (d) An office-equipment firm will give a comprehensive maintenance contract for five years but only if customers agree to purchase all their office materials from the firm.

   (e) Shipping conferences, i.e. those which operate regular services, will agree to give 'deferred rebates', perhaps of 10 per cent, but only if shippers agree to send all their goods to particular destinations by conference lines.

(f) Manufacturers reduce their prices for large companies to a price far below that which smaller companies can obtain. The small companies, therefore, complain about unfair competition, stating that, in many cases, they cannot even buy at the prices at which the larger firms sell to make a normal profit.

(g) Large retailers often use the concept of loss leaders, e.g. they will advertise sugar at prices below cost in order to induce customers to come into the shops and then make large-scale purchases. Other retailers complain that this is unfair practice.

(h) A vertically integrated company has exclusive access to a supply of imports which it sells to competitors only at abnormally high costs.

(i) Firms take out a wide variety of patents to control office-equipment processes, partly to prevent potential competition. This is justified by the firms because of the high costs of research and development.

(j) A computer manufacturer deliberately makes its equipment incompatible with software from independent producers because it wishes to make more profits on sales of its own software.

11. National income

1. Circular flow

Circular-flow diagrams and equations are used to show that *the flows of incomes, output and expenditure within an economy in a given period (perhaps a week or a year) are equal*, i.e. they are used to show that *national income is the same thing as national product (output) is the same thing as national expenditure.*

i.e. $Y \equiv P \equiv E$.

We might assume that at the beginning of a particular week (week 0), within the UK economy, households receive *incomes* (Y_0). These incomes, we might assume, are earned as a result of planned *expenditure* on British goods and services in the previous period.

These incomes (Y_0) encourage households to supply factors of production to British firms, which they require in order to *produce* goods and services. Thus, we assume that households are the owners of factors of production (i.e. land, labour and capital). Supplies of factors of production in week 0 to British firms (whether private or public-sector firms) enable British goods and services to be produced (P_0). There is then assumed to be expenditure (E_0) upon these goods and services.

British goods and services (i.e. P_0) are assumed to be:

(i) bought by British households as a result of *consumption expenditure* (C_0);

(ii) bought by British firms (whether private or public-sector firms) for investment purposes, i.e. as a result of *planned investment expenditure* (Ip_0);

(iii) bought by the British government for consumption expenditure, i.e. as a result of *government expenditure* (G_0);

(iv) or bought by the overseas sector (whether foreign households, foreign firms or foreign governments), i.e. as a result of *export expenditure* (X_0).

(v) However, part of this expenditure (whether consumption expenditure, planned investment expenditure, government expenditure or export expenditure) on British goods and services might be *taxed* (T_0) by the British government.

171

(vi) Furthermore, some expenditure by the UK sector might go on foreign-produced goods and services, i.e. *imports* (M_0).

(vii) Furthermore, part of P_0 might remain unsold, in which case it constitutes *unplanned investment*, i.e. Iu_0.

$$\therefore P_0 \equiv E_0 \equiv C_0 + Ip_0 + G_0 + X_0 - T_0 - M_0 + Iu_0$$
$$\therefore Y_0 \equiv P_0 \equiv E_0 = C_0 + Ip_0 + G_0 + X_0 - T_0 - M_0 + Iu_0.$$

where C_0 is consumption expenditure in period 0,

Ip_0 is planned investment expenditure in period 0,

G_0 is government expenditure in period 0,

X_0 is export expenditure in period 0

T_0 is taxation in period 0,

M_0 is import expenditure in period 0,

Iu_0 is unplanned investment expenditure in period 0

and Y_0 is total or *national income* in period 0, P_0 is total or *national product* (i.e. output) in period 0 and E_0 is total or *national expenditure* in period 0.

Given an income (Y_0), households will either consume or save it.

$$\therefore Y_0 = C_0 + S_0.$$

2. Explanation of terms

(i) *Consumption expenditure* (C) is expenditure by British households on British consumer goods and services.

(ii) *Planned investment expenditure* (Ip) is expenditure by British firms (whether private or public sector) on British investment goods.

(iii) *Government expenditure* (G) is expenditure by the British central or local government on British goods and services. Government expenditure does not include the British government's expenditure on investment goods.

(iv) *Export expenditure* (X) is expenditure by the overseas sector (foreign households, firms and governments) upon British goods and services.

(v) *Taxation* (T) is taxation imposed by the British government upon consumption expenditure, plus planned investment expenditure, plus government expenditure, plus export expenditure.

(vi) *Import expenditure* (M) is expenditure by British households, firms or governments upon foreign goods and services.

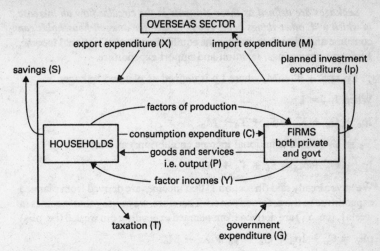

Figure 36. *The circular flow of income*

(vii) *Unplanned investment* (Iu) consists of stocks of British goods and services produced which are left *unsold*, i.e. they are not consumed, bought by firms for investment purposes, bought by government or bought by the overseas sector. It is also known as the *physical increase in stocks* or *stock building*.

(viii) *Savings* (S) is that part of their income households do not spend.

3. National income equilibrium

We assume that national income in one period will be the same as national income in the next period and in the period after that, etc. (i.e. *there will be national income equilibrium*) *as long as planned injections equal planned leakages.*

Injections are defined as those elements in the circular flow an increase in which will, other things being equal, allow households to increase their consumption, and, therefore, raise the equilibrium level of national income. These elements are investment expenditure, government expenditure and export expenditure.

$\therefore$ Jp = Ip + G + X, where Jp is defined as planned injections.

173

Leakages are defined as those elements in the circular flow an increase in which will, other things being equal, reduce the amount households can consume and, therefore, reduce the equilibrium level of national income. Leakages are savings, taxation and import expenditure.

$\therefore Lp = S + T + M$, where Lp is defined as planned leakages.

When $Jp_0 = Lp_0$,

$Ip_0 + G_0 + X_0 = S_0 + T_0 + M_0$.

$Y_0 = Y_1$ (which is national income equilibrium) as long as

$Ip_0 + G_0 + X_0 = S_0 + T_0 + M_0$.

We have already said (in section 1) that incomes are derived from planned expenditure in the previous period. Therefore, we can say that incomes in week 1, (i.e. Y_1) are derived from planned expenditure in week 0 (i.e. pE_0)

$pE_0 = C_0 + Ip_0 + G_0 - T_0 + X_0 - M_0$,

i.e. $pE_0 = E_0 - Iu_0$.

$\therefore Y_1 = C_0 + Jp_0 + G_0 - T_0 + X_0 - M_0 = pE_0$.
$\therefore Y_1 = Y_0$ if $pE_0 = E_0$,

i.e. $Y_1 = Y_0$ if $Iu_0 = 0$. When planned injections equal planned leakages there can be no unplanned investment. Therefore, *there is national income equilibrium from one period to the next if unplanned investment equals zero*. We can show how national income equilibrium is achieved more clearly by building up a circular-flow model, introducing each component of expenditure in turn.

4. A model of the circular flow of income

We can show that

$Y \equiv P \equiv E = C + Ip + G + X - T - M + Iu$

by building up a model of circular flow introducing one element of national expenditure at a time.

We will imagine at the beginning of each stage of our model that

$Y_0 = £5,000m.$

(a) *A two-sector economy in which there are no savings and no planned investment*

We assume that $Y_0 = £5,000m$.

$Y_0 \equiv P \equiv E_0 = £5,000m.$
$= C_0 + Ip_0 + G_0 + X_0 - T_0 - M_0 + Iu_0 = £5,000m.$
$= C_0 + Ip_0 + Iu_0 = £5,000m$ in a two-sector economy
$= C_0 + Iu_0 = £5,000m$ if there is no planned investment.
$_HY_0 = C_0 + S_0 = £5,000m = Y_0$, i.e. households' either spend their income or save it.

If $C_0 = £5,000m$, $S_0 = 0$.
$\therefore Y_0 = C_0$
$\quad = £5,000m.$

Since $Y_0 = £5,000m$, and $C_0 = £5,000m$, $Y_0 = C_0$.

$\therefore Iu_0 = 0$, i.e. all that is produced in week 0 is sold and there is no excess demand.

Thus, UK firms will wish to produce as much in week 1 as was produced in week 0 (i.e. £5,000m of output) and will, therefore, demand the same amount of factors of production from (British) households in week 1 as in week 0. British households will only be willing to supply the same amount of factors of production in week 1 as they supplied in week 0 if they receive an income at the start of week 1 equal to Y_0.

$\therefore Y_1 = Y_0$ (which is national income equilibrium), since $Jp_0 = Lp_0$, i.e. $Ip_0 = S_0$, in a two-sector economy.

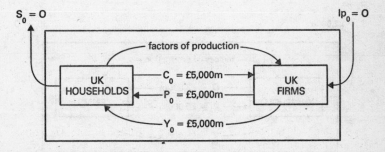

Figure 37. *The circular flow of income in a two-sector economy with no savings and no planned investment*

(b) *A two-sector economy in which there are some savings, but no planned investment*

$Y_0 = £5,000m.$

$Y_0 \equiv P_0 \equiv E_0 = £5,000m$
$\quad = C_0 + Ip_0 + G_0 + X_0 - T_0 - M_0 + Iu_0 = £5,000m.$
$\quad = C_0 + Ip_0 + Iu_0 = £5,000m$ in a two-sector economy.
$\quad = C_0 + Iu_0 = £5,000m$, still assuming no planned investment.
$Y_0 = C_0 + S_0 = £5,000m.$

If households decide to spend (consume) only £3,000m, they are assumed to save £2,000m,

i.e. $Y_0 = C_0 + S_0$
$\quad\quad = £3,000m + £2,000m = £5,000m.$

Given $Y_0 = C_0 + Iu_0 = £5,000m,$

since $C_0 = £3,000m$, $Iu_0 = £2,000m$, i.e. there are unsold stocks totalling £2,000m, i.e. there is excess supply.

Since only £3,000m is sold, U K firms will wish to produce only £3,000m in week 1. Therefore, they will pay incomes at the start of week 1 totalling £3,000m, i.e. $Y_1 = £3,000m,$

i.e. $Y_1 < Y_0$, i.e. there is national income disequilibrium, since $Jp_0 < Lp_0,$

i.e. $Ip_0 < S_0$ in a two-sector economy.

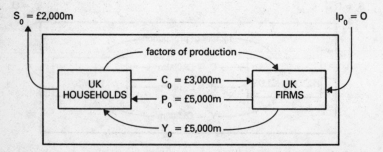

Figure 38. *The circular flow of income in a two-sector economy with some savings, but no planned investment*

(c) *A two-sector economy in which there are some savings and an equal level of planned investment*

Y_0 = £5,000m.
$Y_0 \equiv P_0 \equiv E_0$ = £5,000m
$\quad = C_0 + Ip_0 + G_0 + X_0 - T_0 - M_0 + Iu_0$ = £5,000m
$\quad = C_0 + Ip_0 + Iu_0$ = £5,000m in a two-sector economy.
$Y_0 = C_0 + S_0$ = £5,000m

If C_0 = £3,000m, then S_0 = £2,000m.

$\therefore Y_0 = C_0 + S_0$
$\quad\quad = £3,000m + £2,000m$
$\quad\quad = £5,000m.$

Given $Y_0 = C_0 + Ip_0 + Iu_0$ = £5,000m, where C_0 = £3,000m, if firms plan to buy (for investment purposes) that output that is not bought by consumers (i.e. that output that would otherwise be left unsold) and households' savings are channelled to firms, then Ip_0 = £2,000m. Therefore, Iu_0 = 0.

i.e. $Y_0 = C_0 + Ip_0 + Iu_0$.

$\quad = £3,000m + £2,000m + 0 = £5,000m.$

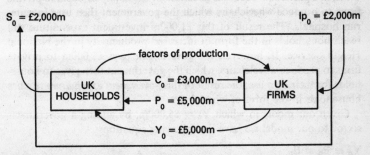

Figure 39. *The circular flow of income in a two-sector economy with some savings and an equal level of planned investment*

Since all that is produced is sold, firms will pay incomes at the start of week (Y_1) equal to Y_0,

i.e. $Y_1 = Y_0$ (which is national income equilibrium),

since $Jp_0 = Lp_0$,

i.e. $Ip_0 = S_0$, in a two-sector economy.

(d) *A three-sector economy in which there is government expenditure, but no taxation*

So far, we have assumed no government sector. By assuming, however, that there is government activity in week 0, we can assume that the government produces goods and services. Thus, in week 0 we can assume that there is not only output from British private-sector firms, but also from the public sector (i.e. nationalized industries, state-run schools, the National Health Service, etc.).

It is important to note that the output of the public sector is included as part of the output of British firms as a whole. Therefore, British firms are defined as private-sector firms plus public-sector firms. This means that any expenditure by the British government on goods to increase the productivity of the public sector (for example, expenditure on textbooks for state-run schools) is said to constitute investment expenditure.

Planned investment expenditure undertaken by the government and included as part of Ip would involve the government purchasing investment goods from other firms which would be used to increase the productivity of public-sector firms. The results of such expenditure reaches households in a different form to the form these investment goods take. Thus, in a particular week, the government might pay £1,000m to private firms to produce wheelchairs which the government then uses in state-run hospitals. The result of this £1,000m investment expenditure will reach households in the form of increased productivity in the National Health Service. If, however, the government pays £1,000m to private firms to produce wheelchairs, which the government then gives to households for their own use, the result of this *government expenditure* reaches households in the form of wheelchairs.

Given our model in which $Y_0 = £5,000m$, by adding a government sector to our model we have the following equations:

$$Y_0 \equiv P_0 \equiv E_0$$
$$= C_0 + Ip_0 + G_0 + X_0 - T_0 - M_0 + Iu_0$$
$$= £5,000m$$
$$= C_0 + Ip_0 + G_0 - T_0 + Iu_0$$
$$= £5,000m \text{ in a three-sector model.}$$

We might assume that $C_0 = £3,000m$, $Ip_0 = £2,000m$ and $G_0 = £1,000m$. If this government expenditure (as distinct from government investment expenditure) is financed by borrowing rather than through taxation, then

$T_0 = 0$.

$$\therefore Y_0 = C_0 + Ip_0 + G_0 - T_0 + Iu_0 = \pounds5,000m$$
$$= \pounds3,000m + \pounds2,000m + \pounds1,000m - 0 + (-\pounds1,000m)$$
$$= \pounds5,000m,$$

i.e. $Iu_0 = -\pounds1,000m$, which means that there is excess demand, whereby had firms produced £6,000m they would have been able to sell all £6,000m of output.

Since $C_0 = \pounds3,000m$, then $S_0 = \pounds2,000m$.

$$\therefore Y_0 = C_0 + S_0$$
$$= \pounds3,000m + \pounds2,000m$$
$$= \pounds5,000m.$$

Given that $Y_0 = \pounds5,000m$, where $Iu_0 = -\pounds1,000m$, firms will wish to produce an extra £1,000m above what they produced in week 0. In order to produce £6,000m of output in week 1, they will require more factors of production from households, requiring them to pay incomes to households of £6,000m at the start of week 1.

$\therefore Y_1 > Y_0$ (which is national income disequilibrium), since $Jp_0 > Lp_0$,

i.e. $Ip_0 + G_0 > S_0 + T_0$ in a three-sector economy.

Given that households have £1,000m extra income in week 1, we can say that they will either spend this extra income or save it. Assuming that

$T_1 = T_0 = 0$, $Y_1 = C_1 + S_1 = \pounds6,000m$.

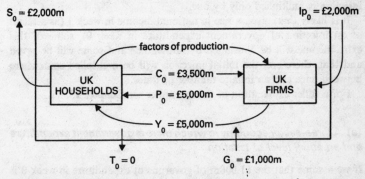

Figure 40. *The circular flow of income in a three-sector economy with some government expenditure, but no taxation*

If all of this extra income is consumed rather than saved, $C_1 = £4,000m$.

$\therefore Y_1 = C_1 + Ip_1 + G_1 - T_1 + Iu_1 = £6,000m$.

$\qquad = C_1 + Ip_1 + G_1 + Iu_1 = £6,000m$, assuming no taxation.

If the government expenditure was for one period only, we can assume that $G_1 = 0$.

$\therefore Y_1 = C_1 + Ip_1 + Iu_1 = £6,000m$, where $C_1 = £4,000m$ and (assuming $Ip_1 = Ip_0$) $Ip_1 = £2,000m$.

$\therefore Iu_1 = 0$.
$\therefore Y_2 = Y_1 = £6,000m$.

Thus, national income in both week 1 and week 2 is £1,000m higher than it would otherwise have been without the one-off injection of government expenditure in week 0 of £1,000m. This means that by the end of week 2 the injection of government expenditure has been multiplied two-fold: Y_1 is £1,000m higher than it would otherwise have been and Y_2 is £1,000m higher than it would otherwise have been.

If $C_1 = C_2 = C_3 = C_4$, etc., then (other things being equal) none of the initial injection of £1,000m will ever be leaked from the economy and the effect of the injection of £1,000m of government expenditure will be multiplied indefinitely.

If, however, none of the initial injection is consumed, but is saved (so that $S_1 = £3,000m$), then Y_2 (other things being equal) will equal £5,000m, i.e. national income will return to its original level and the injection of £1,000m of government expenditure in week 0 will have raised the level of national income only in the first round, i.e. the initial injection is multiplied only by one.

It is likely that, given a rise in national income in week 1 (as a result of an injection of government expenditure in week 0), some of this extra income will be consumed by households and some will be saved and that, therefore, the initial injection will be multiplied somewhere between once and an infinite number of times.

For a fuller explanation of the multiplier see Chapter 13.

(e) A three-sector economy in which there is government expenditure and an equal level of taxation

If we assume that the £1,000m of government expenditure in week 0 is financed through taxation on consumers' expenditure, rather than by borrowing, then $T_0 = G_0 = £1,000m$.

Given $Y_0 = £5,000m$,

where $Y_0 \equiv P_0 \equiv E_0$
$$= C_0 + Ip_0 + G_0 + X_0 - T_0 - M_0 + Iu_0 = £5,000m$$
$$= C_0 + Ip_0 + G_0 - T_0 + Iu_0 = £5,000m \text{ in a}$$

three-sector economy, where $C_0 = £3,000m$, $Ip_0 = £2,000m$, $G_0 = £1,000m$, and $T_0 = £1,000m$.

$\therefore Iu_0 = 0$.

$Y_0 = C_0 + S_0 = Y_0 = £5,000m$.

We have assumed that, given $Y_0 = £5,000m$, $Iu_0 = 0$. Therefore, firms will wish to produce the same amount of goods and services in week 1 as in week 0 and will pay incomes at the start of week 1 totalling £5,000m, i.e. $Y_1 = Y_0 = £5,000m$ (which is national income equilibrium), since $Jp_0 = Lp_0$, i.e. $Ip_0 + G_0 = S_0 + T_0$ in a three-sector economy.

When government expenditure is financed by taxation, the existence of a government sector has no effect on national income, not even in the first round. While, in the absence of taxation, $Y_1 = £6,000m$ (see subsection (e)), when $T_0 = G_0$, $Y_1 = £5,000m$.

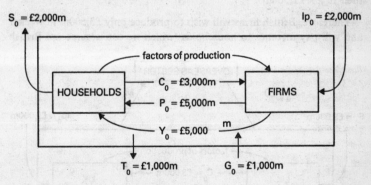

Figure 41. *The circular flow of income in a three-sector economy with government expenditure financed entirely by taxation*

However, in reality, an equal rise in government expenditure and taxation may have a positive effect on the level of national income by redistributing income from those with a high propensity to save to those with a low propensity to save. See Chapter 13 for a fuller explanation of the balanced budget multiplier.

(f) *A four-sector economy, with some expenditure on imports, but no exports*

Given $Y_0 = £5,000m$,

where $Y_0 \equiv P_0 \equiv E_0$
$$= C_0 + Ip_0 + G_0 + X_0 - T_0 - M_0 + Iu_0 = £5,000m,$$

we can show how the existence of an overseas sector might affect the level of national income.

If British households, firms and the government spend a total of £1,500m on foreign-produced goods and services, then we can say that total import expenditure equals £1,500m.

$\therefore Y_0 \equiv P_0 \equiv E_0$
$$= C_0 + Ip_0 + G_0 + X_0 - T_0 - M_0 + Iu_0 = £5,000m,$$

where $C_0 = £3,000m$, $Ip_0 = £2,000m$, $G_0 = £1,000m$, $T_0 = £1,000m$ and $M_0 = £1,500m$, which means that part of household expenditure, firms' investment expenditure and government expenditure is being leaked to the overseas sector.

$\therefore$ £1,500m of U K production is either exported or left unsold. If $X_0 = 0$, then $Iu_0 = £1,500m$.

Therefore, British firms will wish to produce only £3,500m in week 1 and will pay incomes to households (which we can assume are British

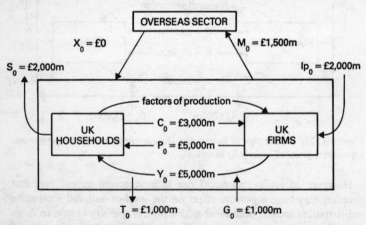

Figure 42. *The circular flow of income in a four-sector economy with some import expenditure but no export expenditure*

households by assuming that only British households, and no foreign households, supply factors to British firms) at the start of week 1 of £3,500m. Therefore, we can assume that national income in week 1 (i.e. Y_1) equals £3,500m (as long as we also assume that British households supply no factors of production to foreign-owned firms),

i.e. $Y_1 < Y_0$ (which is national income disequilibrium), since $Jp_0 < Lp_0$,

i.e. $Ip_0 + G_0 + X_0 < S_0 + T_0 + M_0$.

(g) *A four-sector economy in which exports equal imports*

If expenditure by the overseas sector on British goods and services in week 0 (i.e. X_0) equals £1,500m, then given

$$Y_0 \equiv P_0 \equiv E_0$$
$$= C_0 + Ip_0 + G_0 + X_0 - T_0 - M_0 + Iu_0 = £5,000m,$$

where $C_0 = £3,000m$, $Ip_0 = £2,000m$, $G_0 = £1,000m$, $T_0 = £1,000m$, and $M_0 = £1,500m$,

$$Iu_0 = 0.$$

Therefore, British firms will wish to produce £5,000m in week 1 and will

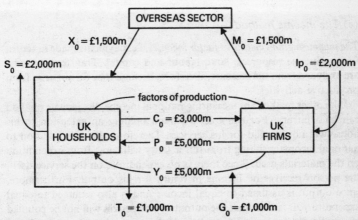

Figure 43. *The circular flow of income in a four-sector economy with some export expenditure and an equivalent level of import expenditure*

pay incomes to (British) households at the start of week 1 of £5,000m.

$\therefore Y_1 = Y_0$ (which is national income equilibrium) since $Jp_0 = Lp_0$,

i.e. $Ip_0 + G_0 + Y_0 = S_0 + T_0 + M_0$.

(h) *Conclusion*

From what we have said, it should be clear that British households' income (Y) is the same as national income and is either consumed or saved, i.e. $Y \equiv Y = C + S$.

This equation is important for our discussions in Chapter 12.

5. National income accounting

We have said, and shown through the development of our circular-flow model, that national income in a particular period is the same thing as national product and as national expenditure in that same period. It therefore follows that we can calculate the level of national income in the UK by calculating all the factor incomes paid, or the output of British firms or total expenditure on UK goods and services. Thus, there are three ways of measuring national income: the income method; the output method; the expenditure method.

(a) *The income method*

The income method measures factor incomes, i.e. payments made in return for productive resources: land, labour and capital. Transfer payments are excluded from the measure, therefore, because they do not arise from productive activities.

Like other methods of measuring national income, the income method can be arbitrary. For example, a person buiding an extension to his house will not be paid for his services. Therefore, the only addition to national income resulting from this activity will come from expenditure on the materials used. Since there is no expenditure on the service itself, the person receives no income in return for his output. Furthermore, since output is assumed to equal income and is also assumed to equal expenditure, it is clear that the output of this person will not be counted in any figures for national product. If, however, this person employed someone to do this same work, the output will be included because an income will be paid and included in national income accounts. There are exceptions to the rule regarding people doing jobs for themselves: farmers who produce food for themselves have the value of this good imputed; similarly, imputed rents are estimated for the value of owner-occupied houses.

Much of the data regarding factor incomes is obtained from the Inland Revenue. However, many services which are paid for may be unrecorded. This is sometimes referred to as the 'black economy'. Apart from illegal tax evasion, individuals may legitimately swap services between themselves without declaring this swapping to the Inland Revenue. In the United Kingdom by far the bulk of income comes from *employment* (*including self-employment*), i.e. in the form of *wages*. Other factor incomes include the gross trading profits of companies, corporations and nationalized industries, rent and the imputed charge for the consumption of non-traded capital. Stock appreciation, i.e. increases in value due to inflation and not to work done, is deducted.

Table 12. National income by category of factor incomes, 1985

	£m
Income from employment	195,350
Income from self-employment	29,859
Gross trading profits of companies	52,977
Gross trading surplus of general public corporations	7,106
Gross trading surplus of general government enterprises	264
Rent	20,541
Imputed charge for consumption of non-trading capital	2,681
Total domestic income	308,778
less stock appreciation	−3,037
residual error	−3,276
Gross domestic product at factor cost	302,465
Net property income from abroad	3,400
Gross national product at factor cost	305,865
less capital consumption	−41,846
National income (i.e. net national product)	264,019

Source: *UK National Accounts* (The CSO Blue Book), HMSO, 1986.

Considerable sums of money come from abroad to the UK in the form of factor payments. Similarly, factor payments are made by the UK to other countries. While the total amounts involved are quite large, the net amount is usually quite small. The gross domestic product at factor cost plus this net property income from abroad equals the gross national product. In order to reduce GNP to net national product, i.e. national income, we have to allow for capital consumption.

(b) *The output method*

The second way of measuring national income is to add up *all outputs by types of industry*. Care has to be taken so as to avoid double counting, i.e. it is important to avoid counting output more than once. Thus, only final goods and services are totalled or the *value added* by each industry. If, for example, we were to add the output of flour from the mills to the value of the output of bread from the bakeries, we would be counting the value of the output of flour twice.

In the UK, as in most countries, the original data regarding the value of output is likely to be obtained from market prices, i.e. the value of output is said to be derived from the price charged. However, the market price may overstate the factor cost value of output (i.e. the amount firms pay in factor incomes to produce a given output), since VAT at 15 per cent is levied on many purchases in the UK and some goods are heavily taxed by excise duties, for example tobacco and alcohol. Conversely, some market prices are less than factor cost because they are subsidized by government. In order to convert national product at market prices to national product at factor cost we must, therefore, subtract indirect taxes and add subsidies.

A further problem which arises with the output method is the problem of measuring the value of the output of the non-commercial public sector, where there is no direct charge made to those who use these services. Charges for services such as education and health care are made through rates and employees' National Insurance contributions. However, it is difficult to tell what proportion of such taxes constitutes a charge for these services. Furthermore, not everyone who pays rates or NI receives these services.

The value of the output of the non-commercial public sector is calculated by measuring the value of the inputs.

Table 13. National income by industry, 1985

	£m
Agriculture, forestry and fishing	5,485
Energy and water supply	34,335
Manufacturing	76,800
Construction	18,651
Distribution, hotels and catering, repairs	40,384
Transport	12,913
Communication	8,044
Banking, finance, insurance, business services and leasing	42,473
Ownership of dwellings	17,775
Public administration, national defence	21,599
Education and health services	26,187
Other services	17,978
Total domestic output	322,624
Adjustment for financial services	− 16,883
Residual error	− 3,276
Gross domestic product at factor cost	302,465
Net property income from abroad	3,400
Gross national product at factor cost	305,865
less capital consumption	− 41,846
National income (i.e. net national product)	264,019

Source: *UK National Accounts* (The CSO Blue Book), HMSO, 1986.

(c) *The expenditure method*

With the expenditure method it is important only to calculate the value of final expenditure. Thus, we count only expenditure on bread and not both expenditure on the flour to produce the bread and the bread itself. Alternatively, we can count expenditure on the flour plus any value added to the value of expenditure on the flour generated by the production of bread using this flour.

The expenditure method calculates final consumption expenditure, final investment expenditure, final government expenditure and final expenditure on exports. Taxation and import expenditure are subtracted and subsidies are added to give a figure for GDP at factor cost. To this

Table 14. National income by category of expenditure, 1985

	£m
Consumers' expenditure	194,673
General government final consumption	69,655
Gross domestic fixed capital formation	55,319
Value of physical increase in stocks and work in progress	−177
Total domestic expenditure	319,470
Exports of goods and services	91,736
Total final expenditure	411,206
less imports of goods and services	−91,852
Gross domestic product at market prices	319,354
less taxes on expenditure	−52,578
Subsidies	7,797
Gross domestic product at factor cost	274,573
Net property income from abroad	3,304
Gross national product at factor cost	277,877
less capital consumption	−38,371
National income (i.e. net national product)	239,506

Source: *UK National Accounts* (The CSO Blue Book) HMSO, 1985.

figure net property income from abroad is added to give a figure for Gross National Product (GNP), and capital consumption is subtracted from this figure to give a figure for Net National Product (NNP) or national income, i.e. NNP = GNP − capital consumption.

The figure for capital consumption shown in Table 14 refers to the level of replacement investment, i.e. the level of investment necessary to replace obsolete or worn-out capital. Replacement investment does not increase productivity and this type of investment was not included in our definition of investment expenditure used in the circular flow models.

(d) *Conclusion*

While each of the three measures of national income should produce the same value, in practice errors do arise. For example, as we have already mentioned, not all incomes are declared to the Inland Revenue and not all outputs are notified to the government. Figures regarding the value of expenditure can be obtained from surveys as well as from those government departments to which taxes on expenditure are paid. Yet distortions in expenditure figures can occur. However, in the United Kingdom the convention is to treat the expenditure method as correct and to adjust for residual error on both the income and output methods.

*

QUESTION

Explain the following terms: (*a*) gross domestic product at market price; (*b*) gross national product at market price; (*c*) gross national product at factor cost; (*d*) national income. Explain the relationship between them.

Gross domestic product at market price is the production within the UK measured at the prices paid by consumers. Some of the incomes generated as measured by GDP may flow overseas because some firms which operate in the UK are foreign-owned. Furthermore, some firms operating in the UK use foreign-owned resources as a result of foreigners lending to the UK or as a result of foreigners working in the UK. These incomes are deducted from GDP, while incomes paid to UK residents working abroad and incomes paid as a result of the UK lending resources abroad, as well as the income generated by British-owned companies operating overseas, are added to GDP to give a figure for gross national product at market price. Thus, GDP at market price plus net property income from abroad equals gross national product at market price.

In order to convert GNP at market price to gross national product at factor cost, we have to deduct taxes on expenditure and add subsidies. We are interested in obtaining figures at factor cost because where taxes on expenditure, such as 15 per cent VAT, exist, the value of expenditure will appear to be greater than the value of production, if we measure the value of expenditure at market price.

GNP at factor cost is converted to net national product or national income by allowing for depreciation, i.e. capital consumption. Net national product is, in many ways, a more useful measure of income than GNP, since it gives a more realistic assessment of whether or not the economy is improving; if, for example, 100,000 houses were built in the UK during the course of a year, while another 100,000 were demolished, the UK would be neither better off nor worse off at the end of the year compared to the beginning of the year, other things being equal.

MULTIPLE-CHOICE QUESTIONS

1. Which of the following are included in GNP:

(A) payment by a parent to a university student;

(B) pensions paid to retired civil servants;

(C) the output of a person decorating their own home;

(D) the food produced by a farmer which he consumes?

    (*a*) A and B only.

    (*b*) C and D only.

    (*c*) None.

    (*d*) D only.

    (*e*) All.

Answer – (*d*)

2. At times of full employment, an increase in government expenditure will:

    (*a*) raise GNP in monetary terms;

    (*b*) reduce GNP in monetary terms;

    (*c*) have no effect on GNP in monetary terms.

Answer – (*a*)

3. National income figures exclude social security benefits.

    (*a*) True.

    (*b*) False.

Answer – (*a*)

4. When calculating national income by the expenditure method we exclude exports.

    (*a*) True.

    (*b*) False.

Answer– (*b*)

5. Net National Product is the same thing as:

    (*a*) GNP at factor cost;

    (*b*) GDP at factor cost;

    (*c*) national income;

    (*d*) none of the above.

Answer – (*c*)

6. GNP at factor cost is the same thing as:
  (a) GDP at factor cost minus imports;
  (b) GDP at factor cost plus imports;
  (c) GDP at factor cost minus net property income from abroad;
  (d) GDP at factor cost plus net property income from abroad.
Answer – (d)

7. Imports are not subtracted from total final expenditure in order to obtain a figure for Gross Domestic Product.
  (a) True.
  (b) False.
Answer – (b)

8. When considering Gross National Product by type of income, stock appreciation rising from inflation is:
  (a) deducted;
  (b) added;
  (c) ignored.
Answer – (a)

DATA RESPONSE

See Table 15, overleaf.

  (a) Instead of consumers' expenditure at market prices, what figure (not included in Table 15) would show how much consumption expenditure actually adds to national income?
  (b) In which years was there excess demand?
  (c) What further information is required to calculate the value of net investment expenditure? See also Chapter 21 to answer this question.
  (d) What further information is required to calculate national income?
  (e) What further information is required to make a reasonable assessment of the real value of GNP at market prices between each of the years shown in the table?

SELF-EXAMINATION QUESTIONS

1. In the *Guardian* in May 1985 there was some correspondence about people employing other people to look after their children while they are

Table 15. Gross national product by category of expenditure (£m)

At market prices	1974	1975	1976	1977
Consumer's expenditure	53,069	65,211	75,675	86,478
General government final consumption	16,714	23,119	27,040	29,473
of which: central government	10,137	13,527	16,180	17,829
local authorities	6,577	9,592	10,860	11,644
Gross domestic fixed capital formation	17,497	21,035	24,504	27,036
Value of physical increase in stocks and work in progress	1,045	− 1,354	901	1,824
Total domestic expenditure	88,325	108,011	128,120	144,811
Exports of goods and services	22,988	27,007	35,210	43,353
Total final expenditure	111,313	135,018	163,330	188,164
less imports of goods and services	− 27,390	− 29,004	− 36,894	− 42,599
Gross domestic product at market prices	83,923	106,014	126,436	145,565
Net property income from abroad	1,507	890	1,557	246
Gross national product at market prices	85,430	106,904	127,993	145 811

Source: *UK National Accounts* (The CSO Blue Book), HMSO 1985.

at work. How is Gross National Product affected by the situation described in the correspondence?

2. What problems are involved in making sure that the income, output and expenditure methods of calculating national income each gives the same value for national income?

3. How might improved national income statistics help national income to be increased?

4. The Legal and General Assurance Group has evaluated housewives' services as if paid for at market rates. How would you evaluate housewives' services?

1978	1979	1980	1981	1982	1983	1984
99,648	118,156	136,995	152,339	166,612	182,207	194,673
33,396	38,852	48,906	55,357	60,380	65,698	69,655
20,134	23,421	29,940	33,859	37,054	40,616	42,892
13,262	15,431	18,966	21,498	23,326	25,082	26,763
31,060	36,855	41,588	41,432	45,390	49,046	55,319
1,804	2,160	−2,875	−2,996	−1,176	772	−177
165,908	196,023	224,614	246,132	271,206	297,723	319,470
47,503	55,023	63,115	67,905	73,060	80,037	91,736
213,411	251,046	287,729	314,037	344,266	377,760	411,206
−45,567	−54,668	−57,718	−60,375	−67,514	−77,171	−91,852
167,844	196,378	230,011	253,662	276,752	300,589	319,354
827	1,188	−219	950	1,115	2,440	3,304
168,671	197,566	229,792	254,612	277,867	303,029	322,658

5. What are the problems of obtaining accurate figures for depreciation when calculating national income? What items does the term 'depreciation' refer to in national income accounting?

6. What is meant by 'GNP in money terms'? What is meant by 'GNP in real terms'? Why might the two differ?

12. The consumption function

1. Factors affecting the division of income between consumption and savings

We have already shown (in Chapter 11) that British households will either spend (i.e. consume) their incomes (i.e. national income) or save (S) them.

$$Y = C + S$$

We would not expect households to either consume all of their income or save all of their income; rather we would expect them to both consume and save.

However, there are several factors which might make households more willing to consume and less willing to save their income or less willing to consume and more willing to save.

(i) Many pre-Keynesian economists believed that *the rate of interest* was the main variable affecting the decision to consume more or to consume less. *The higher the rate of interest, the greater the tendency to save,*

i.e. $S = (f)r$
and $C = (f)r$,

where S is a positive function of the rate of interest and C is a negative function.

(ii) We can also say that the tendency (or *propensity*) to consume partly depends upon *the ease with which credit can be obtained and the rate of interest upon credit*. This factor is particularly important when considering buying a house.

Credit restrictions may, therefore, affect consumption. For example, if the government were to impose tighter credit controls on consumer durables, perhaps by imposing higher deposits, we would expect the demand for such goods to fall. Some economists do not regard credit control as being very effective in practice in the longer term, since both firms and individuals may find ways round these restrictions, such as offering better trade-in deals. The use of readily available credit, on the other hand, such as Access, Barclaycard and other credit cards, may well help to increase consumption.

(iii) When deciding whether or not to buy an expensive item such as a house (which almost certainly involves buying on credit), it is also important that the individual takes account of his or her *likely income in the future* to determine whether or not he or she has the ability to make future credit payments.

(iv) The propensity to consume might also partly depend upon *wealth*. For example, if we were to compare two students, one from a wealthy family and one from a less wealthy family, we might find that the student from the wealthy family is able to spend more money without worrying about the future than the student from the less wealthy family.

(v) *There may be seasonal variations in consumption patterns*, with households more likely to consume in the period between October and December than at any other time of the year.

(vi) Consumption patterns may also be affected by *age*. (See section 9.)

(vii) Keynes believed that the most important determinant in the decision to consume rather than to save is *the level of income* itself. Therefore, the *Keynesian consumption function* is as follows:

$C = (f)Y$
and $\therefore S = (f)Y$.

Keynes said that as households' incomes rise they are inclined to increase their consumption, but not by as much as the increase in income, i.e. the *marginal propensity to consume* is less than one, but greater than zero, i.e. $0 < MPC < 1$.

2. The marginal propensity to consume

The marginal propensity to consume (MPC) is defined as the proportion of an increase in income of one unit which is devoted to increased consumption.

i.e. $MPC = \dfrac{\Delta C}{\Delta Y}$

Given $Y = C + S$, that part of an increase in income which is not consumed is assumed to be saved.

The marginal propensity to save (MPS) is defined as the proportion of an increase in income which is saved

i.e. $\text{MPS} = \dfrac{\Delta S}{\Delta Y}$

Since $Y = C + S$.

$S = Y - C$

$\therefore \dfrac{\Delta S}{\Delta Y} = \dfrac{\Delta Y}{\Delta Y} - \dfrac{\Delta C}{\Delta Y}$

$\therefore \text{MPS} = 1 - \text{MPC}.$

Keynes argued that *the higher an individual's level of income, the greater the proportion of his income that he is likely to save,* i.e. people with low incomes are likely to have fairly high marginal propensities to consume (therefore, fairly low marginal propensities to save) and people with high incomes are likely to have fairly low marginal propensities to consume (therefore, fairly high marginal propensities to save). However, for the sake of simplicity, in the discussion of the Keynesian 45 degree diagram (in Section 4) we assume a constant marginal propensity to consume as income rises.

3. The average propensity to consume

The average propensity to consume (APC) is the proportion of income households plan to consume,

i.e. $\text{APC} = \dfrac{C}{Y}.$

The average propensity to save (APS) is the proportion of income households plan to save,

i.e. $\text{APS} = \dfrac{S}{Y}.$

Given that $Y = C + S,$

$S = Y - C.$

$$\therefore \frac{S}{Y} = \frac{Y}{Y} - \frac{C}{Y},$$

i.e. $APS = 1 - APC$.

The relationship between MPC and APC is discussed in section 5.

4. The Keynesian 45° diagram

The Keynesian 45° diagram shows that *planned consumption* consists of both *autonomous consumption* (that part of consumption which does not vary as income varies, i.e. even if households receive no income we might still expect them to spend a certain amount of money on consumption, whereby they will have *negative savings*) and *income-induced consumption* (that part of consumption which does vary with income). Figure 44 is a 45° diagram which shows expenditure on the vertical axis and income on the horizontal axis. A 45° line is drawn through the origin. Any point along this 45° line represents points at which expenditure equals income. This 45° diagram illustrates the Keynesian consumption function.

The intercept *a* on the vertical axis shows the level of consumption when income equals zero. Given that consumption rises as income rises, there will be at least this level of consumption *a*. This level of income is autonomous consumption. Any consumption above this level will only take place if households are receiving an income.

By assuming that a rise in income of £1 (whether from, say, £1 to £2 or £21 to £22) leads to a fixed rise in consumption, *we assume that the marginal propensity to consume (MPC) is constant and that, therefore, the consumption function is linear.*

Income-induced consumption is said to equal MPC (c) multiplied by the level of income (Y). Thus, at a given level of income, the consumption function (when it is said to be a linear function) is constructed as follows:

$C = a + cY$.

In Figure 44 we have drawn a dashed line, aa^1, below which any consumption is said to be autonomous and above which any consumption is said to be income-induced.

At point P, the level of income equals Y_0 and the level of consumption is C_0. Since this point is on the 45° line, $C_0 = Y_0$. Therefore, at income

197

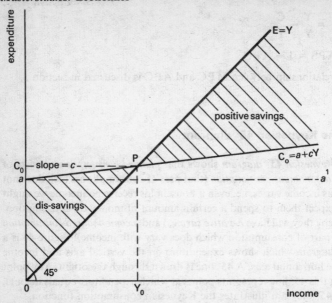

Figure 44. *The Keynesian 45° diagram*

Y_0, households, on average, consume all of their income and save nothing.

At any level of income below Y_0, the level of consumption will be greater than the level of income: *below Y_0 there will be negative savings (i.e. dis-savings).*

Above Y_0, households will, on average, consume less than they receive in incomes: *above Y_0 there will be positive savings.*

It should be clear that the steeper the consumption function (i.e. the greater the MPC) about the point *a*, the greater will be the level of income-induced consumption at a given level of income and the greater will be the level of planned consumption at a given level of income.

5. The relationship between MPC and APC

$APC = \dfrac{C}{Y}$, where $C = a + cY$,

i.e. $C = a + MPCY$.

$$\therefore \frac{C}{Y} = \frac{a}{Y} + \frac{MPCY}{Y} = APC$$

$$\therefore APC = \frac{a}{Y} + MPC$$

At point P in Figure 44, $C = Y$.

$$\therefore \frac{C}{Y} = 1.$$

Therefore, at P, $APC = 1$.

Below point P, $C > Y$.

$$\therefore APC > 1.$$

Above point P, $C < Y$.

$$\therefore APC < 1.$$

Given a linear function, APC will always be greater than MPC unless there is no autonomous consumption.

If there is no autonomous consumption, the linear consumption function passes through the origin, and at each and every level of income $APC = MPC$.

6. The total expenditure function

Since consumption expenditure is not the only element in the total expenditure, i.e. aggregate monetary demand (AMD), equation, income Y_0 is unlikely to be the equilibrium level of income.

Given that $E = C + I + G - T + X - M$, if $I + G - T + X - M$ is positive, we may draw a total expenditure function above the consumption function. Furthermore, we may draw this total expenditure function parallel to the consumption function by assuming that investment expenditure, government expenditure, taxation, export expenditure and import expenditure are determined autonomously and, therefore, not determined by the level of income. This assumption is useful for the sake of simplicity, but it is an unrealistic assumption, given, for example, that we would expect the rate of taxation to rise as income rises.

Point Q in Figure 45 is a point at which income equals expenditure.

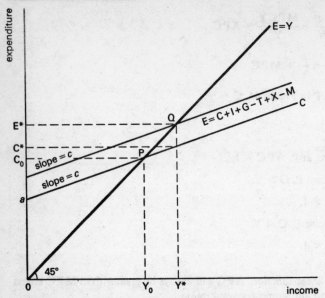

Figure 45. *The Keynesian total expenditure function*

By assuming no unplanned investment, we can call the level of income at point Q the equilibrium level of income (Y*). The level of consumption at income Y* is such that there are positive savings.

7. Full employment equilibrium

It is important to note that in Keynesian economics *national income equilibrium* (Y*) *is not necessarily the point at which there is full employment* (Yf in Figure 46). This is in contrast to the classical economists' theory, which assumed that when the economy is in national income equilibrium, the economy also has full employment, in terms of the number of vacancies equalling the number of unemployed: any unemployment is either frictional or the result of the market not being allowed to function properly (i.e. there would be work for everyone if wage demands were not so high).

Where the level of national income equilibrium is below the point of full employment, Keynes recommended that the government should try

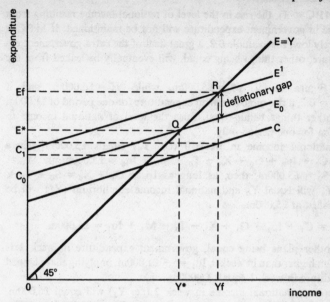

Figure 46. *The deflationary gap*

to achieve full employment equilibrium by reducing taxation, increasing government expenditure or encouraging private investment.

A rise in government expenditure, for example (other things being equal), will increase incomes. Given that this rise in households' incomes will lead to some rise in consumption expenditure, extra government expenditure in one period will push the national income equilibrium level nearer to the point of full employment, even if this level of government expenditure is not maintained in future periods.

When national income equilibrium is below full employment (as is the case in Figure 46 when income is Y^*), there is, according to Keynesian economists, demand deficient unemployment, whereby total incomes are below the level necessary for there to be full employment. There is, thus, a deflationary gap: only by inflating incomes to the level Yf (by increasing injections or reducing leakages), whereby the total expenditure function is increased from E_0 to E^1, is equilibrium achieved at the level of full employment.

Given that a rise in incomes (generated, for example, by extra government expenditure for just one period) will lead to a rise in consumption expenditure which is not as large as the rise in incomes (because

$0 < MPC < 1$), the rise in the level of national income resulting from the rise in government expenditure will not be maintained. If MPC is relatively low, for example 0.2, a great deal of the extra government expenditure, other things being equal, will eventually be leaked from the economy.

In Figure 46, if $Y^* = £5,000m$, while $Yf = £6,000m$, and if $MPC = 0.2$, a rise of government expenditure for one period of £1,000m will, other things being equal, raise the level of national income to £6,000m for one period only.

If national income in week 0 (i.e. Y_0) equals £5,000m, where $Y_0 = C_0 + Ip_0 + G_0 + X_0 - T_0 - M_0 + Iu_0 = £5,000m$ and $Y_0 = C_0 + S_0 = £5,000m$, then, as long as $Ip_0 + G_0 + X_0 = S_0 + T_0 + M_0$, Y_1 will equal Y_0 and national income equilibrium (Y^*) will be established at £5,000m.

$$\therefore Y_1 = C_1 + Ip_1 + G_1 + X_1 - T_1 - M_1 + Iu_1 = £5,000m.$$

If, other plans being equal, government expenditure in week 1 is £1,000m higher than in week 0, $Iu_1 = - £1,000m$, implying that planned expenditure in week 1 equals £6,000m.

Therefore, national income in week 2 (i.e. Y_2) will equal £6,000m, which is full employment national income, i.e. $Y_2 = £6,000m = Yf$.

Given that $MPC = 0.2$, households will only consume £200m of the £1,000m extra income in week 2. Thus, C_2 will be £200m higher than C_1 and S_2 will be £800m higher than S_1.

Since the rise in government expenditure was assumed to be for one period only, other plans being equal, planned expenditure in week 2 will be £5,200m.

Therefore Y_3 will equal £5,200m: the economy tends back towards the original national income level.

This example illustrates that, given $0 < MPC < 1$, a rise in national income resulting from an initial injection cannot be maintained, and it also illustrates that it takes time for the initial injection to be completely leaked out. We return to this in Chapter 13.

At this point, we should note that if the economy is initially in national income equilibrium at full employment, a rise in total expenditure (as a result of an injection) is likely to produce an 'inflationary gap'. (See Chapter 13.)

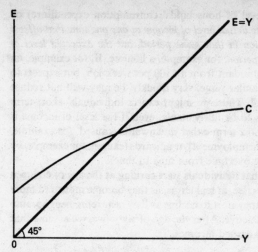

Figure 47. *The consumption function as a curve*

8. The consumption function as a curve

A basic assumption of Keynesian economics, as we have already said, is that as incomes rise people increase their consumption, but not as much as income. In other words, the marginal propensity to consume is less than (or possibly equal to) the average propensity to consume. Although for the sake of simplicity it is useful to assume a constant marginal propensity to consume, in reality it is likely to fall as income rises, although it will still tend to be between zero and one. Thus, it would seem more realistic to draw the consumption function as a curve which flattens out as income increases rather than a straight line.

9. The permanent-income hypothesis and the life-cycle hypothesis

(a) *The permanent-income hypothesis*

Milton Friedman adapted Keynes's consumption function (which assumes that the level of disposable income is the most important determinant of the level of households' consumption expenditure) by stating that *it is not the actual level of income at any one time that affects the level of consumption in that same period, but the expected level of income over a certain period,* for example, a lifetime. If, for example, an individual is made redundant from a £100 per week job, but expects to find a job, paying a similar wage, very quickly, he may well not reduce his consumption at all. Thus, we might expect individuals' short-term consumption patterns to be fairly stable, even if the level of income is fairly erratic in the short term either downwards (caused, for example, by a short period of unemployment) or upwards (caused, for example, by an individual working overtime from time to time).

We might assume that individuals start earning at the age of eighteen and that their earnings rise, in real terms, as they become more and more experienced, but that they start to decline as they near retirement because they become less productive. After the age of sixty-five, we assume that individuals receive no earned incomes.

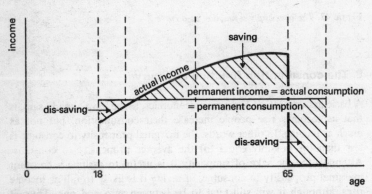

Figure 48. *The permanent-income hypothesis*

In Figure 48 we assume that individuals' planning period covers their lifetime from the age they start earning. Given that the most important determinant of the level of consumption is the level of expected income over the period of planning, we might expect actual consumption over this period of planning to be fairly stable. If we assume that individuals plan to spend eventually all that they earn over their lifetime, we can say that actual consumption at any time equals permanent income. Given that actual income differs from permanent income, there will be periods of saving and periods of dis-saving.

(b) *The life-cycle hypothesis*

The life-cycle hypothesis was developed by *Albert Ando, Aldo Brumberg* and *Franco Modigliani. The life-cycle hypothesis assumes that households' consumption (or savings) plans are affected by age.*

The life-cycle hypothesis assumes that households, during their life cycle, will go through periods of saving followed by periods of dis-saving. It assumes that households' actual consumption will tend to be below their actual income level (i.e. they will save) from the time they begin work (which we might assume is at the age of eighteen) until the time at which they have children, at which time the hypothesis assumes that a period of dis-saving will begin; it then assumes that households will continue to dis-save until their children are reasonably self-supporting, at which time a period of saving is likely to begin. This period of saving is likely to continue until retirement (at sixty-five), at which time a further period of dis-saving is likely to begin.

The hypothesis does not assume that the level of consumption of a household after retirement is higher than the level of consumption of that same household at the age of, say, forty: while the level of savings is lower, the level of consumption is unlikely to be higher because pensioners' incomes are generally lower than the incomes of forty-year-olds.

Note the slight difference in the savings behaviour predicted by the life-cycle hypothesis compared to that predicted by the permanent-income hypothesis.

10. Why there might be changes in consumption

A number of factors are likely to affect the consumption function in the UK as a whole.

(i) During recessions, as in the UK in the 1980s, people may have lower expectations of future incomes than during boom periods. *People who think that they might be unemployed or on lower incomes in the future might be less willing to commit themselves to hire-purchase or other payments.* However, some empirical data seems to suggest that this is not the case. A great deal of expenditure might, in the short term, be relatively fixed. For example, many people have hire-purchase payments or mortgages which they cannot alter.

(ii) However, *consumption patterns are likely to alter as interest rates on HP and mortgage payments change in the longer term.*

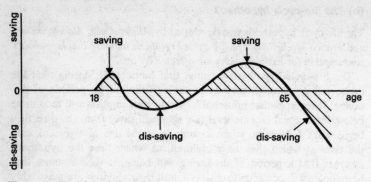

Figure 49. *The life-cycle hypothesis*

(iii) In some cases, *the non-availability of consumer durables, for example in war-time periods, leads to 'pent-up' demand and with the ending of controls people are willing to buy more consumer durables*. It was expected that when the recession of the 1980s ended, people would buy more consumer durables for the same reason.

(iv) As we suggested earlier in the chapter, *changes in expectations regarding the price of certain commodities may influence consumption.* When house prices were rising rapidly in the 1972–3 period, many people, particularly first-time buyers, were probably induced to buy earlier than planned. Conversely, in the mid-1980s, when the price of computers had been falling rapidly, some businessmen and private households tended to delay purchasing in the expectation of being able to buy more cheaply at a later date.

(v) *Changes in income distribution* caused, for example, by changes in the taxation system, may affect consumption patterns.

11. Measuring and forecasting consumption

Governments are very interested in the consumption function, since much of their fiscal and monetary policies, as well as the forecasts about levels of unemployment, depend upon it. Governments will, therefore, wish to carry out their own forecasting. Many other institutes, including NIESR (National Institute for Economic and Social Research), also make forecasts.

Manufacturers might find it helpful to have forecasts for the consumption function. Generally, we would expect much greater fluctuations in the demand for consumer durables (partly because conditions for credit tend to change frequently and partly because it is possible to postpone expenditure on them) than for other commodities, such as food. Therefore, firms which produce consumer durables are more likely to be affected by a recession than firms which concentrate entirely on the production of food.

Conversely, in a boom period, firms in consumer-durable markets are more likely to obtain increased sales than those concentrating on food.

(a) *Problems for forecasters*

(i) One problem for forecasters, whether government forecasters or private forecasters, is that *it is very difficult to know how consumers will react to changes in circumstances*. It would seem intuitively plausible that, in times of very high rates of inflation, consumers might be willing to spend more and save less, especially if interest rates do not keep in line with inflation, since savers will lose in real terms. However, data for the 1976–7 period (a period of high inflation) seems to indicate that during this period the savings ratio was paradoxically higher than normal.

(ii) *It is difficult for forecasters to obtain data about expectations of incomes*. Surveys may be helpful here. None the less, governments may still over-estimate future increases in incomes. This was noticeable with the National Plan in the 1960s.

(b) *Consumption function data*

(i) Data for the consumption function can be found from *cross-section data* taking into account, for example, the size of household being considered and demographic features such as the age of the members of the household.

(ii) Another way of looking at the consumption function is to obtain *time-series data*. While time-series data is generally easier to obtain than cross-section data, one would need to know the various factors, such as rates of inflation and changes in expectations, which might affect it.

*

QUESTION

What are the most important determinants of a household's level of consumption?

The most important determinant is probably the household's level of income: the higher the level of its income, the higher the household's level of consumption is likely to be. But, as income rises, the rise in the level of consumption will probably not be as great, i.e. the marginal propensity to consume will be less than one.

Expected income is likely to be important: if the household's level of income is expected to be fairly steady in the long run, then (even if there are short-term variations in income) both long-term and short-term consumption patterns may be fairly steady. On the other hand, if there are prospects of being made unemployed, the household may start consuming less and saving more.

Interest rates are likely to be important: consumption will rise as interest rates fall, other things being equal.

The ease with which credit can be obtained is likely to affect a household's level of consumption of consumer durables particularly. The level of consumption is likely to vary through the year, and will probably be highest just before Christmas. There might also be pre-Budget spending sprees.

Age is also important. Since incomes are generally likely to rise until just before retirement, we would expect, other things being equal, that a household's level of consumption would rise steadily until retirement. This is not exactly what is predicted by the permanent-income hypothesis. After retirement, the level of consumption is likely to fall, but with there being dis-saving (the household living off past earnings).

MULTIPLE-CHOICE QUESTIONS

1. Given a linear consumption function, the marginal propensity to consume is never less than the average propensity to consume.
    (a) True.
    (b) False.
Answer – (b)

2. A linear consumption function implies that:
    (a) the average propensity to consume is constant;
    (b) the marginal propensity to consume is constant;
    (c) consumption equals income.
Answer – (b)

3. A rise in interest rates will, other things being equal, lead to:
    (a) a rise in the level of consumption;
    (b) a fall in the level of consumption;

(c) no changes in the level of consumption.

Answer – (b)

4. If the marginal propensity to import equals 0.2, the marginal propensity to tax equals 0.3 and the marginal propensity to save equals 0.1, what is the marginal propensity to consume equal to?

    (a) 1.

    (b) 0.9.

    (c) 0.5.

    (d) 0.4.

Answer – (b)

5. Income (Y)	Consumption (C)
0	10
10	14
20	18
30	22
40	26
50	30

Which of the following formulae represents the consumption function tabulated above?

    (a) $10 + 0.4Y$.

    (b) $10 + 4Y$.

    (c) $10 + (C/Y)Y$.

    (d) $C + 0.4Y$.

Answer – (a)

DATA RESPONSE

    (a) Of the items shown in the pie diagram overleaf, which would you expect to have a declining share of consumers' expenditure and which would you expect to have an increasing share of consumers' expenditure in future years? Explain your reasoning.

    (b) Calculate (approximately) the APC as at the beginning of 1983?

    (c) What additional information would you require to calculate MPC?

SELF-EXAMINATION QUESTIONS

1. What is the importance of the consumption function in a modern society?

2. Data for the consumption function can be found through the use of either time-series or cross-section data. Explain the limitations and advantages of both methods.

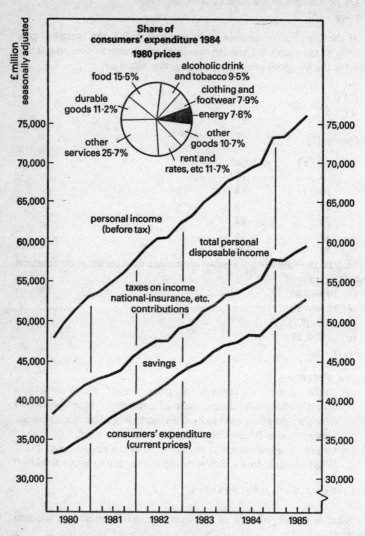

Figure 50. *Personal income and consumption*
Source: *Economic Trends*, no. 390, April 1986 (CSO).

3. Why might the marginal propensity to consume be different in the short run and in the long run?

4. Why might the UK's marginal propensity to consume change over time?

5. Explain, using appropriate diagrams, how the following might affect national income:

   (a) an increase in private-sector investment;
   (b) a decrease in the marginal rate of income tax;
   (c) an increase in the propensity to save;
   (d) an increase in government expenditure unmatched by changes in taxation;
   (e) an increase in government expenditure matched by higher tax.

13. The multiplier and the accelerator

1. The simple multiplier

We have said that, given $0 < MPC < 1$, an initial injection, such as a rise in government expenditure, will, other things being equal, raise the level of national income, but that this new level of national income will not be maintained and the economy will tend back towards its original level. But we have also said that, as long as at least some of the extra income generated is consumed (i.e. as long as MPC is greater than zero), then national income will remain above its original level for more than one period (further assuming that at least some of this extra consumption is on British goods and services).

Let us assume that, originally, the weekly national income equals £5,000m, i.e. $Y_0 = £5,000m$.

If planned expenditure in week 0 equals £5,000m, then $Iu_0 = 0$ and $Y_1 = £5,000m$.

Let us now assume that in week 1 the government spends an extra £1,000m on a particular British good (the level of taxation, import expenditure, etc., remaining constant). If other plans are equal, then this £1,000m extra government expenditure will generate an increase in national income at the start of week 2 of £1,000m: the owners of the factors of production used to make the good bought by the government will receive an extra £1,000m in incomes. This means that $Y_2 = £6,000m$.

If the recipients of this £1,000m extra income spend £200m in week 2 (assuming that government expenditure in week 2 returns to its original level and that other plans, such as the level of import expenditure, are equal), then C_2 is £200m higher than C_1 and planned expenditure in week 2 is £200m higher than it was in week 0, leading to Y_2 being £200m higher than it would have been had there been no injection of government expenditure in week 1.

The extra £200m of consumption expenditure in week 2 generates an extra £200m income, i.e. $Y_3 = £5,200m$. If the recipients of this extra £200m income similarly spend only 0.2 of it, they will spend only £40m of it and, other things being equal, C_3 will only be £40m higher than C_1, so that planned expenditure in week 3 will be £5,040m, leading to Y_4 being equal to £5,040m.

Therefore, a one-off rise in government expenditure in week 1, other things being equal, leads to Y_2 being £1,000m higher than it would otherwise have been, Y_3 being £200m higher than it would otherwise have been, Y_4 being £40m higher than it would otherwise have been, etc., given MPC of 0.2 (other things being equal). This process shows that an initial injection is multiplied, with the added effect of the initial injection getting smaller and smaller.

Had we continued our analysis of the multiplier effect of a one-off injection of £1,000m (in an economy where the marginal propensity to consume is 0.2) into future weeks, we would have been able to show that the initial injection is multiplied 1.25 times, i.e. eventually the injection of £1,000m will have raised national income by £1,250m over time, i.e. by £1,000m in week 2, plus £200m in week 3, plus £40m in week 4, etc.

The extent to which the effects of an initial injection (or leakage) are multiplied over time depends upon the value of the marginal propensity to consume. If the marginal propensity to consume is fairly high, an initial injection will have a fairly large multiplier effect; if it is fairly small, for example 0.2, the value of the multiplier will be fairly small.

If none of an initial injection is either taxed or imported, we can say that the value of the multiplier will depend upon the value of MPC, in which case the multiplier (or k) is defined as $\dfrac{1}{1-\text{MPC}}$ or $\dfrac{1}{\text{MPS}}$,

i.e. $k = \dfrac{1}{1-\text{MPC}}$ or $\dfrac{1}{\text{MPS}}$

If MPC = 0.2, the effects of an initial injection will be multiplied 1.25 times,

i.e. $k = \dfrac{1}{1-0.2} = \dfrac{1}{0.8} = 1.25.$

Thus, if government expenditure rises by £1,000m, the level of national income will be raised by a total of £1,250m over time, if MPC = 0.2, i.e. $\Delta Y = \Delta J \times k$.

Similarly, an initial fall in injections (or rise in leakages) will lower the level of national income over time, other things being equal, by the value of the initial leakage multiplied by the value of the multiplier. Of course, it is possible that while some of the extra income generated by a £1,000m increase in government expenditure will be leaked in the form of savings, it is possible that there will also be expenditure on imports and taxation

213

on expenditure leaking income from the economy. Therefore the value of the multiplier can be defined as

$$\frac{1}{1 - MPC + MPT + MPM} \quad \text{or} \quad \frac{1}{MPS + MPT + MPM},$$

where MPT is the marginal propensity to be taxed and MPM is the marginal propensity to import,

i.e. $$\frac{1}{MPS + MPT + MPM} = \frac{1}{MPL},$$

where MPL is the marginal propensity to leak.

If the value of MPL is assumed to be between 0 and 1, then it can be assumed that an injection will increase the level of national income over time, other things being equal, by more than the value of the initial injection and a leakage will reduce the level of national income over time, other things being equal, by more than the value of the initial leakage.

2. The balanced-budget multiplier

If the government increased both public spending and taxation equally, or decreased public spending and taxation equally, we might assume (wrongly) that this would have no net effect on national income. However, we can show that there is a *balanced-budget multiplier*. Thus, even when government expenditure and taxation are both changed in the same direction by equal amounts (starting from a situation of a balanced budget, i.e. G = T) so that government expenditure still equals taxation, there will be some effect upon national income.

If the government raises both its expenditure and taxation by an equal amount there will be no net effect upon national income only if all of the money paid out by taxpayers to the government in these extra taxes would have been spent by them on British goods and services in the absence of these extra taxes, i.e. an equal rise in taxation and government expenditure in the same period will have no effect on national income only if the marginal propensity to leak equals zero (i.e. if the marginal propensity to consume British goods and services equals one).

If the marginal propensity to leak equals zero, an increase in taxation of £100m will, other things being equal, lead to a fall in expenditure on

British goods and services of £100m, since all of this £100m, if not taxed, would have been spent on British goods and services. In this case, a rise in taxation of £100m, accompanied by an equal rise in government spending, merely replaces private expenditure on British goods with government expenditure and has, therefore, no net effect upon national income, other things being equal. If, however, in the absence of the £100m taxation, £25m had been spent on foreign-produced goods and services (imports) or there had been savings by households totalling £25m, only £75m would have been spent on British goods and services. By raising taxation by £100m, and increasing its expenditure by £100m (all of which it spends on British goods and services or on British households, so that none of this £100m is spent on imports), the effect of this balanced budget approach is to increase national income, in the first round, by £25m (i.e. the £100m increase in government expenditure on British goods and services minus the £75m of private expenditure on British goods and services lost because of the £100m rise in taxation).

In this case, in the absence of taxation, there is a marginal propensity to leak of 25m/100m, i.e. 0.25, whereas the government, given the existence of taxation, has a marginal propensity to leak of 0, i.e. all that it receives in revenue it spends. When the government has a smaller marginal propensity to leak than the rest of the economy, then (other things being equal) a balanced-budget approach will affect the level of national income in the first round.

Given that in our model a balanced-budget approach of raising both taxation and government expenditure by £100m raises households' incomes by £25m, if, in the second round, 0.25 per cent of this income is leaked, the value of the multiplier in the second round (as in the first round) would be 1/0.25, i.e. 4.

If, however, the government spends its original £100m on pensioners (who are likely to have a lower-than-average marginal propensity to save or to import), the value of the multiplier in the second round may well be greater than 4.

3. What are the implications of the multiplier for economic policy?

The implications of the multiplier for economic policy depend partly upon the size of the marginal propensity to leak, since the multiplier

$$(k) = \frac{1}{MPL}, \text{ i.e. } k = \frac{1}{MPS + MPT + MPM}.$$

215

In recent years the average propensity to import has risen sharply (about 40 per cent of GNP is now imported). But MPM is more difficult to determine since as national income and the expenditure on imports change over time, there are other changes taking place at the same time – for example, changes in inflation rates and exchange rates. None the less, MPM is believed to be quite large. In 1988 the marginal rate of taxation for most taxpayers was 25 per cent. Savings have fluctuated quite considerably in recent years.

A reasonable estimate of the value of MPL in the UK at the present time would seem to be about 0.5, so that the value of the multiplier is likely to be quite small: probably less than 2.

In contrast, countries which have a low propensity to import, for example the United States of America, will tend to have higher multipliers, other things being equal, and very small countries with a very high propensity to import will probably have smaller multipliers.

An increase in the construction of roads, which Keynes advocated in the 1930s, would tend to have a fairly high multiplier effect, since, in the first round at least, there would be little marginal propensity to import: the government would tend to employ British workers and use British capital and materials to build the roads since the major objective of public works schemes is usually to employ some of the nation's unemployed resources. Also, as has already been suggested, there would tend to be relatively little propensity to leak in the second round because many of the workers employed on road-building schemes would pay no more than the basic rate of taxation and their relatively low rate of pay would tend to suggest that they would have a relatively small marginal propensity to save. However, problems arise with public works, since there tends to be a time-lag between the decision being taken and its implementation. Usually, public-works schemes are implemented to ease the problems of depressions. However, if a scheme takes a long time to implement, the multiplier effects tend to take a long time to appear. Furthermore, if a public-works scheme is finally implemented when the economy is improving, the multiplier effects are likely to be lower than if the scheme is implemented when the economy is in a trough, because the marginal propensity to save tends to be higher for everyone.

If the government lowered transfer payments, for example to pensioners, the net effect would probably be a fairly high downward multiplier effect. This is because pensioners tend to have a lower propensity to consume consumer durables (which are likely to be imported) and a lower propensity to save than people with higher incomes. If, for example, lower pensions are paid to give people in higher income groups a tax cut, a fairly high reduction in total demand would probably result.

4. The inflationary gap

Some pre-Keynesian economists and some current monetarists have suggested that there is little logic in the government increasing its spending, since this will be at the expense of private investment: government investment 'crowds out' private investment. However, this argument seems to ignore the interaction of private and public expenditure. For example, a public-works scheme to build a road might require the government to contract a private firm to do the work. Also, the argument ignores the fact that if the government did not provide the investment for the provision of public goods, such goods would not be produced, because such goods tend not to be profitable (they do not attract private investment). Furthermore, the argument ignores the fact that government expenditure, as we have already suggested, is more likely to be directed towards those with high marginal propensities to consume (and, therefore, is likely to have greater multiplier effects) than is private investment expenditure.

Government expenditure is only likely to crowd out private investment when there is full or near-full employment. We can use a 45° diagram to explain how inflation rather than increased employment is likely to result from a rise in government expenditure when there is full employment. If the economy is at full employment (Yf), in order for there to be equilibrium, total expenditure must equal Ef. If, however, government expenditure rises, other things being equal, the total expenditure function is shifted leftwards (from E_1 to E_2 in Figure 51).

At full employment, all the nation's resources are fully utilized. Therefore, any rise in total expenditure above the full employment level cannot be met by rises in production, so prices must rise, this being an example of the simple concept of inflation as too much money chasing too few goods. Thus, a rise in expenditure above the level of full employment leads to an '*inflationary gap*'.

It is possible, in practice, for there to be an inflationary gap even if the economy has not reached full employment. For example, if there are vast differences in regional unemployment, with near-full employment in south-east England but high unemployment elsewhere, an inflationary gap might appear. This would approximate to conditions in the late 1960s and early 1970s.

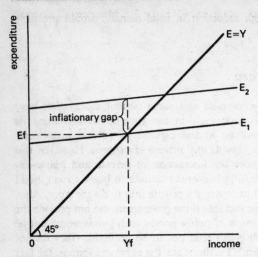

Figure 51. *The inflationary gap*

5. The acceleration principle

We have seen (in Chapter 5) that the level of investment might be determined by expectations or by the current rate of interest, etc. The acceleration principle, however, hypothesizes that the level of investment varies directly with the rate of change of output (i.e. income).

The simplest form of the accelerator assumes that investment expenditure is proportional to the rate of change of output at all levels of output. This form, though, is not completely realistic since as machines become more efficient, fewer machines will be required to produce the same volume of output (i.e. income).

None the less, we might assume, for the sake of simplicity, that there is a fixed ratio between planned investment expenditure (i.e. the demand for capital goods) and the level of income (or output). Assuming that prices remain constant, then (if the demand for firms' products remains constant) firms will have no incentive either to obtain additional capital or to reduce existing capital: any demand for capital goods will merely consist of replacement investment. If, though, demand increases, there will be a tendency to increase the capital stock, particularly if the increase in demand is expected to be permanent. If, on the other hand, demand falls, there will be a lower rate of replacement of existing stock and, therefore, the demand for capital goods and services will fall.

Table 16. How the accelerator affects a road haulage firm when demand increases permanently

Year	Demand for road haulage (tonnes)	Total no. of vehicles required	New demand from firm for vehicles (net investment)	Replacement demand (replacement investment)	Final demand (gross investment)
1	40,000	40	0	10	10
2	50,000	50	10	10	20
3	50,000	50	0	10	10
4	50,000	50	0	10	10
5	50,000	50	0	10	10
6	50,000	50	0	20	20

While many writers refer to the accelerator in terms of capital goods, we can also apply the same principle to the training of individuals.

However, here we will illustrate the accelerator in terms of a road haulage firm. Suppose this firm has forty vehicles and that the life of each vehicle is four years. Suppose also that each vehicle carries 10,000 tonnes during a year. If the demand remains constant at 400,000 tonnes per year, the firm will replace, on average, ten vehicles each year. This means that the firm's investment expenditure consists only of replacement investment: there is no net investment expenditure. Suppose, however, that in a particular year (year 2) demand for road transport grows so that 500,000 tonnes are to be transported by the firm, the firm will not only need to replace ten vehicles but will also need to order an extra ten vehicles to meet the extra demand. The gross investment will, therefore, be twenty vehicles, not ten. In this case, net investment consists not of no vehicles, but of ten vehicles. If the demand the next year remains constant at 500,000 tonnes, the firm will need to replace only ten vehicles. As one can see from Table 16, it will not be until four years later (year 6) that the firm's demand returns to twenty vehicles (all of which is replacement investment), assuming a constant demand for road transport of 500,000 tonnes.

We can show how the firm's demand for vehicles is determined firstly by assuming that at the end of year 1 it has ten vehicles which are three years old, ten which are two years old, ten which are one year old and ten which are brand new. At the end of year 2 the ten oldest vehicles need replacing. Therefore, the firm has a replacement demand for ten vehicles; but the increase in demand for road haulage means that another ten vehicles are also required, so the firm buys twenty brand-new vehicles. At the end of year 3 ten vehicles need replacing. Similarly, at the end of years 4 and 5 ten vehicles need replacing. Similarly, at the end of years 4 and 5 ten vehicles need replacing. However, at the end of year 6 there are twenty vehicles which are four years old and which, therefore, need replacing. Therefore, at the end of year 6 the firm's replacement demand equals twenty vehicles.

If the demand for road haulage, having risen in year 2, falls back to its original level in year 3, there will be no need for replacement of existing vehicles at the end of year 3. Thus, in year 4 the firm will have forty vehicles. Other things being equal, it will have to replace ten of them at the end of year 4. However, if the firm does not anticipate at the end of year 3 that the demand for road haulage in year 4 will be only 400,000 tonnes, it will replace the ten vehicles which are worn out at the end of year 3.

It can be shown, even on the simplified assumptions that we have made, that an increase in demand from consumers can lead to a much bigger increase in demand from firms. Therefore, an initial injection (perhaps of government expenditure) which leads to consumers' demand for road haulage rising by 25 per cent (a rise in demand from 400,000 to 500,000 tonnes) leads to a 100 per cent increase in demand from the firm (a rise in demand from 10 vehicles to 20 vehicles). Other things being equal, this initial increase in demand from consumers will continue to cause fluctuations in demand from firms (compare the firm's final demand for vehicles in year 6 with its demand in year 5 in Table 16). Conversely, a 20 per cent fall in demand (as occurs when consumers' demand for road haulage falls from 500,000 to 400,000 tonnes, as shown in Table 17, leads to a fall in final demand from firms of 100 per cent (i.e. to zero) in year 3 in our example.

In practice, we might make more sophisticated assumptions, for example that if the firms just receive an increase in demand which they do not expect to last they might try to make better use of existing machinery, for example by employing people on overtime or on additional shifts rather than by increasing their investment expenditure. To this extent the fluctuations may not be quite as great as we have been assuming. However, if firms experience an increase in demand and they expect it to last, they may well be over-optimistic and this could lead to larger fluctuations than those illustrated in Table 16.

*

Table 17. How the accelerator affects a road haulage firm when demand increases temporarily

Year	Demand for road haulage (tonnes)	Total no. of vehicles required	New demand from firm for vehicles (net investment)	Replacement demand (replacement investment)	Final demand (gross investment)
1	40,000	40	0	10	10
2	50,000	50	10	10	20
3	40,000	40	0	0	0
4	40,000	40	0	10	10
5	40,000	40	0	10	10
6	40,000	40	0	10	10

QUESTION

What is the importance of the multiplier concept in a modern economy?

The multiplier is the number of times an initial change in aggregate monetary demand has an impact on the subsequent change in national income. If, for example, an increase of government expenditure of £10m were to lead to an increase in national income of £18m, we would say that the value of the multiplier was 1.8.

If the government wishes to use a given injection of government expenditure in such a way that it has the maximum multiplier effect, it is important that it knows the marginal propensity to leak of different groups in society. But MPL is difficult to calculate in a modern society, since a change, for example, in import expenditure over time might be partly explained by changes in inflation rates and exchange rates.

The Treasury has developed a sophisticated model of the economy. Models such as ITEM (Independent Treasury Economic Model) provide sophisticated data about consumption and, thereby, help forecasters calculate the marginal propensity to leak.

It is important that the government knows the value of the multiplier (i.e. knows the value of MPL) not just of society as a whole but of individual groups, since if the government redistributes income from people with high MPLs to people with low MPLs (through the use of taxation and government expenditure) even if there is no net rise in government expenditure, national income can still be raised.

By acquiring more information about, for example, which type of goods are most likely to be imported, a government can try to direct expenditure towards those goods and services which are most likely to be produced by the home country. As information becomes more sophisticated, it should become easier to reduce the marginal propensity to leak and, thus, increase the multiplier.

MULTIPLE-CHOICE QUESTIONS

1. In an economy in which the marginal propensity to import equals 0.2, the marginal propensity to tax equals 0.3 and the marginal propensity to save equals 0.3, what is the value of the multiplier?
   (*a*) 1.4 (approx).
   (*b*) 3⅓.
   (*c*) 1.25.
   (*d*) 5.
Answer – (*c*)

2. The numerical value of the multiplier is likely to rise if which of the following events happen(s):
(A) Import restrictions are loosened;
(B) VAT is raised;
(C) the government raises state pensions?
   (*a*) A only.
   (*b*) A and B only.
   (*c*) C only.
   (*d*) All.
Answer – (*c*)

3. The value of the multiplier will always rise when MPC rises.
   (*a*) True.
   (*b*) False.
Answer – (*b*)

Explanation: MPC might have risen, for example, only because consumption of imports has risen.

4. The accelerator shows that:
   (*a*) a small change in demand will have a greater proportionate effect upon capital-goods industries;

222

(*b*) a small change in demand will have a greater proportionate effect upon consumer-goods industries;

(*c*) a small change in demand will have a greater proportionate effect upon national income.

Answer – (a)

5. If a rise in investment expenditure raises national income over time, it does so because of the workings of:

(*a*) the multiplier;

(*b*) the accelerator principle.

Answer – (a)

DATA RESPONSE

Lord Keynes published his influential book *General Theory of Employment, Interest and Money* in 1936. In this book he argued that aggregate monetary demand would not necessarily equal anticipated aggregate supply of goods and services and that equilibrium of supply and demand could take place at a position well below full employment. This of course was true in the 1930s and would seem to be equally true in the 1980s.

One possible method of altering the equilibrium would be for the government to use expansionary fiscal measures and increase government expenditure and/or reduce taxation (direct or indirect taxation). Governments might need or wish to take account of income distribution: there are advantages in reducing tax rates and increasing personal allowances, including tax thresholds. One of the disadvantages, however, is that income tax can usually be reduced or increased only once a year, so that the time lags between anticipation (following from statistical returns) and actual policy initiative could lead to destabilization.

The government could also alter its fiscal policy through altering corporation tax, though it should be noted that many large firms seem to avoid this taxation altogether. Some economists, particularly in the 1980s have suggested that a reduction in National Insurance contributions might help to increase employment, since these act as a direct cost to firms. The effect of changes in direct taxation upon natural income depends upon the propensity to leak: will any extra disposable income resulting from a cut in direct taxation be spent on imports or saved rather than spent on British goods and services?

(a) Would you expect a £1,000m cut in direct taxation or a £1,000m rise in government expenditure to have the greater multiplier effect? Explain your answer.

(b) In what way might changes in taxation be destabilizing?

SELF-EXAMINATION QUESTIONS

1. 'Transfer payments have no effect upon the level of national income.' Discuss.

2. Explain why, even if a balanced budget is introduced, an increase in government expenditure might increase national income, while a decrease in government expenditure might lead to a contraction of national income?

3. Explain, with an example, why the regional multiplier might be smaller than the national multiplier.

4. Explain the underlying concept of the multiplier. What limitations are there to prevent the multiplier ultimately achieving full employment?

14. Public expenditure

1. Introduction

Public expenditure is defined as the total expenditure of both central and local government plus the expenditure of the public corporations.

2. Why does the government spend money?

(i) Nearly all governments will spend money on *law and order* and *defence*. These services are usually regarded as necessary for any society, but are unlikely to be provided by private firms because there are unlikely to be any returns to the firm from these sectors. Thus, this area of government expenditure can be regarded as *expenditure on public or collective goods*.

(ii) Most governments provide *educational services* (although there is also privately provided education in a number of western-style economies). It is argued that education should be available to everyone, regardless of the ability to pay, because it is a *merit good*. Hence, the need for the provision of education by the state.

(iii) In the United Kingdom since 1909, there has been some provision for *pension schemes*. Most Western governments also provide some form of *social security* for people who are unemployed, poor or disabled. Social security is provided so that those who are unable to earn a living wage are able to purchase essential goods or services. However, some economists and politicians have argued that social security provides a disincentive to work and that the level of social security paid, rather than being a fixed amount, should be related to, say, the amount of savings the recipient has.

In 1988 the government implemented a wide-sweeping change to the social-security system. It should be noted that systems of social-security provision vary from one country to another.

(iv) Many governments provide *subsidies to agriculture*, partly to overcome fluctuations in prices caused by variations in supply and also because it is assumed that the demand for agricultural products is income inelastic.

225

(v) Governments may also provide some money for developing countries in the form of *aid*. However, only a very small proportion of the British government's total expenditure goes to overseas aid.

There has tended to be an increase, in real terms, in public expenditure in the UK since the Second World War. This tendency has occurred partly because of the dominance of Keynesian economics following the publishing of *The General Theory of Employment, Interest and Money* in 1936.

3. Public expenditure and the Medium Term Financial Strategy

The Conservative government, in its expenditure plans, has stated that public expenditure is an integral part of the Medium Term Financial Strategy (MTFS), the aim of which is to reduce inflation and sustain economic growth (see Chapter 17). It has cash targets for public spending, which are designed to hold total public spending fairly level in real terms. The government expects public expenditure to continue to fall as a percentage of national income as the economy grows, which will allow it to reduce taxation, which, it argues, will improve motivation, efficiency and employment.

The government has aimed to reduce public expenditure in cash terms partly because of the anti-inflationary MTFS, since it believes that public expenditure 'crowds out' private expenditure (we argue in section 10, p. 233, that, in fact, 'crowding out' is unlikely when there is high unemployment) and merely adds to inflation. It has also aimed to reduce public expenditure because it believes many areas of the public sector are inefficient: the government aims to get better value for money. However, from the figures in Table 18 it can be seen that in recent years, significantly, both public expenditure on social security and public defence expenditure have risen in real terms and, therefore, by even greater amounts in cash terms. We will go on to discuss these facts in greater detail.

4. Public expenditure on defence

The objective of defence expenditure is to ensure the security of the nation. Since 1979 defence expenditure has more than doubled in money

Table 18. Public spending in real terms by department (£bn, base year 1984/85)

	1983/84 out-turn	1984/85 out-turn	1985/86 estimated out-turn	1986/87 plans	1987/88 plans	1988/89 plans
Defence	16.2	17.2	17.4	16.9	16.6	16.2
Foreign and Commonwealth Office	1.8	1.8	1.8	1.8	1.8	1.8
European Community	0.9	0.9	0.8	0.6	1.0	0.8
Ministry of Agriculture, Fisheries and Food	2.2	2.1	2.4	2.0	2.0	2.0
Trade and Industry	2.0	2.1	1.9	1.4	1.1	0.9
Energy	1.2	2.6	1.0	0.1	-0.5	-0.2
Employment	3.0	3.1	3.2	3.4	3.3	3.4
Transport	4.5	4.6	4.4	4.4	4.3	4.1
DOE – Housing	3.2	3.2	2.6	2.5	2.5	2.5
DOE – other environmental services	3.9	4.0	3.8	3.3	3.1	3.0
Home Office	4.7	5.0	5.1	5.1	4.9	4.9
Education and Science	14.0	14.0	13.8	13.0	12.7	12.4
Arts and libraries	0.7	0.7	0.7	0.7	0.7	0.6
DHSS – health and personal social services	15.4	15.8	15.9	16.2	16.2	16.4
DHSS – social security	36.7	38.1	39.3	39.1	39.1	39.2
Scotland	7.0	7.0	7.0	6.9	6.5	6.4
Wales	2.7	2.6	2.6	2.6	2.6	2.6
Northern Ireland	3.9	4.0	4.1	4.1	4.1	4.1
Chancellor's department	1.7	1.7	1.7	1.8	1.8	1.8
Other departments	1.0	1.2	1.3	1.4	1.5	1.5
Reserve				4.1	5.5	6.8
Central privatization proceeds	-1.2	-2.1	-2.5	-4.3	-4.2	-4.1
Adjustments			-0.1	-0.4		
Planning total	125.7	129.6	127.8	126.7	126.7	127.1
Planning total in cash terms	120.3	129.6	134.2	139.1	143.9	148.7

Source: The Government's Expenditure Plans, 1986/87 to 1988/89, vol. I, HMSO, January 1986.

terms, with spending being switched from manpower to capital equipment. How much the government *should* spend on defence is very much a matter of value judgement. None the less, it seems difficult to see how the government can be getting better value for money as a result of its increased defence expenditure. Furthermore, it is hard to believe that the defence service is any less inefficient than, say, the health service. One of the House of Commons committees in August 1986 for example identified £1bn of over-expenditure on defence.

5. Public expenditure on housing

(a) *Why does the government intervene in housing?*

Since the Second World War, governments have tended to increase public expenditure. One of the major items of expenditure has been that of housing.

(i) This is because partly it has been thought that housing is an example of a *merit good*, i.e. it should be available to all, irrespective of income.

(ii) Intervention in the housing market also takes place because, *if one relied wholly on market forces, it would take a long while for an equilibrium position to be reached.* While some statistics show a crude surplus of housing over a number of households, this may well be misleading. These statistics, for example, take no account of the fact that a young person who is still living with his parents (and is, therefore, included as a member of this one family) wishes to move away (whereby, the statistics would measure two families) when a house is available. Neither do these statistics take into account the condition of available houses and the regions where housing is available.

(iii) The housing market is very susceptible to changes in expectations (*expectations blight*). If a few residents in a particular area expect the price of houses in the area to fall, they might want to sell their houses, starting fears in other residents that the price of property in the area will soon fall and leading to these other residents wishing to sell their houses before house prices in the area fall. This panic selling will, indeed, reduce the price of houses in the area (the high number of houses on the market forces down the market price).

With residents leaving, the area becomes unattractive to industry (since potential customers and employees are moving away). It is important for the government to intervene in such an area (by perhaps buying up the houses for use as council housing or by encouraging people to stay by providing grants) in order to prevent it becoming a depressed area.

In the absence of government expenditure on housing in such a situation, people from other areas might be encouraged to move to the area in question because of low prices, but industry might already have moved away, making job prospects poor.

(iv) Similarly, the housing market is susceptible to *planning blight*. If, for example, the building of a new motorway in a particular area is imminent, many residents will probably wish to sell their houses, leading to a fall in house prices and the moving away of industry from the area and the area becoming a depressed area unless the government intervenes (as above).

(b) *Forms of government expenditure on housing*

(i) Forms of government expenditure in the area of housing include *subsidies to owner-occupiers with mortgages*. Such subsidies tend to take the form of *income-tax relief*.

The system of tax reliefs on mortgages has been absorbed into the *MIRAS* scheme for most domestic housing with mortgages of less than £30,000. Under the old system of tax reliefs someone with, say, a mortgage payment of £2,000 per year (other things being equal) would pay the £2,000 to the building society and would then receive their income-tax relief of, say, £600. Under MIRAS (Mortgage Interest Relief at Source), the tax relief is discounted from the mortgage payment before it is paid, i.e. just £1,400 is paid to the building society rather than all £2,000. Generally, tax reliefs on mortgages are regressive: the higher the value of the house, the greater the mortgage and the greater the tax relief; and the higher a person's income, the more expensive his house is likely to be. Furthermore, since in the 1980s real interest rates have been at their highest ever level, people with mortgages have received even higher tax relief. It is widely argued that a system of relief should concentrate more on people in need, i.e. on the ability to pay. For example, a system of negative income tax for people on particularly low incomes to help them obtain a mortgage would seem to be more progressive than MIRAS. (See Chapter 23.)

(ii) Greater government *expenditure directed towards easing the problems of inner cities and upon investment grants* (see Chapter 24) would be a more progressive form of government housing expenditure than MIRAS.

(iii) The provision of *council housing* has accounted for a large part of government expenditure in the area of housing since the First World

War. It tends to be a more progressive form of intervention than the system of tax reliefs to owner-occupiers.

The Thatcher government favours the selling of council houses without using the money received to build new council houses. Between 1979 and 1985 over 720,000 council houses were sold. Furthermore, high real interest rates have discouraged the building of council (and private) houses at a time when there are long waiting lists for council houses.

6. Public expenditure on education

(a) *Reasons for government expenditure on education*

The government spends money on education partly because it is felt that, in a free market, *not all parents would have sufficiently long time horizons to take account of the benefits of education.* Most governments have felt that *higher levels of education will tend to produce greater economic growth.* It can be shown fairly easily that higher qualifications are correlated to higher salaries, although this does not necessarily prove that better education is directly responsible for higher earnings.

(b) *Is public expenditure on education progressive?*

There is evidence to suggest that public expenditure on education is regressive rather than progressive since, generally, the higher socioeconomic groups tend to receive more education and, therefore, a greater share of this expenditure per capita than people from lower socioeconomic groups.

Also, education expenditure, particularly in further and higher education, tends to be orientated more towards males than to females. This, though, might change as a result of women's greater aspirations in terms of work in the labour market in the last twenty years or so. Some economists have suggested that when considering education at the vocational level the use of discounted cash-flow techniques might help in the evaluation of the benefit of education upon earnings and the type of job obtained. Thus they believe that we can consider the returns on human capital from expenditure on education as we can the returns on any capital from investment.

However, there are immense problems with this approach because further and higher education beyond the age of sixteen might be taken for reasons other than just vocational ones.

If we wish to overcome the regressive aspects of public spending on education, a system of grants for people from working-class families to remain in full-time education beyond the age of sixteen and a similar system of grants for girls might help.

In 1985 the government was trying to encourage more people to enter engineering courses because of the vocational benefits the government felt such courses had in an area of industry it was keen to promote. However, it is difficult to link education to overall manpower planning, especially when there is little indicative planning in any case. Furthermore, time horizons make it difficult to predict which areas of purely vocational education now will be relevant to the needs of the economy in, say, forty years' time.

However, the use of cost benefit analysis might help in the making of more rational decisions.

(c) *Why is public expenditure on education being reduced?*

Real public expenditure on education has been declining in recent years.

(i) Real public expenditure on education has been reduced as part of the government's *Medium Term Financial Strategy*, which (among other things) aims to reduce the Public Sector Borrowing Requirement (PSBR): by reducing its expenditure, the government reduces the amount it has to borrow.

(ii) The present government has argued that expenditure on education should be cut because *the number of children of school age is declining*.

7. Public expenditure on health

There is a need for public expenditure on health care since it is a merit good. From the figures in Table 18, it is clear that real health expenditure has been rising, which indeed it should be: *if public expenditure on education should be reduced because of the rising age structure of the population, it follows that health expenditure should be increased*.

The present government believes that there should be a choice between private medicine and NHS treatment. The government believes that the health service should be able to compete with private medicine: it has reduced the number of ancillary staff in the health service in an attempt to improve efficiency. The government argues that such cost savings coupled with increases in the number of medical staff have led to improvements in health care in at least some areas of the health service's activities, but it can be argued that the provision of public-sector health care is still inadequate. It can also be argued that, in an attempt to help people stay healthy (which the government argues is an objective for the NHS), the government should spend more money on preventing illnesses by, for example, spending more money on discouraging smoking.

8. Public expenditure on social security

The aim of the social security system is to provide financial help to those who need it, such as pensioners. Public expenditure on pensions is expected to continue to rise in real terms partly because of longer life-expectancy. It is expected to rise to £20bn by 1989.

The government plans to replace supplementary benefits by a simple income support scheme and to simplify housing benefits.

Social security expenditure, as a whole, has tended to rise as a proportion of total public expenditure, mainly because of the rapid rise in unemployment, which was well over three million in 1986, but had declined to just over 2½ million by mid 1988.

9. Privatization

From the figures in Table 18 it is clear that privatization proceeds are growing. The privatization programme is part of the government's objective of increasing efficiency.

Despite the growing privatization proceeds, the government's expenditure plans remain fairly level in real terms, suggesting that, if it were not for privatization, public expenditure according to the government's plans would be expected to rise, as it had done up to 1986 at least.

See Chapter 15 for greater detail about privatization.

10. The Public Sector Borrowing Requirement and the Medium Term Financial Strategy

(a) *Why the public sector has to borrow*

Borrowing is necessary for the public sector as for any other sector if the income in any one year is less than the expenditure. This Public Sector Borrowing Requirement is subdivided into three: central government's borrowing requirement; local authorities' borrowing requirements; public corporations' borrowing requirements.

The Public Sector Borrowing Requirement has become more important since the time of Keynes. Keynes suggested that it would probably be necessary for government expenditure to exceed revenue if unemployment was to be alleviated. Borrowing is also important to finance capital expenditure at times when it is inappropriate to raise taxation. Most Keynesian economists would suggest that borrowing is not undesirable if it is necessary for the government to achieve any of the following objectives: full employment; zero inflation; economic growth; balance-of-payments equilibrium.

Monetarists (including the Thatcher government), however, often take the view that growth of the money supply is a major cause of inflation and that the need for the public sector to borrow leads to inflation. Hence the Thatcher government's desire to reduce the PSBR by reducing public expenditure, at least in money terms.

Some monetarists further believe that public-sector investment tends to discourage ('crowd out') private investment and that, therefore, public-sector expenditure (hence PSBR) should be kept to a minimum. While it is possible that public-sector expenditure might crowd out private investment at times of near full employment, crowding out is unlikely to occur in times of high unemployment. Given that public expenditure is likely to be at its highest when unemployment is at its highest (i.e. public expenditure is likely to be counter-cyclical), crowding out to any significant extent is very unlikely indeed. However, some monetarist economists, notably Milton Friedman, regard public expenditure as undesirable in its own right. It is unlikely that all monetarists actually agree with this last argument.

The relationship between the Public Sector Borrowing Requirement and the National Debt should be understood. Whereas PSBR is usually only a record of how much borrowing is required for a year, the National Debt records the cumulative borrowing needs over time.

PSBR tends to be high at the beginning of the financial year because the revenue from any tax changes made in the Budget will not have been collected. However, most of this revenue will have been obtained by the end of the financial year, at which time the government hopes any targets for PSBR made at the beginning of the financial year will not have been overshot. While revenue from taxes tends to be uneven over the year, government expenditure tends to be spread fairly evenly throughout the year.

For a discussion of how the PSBR is financed see Chapter 17.

(b) *What is the importance of PSBR?*

A sudden reduction in PSBR may be undesirable because any reduction in capital expenditure may have unfavourable multiplier and accelerator effects. For example, the present government's attempts to reduce PSBR appear to have been damaging to the construction industry, particularly to the construction of houses. Failure to provide an adequate transport system (indeed, failure to provide an adequate infrastructure in general) may result in higher costs for industry at a later stage.

While it might be argued that it is important for the level of capital expenditure by the public sector to be fairly high, so that, for example, an adequate infrastructure is provided, it would seem to be illogical to argue that capital expenditure is desirable but current expenditure undesirable if, for example, health centres are provided but adequate staffing is not.

11. The National Debt

The National Debt is the accumulation of money borrowed by the government from households, firms and financial institutions (both within the UK and overseas). It has grown partly in line with inflation, but also during periods when the government has a series of budget deficits (particularly in wartime) or when it has needed to finance investment in the nationalized industries or in the local authorities.

While it is sometimes suggested that it is a burden to the country, a great deal of the Debt represents transfer payments, i.e. annual interest is transferred from taxpayers in this country to debt-holders. Above this, there is some money which is paid to people overseas. The National Debt, as a burden for the government, tends to increase in times of high rates of interest.

12. The distinction between local and central government spending

(a) *Central government expenditure*

Central government is responsible for spending about three quarters of the planning total. Local authorities spend most of the rest. The remainder is the net amount public corporations need to finance their activities. About 40 per cent of central government spending goes on social security. The two next largest components are defence and health.

(b) *Local government expenditure*

Local authorities consist mainly of borough councils and county councils. About 40 per cent of local authorities' expenditure is on education. Law and order, housing and other environmental services, personal social services and transport expenditure are the other most important elements of local authorities' expenditure.

The government increased the provision for local authorities' current expenditure for 1986/87 to £26.7bn and for their capital expenditure for 1986/87 to £3.7bn. The rise in the provision for capital expenditure was mainly to allow renovation of houses.

13. Public corporations' expenditure

Part of the public sector's expenditure goes on public corporations' external finance, i.e. their borrowing and government grants to public corporations. This totalled £3.1bn in 1985/86 and fell in 1986/87, largely because no provision was made for external finance of those nationalized industries which were pending privatization, such as British Gas and British Airways.

*

QUESTION

'The selling of council houses is both cost-effective and beneficial to low income groups.' Discuss.

The provision of council houses has generally been thought of as a measure designed to benefit people on low incomes. But the sale of council houses, if accompanied by a system of subsidizing the rents of low-income tenants in private houses (whether or not these houses were originally council houses which were bought by these former tenants), may prove both cost-effective and to have had beneficial redistributive effects. Such a policy, though, requires there to be an adequate supply of private housing. Yet, at the time the Conservative government announced the scheme of council-house selling, the provision of private housing was (and it still is) inadequate relative to the need for housing.

A system of cross-subsidization might be a more cost-effective policy than the selling of council houses: it might even help the government to 'break even' in its housing expenditure. Through a system of cross-subsidization, a greater proportion of the cost of building new council houses could be borne by tenants of older council houses and through local authorities charging higher rates to private house-owners.

Cross-subsidization can also be practised in order to redistribute income, i.e. higher rates could be charged to private tenants to subsidize the rent charged to council-house tenants. This is, to some extent, already done at present. However, in recent times, the subsidizing of council-house tenants' rents has also been financed directly by central government, which may or may not be a more progressive system of subsidizing the rents of council-house tenants than the charging of higher rates to private tenants (it depends on how the central government raises this revenue).

Of course, council houses are sold to existing tenants by the use of discounts (the amount of discount given is geared to the length of time the potential buyers have been council tenants). While this system may have some beneficial redistributive effects, these discounts are not geared to the ability to pay. Furthermore, the government has not replenished the stock of council houses (which it could easily do with the money received from council-house sales), and the waiting lists for council accommodation of people who cannot afford to move into private accommodation are growing.

Given that the tax relief for private house-owners tends to be higher than the subsidy given to council-house tenants, the sale of council houses may well be beneficial to the tenant who is able to buy his council house, but the people who buy their own council homes tend to be those who may well have been thinking about buying a private house anyway. In other words, the selling of council houses does not have a favourable redistributive effect, unless the money received by the government from sales is used to build more council houses.

The effects of the sale of council houses on the distribution of income are also discussed in Chapter 23.

1. The selling of a council house to a tenant who would otherwise have moved into a private house is likely (given that land is scarce and that there are building restrictions) to:
   (*a*) reduce the waiting list for council houses;
   (*b*) increase the waiting list for council houses;
   (*c*) not affect the waiting list for council houses
Answer – (b)

2. If a private houseowner has a mortgage of £20,000 and the annual rate of interest is 10 per cent, how much does he have to pay to his building society per year under the MIRAS scheme if the tax relief is 25 per cent?
   (*a*) £500.
   (*b*) £1,000.
   (*c*) £1,500.
   (*d*) £2,000.
Answer – (c)

3. The provision of education by the state can be justified because education is considered to be:
   (*a*) an inferior good;
   (*b*) a free good;
   (*c*) a public good;
   (*d*) a merit good.
Answer – (d)

See Figure 52 overleaf.
1. (*a*) Which of the above item(s) would you expect to increase their share of public expenditure in forthcoming years the most significantly? Explain your reasoning.
   (*b*) i. Why might you expect public expenditure on housing to decline in real terms (or at least not to rise) in the immediate future?
   ii. What are the implications of such a housing policy?

2. Some economists have suggested that the money supply is partly dependent upon the size of the Public Sector Borrowing Requirement

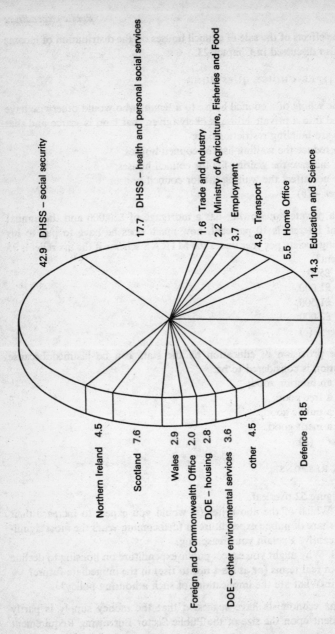

Figure 52. *Planning total by department in 1986/87 (£bn)*
From *The Government's Expenditure Plans, 1986/87 to 1988/89, vol. 1,* HMSO, January 1986.

42.9 DHSS – social security

17.7 DHSS – health and personal social services

1.6 Trade and Industry

2.2 Ministry of Agriculture, Fisheries and Food

3.7 Employment

4.8 Transport

5.5 Home Office

14.3 Education and Science

Defence 18.5

other 4.5

DOE – other environmental services 3.6

DOE – housing 2.8

Foreign and Commonwealth Office 2.0

Wales 2.9

Scotland 7.6

Northern Ireland 4.5

and that, therefore, the latter needs to be controlled. The controls, however, may well be artificial. For example, whereas the borrowing requirement of British Telecom was part of PSBR before it was privatized, since its privatization any borrowing requirements it has are considered as part of private borrowing. It seems difficult to believe, however, that this has any significant effect upon the money supply.

A more crucial consideration would seem to be how much of PSBR is financed by borrowing from UK residents and how much is financed by borrowing from overseas residents, since borrowing from overseas can lead to balance of payments problems in both the short and the long term. Also important is whether or not new debt is taken up through the banks, since the amount of debt taken up through the banks affects the amount of money which they can lend.

(*a*) Critically discuss the conclusions reached in the above article.

(*b*) Some economists have suggested that public investment would 'crowd out' other investment. Is there any reason to believe that borrowing by British Telecom would 'crowd out' other private investment more if it is a private rather than a public institution? Explain your answer.

SELF-EXAMINATION QUESTIONS

1. What are the main items of public expenditure in the United Kingdom at the present time? What changes might be expected in the next ten years?

2. Why do most governments provide compulsory education? What disadvantages are there to such provision?

3. 'The government should only provide health care for the poor and in order to eliminate infectious illnesses.' Discuss this statement.

4. How, if at all, can the optimal allocation of public expenditure be determined?

5. Why have governments in many countries subsidized agricultural production?

6. Is the Public Sector Borrowing Requirement the same as the National Debt? Explain your answer.

7. Why has control of the Public Sector Borrowing Requirement been thought of as more important in recent years? Is the underlying analysis correct?

8. How far is the National Debt an internal transfer payment? How far is it an external burden, i.e. owed to foreigners? Why does the distinction matter?

9. 'The Public Sector Borrowing Requirement is, in itself, no guide for government economic policy since it depends on why it was created. For example, if it is to finance future worthwhile investment, a high Public Sector Borrowing Requirement may be desirable, whereas if it results from inefficiency of the nationalized industries it is undesirable.' Comment critically on this statement.

15. Nationalized industries

1. Introduction

The most direct form of government intervention in the operations of industry is for the government to operate the industry itself. This might be done through a government department (the Post Office was a government department until 1969), but this is generally thought not to result in commercial efficiency. An alternative is to have the industry owned by a public corporation.

Public corporations are, in effect, companies in which the government holds all the shares and appoints the board members. Examples of public corporations include the National Coal Board and the British Railways Board.

2. The changing group of nationalized industries

The nationalized industries are a changing group. Some of the most important industries which have been nationalized in the past or are still nationalized are listed in Table 19, with the year in which they were originally nationalized.

Steel has been nationalized, denationalized and nationalized again. Since the Conservative government came to power in 1979 there has been a period of planned privatization: the National Freight Consortium in 1982; British Telecom (which was part of the Post Office until the 1980s) was privatized in 1984; British Gas was privatized in 1986 and British Airways in 1987.

There are (or have been) a number of major nationalized industries in both the transport sector and in the fuel sector. We discuss the major nationalized industries in these sectors later in this chapter.

Nationalized industries, which form a part of the public sector, are an important part of the total United Kingdom economy. It is difficult to give exact figures for employment in the mid-1980s, as the nationalized industries are changing rapidly, but in the early part of the 1980s they employed over two million people and invested as much as the private manufacturing sector as a whole.

Table 19. The changing group of nationalized industries: major industries which have been nationalized

Year of nationalization	Industry
1908	Port of London Authority
1933	London Transport Board
1946	Coal Board
1946	BEA and BOAC (combined to become British Airways in 1973)
1947	Electricity Board
1947	British Railways Board
1948	Gas Council
1949	Iron and Steel (denationalized in 1953 and renationalized in 1967 under the name British Steel Corporation)
1968	National Freight (denationalized in 1982)
1969	Post Office (had been a government department since the nineteenth century)

3. Reasons for nationalization

(a) 'Natural' monopolies

Nationalization is a way of dealing with '*natural monopolies*' (those industries which are likely to be monopolies whoever owns them). Many governments feel that such industries are better controlled by the government than kept in private hands because *private-sector monopolies are* '*undesirable*': left to the private sector, there is the risk that they will restrict output and raise prices.

(b) 'Commanding heights of the economy'

Labour governments, in particular, have suggested that it is necessary that the government owns the '*commanding heights of the economy*' (i.e. the *key industries*) because the government has the best idea of how to handle these key industries in the national interest rather than for pure profit. It is argued that if these industries do not function properly, then the rest of industry cannot function properly.

These key industries may or may not be 'natural' monopolies.

Rather than nationalize industries (i.e. rather than form public corporations) in order to control the 'commanding heights of the economy', it may be better to have *syndicalism*, whereby the workers themselves control the industry. Paradoxically, while this was regarded in the 1930s as perhaps being too extreme for a Labour government, it has been done, to a limited extent, by the Conservatives in the 1980s: the workers own a substantial proportion of the shares of the former National Freight Corporation, which became the National Freight Consortium in 1982.

(c) *Coordination*

It might be argued that *nationalization can lead to better coordination between industries*, for example, between industries in the fuel sector and industries in the transport sector. But in practice there seems to be little evidence of coordination of investment or pricing policy resulting from nationalization.

(d) *Economies of scale*

In some industries there may be *economies of scale* which can be realized if they are nationalized. Before electricity was nationalized, there were various municipal firms. Since the peaks in demand for electricity may vary in different parts of the country, the nationalization of electricity and the formation of the National Grid meant that there was less wastage of supply (see section 5, pp. 245–7). In 1988 there was intense debate before the government announced that the CEGB would be kept intact but the regional boards could compete.

Industries which are nationalized partly in order to benefit from economies of scale are usually 'natural' monopolies.

(e) *Strategic reasons*

Some industries have been nationalized for *strategic reasons*: the railways were under government control during both world wars (although they were not nationalized until 1947) to speed up the distribution of resources necessary for the nation's security; certain enterprises, such as British Aerospace and the United Kingdom Atomic Energy Authority were nationalized partly because they were very much geared to defence needs.

Yet, despite their strategic importance, very few countries have nationalized their shipping industries.

(f) *Rescue of 'lame ducks'*

Nationalization has been used to *rescue important enterprises* which might not otherwise have survived. Rolls-Royce was effectively nationalized by the Conservative government in 1972 when it faced severe financial difficulties.

Governments may decide to rescue companies in order to avoid the damaging multiplier effects of them having to close. Had British Leyland not been rescued (by setting up a state holding company) there would have been damaging consequences for the West Midlands economy. Under the Thatcher government, the Bank of England was permitted to take over JMB (a banking company which was in financial difficulties) because of the cumulative effects likely to result from a decline in confidence in financial institutions had a substantial financial institution collapsed.

In 1988, British Aerospace took over the Rover group (formerly British Leyland), subject to EEC approval.

(g) *Industrial relations*

Nationalization might be pursued to try to improve industrial relations. Ironically, one of the reasons for nationalizing the coal industry in the 1940s was poor industrial relations in the industry.

A Royal Commission, considering the future of the coal industry in the 1920s (when it was still private), suggested that the workers might work harder if they were not having to make a profit for other people. It is perhaps surprising that, in the light of such an argument, the syndicalist suggestion that workers should control their own industry has not been considered more seriously as an alternative to nationalization.

(h) *Divergence between private costs and social costs*

Another reason for government control, though not necessarily government ownership, is where there is a *divergence between social and private costs,* i.e. if firms, in the absence of government control, lose revenue if they employ more workers, reduce air pollution or increase their safety standards. But there is little evidence that nationalized industries are necessarily any better or any worse than their private counterparts in considering the effects of any divergence between private and social costs. In practice, some former nationalized industries, notably the National Freight Corporation, operated very much on commercial lines and seemed to ignore most externalities.

Furthermore, one of the reasons for the long coal strike in 1984 was that the National Coal Board seemed to be concentrating on private costs and benefits rather than social costs and benefits. However, the National Coal Board has kept open uneconomic pits. British Rail has kept open railways that would have been closed under a pure price mechanism. Yet it would be possible to achieve much the same effect through the provision of subsidies or taxation. For example, by subsidizing private firms to boost employment, while taxing externalities such as pollution and noise.

4. Nationalized industries and economic policies

We have seen that some industries might be nationalized in order to avoid rising unemployment and some even to help control prices. But whether or not industries have been nationalized primarily for these reasons, it may well be that *the activities of nationalized industries can be manipulated by governments in order to help them in any anti-inflationary policies or in order to help counteract unemployment.*

The Conservatives in the early 1970s, for example, aimed to control prices charged by nationalized industries in its attempt to reduce inflation. Paradoxically, the Thatcher government has sometimes increased prices within the nationalized industries, for example in the gas industry, partly to keep down the Public Sector Borrowing Requirement as part of its counter-inflationary policy. Furthermore, it has often been argued that the Thatcher government (while not openly having an incomes policy) has a 'hidden' incomes policy for the public sector, of which the nationalized industries are a part.

There are objections to governments using the activities of nationalized industries in the pursuit of their policy objectives:

i. *it is difficult to see how far the nationalized industries are efficient*;
ii. *there is also the danger of governments using nationalized industries in their pursuit of short-term expediency* (such as making large-scale investment plans at a time of a key election) rather than taking a longer-term view.

5. The electricity industry

(a) *The derived demand for electricity*

The electricity industry grew rapidly during the 1960s and 1970s. As with other industries in the fuel sector, *demand is derived*, and for a long while it tended to be assumed that economic growth would be at the rates to which the United Kingdom had become accustomed from about 1945 to 1970 and that the demand for electricity would grow proportionately with this. A number of economists, notably *Lovins* in his book *Is Nuclear Power Necessary?*, have criticized the Electricity Board for consistently overestimating demand.

Overestimation of the demand for a commodity such as electricity is particularly undesirable, given that there is no adequate means of large-scale storage.

(b) *The supply of electricity*

The electricity industry has to estimate how much surplus capacity it needs to meet the potential peak demand on the coldest winter day. *Load factors* (which are defined as the amount of electricity sent out during the year as a percentage of the amount that would be sent out if generation was at its peak level throughout the year) are often quite low, such as 50 per cent. In general, the average level of demand in the winter is considerably above that in the summer.

Furthermore, the CEGB (Central Electricity Generating Board) needs to know the daily peaks in demand. Because those peaks may vary between one area of the country and another, and because it is so difficult to store electricity, if might be argued that the creation of one central Electricity Board and the establishment of the National Grid should lead to economies of scale. However, it has been argued that the CEGB's spare capacity is higher than is necessary for purely commercial reasons. The CEGB's capacity is usually about 30 per cent higher than demand. The CEGB can reasonably predict daily peaks in demand: the demand for electricity is at its highest between 8.30 a.m. and 9 p.m.; there is unlikely to be that much regional variation in demand. Therefore, the CEGB could reduce its spare capacity (thereby cutting its variable costs) and so reduce prices. Some economists argue that the price of electricity would be lower if the CEGB were not a monopoly (i.e. if the electricity industry were not a nationalized industry).

(c) *Has, in fact, the CEGB got a monopoly?*

To answer this question we may look at *the degree of substitution between electricity and other fuels* which might take place at different price levels. There is little possibility of using fuels other than electricity for items such as lifts or electrified railways, but for space heating it is often wasteful to use electricity and there are a number of substitutes for electricity.

6. The gas industry

(a) *Economies of scale resulting from nationalization*

Before nationalization, the gas industry consisted of hundreds of undertakings, which generally served limited areas. The average size of gas plants was below the optimum, so a potential advantage of nationalization was that gas plants would reach a size that was nearer their optimum.

(b) *The demand for gas*

During the 1950s gas sales rose much more slowly than those of either electricity or oil, but from the 1960s onwards there were rapid changes which helped the gas industry. One of these was that newer processes for gas production were used, which used lower grade, cheaper coal and thus the relative price of gas became more competitive. Partly because of the low costs of gas, gas central heating rapidly became the cheapest and one of the most popular forms of central heating. This was partly offset from 1979 onwards, when the price of gas was pushed above the rate of inflation by the government in its attempt to control PSBR as part of its Medium Term Financial Strategy. The price of gas has been raised for reasons other than profit.

(c) *Why did the government privatize the gas industry?*

i. *The Thatcher government believes that industry functions better under competitive conditions.*
ii. *The sale of gas brought in a lot of revenue*: because gas is profitable, there was a high demand for shares.

7. The coal industry

The coal industry was nationalized at the end of 1947. From then until 1957 there was an acute coal shortage in the United Kingdom and the main emphasis was on supplying coal almost irrespective of the cost. Less coal would have been supplied (because of the high costs involved) had coal remained in private hands.

Partly as a result of this shortage, British fuel policy was geared towards saving coal and the railways were encouraged to switch to diesel engines. The coal industry faced reduced demand from the late 1950s onwards, partly for this reason and partly because of the Clean Air Act 1956, which prohibited the use of coal, as such, in many areas, although many coal-based products were still used and coal could still be used for central heating.

The coal industry tended to concentrate on better pits and on fewer coal faces, which gave rise to greater prospects of using equipment more fully. The prospects for the coal industry seemed brighter after the rise in oil prices, in 1973, though this was partly offset by the exploitation of North Sea oil from the mid-1970s onwards. The coal strike in 1984, partly as a result of fears of redundancy amongst miners, showed that the future is more uncertain.

8. The railways

(a) *Why were the railways nationalized?*

Prior to 1921 there were about 120 private railway companies and so it was difficult for them to make the best use of their facilities, especially for long-distance, large-scale consignments. In 1921 voluntary mergers into four companies (the Great Western Railway, London Midland Scottish, the London North Eastern Railway and Southern Railways) meant that there were more potential economies of scale, though at this time, as later, the railways complained of unfair competition, since road hauliers did not have to finance roads.

The railways were nationalized in 1947, when they were in a dilapidated state because there was virtually no replacement or investment during the Second World War. The Transport Act 1947 set up the British Transport Commission, which had overall financial control over a large number of different transport undertakings, including the railways, docks and inland waterways, London Transport Executive Hotels and road haulage. The Act recommended a break-even policy, i.e. their revenue was supposed to be sufficient to meet their costs, taking one year with another. But an independent Transport Tribunal had control over rates and charges, and could veto any proposed changes.

(b) *The effects of nationalization*

As a nationalized industry, British Railways felt they had obligations which a private railway company would not have, such as the obligation to run Sunday services, for which there was relatively low demand and for which higher wages had to be paid. These obligations were hardly justifiable on commercial grounds, Furthermore, the railways were obliged to carry awkward loads for rural journeys, while road haulage firms (which were likely to be better equipped) could refuse on the grounds that such a service was unprofitable. There was no way the railways could break even. It was not until the 1962 Transport Act that the railways were given commercial freedom: freight rates and passenger fares were freed from any special control.

The move towards greater commercialism was illustrated in 1963 when, as a result of the Beeching Plan, unprofitable lines were closed and 70,000 jobs cut.

Nationalization had therefore failed to save jobs. It also failed to integrate the railways, until the 1968 Transport Act, when an attempt was made to have common timetables, common fare structures, etc. Also, as a result of the 1968 Act, the government took greater responsibility for the railways' role as a social service.

The 1974 Railways Act modified the 1968 Act: the social obligation of the railways was further emphasized: it was stressed that railway services were a *merit good* and should, therefore, be available in all parts of the country, including rural areas.

9. British Airways

British Airways was denationalized in 1987. It was an unusual nationalized industry, in that the majority of its main competitors were outside the United Kingdom. Many of its competitors were also nationalized, although notable exceptions were the American airlines.

While the demand for air travel is usually thought to be very income elastic (and for a long while depended largely on business passengers), this opinion has been changing since the 1960s; by the mid-1980s about half the passengers were social travellers rather than business travellers. This has meant that airlines, including British Airways, have had to concentrate far more on charging competitive fares than in the past, when competition in terms of comfort and convenience was perhaps more important.

British Airways has contributed considerably to the UK's balance of payments and is one of the world's largest airlines. However, in the early 1980s British Airways was making large-scale losses, partly the result of having to make redundancy payments and partly because of its excessive writing down of the depreciation of aircraft in the accounts (if, for example, an aircraft was expected to last for ten years but depreciates in value each year by £1m, instead of British Airways writing down that the depreciation value, which is defined as a cost, was £1m each year, it wrote down that the depreciation value in the first year was £10m and that in future years it did not depreciate at all). By 1985 British Airways' position had been reversed.

The future of British Airways, like that of other airlines, will be partly determined by how it views and reacts to other firms' moves – reducing prices (like the former Laker Airways and Virgin Atlantic) or improving the quality of service (perhaps providing extra shuttle services).

Policy on fares has not always been wholly in the hands of British Airways: IATA (International Air Transport Association) for a long while set a series of prices between most major destinations. In practice, these scheduled fares often meant that fares were higher than they would have been had there been competition and that load factors were poor (i.e. there were many empty seats on most flights). It also meant that airlines tended to compete more on non-price factors than on price factors.

As with most other service industries, because the marginal cost of unused space is very low, some form of price discrimination, for example standby fares, would be desirable if it did not lead to a loss of revenue from regular customers. Price discrimination has often been tried and British Airways has sometimes charged lower fares to people who book well in advance or to people who are willing to take a standby flight than to businessmen who often do not know long in advance when they will need to fly.

Like other airlines, British Airways has gradually introduced larger aircraft, partly because of potential economies of scale – though this too has made it more difficult to obtain high-load factors.

*

QUESTION

'Profit-making in nationalized industries is a sign of success. A deficit is automatically a sign of failure.' Discuss.

This may not always be true, since one needs to consider the factors leading to either a financial surplus or a financial deficit. A nationalized industry which has a strong monopoly position and which, as has happened since the Conservative government took office in 1979, is encouraged to raise prices, might make large-scale monopoly profits. This, for example, would have been true to some extent of British Telecom before it was privatized. However, even large-scale profits do not necessarily indicate that it was efficient.

Nationalized industries which are not in a monopoly position, such as the National Freight Corporation before its privatization, are of course not in a position to make monopoly profits and therefore financial surpluses are more likely to represent efficiency.

Similarly deficits, such as occurred in the early 1970s when nationalized industries' prices were held down by the Conservative government below the prices determined by commercial criteria, do not necessarily reflect failure on the part of nationalized industries. Unless all firms' prices are held down or unless price elasticity of demand is very high, such a policy will almost certainly lead to large-scale deficits.

Sometimes nationalized industries may have other objectives, for example, rural services of the Post Office or of some of the nationalized transport sectors would either not be provided or would be provided at a higher price if purely commercial criteria were to apply. If, therefore, one wished to judge the efficiency of nationalized industries, perhaps the government should provide direct subsidies for such unprofitable, but necessary, services. Such subsidies would be useful to help British Rail fulfil its public-service obligation. The EEC has suggested that there should be transparency of subsidies, whereby it should be obvious why subsidies have been paid.

In the United Kingdom, many economists and some White Papers have suggested that pricing should reflect the marginal cost. If the government accepted this criteria, then such pricing policies would affect the accounting definition of profits or losses.

MULTIPLE-CHOICE QUESTIONS

1. Nationalized industries are usually bound by *ultra vires* rules. This means that they cannot carry out activities unless they have been specified in the appropriate Act.

    (*a*) True.
    (*b*) False.
Answer – (*a*)

2. The marginal cost at peak times of British Rail providing additional capacity is much greater than at off-peak times.
    (*a*) True.
    (*b*) False.
Answer – (*a*)

3. Short-run marginal-cost pricing is a useful method of evaluating whether investment is worthwhile.
    (*a*) True.
    (*b*) False.
Answer – (*b*)

4. One of the most important differences between nationalized industries and private-sector firms is that:
    (*a*) nationalized industries are always monopolies;
    (*b*) nationalized industries always have social obligations imposed upon them;
    (*c*) nationalized industries are always unprofitable;
    (*d*) the profits of nationalized industries are always ploughed back into future investment;
    (*e*) nationalized industries do not generally offer shares to the public.
Answer – (*e*)

5. If a nationalized industry charges marginal costs for its services when its average cost curve is declining, it will:
    (*a*) break even;
    (*b*) make a loss;
    (*c*) make a profit.
Answer – (*b*)

6. The government in the 1960s specified a 'test discount rate' for most nationalized industries. The test discount rate refers to:
    (*a*) the returns which the nationalized industries should make on capital employed;
    (*b*) the returns which they should make on new investment;
    (*c*) the discount they give to their most favoured customers.
Answer – (*b*)

DATA RESPONSE

1. When looking at nationalized industries it is important to have some measures of efficiency. Efficiency might be measured by comparing nationalized industries to other industries within the United Kingdom, although for electricity, rail, gas, etc., this may be difficult since there are no industries in the private sector of comparable size. An alternative, therefore, is to look at similar industries elsewhere.

It is important to look at efficiency, for example in the electricity industry, to see whether there is too much spare capacity contributing to increased costs or too little spare capacity, which could pose problems for consumers, both domestic and industrial. If possible, prices should relate to the allocation of resources. This is particularly difficult in industries where the services cannot be stored, as, for example, with electricity and railways.

It is also important to know the effects of government intervention, for example through monetary policy or prices and incomes policies, cash limits, etc., on nationalized industries. There has often been too little coordination between the sponsoring ministries and their undertakings over long-term strategies. For example, on the railways there is the need to consider the long-term electrification of many of the main-line routes. This is partly because of the need to save fuel, although the main effects would be reduced maintenance costs.

When looking at the effects of differing pricing policies of the nationalized industries, competitors' costs should be taken into account. For example, a feature often overlooked when criticizing British Rail is that road users, especially company car drivers, do not pay their full social costs. This poses problems for a sensible pricing system.

(a) What measures can be used to look at the efficiency of a nationalized industry? In what ways, if at all, do these differ from those of private industries?

(b) In the early 1970s the government held down prices in the public sector in an attempt to reduce inflation. What effects might this have had on the rivals of the nationalized industries and those industries which used the services or goods as factors of production?

(c) The Conservative government in the early 1980s tended to raise nationalized industries' prices in order to reduce the Public Sector Borrowing Requirement. What effect would this have had on the nationalized industries' competitors and on those firms which used nationalized industries' services or goods as factors of production?

(d) What effect would cash limits have on the investment policies of nationalized industries?

2. One of the problems which arise for the nationalized industries is that they are bound by an *ultra vires* clause which usually prevents them from diversifying. For example, while the pre-war (privately owned) railways in the United Kingdon diversified into owning road-freight vehicles, buses and even, on occasions, air transport, British Rail is not allowed to do this. If, therefore, demand for rail travel declines, the workforce is likely to be more concerned about saving jobs than about any attempts to modernize the industry.

The reasons given for the *ultra vires* clause are that, without it, the nationalized industries would be competing on unfair terms with other industries. This, however, does not seem to be valid. The situation has been made even worse in the United Kingdom by divesting the nationalized industries of many of their profitable activities. There is, therefore, little incentive for either management or workers to become more efficient, since such activities lead to them being hived off. It also has a bad effect on the morale of the workers and managers in the nationalized industries, since they are likely to be seen as inefficient, loss-making industries.

The nationalized industries have also suffered from being 'political shuttlecocks', i.e. being changed at the whim of different governments or even by the same government. Sometimes, nationalized industries' prices have been held down by the government in an attempt to reduce inflation. Holding down prices in industries with a high proportion of fixed costs and often low price elasticities of demand will almost certainly lead to losses, as occurred in the early 1970s. One concept stressed in the late 1970s was that there should be more consultation between the sponsoring departments, trade unions and management in terms of a policy council which would then set an agreed set of policies. This would remove the problems of governments treating nationalized industries as political shuttlecocks. However, it seems unlikely that any government would allow this degree of independence and more probable that they would often intervene for allegedly macroeconomic reasons. In practice, because of by-elections, general elections and so on, governments often take shorter time horizons in their planning decisions than managers of nationalized industries would.

(a) What are the implications of nationalized industries being political shuttlecocks? What effects might these have on the costs of the nationalized industries and the demand for their products?

(b) Why does the writer argue that diversification of the nationalized industries might be desirable? What are the disadvantages of diversification?

(c) What would be the effects of the government holding down prices in the nationalized industries in an attempt to reduce inflation? What are the effects if it raises prices in order to reduce the Public Sector Borrowing Requirement in an attempt to reduce inflation?

3. The electricity supply industry is an example of a high-fixed-cost, relatively *low-variable-cost industry*. One of the problems faced by the electricity industry is whether or not it should try to meet the highest possible demand at any given time and thus have spare capacity for most periods of the year. Even the highest possible demand cannot be known with any great degree of certainty since, for example, the demand for heating will depend upon weather conditions. The industry has been criticized by some environmentalist bodies for having far too large an excess capacity which means that fuel costs are unnecessarily high and there is a great deal of waste. The problems are compounded since the electricity industry cannot store electricity in large quantities.

The industry, therefore, has a strong incentive to try to encourage demand during off-peak periods. One of the ways of doing this is through the use of night storage heaters where, providing the electricity supply industry covers its variable costs, the additional revenue is worth having.

The electricity supply industry is a good example of an industry in which there is price discrimination. The two major markets, i.e. the industrial and the domestic markets, are likely to have different price elasticities of demand. There is little possibility of re-selling and, thus, the markets can be effectively segregated. This enables the electricity supply industry to gain a higher overall revenue than if it merely charged one price for its product.

(a) Explain the term in *italic* type.

(b) Why, for price discrimination to be profitable, is it necessary to be able to segregate the markets? Why is it generally easier to do this for services than for goods?

(c) Explain why the different charges in the peak and the off-peak periods would not be defined as price discrimination by the economist.

(*d*) Explain, with the use of diagrams, why revenue will be higher with price discrimination than if a single price were charged.

4. During 1984 privatization, i.e. the selling of nationalized industries, increased. The Financial Secretary to the Treasury suggested that if Mrs Thatcher were elected for a third time, the only thing left to sell would be the Treasury. Not all economists would necessarily approve either of the pace or of the timing of privatization. Furthermore, while the government suggests that privatization increases competition, this does not always seem to be true. For example, the National Freight Consortium (formerly the National Freight Corporation) accounts for less than 10 per cent of the total road freight market and, in any case, competed with the large own-account firms (those firms which transport goods for themselves). Similarly, it seems likely that British Telecom, which was sold in 1984, is to be a near-monopoly, and many economists are as worried about private monopoly as about public monopoly. Internationally, competition in the air-travel market depends far more on I A T A and on bilateral negotiation between governments than on the British government alone.

In some cases, the conditions of sale have also caused some concern. For example, the sudden rise in share prices immediately after the privatization of British Telecom caused concern. The short-term capital gains to the private shareholders have been at the expense of the taxpayer. If the government had pitched the price at a slightly higher level, more money would have been available for aid to developing countries or to worthwhile social projects. The sale of British Telecom, however, did widen the number of shareholders quite considerably and this has been perhaps the main achievement. Similarly, by late 1984, about 750,000 council homes had moved into private ownership, partly because of the discounts given. The greater freedom of choice in private ownership might well be beneficial to the occupiers, though the overall position will depend partly upon whether new council housing or other forms of housing are available to families on the waiting list.

The Consumers' Association would like to see increased consumer protection once the nationalized industries are privatized. This is particularly important in the case of British Telecom. For example, had it remained in the public sector, it would almost have certainly have made losses on rural telephone boxes and, to some extent, upon general rural services. A profit-maximizing firm would almost certainly either reduce these services or increase charges considerably.

(*a*) How far has privatization increased competition? (Refer in your answer to different industries.)

(*b*) Why might the Consumers' Association suggest that there should be more safeguards against a private monopoly?

(*c*) What would be the effect on consumers of a profit-maximizing British Telecom? How can there ever be effective competition in the telecommunication industry without inefficient duplication?

(*d*) What should be the economic guidelines for the sale price of shares in an industry about to be privatized?

SELF-EXAMINATION QUESTIONS

1. What are the main nationalized industries in each of the following sectors:
   (*a*) the transport sector;
   (*b*) the energy sector;
   (*c*) other sectors?

2. Some Acts of Parliament in the United Kingdom in the past have specified 'break-even' policies for nationalized industries. How does the economist's definition of break-even differ from that of the accountant? Under what circumstances does break-even imply cross-subsidization?

3. In the past nationalized industries, including British Rail and the Post Office, have often used an average-cost pricing policy for their services. What are the different effects of this in:
   (*a*) a competitive position;
   (*b*) a monopolistic position?

4. What possible economies of scale might arise from having all the nationalized energy industries in one organization and all the nationalized transport industries in another? What possible dis-economies of scale might arise?

5. What problems do large fixed costs such as those in the electricity and the railway industries pose when considering pricing policy? How, if at all, can any problems which arise be overcome?

6. A Green Paper issued in the 1970s on transport suggested that prices on roads should reflect their marginal social costs. What would be the implications of such a move for the nationalized transport industries?

16. Taxation policy

1. Introduction

Taxation and government-expenditure policy is often referred to as *fiscal policy*. Originally taxes were levied solely to meet the expenditure of the state or the monarch, but in modern society taxation policy is more complex. For example, the government might wish to redistribute income, and fiscal policy is one method of doing this. Taxation policy has also become more important since Lord Keynes demonstrated that taxation policy could have an effect on employment. In Chapter 13 we explained how changes in the level of taxation might affect the level of unemployment.

2. Purposes of taxation

(i) One of the purposes of taxation is to allow the government to *raise revenue in order to be able to provide goods or services which would not generally be supplied by the market*, i.e. *public goods*, such as parks and open spaces and defence. Taxation policy for these purposes could be determined through a series of questionnaires asking how much money collectively the government should spend on certain measures. However, this has rarely been done and usually the government will have to make a value judgement about the benefits of one public good compared to another.

If the main purpose of indirect taxation, such as the taxation imposed upon cigarettes, is to raise revenue, then we would expect the government not just to impose the tax on the good in question, but also on its immediate substitutes.

(ii) The second main purpose of taxation is to *redistribute income*. While in the United Kingdom the taxation policy is assumed to be *progressive* (i.e. more is taken from the rich than from the poor), we need also to look at the distribution of *benefits*. There is a considerable degree of evidence in this country to show that many of the benefits, particularly that of state-provided education, go to the richer sections of society.

(iii) A third main purpose of taxation might be to *influence the market when the market, by itself, does not lead to the optimum distribution of the allocation of resources*. This will apply where there are *externalities*, such as noise, pollution and accidents. In order to *maximize social welfare*, the government should raise taxes or give subsidies up to the point where *marginal social costs equal marginal social benefits*. We discuss this more fully in the chapter on cost benefit analysis (Chapter 22).

(iv) The other main purpose of taxation in Keynesian economics is to try to *influence unemployment, inflation, economic growth and the balance of payments*. However, it may be very difficult to achieve all these objectives simultaneously.

Furthermore (as suggested in Chapter 13), a rise in government expenditure is likely to have more effect upon the level of unemployment than a fall in the level of taxation by the same amount.

A rise in levies upon goods which the UK is likely to import may, in fact, lead to some fall in unemployment by reducing the amount of money consumers spend on imports and increasing the amount spent on home-produced goods. Such a policy is likely, though, to lead to retaliation. Also, the legality of such a policy may be contested. For example, the EEC recently deemed that the high taxation levied by the UK on wine (which is more likely to be imported than produced in the UK) was against the principles of the Treaty of Rome.

(v) Taxation, whether direct or indirect, will reduce purchasing power. *The high taxation placed upon tobacco may be designed partly to deter consumption*. In the 1984 Budget the Chancellor claimed that the taxation on cigarettes was to be increased for health reasons. However, the fact that the demand for cigarettes is very inelastic means that a rise in price, as a result of a higher levy, increases revenue.

3. Problems of taxation policy

(i) As we have already suggested, *a rise in taxation will reduce purchasing power*. If the taxation on a good for which the demand tends to be elastic is increased (leading to an increase in price), then revenue to the government will fall. However, raising the taxation on goods for which the demand is inelastic will increase revenue.

(ii) For changes in direct taxation, the Chancellor has to take into account possible effects on *the incentive to work*. It is often claimed that a rise in income tax will reduce the incentive to work. Yet there is very little evidence available to support this claim. In fact, a rationale which assumes that work can be substituted for leisure asserts that a fall in income will lead to more hours being worked to achieve the same income as previously. If this is the case, we can refer to the substitution effect of a change in taxation: if taxation increases, the substitution effect will lead to less time being spent in leisure activities and more hours spent at work. If the individual is prevented from working more hours in his present job he may either change his job or 'moonlight'. If a progressively higher marginal rate of income tax exists, this may deter overtime, although if people are saving for a fixed sum, it could, paradoxically, increase the number of hours worked.

(iii) *A very high rate of income tax may encourage people to carry out services for themselves* rather than hire someone to do them. For example, if it would cost £10 labour expenses to hire someone to carry out minor house repairs and the house-owner's marginal rate of income tax is 60 per cent, it may be worth while for the owner to carry out the repairs himself, since the true labour cost of these repairs is £4 (whereas it would cost him £10 to hire someone). It is possible that a high rate of marginal income tax, combined with the effect of VAT on materials, may also lead to the growth of a 'black economy'.

4. Direct taxes

(a) *Types of direct tax*

i. Income tax

Direct taxation includes *income tax.* Income-tax systems are usually, as in the United Kingdom, *progressive*. This means that, in general, people on higher incomes pay proportionately more than those on lower incomes. In the United Kingdom this is achieved partly through personal allowances, whereby people on very low incomes do not pay any income tax. Beyond this there is a marginal rate of tax, which in 1988 was 25 per cent for the majority of taxpayers. The 'pay-as-you-earn' principle, which applies to most income taxpayers (but not the self-employed), means that it is comparatively easy to pay. Different taxes may sometimes be imposed on unearned income such as commercial rents.

Income tax accounted for about 25 per cent of the public sector's receipts in 1985.

ii. Corporation tax

Corporation tax is levied on companies' profits. Until 1972 there was a higher tax on distributed than on undistributed profits within the United

Kingdom. The effect of this was to make it more difficult for the smaller, growing firm to be able to obtain capital.

It has sometimes been claimed that if there is a high rate of corporation tax, many owner-managers prefer to spend money within the firm for their own benefit rather than to have more profits, on which tax is levied.

iii. Capital gains tax
Capital gains tax was originally introduced in the 1960s on speculative gains, but has since had much wider coverage. The logic behind capital gains tax seemed to be to close a loophole in the system, since previously people who invested in shares from which they received dividends were taxed, whereas people who invested in shares which showed capital gains were not taxed. Some critics have suggested that the system would be improved, or at least be made more equitable, if exemptions were given for capital gains below the rate of inflation. However, this ignores the point that dividends may also be below the rate of inflation and yet still be taxed.

A number of items are exempt from capital gains tax, notably owner-occupied first houses. This has perhaps distorted investment, since for many people it has become more worth while to buy an expensive house, which is free from capital gains tax, than to invest in shares or unit trusts, etc.

iv. Inheritance tax
Inheritance tax (which was formerly known as *capital transfer tax*) replaced estate duty. Whereas estate duty was only payable on property left at death, inheritance tax is payable if large sums of money are paid from one person to another a number of years before death. It could be made more progressive if the Chancellor imposed the tax upon the recipient rather than on the donor: at present a poor recipient has to pay the same rate of inheritance tax on a given sum as a wealthy recipient.

(b) *Advantages of direct taxes*

(i) They tend to be *progressive* and so to reduce inequalities in wealth.

(ii) They *reduce* purchasing power rather than increase prices and tend, therefore, to be *non-inflationary*.

(iii) *Tax liability is fairly easily calculated.*

(iv) *Revenue is guaranteed*, as the supply of labour, for example, is fairly inelastic.

5. Indirect taxes

(a) *Types of indirect tax*

i. Value added tax

An example of an indirect tax in the United Kingdom is that of *value added tax* (VAT). This is levied on a wide range of goods and services, currently at the rate of 15 per cent. Some goods are zero-rated, although in mid 1988 press reports suggested that some items on which the tax had not previously been paid would soon incur VAT. Thus, in particular, fears were expressed about VAT being levied on books. Value added tax is levied at all stages of production, unlike purchase tax (which VAT replaced), which was levied at the wholesale stage of production. The administrative costs of VAT are much higher.

The logic of levying taxes on both services and goods is that there seems to be no reason, in principle, why for example, if one watches football on television, the television should be subject to VAT, while watching live football is not taxed (as was the case under the previous purchase tax system).

It is sometimes claimed that value added tax is *more regressive* than purchase tax, since everyone has to pay and the poor pay proportionally as much as people in higher income brackets. However, this depends on how VAT is levied. For example, if higher rates of VAT were imposed upon luxury goods than upon necessities, then the tax would be made more progressive; alternatively, goods and services which the poor are more likely to purchase than the rich could be made exempt from VAT.

Because value added tax is a wide-ranging tax, it probably has relatively little effect on the allocation of resources. However, when, for example, VAT was levied on building repairs in 1984, it had the effect of making do-it-yourself services cheaper relative to the cost of contracting outsiders. Therefore, it may have had the marginal effect of raising unemployment. As the tax is not levied on very small firms, employment in small firms may be increased at the expense of employment in larger firms. One important consequence of VAT is that, if the government decided to increase indirect taxes rather than direct taxation, this would have an immediate inflationary effect.

ii. Duties on petrol, alcohol and tobacco

In the United Kingdom there are usually *separate taxes on petrol, alcohol and tobacco*, though the principle here is not different from that of value added tax. Taxes on tobacco and alcohol are high, partly because it is assumed that they are price inelastic and partly because of the desire to deter the purchase of such commodities. (The Royal College of Physicians' report on *Smoking or Health* shows that a large number of people in the United Kingdom die each year from illnesses related to smoking.)

iii. Vehicle excise duty

Another important tax which is an indirect tax is *vehicle excise duty*. This is currently levied at a flat rate and in 1988 it was £110 per vehicle. This again seems slightly regressive, and it could be made more progressive, for example by levying it according to the length of vehicle or cubic capacity, since, in general, it might be assumed that higher-income groups would buy bigger vehicles.

(b) *Specific taxes and* ad valorem *taxes*

Taxes on goods or services, i.e. *expenditure taxes*, can usually be said to be either *specific* or *ad valorem*.

(i) *Specific taxes* are levied in terms of a fixed amount of money upon a particular good or service. They fail to take account of the quality and pre-tax market price of the product. Excise duties on alcohol, tobacco and petrol are examples of specific taxes. If a tax of £1 is levied upon each bottle of wine, the cheapest, poorest quality wine is taxed as heavily as the most expensive, highest quality wine. Similarly, the television licence and the vehicle excise duty are specific taxes: the vehicle excise duty takes no account of the type of the car nor of the amount of use.

(ii) *Ad valorem taxes* are levied as a percentage. For example, the current rate of VAT is 15 per cent. Therefore, those goods and services with the highest market value pay a higher amount of tax in monetary terms than those goods and services with the lowest market value.

Ad valorem taxes are responsive to inflation, whereas specific taxes are not. Thus, when the market price of a good or service rises because of inflation, the Exchequer receives a higher monetary sum than before if the tax levied upon it is an *ad valorem* tax.

(c) *Advantages of indirect taxes*

(i) From the government's point of view, indirect taxes have the merit of being perhaps *less noticeable than direct taxes* such as income tax: most people are unaware, for example, just how much tax they are paying when they buy a gallon of petrol. This is an advantage to the government, but a disadvantage to the consumer.

(ii) Indirect taxes tend to be *fairly quick regulators of the economy*, since the government can alter the rates fairly quickly: downwards if it wishes to stimulate the economy; upwards if it wishes to deflate the economy or a part of it. However, because value added tax is levied at different stages of production, it is generally more difficult administratively to alter the rate quickly than it was with the former purchase tax.

(iii) Indirect taxes can be used to *discourage the consumption of 'harmful' goods or of imports.*

(iv) *Tax evasion is difficult* on goods (this is probably less true of services).

6. Local government revenue

(a) *Rates*

Rates are based upon the hypothetical value of rent obtained. The rateable value of a property depends partly upon its size, the age of the property and its location. Rates are advantageous to local authorities in that *revenue is certain* (except where the property is empty) and the *administrative costs are low.*

Rates do have a degree of *unfairness* about them. For example, *the ability to pay is ignored,* although generally richer people have bigger, more expensive houses with higher rateable values. Also, property values quickly get out of date and *the rate payable may not truly reflect the market value of the property.* Rates are also criticized for *not taking full account of who makes the most use of the services provided by the local authority.* Individuals between the ages of eighteen and thirty tend to use these services a lot, but many of these people are not houseowners and so are not directly rate-payers. It is also claimed that *rates provide a disincentive to improve property,* since the property might, after improvement, have a higher rateable value.

Rates are payable on work premises as well as on houses. During periods of recession, firms in the most depressed areas are the most likely to go bankrupt or move away, reducing the revenue of local authorities in such areas.

(b) *Alternative sources of local government revenue*

Many alternative sources of revenue to replace rates have been suggested over the years.

(i) A *local income tax* would be more progressive than the rating system, but the administrative costs would probably be high and the tax would not necessarily fall most heavily on those who use the services the most. Also, there is the problem of deciding which area does the taxing, i.e. whether the tax is levied by the authority in which the person concerned is resident or whether the tax is levied by the authority responsible for the area in which the person concerned works, where these two areas are different. Also, some people work in more than one area.

(ii) A *local sales tax* would have high administrative costs and, once again, there is the problem that it would not necessarily reflect who uses the services provided by local authorities the most. It would probably prove regressive and, anyway, there is already VAT on a wide range of goods and services.

(iii) A *local poll tax* (which is levied equally on each adult in the area) has been given serious consideration recently as an alternative source of local government revenue. A poll tax, though, would be very regressive because of the fixed rate. In 1988 the government legislated for this system, to be called the community charge.

(iv) *Vehicle excise duty* is collected locally on behalf of the central government, and it has been suggested that some or all of this money could instead go to the local authorities. However, this duty has a fixed rate and so is regressive. Also, the fact that it has a fixed rate means that when there is inflation the real value of the duty falls. If the duty charged was not the same in each area there would be the problem of where to register the vehicle. A system of local authorities raising revenue from vehicle excise duty also has the major disadvantage that the richer authorities, where there are most cars per head, would gain at the expense of the poorer authorities.

(v) Alternatively, local authorities could place a *tax upon the services* they provide so that tax is paid on use. However, some services, such as medical services, may be required most by those who are least able to pay for them. Also, many services, such as the provision of open spaces, are collective goods, and it is difficult to prevent people from using such facilities without paying, i.e. there is the problem of free-riding.

Table 20. Finances of the public sector (£bn)

Receipts		1985/86 estimate, Budget 1986
Income tax		35.6
Corporation tax, excluding North Sea oil		8.4
Capital taxes		2.5
Expenditure taxes		56.6
of which: VAT	19.3	
local authority		
rates	13.7	
petrol	6.5	
alcohol	4.2	
tobacco	4.3	
others	8.6	
North Sea oil		10.1
Total taxes and royalties		113.1
National insurance and other contributions		24.3
Interest and dividend receipts		6.4
Gross trading surpluses and rent		2.9
Other		2.9
General government receipts		149.6

Source: *Financial Statement and Budget Report, 1986–87*, HMSO, March 1986.

(c) *Other current sources of local-government revenue*

Rates, or poll tax, are not the only source of revenue for local authorities.

(i) There is the *rate support grant* from central government. However, there is a policy of *rate-capping* by the Thatcher government, whereby it lays down a limit to the rates each local authority is allowed to charge; if a local authority charges a higher rate than this, it is liable to have its grant from central government stopped.

(ii) Local authorities obtain some revenue from *loans* from various sources.

(iii) Local authorities make *direct charges for some of the services they provide*.

Table 21. Local authority receipts (£bn)

	1985/86 estimate, Budget 1986
Rates (net of rate rebates)	13.7
Rate support grant	11.2
Other grants from central government	9.6
Other	5.1
Total receipts	39.6

Source: *Financial Statement and Budget Report, 1986–87*, HMSO, March 1986.

QUESTION

What are the merits and demerits of income tax?

Income tax tends to be progressive since the highest wage earners pay the highest rates of income tax, whereas the very lowest paid workers pay no income tax. As well as paying no income tax, the lowest wage earners receive means-tested benefits. One serious disadvantage of this system of benefits is that it is all or nothing: a low-wage earner may receive a pay rise of just a couple of pounds which takes him above the income-tax threshold, so that he has to start paying income tax and he loses a large number of benefits; as a result, he becomes worse off than he was before receiving the wage increase. To try to prevent this 'poverty trap' a system of gradually decreasing benefits and gradually rising income tax has been advocated to replace the 'all-or-nothing' system (see Chapter 23).

The progressive nature of income tax (the fact that as a person's income rises, his rate of income tax rises) may be a disincentive to work harder. Furthermore, a rise in the marginal rate of income tax may make work a less attractive proposition, encouraging individuals to spend less time at work and more time pursuing leisure activities; on the other hand, a rise in the marginal rate of income tax may lead to individuals working harder and working longer hours in order to receive the same level of income as before the income-tax increase.

Very high rates of income tax might encourage people to look for benefits in kind rather than for additional direct income. This is one of the reasons why company cars are a very common form of perk, since the taxpayer pays less, generally, on these benefits than if he were to receive the equivalent amount in cash. Other methods of tax avoidance include 'moonlighting'.

None the less, income tax does have the advantage to the government of a high yield: the supply of labour tends to be inelastic. It also has the advantage that the Chancellor is able to estimate fairly precisely the likely revenue from income tax.

MULTIPLE-CHOICE QUESTIONS

1. If income-tax thresholds remain unchanged during a period of inflation and income distribution remains unaltered, this will result in which of the following:
   - (*a*) the Chancellor of the Exchequer receiving a higher proportion of total incomes;
   - (*b*) the Chancellor of the Exchequer receiving a lower proportion of total incomes;
   - (*c*) the Chancellor of the Exchequer receiving the same proportion of total incomes?

Answer – (*a*)

2. Which of the following would be *least* likely to produce an immediate inflationary effect:
   - (*a*) a rise in prescription charges;
   - (*b*) an extension of value added tax to cover items previously exempted;
   - (*c*) a higher rate of tax imposed upon future pensions;
   - (*d*) an increase in taxation of vehicles?

Answer – (*c*)

3. If the income tax payable by a household with a gross income of £10,000 is £1,000 and the same household would pay £1,300 upon a household income of £11,000, the marginal rate of tax is:
   - (*a*) 12 per cent;
   - (*b*) 30 per cent;
   - (*c*) 10 per cent.

Answer – (*b*)

4. If a specific rate of tax imposed on tobacco is unchanged, increases in the prices of cigarettes due to inflation will bring in more revenue to the Chancellor of the Exchequer.

(*a*) True.

(*b*) False.

Answer – (*b*)

5. If an *ad valorem* rate of tax is applied and prices rise because of inflation, the Chancellor of the Exchequer will receive:

(*a*) a higher proportion of total income;

(*b*) an unchanged proportion of total income;

(*c*) a decreased proportion of total income.

Answer – (*b*)

DATA RESPONSE

Immediately before the Budget in 1985 there were suggestions that there should be taxation on banks, particularly in view of the large profits which they had made. These arose partly because of the high level of interest rates, which had been imposed in order to stabilize the value of the pound. Banks' profits were, therefore, regarded partly as windfall profits, on which a tax could be imposed without any effects on the efficiency of banks, and which would generally be less unpopular than taxing pensions funds, which was also suggested.

The Chancellor of the Exchequer could, perhaps, have gone further in taxing financial services. This again might be more popular politically than extending value added tax (as when it was extended to takeaway meals in 1984, which was generally thought to be a regressive measure).

(*a*) What is meant by windfall profits and why might a tax on banks have little effect on efficiency?

(*b*) What problems might occur with having value added tax on financial services? Why might it be more progressive than value added tax generally imposed?

(*c*) In 1981 the selective excess profits tax introduced in the United Kingdom, and fixed at 2½ per cent of the tax base rate, was criticized as being 'retrospective'. What is meant by such a term? What are the disadvantages of retrospective taxation?

(*d*) Some economists have suggested that an excess profits tax should not be applied, since higher profits may not be excessive. How can one determine the truth or otherwise of such a statement?

SELF-EXAMINATION QUESTIONS

1. What are the potential advantages of index-linking tax thresholds? What are the disadvantages?

Masterstudies: Economics

2. What are the merits of a tax system which taxes both businesses and individuals?

3. What would be the advantages of a wealth tax, which was suggested in the 1970s? What problems might occur imposing such a tax?

4. What advantages and disadvantages might there be in having a tax paid by individuals when receiving capital rather than the present system of gift taxes which are imposed upon the size of the estate?

5. It is sometimes suggested that, during inflation, capital gains tax is imposed upon illusory gains. What is meant by such a statement?

17. Money and monetary policy

1. The qualities of money

(i) Money needs to be *durable*. Therefore, coins made from metal have been developed in place of less durable commodities which have been used as currency, such as livestock.

(ii) A note or coin also needs to be *divisible* in order that part of it may be spent now and part of it later.

(iii) Coins of little face value tend to be made of bronze and silver rather than gold so that *the cost of production of each coin does not exceed its face value.*

(iv) In order to have value, money needs to be *fairly scarce*. Metals such as gold and silver have often been used to make coins.

(v) There is also the need for money to be *uniform* so that it can be recognized and *generally accepted* for what it is.

(vi) Also, money needs to be *portable*.

These are all *qualities* which money should possess so that it can perform the *functions* of money.

2. The functions of money

(a) *A medium of exchange*

One of the main functions of money is as a *medium of exchange*. While one can have a bartering system (this still exists in some primitive societies, as well as in some international trade), bartering needs a *double coincidence of wants*. This means that a firm or country wishing to sell grain and buy cars has to find someone wishing both to sell cars and to purchase grain. The existence of money tends to reduce the time required to obtain information about possible purchasers and sellers: *money simplifies the system of exchange* (the complicated trans-action of finding someone with cars to sell in exchange for grain is replaced by two simple transactions, i.e. the sale of grain to one person and the purchasing of cars (from someone else). The existence of *money reduces the costs of searching* for someone with whom one can exchange.

(b) *A store of value*

The breaking down of exchange into two separate transactions (namely, selling and purchasing) means that *the two transactions can be carried out at different times*. The advantage here is that an individual does not have to decide what to purchase when he sells his commodity. Thus, *decisions can be put off*. This function of money (i.e. *as a store of value*) is a very useful function. For example, under a bartering system an individual might exchange some grain he has for a pig, with the intention of consuming it in the future; if, however, he is in the meantime converted to Judaism, the pig will become useless to him. Decisions to purchase a particular commodity should, therefore, be put off for as long as possible, because *information about the future is imperfect* (i.e. *the future is uncertain*).

(c) *A unit of account*

Money is also used as a *unit of account: prices of goods and services can be compared in terms of money*. However, in times of inflation, especially hyper-inflation, this function might prove a difficult one for money to perform. Money's function as a store of value might also be less effective in such circumstances.

(d) *A standard for deferred payments*

Money can also perform the function of a *standard for deferred payments*, whereby a deal might be struck today, but payment does not have to be made straight away. Money provides a standard by which future payments can be measured.

The function of a standard for deferred payments may be treated as a separate function of money, but it is commonly included within the three previous functions.

3. The importance of confidence in money

In most Western societies, the main forms of money have little *intrinsic* worth but are '*token*' forms of money. Most money in the UK is in the form of notes or coins which have little or no intrinsic worth. What is meant when it is said that notes and coins have little intrinsic worth is that they are only worth the paper or metal they are printed on. Thus, the face value of these notes and coins is generally much higher than the value of the metal or paper used. These notes and coins are accepted for their face value only because there is *confidence* in them. However, for a long time (even after the 1844 changes in the Bank of England) notes and coins had to be nearly fully backed by the amount of gold which was available in the Bank of England. However, in 1844 the concept of *fiduciary issue* came about. *Fiduciary issue means that notes and coins are issued without being fully backed by gold or silver*, the issuing of notes and coins being reliant upon faith in the institution.

For England and Wales, the Bank of England has a monopoly of the issue of cash, to try to prevent the over-issuing of notes and coins without the backing of gold, whereby confidence in money would be lost. However, there are a few Scottish banks which issue their own notes.

Without confidence, bank deposits (see below) would not be accepted as money because they are not *legal tender*. Where money is legal tender, it *has* to be accepted in payment for goods or services. Some coins are legal tender up to a certain limit, but above these limits they can be refused, as can bank deposits, as payment in transaction.

4. Definitions of money supply

While it might seem easy to define money, modern society has made it increasingly difficult. However, the rise of monetarism has made it particularly important to be able to define money: with governments trying to control the money supply we need to know just what it is they are trying to control. Cash and current accounts are usually considered to be money, but in some definitions of money, bank deposit accounts are not counted. Similarly, building-society deposits are not usually regarded as money. A common argument against including deposit accounts and building-society deposits in the definition of money is that these deposits earn interest and that money should be held for what it is and should not require some other incentive such as interest. However, with an increasing number of cheques being issued by building societies, it is becoming increasingly difficult to distinguish between building-society deposits and current accounts; building-society deposits are able to circulate more and more freely as mediums of exchange.

Similarly, credit cards are not usually included as part of the money supply even though they are widely accepted as a means of obtaining a good or service.

It is clear that there are a number of different definitions of money. Below we give details of some of the most important.

(i) One of the most commonly quoted definitions of money is the *M1 definition of money stock*. This is a *narrow* definition of money. *M1 is the sum of notes and coins in public circulation plus private-sector 'sight' deposits or current accounts* (*i.e. those deposits which can be withdrawn on demand*) *at UK banks*. Those sight deposits which earn interest are included in this definition.

(ii) Another common definition of money, which is also known as a *money stock definition*, is *sterling M3* (*£M3*). This is the *broad* definition of money. *£M3 is the sum of notes and coins in public circulation plus all sterling deposits held by UK residents in the private sector*. Thus, *£M3 equals M1 plus private-sector sterling time-deposits* (*i.e. deposits which can be withdrawn only after having given some notice*) *at UK banks*. It should be noted that the government changed the definition of £M3 at the start of the 1984/5 financial year: previously £M3 had also included all public-sector sterling deposits at UK banks.

(iii) *Domestic Credit Expansion* (*DCE*) looks at the credit which is generated within the economy. *DCE is approximately equal to the increase in £M3 plus the balance of payments deficit* (*or minus the BOP surplus*). DCE is used to measure a *flow*, whereas £M3 is used to measure a stock. The *change* in £M3, rather than its level, is included in the definition of DCE because a stock cannot be used to measure a flow.

DCE might be regarded as a better indication of monetary policy than a definition of the money stock because a policy which allows a large BOP deficit to achieve a fall in the money supply is shown up in the DCE measure.

(iv) As part of its Medium Term Financial Strategy (see section 7), in 1984 the Conservative government introduced an even narrower definition of money than M1: *M0*, which is known as the *monetary base*. *M0 is the sum of cash in banks' tills plus deposits with the Bank of England plus currency in public circulation. M0 is virtually only notes and coins in circulation* because notes and coins in circulation form 90 per cent of M0.

5. The demand for money

According to Keynes, money is demanded for three purposes: (a) *trans-*

actions; (b) *precaution*; (c) *speculation*. When Keynes talked about money in these terms he was really referring to notes and coins in people's pockets and bank accounts. He said that people held money in order to carry out transactions, to hedge against risks and/or to take risks.

(a) *The transactionary demand for money*

Money held to make *transactions* is simply money held to pay for those goods and services an individual expects to pay for between receiving one pay packet and the next. Such expenditures include food, rent and the train fare to work.

The demand for money for transactionary purposes depends upon: (i) *the level of the individual's income*; (ii) *payment conventions*; (iii) *transactions costs*.

(i) *The higher a person's income, the smaller the proportion of his income he is likely to require for transactionary purposes*, but a person on a high income is likely to have a higher absolute demand for money for transactions than someone on a low income. Thus, someone earning £100 per week might demand £75 per week (i.e. 75 per cent of his income) for transactionary purposes, while someone earning £200 per week might use £100 (i.e. 50 per cent of his income) for transactionary purposes.

(ii) By quoting an example, we can show how *payment conventions* might affect the transactionary demand for money. If we assume that a person makes transactions at a constant daily rate, that he has an income of £100 per week and that he holds £70 for transactionary purposes, we can say that he spends £10 per day on transactions and that the average amount of money he holds for transactionary purposes is £35, i.e. the amount of money he holds for transactionary purposes in the middle of the week. If the individual is paid monthly rather than weekly, with a wage of £400 per month, assuming that he spends £10 per day on transactions, the amount of money he holds for transactionary purposes on average is £140, i.e. the amount of money he holds for transactionary purposes in the middle of the month. The individual's demand for money for transactionary purposes, therefore, appears to be different under different payment conventions.

(iii) *If there were no transactions costs, there would be no need to hold money at all for transactionary purposes:* goods and services could be purchased without time or effort. Therefore, it would pay an individual to transfer his money into gilt-edged securities (which are not money under any accepted definition of money) and transfer the gilt-edged securities back into money when he wants to make a transaction. This way he would earn interest on his money. If 'money' in a building-society account is not defined as money and there are no transaction costs in physically depositing and withdrawing money from a building society, an individual could put the money which he requires for transactionary purposes into a building society and withdraw it when required and he would be said to hold no money for transactionary purposes.

Once an individual has put aside the money he demands for transactionary purposes, he might use any income he has left over to speculate or for precautionary purposes. Alternatively, he might use it to buy gilt-edged securities or he might put it in a building society, in which case it might not be known as money at all.

(b) *The precautionary demand for money*

Individuals are likely to be *averse to risk* and will wish to hold some money for *emergency* use, to purchase goods and services which they do not normally purchase during the week. Such commodities may include clothes and washing-machines.

While money spent on petrol for travelling to work each day is money required for transactions, the money for purchasing a new car battery is money which is required for emergencies (money which is demanded for *precautionary* reasons).

An individual may decide that money he is intending to use for precautionary purposes can be transferred into gilt-edged securities. If he does this, this 'money' is no longer defined as 'money' until it is transferred back into money in his pocket. Alternatively, the individual may decide to keep this 'money' in a building society, in which case once again (under most definitions of money) it is not defined as money. The demand for money for transactionary plus precautionary purposes is sometimes called the demand for *active balances*.

(c) *The speculative demand for money*

Money may also be held for *speculative* (or *passive* reasons). The demand for money for speculative reasons is sometimes called the demand for *idle balances*.

Individuals who have some *preference for risk* might decide to hold money for speculative purposes in the hope of making a profitable return, i.e. they might decide to hold money with which to purchase physical

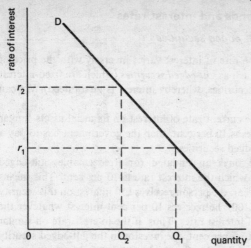

Figure 53. *The demand for money*

assets, such as works of art or property, which they hope to sell in the future for a profit.

Keynes said that individuals with some preference for risk will (after allowance has been made for their transactionary and precautionary demand for money) either hold any money left over for speculative purposes or buy bonds (which are not money).

If interest rates are rising, then the price of bonds is falling, (since the price of bonds is defined as being inversely related to interest rates (see Section 6), so that (other things being equal) individuals will buy more bonds and hold less money for speculative purposes. If, however, interest rates are very low, bond prices are very high and there is more incentive to speculate: the *opportunity cost* of this action is not very high, since buying bonds is not a very attractive proposition.

It should be noted that affluent individuals are likely to have more preference for risk (i.e. less aversion to risk) than poor people and are, therefore, likely to have a greater speculative demand for money, other things being equal.

From what we have said, it should be clear that *the higher the rate of interest, the lower the demand for money*, other things being equal.

6. Government bonds and interest rates

(a) *Irredeemable gilt-edged securities*

We have said that the rate of interest varies inversely with the price of government bonds, such as *gilt-edged securities* (which are fixed-interest British government securities, whereby interest is guaranteed). We can show why this is.

If, for example, the current rate of interest on financial assets similar to gilt-edged securities is 10 per cent, then the government has to pay a similar rate on gilt-edged securities.

Suppose someone buys an undated (or irredeemable) gilt-edged security for £100 on which the interest rate is 10 per cent. This means that each and every year, the person receives £10 interest on this security (i.e. 10 per cent of £100): he receives 10 per cent interest whatever the general movement of interest rates. Thus, if the interest rate on similar financial assets falls to 5 per cent, the investor in the gilt-edged security will still receive £10, while other financial assets are only paying interest of £5 on a £100 investment. Given that the highest available interest payment on a £100 investment in any asset other than a government bond is only £5 (i.e. 5 per cent of £100), new investors would be willing to pay up to £200 for gilt-edged securities paying 10 per cent interest.

If, however, the general rate of interest rises to 20 per cent (while gilt-edged securities priced at £100 are only paying 10 per cent interest), new investors will not be attracted to buy these existing irredeemable gilt-edged securities unless their price falls to £50.

Investors who bought £100 of war loans in the immediate post-war period at an interest rate of $2\frac{1}{2}$ per cent find that (because they are of fixed interest) they are only receiving £2.50 interest per year from their initial investment of £100.

(b) *Redeemable gilt-edged securities*

If a redeemable gilt-edged stock has one year to run, an investor who is considering buying it will consider whether, by purchasing it, he will make a capital gain or a capital loss.

If the security was originally issued for £100 and the nominal rate of interest (which is fixed) is 10 per cent, but the price has now fallen to £98, an investor who purchases the bond at the price of £98 will receive in this year before redemption an interest payment of £10 (i.e. 10 per cent on the initial £100) plus the £2 capital gain (i.e. the price of £100 at which the security was originally issued minus the price of £98 which he paid for the security). Thus, he receives £12, which means that the current yield is $\frac{£12}{£98} \times 100 = 12.2$ per cent (approx).

7. The Medium Term Financial Strategy

The Chancellor of the Exchequer announced in the 1980 Budget the government's intention of adopting the *Medium Term Financial Strategy* (*MTFS*), the main aim of which was to reduce the growth of the money supply. Control of the money supply was seen as an instrument for achieving the objective of reducing inflation, but control of the money supply is seen as an objective in its own right as well.

The adoption of the MTFS required the government to have a clearly defined definition of money, so that it could trace its progress in reducing the growth of the money supply. The definition of money supply the government adopted as its target of control was *Sterling M3* (*£M3*). The £M3 definition of money was, at that time, notes and coins in circulation plus all sterling deposits held by both the private and public sectors in UK banks.

(a) *How did the government attempt to reduce the growth of the amount of money in the economy?*

(i) The government's adoption of the MTFS was based on the *belief that the growth of the money supply is the most important determinant of inflation.* Therefore, the government attempted to reduce the growth of money in the economy mainly by *attempting to reduce the growth of the money supply.* The Chancellor announced gradually diminishing target growth rates for £M3 in the March 1980 Budget. These target growth rates were as follows: for 1980/81 the target band was between 7 and 11 per cent; for 1981/2 it was between 6 and 10 per cent; for 1982/3 it was between 5 and 9 per cent; for 1983/4 it was between 4 and 8 per cent.

Reducing the growth of the money supply has the effect of forcing interest rates upwards. In the diagram below (Figure 54) we show that a fall in the growth of the supply of money from Q_1 to Q_2 results in interest rates rising from r_1 to r_2.

(ii) However, the government did not want the burden of a falling growth of money supply to fall completely upon interest rates. *The government, therefore, decided that it would also attempt to reduce the demand for money.*

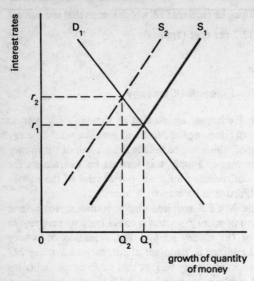

Figure 54. *The effect of a fall in the growth of the supply of money*

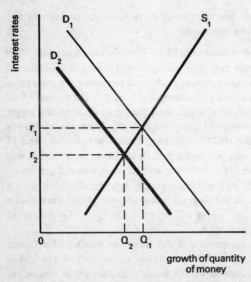

Figure 55. *The effect of reducing the demand for money*

By reducing both the growth of the money supply and the demand for money, the government hoped to reduce the growth of money without interest rates rising too much.

(b) *How did the government attempt to reduce its demand for money?*

The government attempted to *restrict its demand for money by cutting the Public Sector Borrowing Requirement (PSBR)*. This basically involved the government *cutting public expenditure*. The government announced declining targets for PSBR, but was prepared to allow PSBR to fluctuate from these targets whenever the pattern of economic activity made this necessary.

The targets for PSBR as a percentage of GDP announced in the 1980 Budget were as follows: 1980/81, $3\frac{3}{4}$; 1981/2, 3; 1982/3, $2\frac{1}{4}$; 1983/4, $1\frac{1}{2}$.

(c) *How did the government attempt to control the money supply?*

(i) The government attempted to control the supply of money in a number of ways, the most basic and most central to the government's plans being *a reduction in the printing of notes and coins, to reduce the growth of the number of notes and coins in public circulation*.

(ii) *Selling securities on the open market (open-market operations) by the Bank of England was encouraged by the government in an attempt to control money in UK banks*.

These securities (which are not defined as money) are bought by commercial banks, financial institutions and companies. Particularly important to the government in its attempt to control money was the concern that commercial banks should buy these securities because, in the act of buying these securities, cheques are drawn on the buyer. Thus, when the buyer is a commercial bank, the drawing of cheques reduces its deposits at the Bank of England and, thus, the commercial bank's cash reserves are reduced. The Bank of England then is able to withdraw this 'money' from the money supply.

The selling of government securities is the main way the government finances the Public Sector Borrowing Requirement: in 1979 the selling of government securities financed 69.7 per cent of PSBR. This method of financing PSBR is claimed to be non-inflationary: it does not add to the money supply; indeed, the more PSBR is financed by the selling of government securities, the more the growth of £M3 is reduced (hence the government's desire to increase the sale of securities). However, the logic of the argument depends partly upon who buys the securities: the bank or the non-bank sector.

(d) *Why did £M3 exceed its target rate?*

During the first year of MTFS, despite the fact that monetary policy was undoubtedly tight, £M3 grew much faster than the government's target for it. Between February 1980 and April 1981 £M3 grew by 18 per cent.

(i) Among the reasons for £M3 growth greatly exceeding the target path for it was *the presence of several 'distortions' to £M3* caused by, for example, the ending of exchange controls in 1979, the raising of VAT to 15 per cent in 1980 and the monetary changes of 1981.

Other money supply definitions, such as M1, appeared to give a clearer indication of the tightness of monetary policy: M1 was growing more slowly than prices. However, the retail price index for 1980 was 18 per cent, so inflation was not under control. This suggests that distortions to £M3 were not the main reasons for £M3 greatly exceeding its target growth path.

(ii) Perhaps the main reason for £M3 exceeding its target growth path was *the rise in PSBR*. The forecast for PSBR made in the 1980 Budget was that it would be £8.5bn (3¾ per cent of GDP) for the financial year 1980/81. The actual PSBR for that period was £13.2bn (5¾ per cent of GDP). Thus, the greater than forecast rise in £M3 can be partly explained by a movement up the supply curve (i.e. an upward shift of the demand curve).

PSBR rose mainly because the government had to pay out more and more social security because of rising unemployment, while receiving less and less from taxes (also largely because of the rising unemployment). For 1986–7, the Chancellor, in his 1985 autumn statement, estimated that social security payments would account for 30 per cent of government expenditure.

Given that monetary policy was tight, the actual effect upon money supply of the government's monetary and fiscal policies during the period 1980/81 was something like that shown in Figure 56 opposite. This diagram is perhaps a fair appraisal of the actual outcome of the government's policy for much of its Medium Term Financial Strategy, with the supply of money being restricted but the government's demand for money being forced upwards by a rising PSBR (in 1979/80 PSBR was £9.9bn and for the 1980/81 financial year it was £13.3bn), despite the cutting of government expenditure on many items, particularly invest-

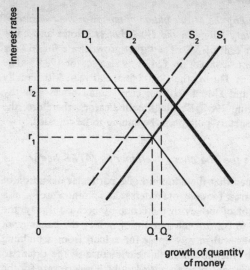

Figure 56. *The outcome of the MTFS over the first few years*

ment in sectors such as education. One outcome of this policy (evident in Figure 56) is the rise in interest rates. Interest rates in the early eighties were at their highest ever levels in real terms.

(e) *A revision of targets*

(i) Although the actual growth of £M3 in 1980/81 greatly exceeded the target for it, targets for £M3 were not revised in the *1981 Budget*: the target path for £M3 for 1981/2 remained at 6–10 per cent (it actually grew by 14½ per cent). However, *the projected path for PSBR was revised upwards*.

(ii) The fact that M1 had been giving a more encouraging picture of monetary tightness than £M3 led the government to abandoning the single definition of the money supply and to have targets for both M1 and £M3. *This multiple target approach was adopted in the 1982 Budget*.

However, the actual growth of M1 exceeded the target growth rate for 1982/3: M1 grew by 12.1 per cent (the target was 8–12 per cent). M1, like £M3, proved not to be a particularly good measure of the tightness of the government's monetary policy. By this time inflation was beginning to fall: in 1981 it was 11.9 per cent; in 1982, it was 8.6 per cent; in 1983 it was 4.6 per cent.

(iii) *M1 was replaced by the M0 definition of money as the measure of the tightness of monetary policy in the 1984 Budget.* Notes and coins make up about 90 per cent of M0. The target growth rate for M0 for 1984/5 was 4–8 per cent. A target for £M3 was also set for 1984/5. The target was 6–10 per cent. During the 1984/5 financial year, M0 actually grew by 5¾ per cent and £M3 by 10 per cent. Retail prices grew by about 5 per cent during 1984. By all three indicators, therefore, the actual tightness of monetary policy was beginning to be revealed.

(f) *How effective has the Thatcher government's MTFS been?*

It has often been argued that the adoption of a particular definition of money supply as the target for control renders that definition useless as a measure of the amount of money in the economy because if, say, the government attempts to control the amount of money the banks lend, people who want loans will merely apply for a loan from a building society. Therefore, in order to obtain a clear picture of the extent to which the government is controlling money supply, it is necessary for the government to adopt broader and broader definitions of the money supply. However, the Thatcher government has actually adopted narrower and narrower definitions of money supply. This can be explained partly by the fact that £M3 and M1, concentrating mainly on notes and coins in circulation, did not appear to reveal the true tightness of monetary policy. However, it might be argued that monetary base control enables the Bank of England to have a better chance of meeting targets, since all the components of M0, unlike, say, £M3, are directly under its control.

(i) By 1986, *targets for the growth of M0 were beginning to be met,* but originally (i.e. in the 1980 Budget) the government had hoped to have the growth of £M3 between 4 and 8 per cent by 1983/4.

(ii) In 1986, *monetary policy continued to be tight, so interest rates were still high, discouraging borrowing and, therefore, discouraging investment.*

(iii) *The government was unable to keep to the targets for PSBR it set in 1980.* PSBR was forecast to be 3¼ per cent of GDP during 1980/81, but was in fact 5¾ per cent. The forecast for 1983/4, made in 1980, was for PSBR to be 1½ per cent of GDP; it turned out to be 3¼ per cent of GDP. PSBR in 1983/4 was £9.7bn. PSBR rose to £10½bn during 1984/5, but was forecast in the March 1985 Budget to fall to £7bn. However, the forecast for 1985 was revised in the Chancellor's autumn statement to £8bn. The Chancellor blamed the upward revision of the PSBR forecast for 1985 upon lower sterling oil revenues than expected, but said that PSBR would be the smallest it had been, as a percentage of GDP, since 1971/2. The proceeds from privatization have meant that PSBR is lower than it might otherwise have been.

The PSBR remained higher than the government hoped largely because of the rise in social security the government had to pay and because there were fewer and fewer taxable assets. Similarly, money supply remained higher than the government wished because notes and coins were still required, to some extent, to finance PSBR.

*

QUESTION

Tight monetary policy tends to lead to high interest rates. What effects do high interest rates have on the economy?

The effects of monetary policy may have added considerably to the United Kingdom's National Debt charges, particularly for short-dated Treasury bills, though the Treasury may be reluctant to issue long-term gilt-edged stock at times of high real rates of interest. High interest rates tend to add considerable burdens to the public sector, including public utilities. For example, modern power stations cost large sums of money, for which finance has to be available through borrowing. High interest rates tend to affect adversely the price of gilt-edged stock (as interest rates rise so the price of bonds falls). For example, people who bought war loans at $2\frac{1}{2}$ per cent find the capital values falling as a result.

The problems are not confined to people who have invested in the public sector, since the price of preference shares will also fall if interest rates rise. The effects of higher interest rates, therefore, may mean that people will transfer assets from shares to bonds. These problems of income distribution are frequently ignored by many advocates of monetarist policy, even though they look very keenly at the redistributive effects caused by inflation. When testing whether or not such redistributive effects are desirable we might wish to consider who invests in fixed-income assets (such as preference shares, annuities and investment trusts) and who tends to borrow money, for example for buying houses.

Money restraint may also encourage people to switch between different types of assets according to changes in interest rates. This could lead to an increased velocity of circulation, which might be important when considering the underlying formula $MV = PT$. (See Chapter 19.)

We might also expect high interest rates to have a destabilizing effect

285

on the construction industry and this has been shown, to some extent, in the recession of the early 1980s.

One possible way of overcoming some of the problems mentioned would be to have much more index-linking, which would mean that people did not have to choose between long-term and short-term dated stock in order to avoid: (*a*) the problems of anticipating inflation; (*b*) the problems of anticipating future interest rates. It would also prevent both some of the redistributive effects of inflation and some of the problems of unanticipated changes in monetary policy.

MULTIPLE-CHOICE QUESTIONS

1. If the demand for money is perfectly interest inelastic (where the interest rate is defined as the price of money), then a rise in the rate of interest will:
   (*a*) increase the quantity of money demanded;
   (*b*) reduce the quantity of money demanded;
   (*c*) not affect the quantity of money demanded.
Answer – (*c*)

2. A government bond was bought for £100 and had a nominal interest rate of 5 per cent. If the price became £90 with one year to run, the current yield would be, to the nearest 5 per cent:
   (*a*) 5 per cent;
   (*b*) 10 per cent;
   (*c*) 15 per cent;
   (*d*) 20 per cent.
Answer – (*c*)

Explanation. The interest payment in the final year equals £5 (i.e. £100 × 5 per cent). There is also a capital gain of £10 (i.e. £100 − £90).

The current yield $= \dfrac{£15}{£90} \times 100 = 16\frac{2}{3}\%$.

3. If irredeemable gilt-edged securities were bought for £100 with a nominal interest rate of 10 per cent and their price is now £80, the current yield is:
   (*a*) 10 per cent;
   (*b*) 12½ per cent;
   (*c*) 15 per cent;
   (*d*) 20 per cent.
Answer – (*b*)

Explanation. The current yield $= \dfrac{£10}{£80} \times 100 = 12\frac{1}{2}\%$.

There is no capital gain because the securities are irredeemable.

4. A rise in interest rates will affect the market for gilt-edged securities by:
   (*a*) increasing price and yield;
   (*b*) increasing price and reducing yield;
   (*c*) reducing price and yield;
   (*d*) reducing price and increasing yield.
Answer – (*d*)

5. A tight monetary policy will lead to:
   (*a*) a rise in the price of bonds;
   (*b*) a fall in the price of bonds;
   (*c*) neither a rise nor a fall in in the price of bonds.
Answer – (*b*)

DATA RESPONSE

While some textbooks seem to suggest that the rate of interest is a quantity which can be easily ascertained, this is far from being the truth. For example, in November 1985, there was a wide variety of fairly safe forms of investment for investors which paid a wide variety of rates depending upon how quickly people wished to withdraw their money and upon whether the amounts were for regular or for lump-sum savings and personal taxation. Amongst the lowest rates paid for individuals who can claim the basic rate of tax (which was 30 per cent in 1985) are those for bank deposit accounts, which paid about 6 per cent in November 1985.

Those who deposit their money in current accounts generally receive no interest at all. However, people may feel that it is worth putting their money in a current account because it is easy to withdraw the money. While theoretically some interest is lost or seven days' notice is required in order to withdraw money from deposit accounts, in practice this may not necessarily be the case. National Savings Certificates (which can be withdrawn on demand) were being issued at a rate of return of about 8 per cent, although this depended on the certificates being held for five years.

British government stocks gave higher rates of return for the best short-dated stocks of approximately 8 per cent. The price was, of course, not guaranteed and tended to fluctuate in line with interest rates. Those who held British government stocks in late 1984 would have found that the violent fluctuations in interest rates in early 1985 could have meant that the price oscillated quite considerably. They could have put money into alternative assets, such as preference shares or debentures (where the rates of interest might generally be expected to be higher) or even into equities. The rates of these, of course, are more likely to be uncertain.

For borrowers, the rates of interest fluctuated considerably. Bank overdrafts were available in November 1985 at between 15 and 20 per cent for the typical borrower, although in exceptional circumstances this could have been less. Overdrafts, however, were not subject to tax relief, whereas bank ordinary loans charged slightly lower rates and were subject to tax relief, as were bank personal loans, though these are usually at a much higher rate of interest. Those who wish to borrow on their insurance policies generally find this a cheaper way to borrow (the rates were between 5 and 11 per cent in November 1985). These may be subject to tax relief depending upon the purpose of the loan, as with bank loans. Credit cards may be generally more convenient, but the rate of interest charged is very high (27 per cent in November 1985). Hire purchase is a very common method of borrowing although the rates again are very high, typically about 30 per cent. From this, it must be seen that to depict the rate of interest as something which is easily determined is, to say the least, an over-simplification.

(a) Explain, in the light of the above text, why savers might be willing to receive some of the lower interest payments mentioned rather than larger interest payments.

(b) Explain why the price of government stocks varies according to interest rates. Explain also why long-dated stocks generally fluctuate more in price than short-dated stocks.

(c) Why, if hire-purchase interest rates are usually very high and not subject to tax relief, do people use this method to borrow rather than obtain bank overdrafts or loans?

SELF-EXAMINATION QUESTIONS

1. How far is it true that the changing patterns of control of the money supply by the government reflect changing definitions of money in a modern society?

2. Does the introduction of the widespread use of credit cards mean that it is impossible to control money supply effectively?

3. The British government abolished most exchange controls in 1979. How, if at all, does this affect the problem of controlling money?

4. Lord Keynes suggested that the demand for money can be divided into the precautionary motive, the speculative motive and the transactions motive. How far is this still valid and what factors will affect the demand under each of these motives?

5. 'If the government is not careful, increases in money supply lead to speculation for goods and services rather than productive investment.' How far is this true?

18. Financial institutions and monetary control

1. Types of banks

The *1979 Banking Act* defined banks as either *recognized banks* or *licensed deposit-taking institutions*. Recognized banks have to offer a wider range of banking services than licensed deposit-taking institutions. The distinction is largely unimportant at this level, especially given that the distinction was reviewed in 1986.

(a) *The London clearing banks and the Bank of England*

The most important banks are the *London clearing banks and the Bank of England*, which is also defined as a *clearing bank*. The London clearing banks are all *commercial banks* (i.e. *their main aim is to make a profit*). The Bank of England, on the other hand, is not a commercial bank. The main London clearing banks are Barclays, Coutts, Lloyds, Midland, National Westminster, Williams and Glyns, and the National Girobank.

(b) *Other banks*

There are *other commercial banks which are not clearing banks*, such as the Trustee Savings Bank. The TSB already has a large number of customers (although, until its sale in October 1986, it did not have a proportionate amount of assets). In the future the TSB may also become one of the main clearing banks. At the time of writing, the status of the TSB is slightly different to that of the other commercial banks.

2. Functions of the London clearing banks

The London clearing banks carry out a very large percentage of their business within the UK. *At the end of each day transfers between the banks to settle net indebtedness is done through the London Clearing House.* Any deposits which are held by, say, Lloyds and owed to Barclays are weighed up against debts owed to Lloyds by Barclays and the net debt is transferred from the net debtor to the net creditor via the London

Clearing House. Because one clearing bank tends to have similar debts to the other banks, there is actually very little money transferred through the London Clearing House at the end of each day.

Since the London clearing banks are also commercial banks, it is important to note that *their main objective is to make profits for their owners. However, they are also interested in having some liquid assets* so that they can meet any likely demands on their liabilities. These two objectives usually conflict. Generally, *the shorter the loan, the greater the bank's liquidity but the smaller the rate of interest and the smaller the profit*. Notes and coins and balances at the Bank of England are examples of extremely liquid assets. They do not, however, earn interest. Conversely, long-term loans to customers and investments will tend to be very profitable, but are examples of fairly illiquid assets. The banks will, therefore, have to consider how much liquidity they need to be able to cover their day-to-day transactions, how much they may need within a period of, say, one year and how much can be advanced on a longer-term basis. It is usually unwise to borrow short and lend long, although, for various reasons, the building societies tend not to follow this rule.

3. Assets held by the London clearing banks

The London clearing banks tend to have their assets in a variety of forms.

(i) Some money is held as *cash in tills*.

(ii) Some money is *held at the Bank of England*. Money is kept at the Bank of England partly because the Bank of England acts as the banks' bank and partly because the Bank of England sometimes forces the banks to hold some of their assets there. Since 1981 about $\frac{1}{2}$ per cent of banks' assets have had to be held in special deposits at the Bank of England and these do not yield any interest.

(iii) Other money is in the form of *money at call or short notice*, which is usually lent to the *discount houses* (see section 6) at very low rates of interest. The clearing banks act quickly if they wish to recall money from the discount houses. Thus, this form of money is a very liquid asset.

(iv) Some money is *lent on discounted bills to central and local government and to industry*. This tends to yield a slightly higher interest rate than money at call or short notice, but less than *longer-term investments in government and local-authority stock*. The most profitable form of money of all is *advances to nationalized industries, private industry and households.*

(v) The London clearing banks will also have some money in *government stocks with one year or less to maturity.* Until 1981, this money formed part of eligible reserve assets. These stocks are very liquid. If the interest rates on these stocks were to rise, there could be small losses on these stocks to the banks. A rise in the interest rate of stocks with longer to run to maturity will lead to larger losses.

4. Sources of banks' assets

The banks obtain their assets from two main sources: (i) *current accounts* (*sometimes referred to as sight deposits*), which are withdrawable upon demand and which generally do not yield interest to the depositor; (ii) *time deposits*, the best known example of which is probably *deposit accounts.* There are, however, a number of different time deposits, including *wholesale deposits* for large sums of money, which yield much higher rates of interest. They may have time periods of from one week to over five years.

5. Creation of credit

Banks are not merely cloakrooms where money or assets are deposited: they can *create credit. The extent to which banks can create credit depends upon the ratios of cash which they may hold, either in their tills or at the central bank.* This may be determined by the central bank to some extent. For example, between 1972 and 1981 $12\frac{1}{2}$ per cent of a bank's *eligible assets* had to be held in *reserve.* However, the banks may have tended to hold more than just $12\frac{1}{2}$ per cent in reserve to ensure stability.

In the absence of government controls, we might assume that banks would keep 10 per cent of their total deposits in cash to cover any likely withdrawals. In practice, this has become the requisite sum.

If a firm *deposits* £100 in cash in the bank, a simplified balance-sheet will show that the bank's *liabilities* are £100, while the bank's *assets* are also £100, since this amount has been deposited and, thus, the bank has £100 in its till. Experience has shown banks that not all customers depositing money will require the withdrawal of their money at the same time. The bank can, therefore, lend other potential or existing customers more than £100 which it has in cash by the process of *credit creation*.

If the bank keeps 10 per cent of its eligible liabilities in reserve, it can lend £90 of the original £100, while keeping the other £10 in reserve as cash in tills. When this £90 is repaid to the bank by the borrower it is deposited in the bank. Of this £90 returned, the bank will keep £9, i.e. 10 per cent, in reserve and will lend the other £81. When this £81 is returned to the bank it in turn is deposited; 10 per cent will be kept in reserve and the other £72.90 lent. So this process of credit creation continues. It can be worked out that, from the initial deposit of £100, £900 can be created, while allowing for a 10 per cent reserve asset ratio. The formula for how much credit can be created from an original deposit is

$$\frac{(1 \times \text{deposit})}{r} - \text{deposit},$$

where r is the reserve asset ratio. For our example above, it can be seen, therefore, that the amount of credit that can be created is

$$\frac{(1 \times £100)}{10\%} - £100,$$

i.e. £900

The amount of money the bank has in terms of liabilities and assets equals

$$\frac{1 \times \text{deposits}}{r}.$$

In our example this amount is £1,000.

This process of credit creation is shown in Table 22.

6. Other money-market institutions

Money-market institutions are those institutions which buy and sell *short-term money*, whereas *capital-market institutions* are those institutions which buy and sell *long-term money*.

Commercial banks deal with both short-term and long-term money.

Table 22. Credit creation

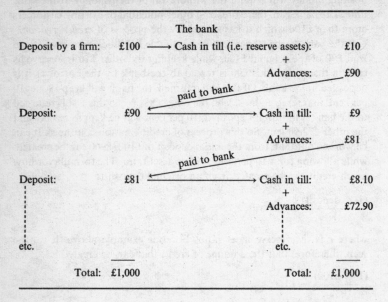

However, other institutions in the money market, such as *discount houses*, are exclusively money-market institutions.

(i) *Discount houses* are institutions (in fact public companies) within the *London discount market*. The *discount market is the market dealing in Treasury bills, commercial bills (or bills of exchange) and short-dated bonds.*

Discount houses buy bills of exchange at face value minus a *discount* (or rate of interest); they then resell them or hold on to them until maturity. The discount houses finance their purchases of bills of exchange mainly by borrowing short term from banks and other financial institutions and then selling securities at a slightly higher rate of interest (or discount). As a result of their activity, *discount houses provide a medium through which the Bank of England can influence the movement of interest rates.* During the 1970s discount houses were the main dealers in securities comprising *eligible reserve assets.* The *reserve asset ratio* was abolished in 1981 (see section 7).

(ii) *Accepting houses* are institutions which specialize in guaranteeing (*or accepting*) *bills of exchange* in return for a commission. Originally *merchant banks* carried out the function of accepting bills of exchange.

7. Monetary control by the Bank of England

(a) *The Minimum Lending Rate*

The rate of interest at which the Bank of England lends to the banking system was known as the *Bank Rate* until 1972. In 1972 the then Conservative government replaced the Bank Rate with the *Minimum Lending Rate* (*MLR*). It was intended as a means of controlling the money supply: a rise in MLR would tend to increase short-term interest rates, so reducing the demand for credit. The rate was meant to be determined by the market so that it would not be left to the Bank of England to determine interest rates: *MLR was, in theory, a market-determined interest rate*. In practice, however, the Bank of England has frequently intervened in interest rates. M L R was abolished in August 1981.

(b) *Special deposits*

The scheme of *special deposits* was introduced in 1958 and became effective in 1960. Special deposits are cash deposited at the Bank of England by the clearing banks in response to a special directive. The scheme was designed as a means of reducing clearing banks' *liquidity ratio* (i.e. the proportion of a bank's assets held in the form of cash and liquid assets), so reducing their ability to lend.

The special deposits scheme did not have much effect in reducing banks' ability to lend because they possessed reserves of liquid assets which they were able to lend instead.

(c) *The 1971 Competition and Credit Control Act*

It was clearly necessary, if there were to be controls on the creation of credit, for controls to be extended to cover a wider range of assets. The *1971 Competition and Credit Control* (*CCC*) *Act* replaced the special deposits scheme of liquidity control with a system of credit controls covering a wider range of assets. The liquidity ratio (of 28 per cent) was replaced by a $12\frac{1}{2}$ per cent *reserve asset ratio*. The CCC Act required that at least $12\frac{1}{2}$ per cent of each bank's *eligible deposit liabilities* had to be kept in reserve. *Eligible liabilities* consisted of *sterling deposits* and *certificates of overseas net liabilities*, whereas the liquidity ratio consisted of 'liquid' assets (i.e. money at call or at short notice and short-term bonds) and cash. *Cash in banks' tills and special deposits were excluded from the reserve asset ratio.* Under the CCC Act, $1\frac{1}{2}$ per cent of banks' eligible liabilities had to be kept in the form of *non-interest-bearing balances at the Bank of England.*

Another feature of the CCC Act was that *the range of banks controlled by the Bank of England was extended.* Prior to this only the London clearing banks were subject to control, while other banks were free to increase the creation of credit. Thus, prior to 1971 a number of *secondary banks* had emerged, which were able to take business away from the clearing banks. The Competition and Credit Control Act, as its name suggests, aimed to stimulate greater competition among banks, hence the extension of credit controls to more banks.

CCC consisted of indirect, rather than direct, government control over credit. For example, the MLR (introduced as a result of the CCC Act) was, in theory, market-determined. Essentially, CCC was designed to rely upon traditional techniques of *open-market operations*, with *reliance upon interest rates as a means of controlling credit.*

The money supply was not efficiently controlled by this system of indirect controls. As a result, there was recourse, from time to time, to more direct forms of control. For example, on a number of occasions MLR was fixed by administrative decisions rather than by the market and in 1973 a *supplementary special-deposits (SSD) scheme* was introduced.

The SSD scheme required those banks whose interest-bearing deposits grew faster than the prescribed rate to place non-interest-bearing deposits with the Bank of England. The faster banks' interest-bearing deposits grew in excess of the prescribed rate, the more deposits they had to make with the Bank of England. SSDs were called for not only in 1973, but also in 1976 and 1978.

The SSD scheme (which was also known as the '*corset*') led to *disinter-mediation*, i.e. financial institutions not subject to this scheme were able to increase their lending activities at the expense of banks. The problem of disintermediation had also applied to the special-deposits scheme.

(d) *The abolition of the reserve asset ratio and of the MLR in August 1981*

The system of competition and credit control failed to control the money supply. The monetarist Conservative government which came to power in 1979 was eager to control the money supply, yet did not wish to use direct controls (principles similar to those behind the 1971 CCC Act). By 1979, however, the CCC Act was coupled with a number of direct controls. The Conservative government, therefore, endeavoured to make a number of changes to the system of monetary control. *In August 1981 the reserve asset ratio and M L R were abolished.*

(i) The reserve asset ratio was replaced by the principle that *banks had to hold at least ½ per cent of eligible liabilities in non-interest-bearing accounts at the Bank of England.*

(ii) In place of M L R, *the Bank of England announced that it would keep short-term interest rates within a reasonable range, but would not publish the band.*

The changes introduced in 1981 represent a move towards a *monetary-base system of control*: the authorities concentrate mainly on controlling cash. Although the principle behind the 1981 changes was to allow market forces, where possible, to control the money supply, the monetary authorities still possessed the powers to impose direct controls on credit by means of instructions to banks, influence over interest rates, the use of special deposits and *debt management* (i.e. control of the Public Sector Borrowing Requirement, PSBR).

See also section 7 of Chapter 17.

*

QUESTION

'If control is to be exercised by the monetary authorities, in order to reduce the growth of the money supply successfully, a wide range of financial institutions must be subject to the control.' Discuss.

For most purposes, if we were to ask people how much money they have, they would refer not to the notes and coins in their pockets, but also to the amount they have in a current account. The amount of money in current and deposit accounts in banks partly governs the amount of lending which the banks wish to carry out for commercial reasons. Governments have become increasingly aware of this and, during the 1950s and 1960s, the United Kingdom authorities often sought to deflate the economy by restricting the amount of money which could be lent. However, institutions which escaped these credit restrictions, for example building societies and overseas banks, were able to increase their lending activities. The number of overseas banks increased and the building societies tended to extend their networks and grew more rapidly in terms of total savings than those banks which were subject to the credit restrictions. Building-society deposit accounts became, for most practical purposes, a form of money, although building societies have less credit-creation potential than banks because of the higher reserves they are required to have.

While the exercising of control over banks alone, rather than over all financial institutions, might prove successful in reducing the growth of the money supply as defined by, for example, £M3, it might not be successful in reducing the money supply if it is defined as including building-society deposits. The argument for including in the definition of money all interest-bearing accounts, whether at banks or other financial institutions, is largely based on the fact that the distinction between current accounts and deposit accounts at banks is becoming blurred. While theoretically banks ask for about seven days' notice of withdrawal from deposit accounts, this requirement is often waived, perhaps in an attempt to compete with building societies' instant-withdrawal interest-bearing accounts. Because of this blurring of the definition of current and deposit accounts, and because of the competition between banks and other financial institutions (especially building societies), for most purposes, building-society deposit and share accounts, as well as deposit accounts in commercial banks, have become part of the money supply (even if not officially defined as such). Therefore, attempts at credit control in order to reduce the growth of the money supply should be directed towards all financial institutions and not merely at banks.

MULTIPLE-CHOICE QUESTIONS

1–3. Commercial banks have the following main assets:
   (a) special deposits at the Bank of England;
   (b) cash in tills;
   (c) cash at the Bank of England;
   (d) money at call to the discount houses;
   (e) holdings of short-term government securities;
   (f) holdings of medium-term government securities;
   (g) overdrafts from private customers;
   (h) overdrafts of industrial companies;
   (i) loans to individuals;
   (j) loans to firms.

1. Which of the above items are the four most liquid assets?
Answer – (b), (c), (d), (e).

2. Which four of the above items can be regarded as the most profitable assets?

Answer – (g), (h), (i), (j)

3. Which of the above is neither profitable nor liquid?

Answer – (a)

4. Other things being equal, if the Bank of England buys securities in the open market, this will:

    (a) increase interest rates;

    (b) decrease interest rates;

    (c) leave interest rates constant.

Answer – (b)

5. If the Bank of England wished to restrict money supply, which of the following actions might it *not* take:

    (a) increase interest rates, through temporarily bringing back the Minimum Lending Rate, as in early 1985;

    (b) increase the proportion of special deposits required from commercial banks;

    (c) extend controls over money supply to financial institutions not currently covered;

    (d) issue a new long-dated stock?

Answer – (d)

SELF-EXAMINATION QUESTIONS

1. 'Banks are merely cloakrooms for the depositing of money and assets.' Discuss.

2. How far, in a modern society, can banks decide to trade off liquidity and profitability?

3. 'It is unwise to borrow short and lend long.' Why, therefore, do building societies generally ignore this rule?

4. What are the main objectives of the commercial banks?

5. What are the main roles of a central bank? What are the conflicts between its role as a banker and its role as adviser to the government?

6. Explain the Bank of England's role as the central bank.

7. What are the comparative advantages and disadvantages of directives to the commercial banks?

8. Why has the central bank often used special deposits in its attempts at controlling money supply?

9. What assets does the Bank of England have to back the note issue?

10. The Bank of England is sometimes described as the 'bankers' bank'. What is meant by this definition?

DATA RESPONSE

(a) Explain the following terms: (i) 'eligible liabilities'; (ii) 'reserve assets'.
(b) Calculate, to the nearest whole number, the reserve asset ratio as at 10 December 1980 for the banks in Table 23.
(c) What assets are held by London clearing banks?
(d) Why was the reserve asset ratio abolished in 1981?

Table 23. Banks' liabilities and assets, 10 December 1980

	London and Scottish clearing banks and Northern Ireland banks (£m)
Liabilities	
Sterling deposits	48,911
Other currency deposits	13,039
Other liabilities	11,082
	73,032
Assets	
Sterling assets	51,770
Other currency assets	13,579
Other assets	7,687
	73,032
Total liabilities or assets	
of which: Eligible liabilities	39,550
Reserve assets	5,276

Source: *Bank of England Quarterly Bulletin*, September 1981.

19. Inflation

1. Introduction

Although in recent years, most Western governments have regarded inflation as one of the major economic problems, this has not always been the case. For example, in the 1930s the problems of unemployment seemed much greater than those of inflation. We should note that when we talk of inflation we mean a *general* rise in prices rather than a rise in the price of particular items.

2. Is inflation really a problem?

(i) *Inflation tends to redistribute incomes.* Inflation tends to affect those on low fixed incomes (such as old-age pensioners and students) and people who have bought securities with fixed interest rates, war loans or gilt-edged securities. As interest rates rise with inflation, the price of such securities falls, i.e. their value falls.

It might be possible to overcome many of the problems for people on fixed incomes caused by inflation with the use of *indexation*. The former issue of 'Save As You Earn' certificates, which kept in line with the retail price index, helped overcome the problems caused by inflation. There are also issues of index-linked National Savings Certificates. The use of index-linked pension schemes also helps reduce the problems of inflation for pensioners.

Index-linking tends to transfer the problem of inflation from one section of the community to another. An index-linked benefit scheme, such as old age pensions, requires increasing government expenditure. If the government increases income tax to cover this extra expenditure, the burden of inflation is passed on to taxpayers.

(ii) If the tax thresholds are unchanged, *substantially more people pay income tax* in times of inflation than before (people are pushed up into higher tax brackets if their wages rise with inflation). Income tax acts as an automatic stabilizer. If tax thresholds are unchanged, those people who receive wage increases will tend to pay more tax, so that those on fixed incomes will tend not to lose out too much, in terms of a share of national income.

(iii) Inflation may also have another redistribution effect, with a *greater amount of firms' revenue going in the form of wages* and less going to entrepreneurs in the form of profits.

(iv) If there is *hyper-inflation*, there is the possibility that *confidence in the currency will be lost*, as confidence in the mark was lost in Germany in the 1920s.

In some cases, firms have invested in items of value rather than productive assets; for example, British Rail is known to have invested in paintings because of fears of inflation. Thus, inflation may cause money to lose its role as a store of value, showing that, to some extent, a loss of confidence in money may not be confined merely to times of hyper-inflation.

(v) *Inflation can lead to distortions in the market.* For example, property owners might leave property empty rather than rent it, because rising property prices make it possible for property owners to make significant capital gains on the future sale of their property and they are not prepared to tie up their property by renting it. Centre Point in London and a number of ordinary houses have been left empty in the past for this reason.

(vi) *Inflation can also lead to problems of pricing*, especially for contracts which take a long time to fulfil. For example, because of inflation many construction and shipbuilding schemes have cost a lot more than originally estimated. Some firms (such as Leyland Buses, which are now part of Volvo) have tried to overcome pricing problems by having '*rise and fall' contracts*, but this merely transfers the problem of inflation from the seller to the buyer.

(vii) *Inflation can also lead to problems in defining profits.* The accountancy profession has produced a number of reports about the use of *inflation accounting*.

(viii) It is often suggested that *inflation is a particularly important problem for exporters*, who find that the costs of their products (and, thus, the break-even prices of their products) are higher than those of their international competitors.

(ix) *The problem of inflation is particularly significant where wages rise even though productivity does not.* Where wages rise in line with increases in productivity, the problem of inflation tends not to be as big a problem as where wages rise in excess of productivity growth.

(x) It has also been claimed that *thriftiness (saving) is discouraged by inflation* because the value of savings falls in real terms. However, the savings ratio in the UK in 1975 and 1976 was higher than in other years, even though inflation was at its highest post-war level.

3. The possible causes of inflation

(a) *'Cost pushing'*

One of the possible causes of inflation is '*cost pushing*'; for example, trade unions or other groups of workers push up wages and this increase in wages is then passed on to the consumer in the form of higher prices. If just one industry or firm was subject to such wage increases, we might expect there to be a rise in unemployment rather than a rise in prices, assuming that the market is fairly competitive. If, however, all employers in an industry are subject to such pressures, then there is no reason to assume that, in a comparatively closed economy, it would affect employment. Even in an open economy, such as the United Kingdom, the effects on employment would be minimal if other countries are experiencing the same inflationary pressures.

Many commentators, noticeably Stuart Holland, MP, have suggested that monopolistic or oligopolistic institutions are the most likely to add to cost-push inflationary pressures. The increasing of employers' National Insurance contributions by the government would also tend to add to cost-push inflation in a manner similar to that where trade unions force wage increases.

(i) There may be '*leapfrogging*' of wages between different trade unions, with one trade union anxious to maintain its differential with other workers. The result is that wages tend to rise irrespective of productivity. If the UK had industry-wide unions, as West Germany has, there would be less scope for 'leapfrogging'.

(ii) Part of the problem of cost-push inflation may be caused by '*wage drift*', i.e. there may be a difference between the centrally negotiated wage and the wage actually paid by the employer to an individual worker. This problem has arisen in the past partly because of pressure put on centrally negotiated wage settlements by prices and incomes policies.

(b) *'Demand pulling'*

Another possible cause of inflation is 'demand pulling'. If total demand is greater than the total supply of goods and services at full employment, there is likely to be an *inflationary gap*. Note, however, that this could arise even if the whole economy was not at full employment. For example, if employers in the South-East cannot get the amount of labour they require, they may boost wages or salaries in that region for certain groups of workers, even if there is unemployment for other groups of workers in the region and unemployment in other regions of the country.

(c) *Monetarists' explanation of inflation*

In recent years, *the monetarist view of inflation* (*that it is due to the presence of institutions such as trade unions which prevent the market from working properly*) has predominated in government policy recommendations. The underlying assumptions of the monetarist position are contained within the equation $MV = PT$

where M is the total stock of money in the economy,

     V is the velocity of circulation of money, i.e. the number of times that money changes hands during a given period,

     P is the price level

and   T is the total number of transactions or the level of national income or national product.

Most monetarists claim that the number of transactions and the velocity of circulation are likely to be constant and so claim that there is a relationship between the general price level and the money supply. They claim that a fall in the supply of money will lead to a fall in prices; they also claim that a rise in the money supply will, at least in the long run, have no effect upon total output and will, therefore, not reduce unemployment, but will only increase prices. Monetarists believe that increasing money supply will generate no increase in employment: increasing government expenditure leads to a crowding out of private investment by the same amount.

While most monetarist economists (most noticeably Milton Friedman) have suggested that money supply is virtually all-important in determining inflation ('control money supply and you control inflation'), it should be noted that *restrictive money-supply policy tends to raise interest rates, and higher interest rates may themselves add to inflation* through the higher costs of borrowing and investment. It should also be noted that a *government attempting to control the money-supply market might not actually control all money, but might just concentrate on notes and coins.*

The relationship between the money supply and prices is, perhaps, more complex still when there is less than full employment. When there is full employment, the number of transactions (T) – see above – is fixed upwardly, but *when there is less than full employment there is no reason to suppose that T is fixed*. There is evidence to suggest that, when there is less than full employment, a reduction in M is more likely to lead to a reduction in T (for example, a reduction in the number of houses being built) than in a reduction in the price level (P). Therefore, in times of less than full employment, it appears that restrictive monetary policy is more likely to increase unemployment than reduce inflation.

The monetarists argue that an increase in money supply leads to an increase in prices. They tend to argue that the government can control money supply. However, Cairncross, for example, has argued that at Christmas the money supply rises because of an increase in the number of transactions taking place. Thus, not only might a rise in M lead to a rise in T, but a rise in T might lead to a rise in M.

If it is believed that the level of aggregate demand is a determinant of the level of inflation (i.e. 'too much money chasing too few goods'), it can be argued, as it is by the Cambridge School (a group of Keynesian economists) that, given that a rise in M must lead to either a rise in P or in T, if more goods can be produced the effect of a rising money supply will fall less on prices and more on the number of transactions.

Furthermore, *there is no reason to believe that the velocity of circulation is constant*. Changes in interest rates, changes in the expected rate of inflation, changes in wealth and changes in asset preferences might all cause velocity to change. For example, during a period of high inflation, an individual might make all his purchases as soon as he is paid his monthly wage.

(d) *Expectations*

Some economists argue that *when people expect there to be inflation in the future, there will be inflation in the future* because, for example, wage bargainers will allow for inflation in their wage negotiations. Furthermore, when contractors enter into negotiations with a potential customer, they will take account of what they expect the effect of inflation will be upon wage costs and the cost of materials. Expectations also affect the price of housing significantly. If people expect the price of housing in a particular area to rise they will wish to buy property in that particular area before the price goes up. This increase in demand will, indeed, lead to a price rise, which will fuel expectations that the price of houses in this particular area will continue to rise, encouraging people to buy a house now rather than later. This increase in demand leads to a further price rise and this trend continues. The effect of expectations is more important in the case of houses than with most other commodities because of the large increase in price, in absolute terms, a 10 per cent price rise, for example, has.

A report by the Nationwide Building Society (now Nationwide Anglia) suggested that expectations of high price rises have probably contributed more to the rise in house prices than a growing money supply.

(e) *Other factors*

(i) Other factors which might help to explain the existence of inflation include *advertising*, which contributes to inflation by persuading people to buy commodities they would otherwise not want (i.e. advertising adds to demand-pull inflation) and by adding to firms' costs (i.e. advertising adds to cost-push inflation).

(ii) *Inefficient consumption* may add to inflationary pressures. This factor applies particularly to energy: heating bills are much higher than they need to be when pipes and lofts are not insulated.

(iii) There is also evidence to suggest that, particularly in the mid-1970s, *imports* were a major source of inflation. This may, however, be considered as part of cost-push inflation.

4. Policies designed to reduce inflation

(a) *Increasing taxation*

Keynesian economists have tended to concentrate on the problems of aggregate demand rather than on the problem of inflation itself. Thus, where there is an inflationary problem, *the use of fiscal policy* – altering the taxation system – tends to be advocated to try to reduce any excess demand there might be in the economy.

However, if, say, VAT were increased in a bid to cut expenditure, the burden of the increase would probably fall most heavily upon the poorest people in the economy. Such a policy, therefore, would tend to be self-defeating, since probably the biggest problem with inflation is the fact that it tends to burden people on low incomes the most. Furthermore, increasing VAT will lead to, at least initially, a rise in retail prices. Also, it is probably more difficult to alter VAT than it was to alter purchase tax (which VAT replaced) because of the number of traders involved.

It should be noted that, in some cases, deflationary measures may in fact increase firms' unit costs because of reduced demand.

(b) *Reducing inflationary expectations*

Attempts to reduce people's inflationary expectations might include the government trying to convince the public that inflation will be lower than the government actually expects it to be. However, the government will probably be unable to fool the public all of the time.

By setting targets for inflation the government might be able to reduce inflationary expectations. Such targets are likely to be included in prices and incomes policies. Prices and incomes policies are perhaps the best way of reducing expectations. Prices and incomes policies are discussed later on in this section.

(c) *Increasing unemployment*

Given the evidence of *an arithmetic relationship between inflation and unemployment* for much of this century, it seems that *inflation might be reduced if unemployment is increased*. However, this 'Phillips relationship' did not seem to hold in the 1970s and so the Phillips-curve analysis has lost some credibility. Yet in the 1980s inflation has indeed fallen, with rising unemployment seeming to be a consequence of this.

It is important, though, that the suggested cures for inflation should not be worse than the disease. My own opinion is that if economists were as likely to be unemployed as the average unskilled person, they might not be so keen to suggest unemployment as a cure for inflation.

(d) *Indexing*

The Conservative government introduced the concept of *indexing* in 1972/3. They introduced 'threshold agreements', which allowed wages to increase in relation to higher prices. This policy, rather than reducing inflation, though, tended to add to it. However, such a policy was designed to deal with the problems which inflation causes rather than with the causes of inflation.

(e) *Prices and incomes policies*

Prices and incomes policies are usually introduced to reduce expectations of future wage and price rises and to avoid the unemployment/inflation dilemma (see the next section).

5. Prices and incomes policies

(a) *The aims of prices and incomes policies*

(i) One of the aims of prices and incomes policies is to *keep aggregate wage increases in line with aggregate productivity increases.* Under these circumstances unit labour costs remain stable and this would be consistent with stable prices, as long as there were no other sources of inflation present within the economy.

(ii) Another aim of prices and incomes policies is to *reduce inflationary expectations.* Many economists, notably Lord Kahn, have suggested that trade unions have partly added to inflation because of the 'leapfrogging' of wage demands. This is particularly likely to happen in industries where there is more than one trade union representing members of the workforce. An incomes policy would help to reduce this pressure.

(b) *Problems in controlling inflation through prices and incomes policies*

(i) One of the problems which arises in the attempt to control prices and incomes through a prices and incomes policy is the problem of determining *what is actually meant by 'incomes'.* Do we, for example, mean the national negotiated rates or do we mean average earnings, which would mean including the effect of local agreements, overtime payments and the different rates paid for shiftwork and for working unsocial hours?

(ii) However, *a prices and incomes policy must be able to respond to supply and demand conditions in the labour market.* For example, an expanding firm might wish to pay higher wages in order to attract new workers. This might be difficult to achieve within the framework of an incomes policy and may lead to the growth of fringe benefits if a statutory policy is imposed.

(iii) *Should an incomes policy set a limit to rises in incomes in terms of a flat rate or in percentage terms?* The important issue here is that of *union-imposed differentials.* If *a maximum flat-rate increase* is allowed, for example of £6 per week, this will tend to reduce percentage differentials between lower and higher paid workers. However, *a maximum percentage increase* of, say, 5 per cent would tend to increase the differential in monetary terms, so some incomes policies set a maximum increase of so many pounds, while also including some maximum percentage increase. For example, Phase II of the 1972–4 policy permitted an increase of £1 plus 4 per cent.

Following this line of reasoning, it is clear that *a maximum flat-rate increase will tend to redistribute income from highly paid to lowly paid workers* in percentage terms, whereas *a maximum percentage increase will tend to redistribute income from lowly paid to highly paid workers* in monetary terms.

(iv) An incomes policy needs to take into account whether *incremental allowances are to be controlled.* Incremental allowances are salary increases which are paid each year. They are common in many areas of the public sector (including local authorities) and in many insurance companies. Incremental allowances may be either formal or informal. Where they are formal, as they tend to be in the public sector, the government is aware that they are being paid and so can control them; where incremental allowances are informal, as they tend to be in insurance companies, the government is unaware that they are being paid and thus cannot control them.

(v) *An incomes policy may well distort the price mechanism* and lead to some loss of efficiency, since, *unless allowances are made for productivity increases, workers have little incentive to increase their productivity.* However, making allowance for productivity increases has been criticized by some economists who believe that it is the most inefficient firms which have the greatest scope for increasing productivity; an incomes policy which makes allowances for productivity increases might therefore be unfair to workers in industries which are already efficient.

(vi) *There is also the problem of trying to define efficiency and productivity,* particularly in many of the service industries, whether these are in the public sector (such as teaching) or in the commercial sector (such as banking).

(vii) It is also argued that the use of a *prices and incomes policy may affect the efficiency with which the price mechanism allocates resources.* In practice, however, there are often many distortions within the labour market preventing labour being allocated efficiently anyway. These arise because of restrictive practices by both trade unions and professional associations and prejudices by both employees and employers.

Even without having an incomes policy, the government still has some control over incomes in that both central and local government employ a large number of workers both directly and indirectly.

(viii) One of the practical problems of trying to arrange a satisfactory prices and incomes policy is that *it needs at least the tacit support of both employer's associations and trade unions.* This means not only the TUC and the CBI but also individual union leaders and individual firms, since the TUC and CBI have relatively little control over their members. Although there has been fairly wide publicity in the past about trade unionists not keeping to such agreements, the less well publicized problem of persuading employers to keep to the same agreements has also constituted a fairly major problem.

The last Labour government tried to gain the support of individual trade-union leaders through the '*Social Contract*', which included a wide range of objectives, including repeal of the 1971 Industrial Relations Act. This improved the political climate slightly but did not alter the rate of inflation much.

(c) *Problems of assessing the effectiveness of prices and incomes policies*

There have been relatively few attempts to assess the effectiveness of prices and incomes policies.

(i) One of the problems of trying to assess the effectiveness of incomes policies is that, while we can test wages and incomes throughout the duration of a policy, *it may well be that wages will be raised immediately after such a policy ends*.

(ii) Where trade unions and employers expect a prices and incomes policy to come into force, *they may try to hurry through wage negotiations immediately before such a policy comes into operation*.

(iii) There is also the point that *we might generally expect wages and salaries to be higher during prices and incomes policies than at most times, because if they were low, the prices and incomes policies would not have been introduced in the first place*.

(iv) It might be possible to have some form of *national job evaluation*, which would try to take into account relative wages in both the private and the public sector before and during the policy's operation, and for a period after its ending. While *this has sometimes been rejected as being unrealistic*, job evaluation already takes place in the army, which comprises a wide range of occupations, and in large-scale private industry, which in many cases includes most of the categories of workers to be found throughout the private sector.

(v) There is also the problem of determining *just what is meant by a prices and incomes policy*. For example, while the current Conservative government claims not to have a prices and incomes policy, there is an 'incomes policy' *de facto* for the public sector, though not for the private sector. This can be clearly shown in terms of the teachers' dispute in 1985, when the government was determined to keep fairly rigidly to a wage limit of 4 per cent. Thus, even without having a declared incomes policy, a government may still have some control over wages because a

Table 24. UK incomes policies since 1948

Period	Name	Voluntary/compulsory	Wage norm
Feb. 1948–Sept. 1950	Statement on Personal Incomes, Costs and Prices	voluntary	None, but proposed wage standstill in Sept. 1950
July 1961–March 1962	Temporary 'Pay Pause'	voluntary	zero
April 1962–Oct. 1964	Incomes Policy: the Next Step	voluntary	2–2½% 'guiding light'
Dec. 1964–July 1966	Joint Statement of Intent on Productivity, Prices and Incomes	voluntary	3–3½% p.a., with criteria for exceptional pay increases
July 1966–June 1967	Prices and Incomes Standstill	compulsory	zero for six months, followed by six months' 'severe restraint'
July 1967–April 1968	Prices and Incomes Policy	compulsory	none, but increases had to be justified by same criteria as in 1965
April 1968–Dec. 1969	Productivity, Prices and Incomes Policy in 1968 and 1969	compulsory	3½%, with exceptions for genuine productivity agreements
Dec. 1969–June 1970	Productivity, Prices and Incomes Policy after 1969	compulsory	2½–4½%
Nov. 1972–Feb. 1974	A Programme for Controlling Inflation		
Nov. 1972–March 1973	Stage 1 of counter-inflation policy	compulsory	zero
April–Oct. 1973	Stage 2 of counter-inflation policy	compulsory	£1/week plus 4% with upper limit of £250/year. Some flexibility for moves towards equal pay
Nov. 1973–Feb. 1974	Stage 3 of counter-inflation policy	compulsory	7% or £2.50/week with upper limit of £350/year. Threshold agreements of 40p for each 1% rise in RPI

Table 24. (cont.)

Period	Name	Voluntary/compulsory	Wage norm
July 1975–March 1979	The Social Contract		
July 1975–July 1976	The Attack on Inflation: Phase 1	compulsory	£6/week, but no increases for those earning over £8,500/year
Aug. 1976–July 1977	The Attack on Inflation: Phase II	compulsory	£2.50 for those earning up to £50/week; 5% for those earning £50–£80; £4 for higher earners
July 1977–July 1978	The Attack on Inflation after July 1977: Phase III	compulsory	10% max., with exceptions for self-financing productivity schemes
July 1978–March 1979	Winning the Battle Against Inflation: Phase IV	compulsory	5% max., with exceptions for self-financing productivity schemes

large number of workers are employed by both central government and local government.

6. Measuring inflation

In the UK the most commonly used measure of inflation is the Retail Prices Index. This attempts to measure the price of a typical basket of goods and services over a certain period. For the sake of simplicity, we shall assume that this typical basket includes bread, potatoes, tomatoes, carrots, meat, gas, electricity and meals out. The price of these commodities in January in year 0 might be as follows:

Bread	40p per loaf
Potatoes	20p/kg
Tomatoes	£1.00/kg
Carrots	30p/kg
Meat	£1.00/kg
Gas	40p/therm
Electricity	6p/kilowatt hour
A meal out	£5.00

In July of the same year, we might find the prices of these commodities to be as follows:

Bread	45p per loaf
Potatoes	10p/kg
Tomatoes	30p/kg
Carrots	20p/kg
Meat	£1.10/kg
Gas	48p/therm
Electricity	6p/kilowatt hour
A meal out	£6.00

In January of the following year (year 1) prices might be as follows:

Bread	50p per loaf
Potatoes	22p/kg
Tomatoes	90p/kg
Carrots	35p/kg
Meat	£1.20/kg
Gas	48p/therm
Electricity	6.3p/kilowatt hour
A meal out	£6.50

A 10 per cent rise in the price of a loaf of bread might not have the same effect as a 10 per cent rise in the price of a kilogram of potatoes: the effect depends upon how much of a consumer's income is spent on bread and how much is spent on potatoes. Therefore, the proportion of income consumers spend on each item has to be considered.

The level of income is important in determining what is bought: the richest members of society (say, those people with an annual income of over £100,000) might spend only 0.5 per cent of their income on food, and 40 per cent of their income on meals out whereas a person with an annual income of £5,000 might spend 10 per cent of his income on food. Furthermore, a person with an annual income of £1,500 might spend about 30 per cent of his income on food and nothing on meals out. The inclusion of the spending of the very rich and of the very poor in the Retail Prices Index will distort the index if the Index is intended to show the effect of a rise in, say, the price of bread on most people, bearing in mind that most people will spend say between 5 per cent and 20 per cent of their income on food rather than about 0.5 per cent or 30 per cent.

For this reason, the spending of the very poor and of the very rich are not included in the calculations for the Retail Price Index. We might, therefore, decide to calculate a price index by using only the spending patterns of people with annual incomes of between £2,500 and £50,000.

We might find that the proportion of income the average consumer within this group spends upon each of the items included in our price index is as follows, given the income of the consumer at the beginning of year 0:

	%
Bread	2
Potatoes	1
Tomatoes	0.5
Carrots	1.5
Meat	5
Gas	17
Electricity	20
Meals out	3
All items in index	50

We assume that the rest of people's income is either saved or spent on items not included in the index. We also assume that the only items of food are those mentioned. Thus, the amount spent on food, by the average consumer in the group, is 10 per cent of income.

We assume that in January of year 0, the average consumer spends 2 per cent of his income upon bread. Over the course of the year the price of a loaf of bread rises by 10p. To show the effect of this price rise upon the cost of living we assume that the consumer demands a fixed number of loaves each month, whatever the price. In order to buy the same number of loaves in January year 1 as in January year 0, the consumer has to spend more money on bread.

By considering an individual with an annual income of £5,000 (i.e. a monthly income of about £417), we can say that, assuming this individual spends 2 per cent of his monthly income on bread in January year 0, he will spend 2 per cent of £417 on bread, i.e. £8.34. Thus, he buys 20.8 loaves. In order to buy 20.8 loaves the following January, he will have to spend (given that the price of a loaf is 50p) £10.40 on bread. Thus, the cost of living in terms of bread for this individual rises by £2.06. Since only 2 per cent of income is spent on bread, the rise in the cost of living caused by this 25 per cent rise in the price of bread is only 2% × 25% i.e. 0.005 (or 0.5%). However, since only 50 per cent of income is spent on items included in our price index, the weight given to bread is 2% ÷ 50%, i.e. 0.04. Therefore, the rise in the cost of living, as measured by the price index we are forming, caused by a 25 per cent rise in the price of bread, is 0.04 × 25%, i.e. 0.01 or 1%. Similarly, a 10 per cent rise in the price of potatoes over the year, given that 1 per cent of income is spent on potatoes, has an effect upon the cost of living by raising it by (1% × 10%) ÷ 50%, i.e. the cost of living is raised by 0.002, i.e. 0.2 per cent. The effect upon the cost of living of changes in the price of the other items included in our index can be calculated in the same way (see Table 25).

From Table 25 it is clear that the annual rate of inflation for year 0 is 14.2 per cent (see column 6). Had prices followed the trend they followed in the first six months over the second six months as well, the rate of inflation would have been 13.6 per cent, i.e. 6.8 per cent × 2 (see column 5).

Weaknesses of the Retail Prices Index

The Retail Prices Index actually covers about 350 items, subdivided (for convenience) into eleven sections as follows: I, Food; II, Alcohol; III, Tobacco; IV, Housing; V, Fuel and light; VI, Durable household goods; VII, Clothing and footwear; VIII, Transport and vehicles; IX, Miscellaneous goods; X, Services; XI, Meals out.

(i) The assumption of a constant demand throughout the whole year (given a constant price) made for the purpose of constructing the Retail Prices Index (and made for the purpose of constructing our price index) is an unrealistic one. This is because there is no allowance made for seasonal variations in demand.

The assumptions made in our price index that the rise in the cost of living between July (year 0) and January (year 1) was 7.4 per cent (i.e. 14.2% − 6.8%) is unrealistic since in the winter a consumer may well spend nothing on tomatoes. Furthermore, consumers who use gas to heat their homes are more likely to use gas in the winter than in the summer.

(ii) *A more acute problem with the Retail Prices Index occurs when trying to measure inflation over long periods of time.* For example, in the early part of the twentieth century a great deal of money was spent on candles. Nowadays, however, very little is spent on this item. *There are problems, therefore, of assuming that people are spending a large proportion of their total expenditure on a certain product when in fact they are not.*

(iii) Furthermore, *it is difficult to compare inflation in one year with inflation in another when products consumed in one year have since been discontinued or when there are new products.* For example, it is difficult to compare inflation in the 1980s with inflation in the 1960s, since in the 1980s a large proportion of expenditure may go on home computers and

Table 25. How a retail price index is constructed

	1 Proportion of income spent on item	2 Weight	3 Price rise to July (%)	4 Price rise to Jan. (%)	5 Weighted rise to July (%)	6 Weighted rise to Jan. (%)	7 Index Jan. 0	8 Index July 0	9 Index Jan. 1
Bread	0.02	0.04	12.5	25	0.5	1	100	112.5	125
Potatoes	0.01	0.02	−50	10	−1	0.2	100	50	110
Tomatoes	0.005	0.01	−70	−10	−0.7	−0.1	100	30	90
Carrots	0.015	0.03	−33.33	16.67	−1	0.5	100	66.67	116.67
Meat	0.05	0.1	10	20	1	2	100	110	120
Gas	0.17	0.34	20	20	6.8	6.8	100	120	120
Electricity	0.2	0.4	0	5	0	2	100	100	105
Meals out	0.03	0.06	20	30	1.2	1.8	100	120	130
All items	0.5	1.00			6.8	14.2	100	106.8	114.2

the software for those computers whereas in the 1960s there was no consumption of such products.

(iv) *There are also problems in comparing inflation in different periods when the quality of products changes over time.* For example, how can we compare the price of a typical 1986 car with the price of a car from 1966, when the design and quality of cars have changed so much over this period?

(v) *Problems might occur when the base year chosen is not a typical year.* If the base year is in the middle of a boom, inflation is likely to be high and as the economy tends towards recession the fall in the rate of inflation which might be expected would tend to be exaggerated.

(vi) *Do we include changes in taxation or social benefits in our measure of inflation?* If we do not, we may be giving an incomplete picture of what happens when prices and earnings are changing.

(vii) Another of the problems with the Retail Prices Index is that *it looks at pre-tax income.* Mrs Thatcher attempted to introduce the *Tax and Prices Index*, which looks at post-tax income. Thus, if a person's income rises from £5,000 (at which level, let us assume, he pays no tax) to £6,000 (at which level he pays £1,000 tax) he gains no extra spending power. The Tax and Prices Index takes account of the fact that no extra spending power is derived, but fails to measure the '*social wage*', i.e. it fails to note the benefits derived from the individual paying this £1,000 extra taxation (benefits such as better health and education facilities which can be provided by the government as a result of receiving this extra £1,000 revenue).

QUESTION

How do Keynesians and monetarists differ on the question of the relationship between the money supply and the price level?

The differences between Keynesians and monetarists are often stressed in the media. In practice, the differences may be quite difficult to analyse. Many monetarists and Keynesians may hold similar views about the effects of money supply upon inflation, but would not necessarily hold similar views about all public-sector activity. Furthermore, monetarists may be divided on some issues: some monetarists suggest that control of the money supply is a sufficient condition for controlling inflation, but other monetarists would tend to suggest that it is not necessarily suitable for fine tuning of the economy, since there is no unique rate of inflation consistent with one particular growth rate of money supply. From empirical evidence, A. A. Walters suggested that the growth of money supply and the rate of inflation will tend to differ by as much as 6 per cent. Thus, starting from a base year in which we can index the money supply at 100 and prices at 100, if in the next year money supply is still 100, prices could be between 94 and 106. He further argued that in one year in three, inflation will be outside these limits.

Keynesians are also divided on certain issues. For example, some Keynesians feel that control of the money supply is a necessary but not a sufficient condition for controlling inflation, while other Keynesians would suggest that prices and incomes policies might be a more sensible way of tackling inflation. Even amongst those who advocate prices and incomes policy, there is disagreement: some advocate voluntary policy; some advocate statutory policy. Furthermore, some reluctant converts to prices and incomes policy have favoured long-term policies rather than short-term policies because of the greater flexibility long-term policies tend to have. For example, short-term policies might not allow expanding firms to pay the higher wages needed to attract more labour. Such a restriction imposed by a long-term policy would seriously restrict the growth of such firms. For this reason long-term policies are unlikely to impose such restrictions.

Both Keynesians and monetarists would probably agree that when there are large increases in the quantity of money, as when major sources of gold and silver were discovered in the New World, there tends to be a major rise in prices. The underlying quantity theory, i.e. $MV = PT$, cannot really be disputed since it is an identity rather than a theory. However, monetarists would tend to suggest that V is fairly stable and predictable. Therefore, they argue that, if T can also be predicted as being fairly stable, it can be shown that there is a direct link between M and P (money supply and prices). They argue that the only effect of increasing the money supply is an increase in inflation.

However, some Keynesians suggest that if the government tries to restrict M, what will happen is that T itself will alter (the volume of transactions will fall). This fall in T is shown through rising unemployment and/or declining economic growth. In particular, a restrictive monetary policy will tend to hit hardest rapidly expanding new firms, which borrow the most money. Such a policy will also affect capital-goods industries, such as the construction industry, since these are much more vulnerable to changes in interest rates than other sectors, such as the clothing industry, because of the need for long-term borrowing.

Many Keynesians would suggest that, while at one stage money supply did determine prices, in most cases now the money supply adjusts to changes in prices and the volume of transactions rather than prices adjusting to changes in the money supply. For example, money supply will tend to increase at Christmas in accordance with the increase in the volume of transactions.

The issue of differences between Keynesianism and monetarism is further complicated because there is often a difference between the rhetoric and the reality. For example, monetarism is often linked with the concept that governments should balance budgets, yet the Reagan administration in the US (which is assumed to be monetarist) has, in practice, had large-scale budget deficits, which have been identified by most European countries as one of the main causes of Europe's problems. Paradoxically, governments usually thought of as Keynesian, such as that of President Mitterrand in France, have criticized the American regime for tackling its problems in a way which would usually be regarded as Keynesian.

Differences between Keynesianism and monetarism are also clouded by extremism by some of the parties involved. For example, if a monetarist takes a particularly right-wing stand on one area of policy, Keynesians might tend to believe that this monetarist has right-wing views on all areas of policy. Indeed, monetarism now tends to be connected with a whole series of right-wing policies.

MULTIPLE-CHOICE QUESTIONS

1. If there is a sudden upsurge in inflation which was not anticipated, who would gain?
    (a) People who have taken out fixed-interest loans to buy their house.
    (b) People who have taken out life-assurance policies for a fixed sum.
    (c) People who have invested money in irredeemable gilt-edged securities.
    (d) None of the above.
Answer – (*d*)

2. If inflation is higher than anticipated, the number of people paying income tax will, other things being equal:
    (a) rise;
    (b) fall;
    (c) remain the same.
Answer – (*a*)

3. When will an increase in the money supply most likely lead to an increase in the price level?

    (*a*) When there is unemployment;

    (*b*) When there is full employment;

    (*c*) When interest rates are unstable.

Answer – (*b*)

4. An incomes policy which sets a limit to wage increases in percentage terms will tend to reduce monetary differentials.

    (*a*) True

    (*b*) False

Answer – (*b*)

DATA RESPONSE

1. Since the Second World War, governments have tried a variety of different ways of solving inflation. Some have used prices and incomes policies. These, however, have broken down, partly because of opposition from individual trade unions. Others have used mainly fiscal policies, whereby government expenditure, in particular, is used counter-cyclically, i.e. it is increased during recessions and reduced during booms. Counter-cyclical fiscal policies have the disadvantage of leading to stop/go policies, which make investment decisions difficult for private-sector firms (as well as for public-sector firms) because of uncertainty of expectations. These policies also tend to reduce economic growth because, instead of letting things boom, they stop booms.

Other governments, such as the Thatcher government, have used monetary policy in an attempt to reduce inflation. Inflation may be reduced, but only at a very high cost, i.e. at the expense of other objectives, including employment.

It might be better to look and see whether we can reduce most of the bad effects of inflation, even if we do not actually reduce inflation itself. Some economists have argued that one of the main problems with inflation is that its extent is often not fully anticipated. If, therefore, the government attempted to index-link both savings and incomes, most of the effects of inflation could be reduced without infringement upon other objectives.

Index-linked savings schemes have been used since 1975. Originally, these schemes were limited to people of retirement age or over, but they have since been extended to the whole community. However, as inflation has been reduced, the interest rates on these schemes have become less attractive and some of the schemes have been withdrawn.

It has often been claimed that inflation has caused distortions, particularly in the housing market. In times of high inflation, some people may become home-owners partly to hedge against inflation, i.e. in the expectation of future capital gains. The poorer sections of the community are unable to hedge against inflation in this way and thus tend to lose out in relative terms. An index-linked scheme for building-society savers and mortgage payers would help to reduce the cost of inflation to them. If inflation is high and rising, labour might demand wage increases of 12 per cent when inflation is only 10 per cent. By index-linking wages, this problem of expectations might be mitigated. If inflation is falling, index-linking might prolong inflation.

The use of index-linking for wages would, if applied on a national scale, avoid the problems of leapfrogging and the unfairness of some past prices and incomes policies, when some people were given wages increases just before a freeze on wages came into effect. There were further problems when the prices and incomes policies ended: workers would scramble for wage increases. The index-linking of wages would help reduce the unfairness caused by some workers having their incomes reduced in real terms, while the wages of other workers, those who are in a stronger bargaining position, keep pace or more than keep pace with inflation.

(*a*) Critically evaluate the likely benefits and dis-benefits of index-linking, with regard to savings, investment and wages.

(*b*) Would index-linking, as some economists and politicians have suggested, merely lead to institutionalized inflation?

(*c*) What problems might occur for firms which were expanding rapidly if wages were linked to inflation? What problems might it cause to firms which needed to contract?

2. Prices and incomes policies came into vogue in the United Kingdom during the 1960s and 1970s under a wide variety of names. One of the reasons for the use of such policies was the assumption, under the *Phillips curve*, that there would normally be a *trade-off* between inflation and unemployment. It was hoped that prices and incomes policy would be a method of overcoming the dilemma of choice between the objectives of either controlling inflation or controlling unemployment.

However, not all economists accepted the Phillips curve analysis. For example, some economists have pointed out that if the price of one product rises, we might expect demand to fall and unemployment in that industry or firm to rise. However, if all prices in the economy rise, there is no reason to expect demand to fall, except where a fixed exchange rate leads to a fall in the demand for exports.

If it is accepted that rising general inflation tends not to increase unemployment, a reflationary policy (whereby the government increases its expenditure to create more jobs) in times of high unemployment, backed by a prices and incomes policy, could reduce unemployment while controlling inflation.

Even if one accepts the need for a prices and incomes policy, it must also be accepted that there are problems in implementing such a policy. One such problem is to decide whether incomes should be restrained on a monetary basis (in which case *differentials* would tend to decline in percentage terms), or on some other basis.

For a prices and incomes policy to be most effective, all forms of income, rather than just wages, ought to be considered. Therefore, it might be helpful to limit *dividends*. However, dividends will probably be paid eventually and a prices and incomes policy would merely postpone the payment of dividends. If the government wants to try to control fringe benefits, in a prices and incomes policy, it may have problems because not all fringe benefits are declared by firms.

A further point which has not always been fully considered is the definition of 'incomes'. Should a government define income as the basic weekly wage without overtime or should overtime be included? There are problems involved in trying to control piece rates (where wages are paid per unit of output rather than per hour), where an individual may do one task one year and a different one the next year.

(a) Explain why the definition of incomes may be difficult but important.

(b) Why is it difficult to control fringe benefits?

(c) Should prices be controlled?

3. See Figure 57.

(a) Explain why incomes policies seemed to be more successful in reducing prices and incomes in the late 1970s than in the early 1970s.

(b) Why have prices and incomes generally fallen since 1980 in the absence of any incomes policy?

(c) Explain the large gap between earnings and prices between 1982 and 1985.

4. Some economists have mentioned the idea that militant trade unions

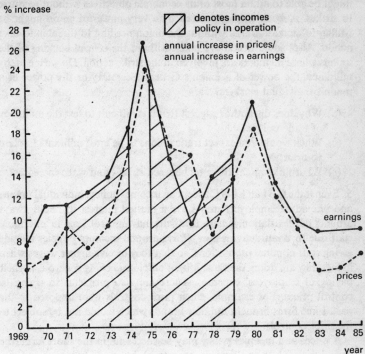

% increase

denotes incomes
policy in operation

annual increase in prices/
annual increase in earnings

earnings

prices

Figure 57. *Trends in prices and earnings*
Source: *Monthly Digest of Statistics*, CSO, various editions.

have added to inflation. However, there are a number of problems in testing such a hypothesis. How, for example, can we measure the militancy of trade unions? Is there any evidence to show that trade unions were more militant in the late 1970s, when inflation was running at very high rates, than during parts of the inter-war years when inflation was either low or, in some cases, negative?

Some economists have suggested that strikes might be used as a proxy variable to measure trade-union militancy. However, this suggestion seems to assume that all strikes are about pay, but the lengthy coalminers' strike in 1984–5 was not about pay. Even if we analyse the Department of Employment's data about the causes of strikes, can we be sure that the grievance which triggers off a strike is in fact the main underlying grievance? In any case, it seems likely that a very powerful trade union might be able to attain most of its economic objectives without recourse to strikes. A weak employer faced by a very powerful union might be willing to increase wages without the union needing to threaten to take action. Also, some strikes are taken without the official backing of the unions whose members are involved in the strike action. Do we mean, by militancy, the power of a union's General Secretary or the power of a union's individual workers?

(a) Why does the author suggest that it is difficult to test the militancy of trade unions?

(b) When would you expect trade unions to be most militant? Explain your answer.

(c) What links might there be between strikes and wage increases?

5. Even if the CBI and TUC accept an incomes policy, individual unions and individual employers may have a mutual interest in finding ways around the legislation, where firms are having problems in obtaining staff due to unattractive wages. Ways around incomes policies include giving staff nominal promotions, so that they receive higher wages when in fact they are doing the same job, or employers being generous in their paying of employees' expenses. There are also problems in trying to control prices. For example, when price controls were imposed in the past, some firms brought out new brands which would not be subject to the price controls.

A prices and incomes policy may be successful in the short term (the period in which the policy is in operation), but trade unionists and employees might agree to wage claims immediately before or after the duration of the policy, with such claims being exaggerated to take account of the imposition of the incomes policy. Those people who have their wage claim accepted immediately before the imposition of an incomes policy have an advantage over those whose wage claims are postponed.

(a) How might expectations affect the rate of inflation?

(b) How might the success or failure of incomes policies be evaluated?

SELF-EXAMINATION QUESTIONS

1. Which groups does inflation tend to affect most adversely? What are the advantages and disadvantages of index-linking fixed incomes?

2. 'Since inflation is mainly undesirable because of the ways in which it redistributes income, the government should be concerned to reduce these effects, for example through indexation, rather than with many of

the so-called "cures" for inflation, which are worse than the disease.'
Discuss.

3. Should pensions be linked to prices or earnings or neither? Explain
your answer.

4. 'While economists have sometimes commented about the adverse
effects of inflation on old-age pensions, students and people who have
bought gilt-edged securities, the selective effects of tight money-supply
policy, for example the disproportionate effect on housing and the
construction industry generally, have often been overlooked.' Discuss.

5. It is sometimes suggested that if income-tax thresholds remain constant, income tax will act as a stabilizer to inflation. Analyse why this
might be true.

6. How far is it true that inflation is a problem for exporters under a
fixed rate of exchange but not under a free-floating exchange rate?

7. Some economists have suggested that prices and incomes policies
have the advantage of overcoming the inflation/unemployment dilemma.
How far is this true?

8. What are the comparative merits and demerits of prices and incomes
policies for restraining inflation compared to contractionary monetary
policy?

9. Some economists have suggested that with prices and incomes policies
there are problems for the fast-growing industries which need to recruit
additional workers. How far is this true?

10. It has sometimes been suggested that under the present government
there is a hidden incomes policy for people in the public sector. What is
meant by this and how far is it true?

11. 'We should concentrate less on worrying about wages and more
about wages in relation to productivity, since in an industry where
productivity is rising higher wages could be afforded without them
contributing to inflation.' Critically discuss this statement.

12. Would higher productivity reduce inflation? How can we tie this in
with the general Keynesian model?

13. 'The control of money supply is a necessary but not a sufficient
condition for the control of inflation.' Discuss.

14. 'Monetarism is slightly self-defeating because the higher interest
rates which are necessary to control money supply are, in themselves,

inflationary, as firms add the cost of borrowing to their prices.' Discuss.

15. What are the definitions of money supply? Why might they be important when considering inflation policy?

16. In the past, governments have occasionally given subsidies to the building societies in order to reduce interest rates. What are the reasons for this policy?

17. Does V or T ever change in the formula $MV = PT$? Explain your answer.

18. Would the Cambridge School's idea of producing more goods solve the problem of inflation? Explain your answer.

19. How far does a switch from direct to indirect taxation affect inflation?

20. It is sometimes suggested that inflation is mainly a problem only when it is unanticipated. What is meant by this and how far is it true?

21. Do expectations of inflation help to continue inflation? What would be the expectations of inflation now and what would they have been two years ago?

22. Is Stuart Holland, MP, correct in suggesting that monopolies contribute to inflation? Explain your answer? What, if anything, can be done about any inflationary tendencies monopolies might have?

23. How does marketing and advertising contribute to inflation?

24. How does inefficient consumption lead to inflation?

25. How does 'leapfrogging' of wage claims add to inflation? What, if anything, can be done to prevent 'leapfrogging'?

26. How, if at all, have imports into the UK contributed to inflation?

27. What is meant by 'wage drift'?

28. 'The effect of higher interest rates is to discourage investment in assets and thus inflationary policy now is at the expense of economic growth in the future, whether this counter-inflationary policy takes a fiscal or a monetary form.' Discuss.

29. Is there a conflict between unemployment and inflation? If so, where should the balance be struck?

20. Unemployment

1. Types of unemployment

(a) *Frictional unemployment*

There are several types of unemployment. One is *frictional unemployment*, which occurs where there are *time-lags* between workers leaving one job and finding another, assuming that there are suitable vacancies. Part of the reason for frictional unemployment may be imperfect information, although Job Centres, the Professional and Executive Register and employment agencies may help to remedy this problem. Frictional unemployment may also occur because time may be needed for a worker to move between different areas. It would also occur if the worker needs to acquire slightly different skills for another job: it might take some time for him to acquire these new skills. The costs of moving could also contribute to frictional unemployment. It could be argued that inadequate provision of council housing, the high cost of housing in the private sector and the subsequent delays in moving between areas also contribute to frictional unemployment. Frictional unemployment can be said to be the result of the *costs of searching*.

(b) *Seasonal unemployment*

This occurs in many industries, notably the building industry and the tourist industry, which tend to have fewer jobs in the winter period than in the summer. Sometimes firms may take steps to overcome the problem of *seasonal unemployment*. For example, Walls began manufacturing sausages (which were originally consumed mainly in the winter) to complement the sales of their ice-cream (which is mainly consumed in the summer).

Central or local government may be able to assist by providing offsetting employment. For example, the building of a university or a college in a seaside resort might help to overcome the problem of seasonal unemployment there.

(c) *Structural unemployment*

This occurs when either a particular firm or a particular industry loses employment either because of *changing demands* or because *capital replaces labour.* In the 1950s and 1960s the shipbuilding industry lost a lot of employment because of a fall in demand for its products. An example from the 1980s of an industry suffering *structural unemployment* is the steel industry. Structural unemployment is often linked to regional unemployment and explains why areas such as the north of England and Wales have especially high rates of unemployment.

(d) *Cyclical unemployment*

This occurs because of the operation of the *trade cycle.* In a boom, relatively few people will be unemployed, whereas in a depression far more will be unemployed. Governments may be able to offset this type of unemployment by *counter-cyclical policies,* although the problems of obtaining information and implementing decisions on time can mean that in some cases governments have contributed to rather than prevented cyclical unemployment.

This type of unemployment is also referred to as *demand-deficient* unemployment. Keynes argued that this is the type of unemployment that should be countered by injections into the economy and, in particular, he urged governments to increase their expenditure. Thus Keynes argued that demand-deficient unemployment could be reduced by increasing national expenditure: as expenditure rises, output rises.

Demand-deficient unemployment is caused by there being insufficient demand in the economy as a whole, whereas structural unemployment may be caused by changing demand patterns, resulting in insufficient unemployment in certain regions or sectors of the economy.

(e) *Regional unemployment*

This may, as we have mentioned, be due partly to structural unemployment. It could, however, be due to a poor-quality labour force in certain parts of the country, due to inefficient educational or training facilities. *Regional unemployment* may also be partly caused by a particular area having high transport costs, preventing cost-effectiveness. While the unemployment rate in one region in the UK might be very different to the rate in another (for example between Northern Ireland and south-east England), the differences are small when compared with regional differences in some other countries, notably Italy.

Table 26. Recent trends in unemployment in the UK

Year	1 Working population (m)	2 Employed labour force (m)	3 Total unemployed (m)	4 Vacancies (m)	5 Percentage unemployed i.e. column 3 ÷ column 1
1965	25.50	25.20	0.30	0.27	1.12
1975	25.87	25.04	0.84	0.15	3.24
1980	26.82	25.31	1.51	0.14	5.64
1982	26.66	23.89	2.77	0.12	10.39
1985	27.42	24.25	3.18	0.17*	11.59

* Figure calculated for 1984.
Source: Central Statistical Office, *Economic Trends, Annual Supplement*, HMSO, 1986 edition.

A regional policy to reduce unemployment in the most depressed areas has to be designed either to take work to the workers or to take the workers to the work (see Chapter 24).

2. Why has unemployment risen in recent years?

There are problems in defining the total number of people who are unemployed. Government figures show the number registered unemployed, but certain people (such as many housewives and pensioners) who may be looking for work, are not registered as unemployed. This underestimating of unemployment is partly offset by the number of people registered unemployed who are not really seeking work.

The rise in unemployment since the early 1970s has probably been caused by a number of factors.

(i) *There has been some rise in the size of the working population.* However, in the period since 1979, when unemployment has risen dramatically, the increase in the size of the working population has not been very significant: the fall in the total number employed has been greater than the increase in the size of the working population. However, *the rise in the activity rate of women* (which has helped to increase the size of the

329

working population) has probably had some effect in reducing the employment of men.

(ii) Governments have given *priority to other objectives* (especially to the control of inflation) rather than to the reduction of demand-deficient unemployment. Many of the measures employed by governments designed to reduce balance of payments deficits or to reduce inflation appear to lead to unemployment, at least in the short term.

Keynesian economists would suggest that a lack of aggregate monetary demand has been the major cause of the recent rise in unemployment. They advocate more government expenditure or less taxation as means of reducing this unemployment. Alternatively, they suggest that the government should encourage more private consumption, more investment, more exporting and less importing.

That *deficient demand may be a cause of the current high unemployment* levels can be shown by the fact that during the Second World War unemployment in Western Europe declined dramatically.

(iii) Some economists have suggested that unemployment has risen in recent years partly because of *a mis-match of supply and demand*, part of which is *structural unemployment*. Thus, part of the relatively high unemployment rate in the North-East (compared to the rate of unemployment in the South-East) can be explained by virtue of the fact that many of those who are unemployed in the North-East have skills which are no longer required by employers.

(iv) Some economists, particularly those associated with the Chicago School, have suggested that *higher social-security payments* might contribute to higher unemployment. However, it seems unlikely that higher social-security payments have in fact contributed very much to the rise in unemployment.

(v) A further possible cause of the rise in unemployment, cited by some government ministers, could be *higher real wages*. It is certainly true that real wages in manufacturing have tended to rise in the United Kingdom even though there has been a decline in employment. Some economists, particularly classical economists, have suggested that people made unemployed in such industries have *priced themselves out of a job*. However, the burden of unemployment tends to fall most on those people with the lowest incomes.

(vi) There has been a decline in employment opportunities in mining, construction and public utilities, as well as in manufacturing. Many economists have commented on a *natural de-industrialization process* whereby the penetration of imports has reduced the demand for the

330

products of these industries, leading to a *structural decline* of these industries. *Structural unemployment* probably explains declining employment in these industries better than rising real wages.

(vii) For some countries, including the United Kingdom, *external factors* may have played a minor part. For example, if the terms of trade worsen this could lead, in some cases, to more unemployment; a very high exchange rate might make it difficult for firms to export their goods or services. However, there was a considerable rise in the value of the dollar in 1984, yet American unemployment fell.

(viii) Some people may find it difficult to obtain jobs because of *prejudices of employers or of other workers*. Prejudices apply towards older people, women and some ethnic minorities: unemployment among some ethnic groups is extremely high. Legislation such as the Equal Pay Act 1975 may have led to greater unemployment among women, with employers preferring not to employ women at all if they have to pay them at wage rates equal to those paid to men.

3. Policies to reduce structural unemployment by reducing labour costs

Some of the rise in unemployment has probably been the result of people, particularly in industries suffering structural decline, pricing themselves out of a job.

(i) The labour costs to firms in such industries may be reduced by the government *reducing employers' National Insurance contributions*. However, protecting or creating jobs in this way is very expensive.

(ii) A system of *direct subsidies* is a more effective way of protecting and creating jobs. One such direct subsidy was the *Temporary Employment Subsidy (TES)*, which was in force in the UK between 1975 and 1979. TES did not, however, create new jobs, it merely protected existing jobs: a subsidy of £20 per week was paid to employers who protected jobs where they would otherwise have made employees redundant. *TES therefore acted as an economic rent for existing employers*.

(iii) *The Industrial Development Act 1982* provided for a system of *grants to firms in mining, manufacturing and construction undertaking investment projects*. Firms have to show that the projects would not take place without such assistance and that they will lead to additional employment or safeguard existing employment. A condition is that project costs should be met mainly outside the public sector and attention must be paid to the contribution of each project to the economy as a whole.

(iv) In 1984 a *subsidy designed to create extra employment* (rather than merely to protect existing jobs) was introduced. It was *a subsidy of £40 per week, available for one year, to encourage unemployed people to establish themselves as self-employed.* Subsidies have also been paid to commercial firms creating new jobs, whereby the more employment created, the larger the subsidy received. These subsidies are known as *marginal employment subsidies.* They have the effect of reducing firms' marginal costs and so encouraging them to employ more labour. Marginal employment subsidies are advocated by Keynesian economists, but they are based on the classical view of competitive markets that the excess supply of labour can be reduced if the wage is reduced.

(v) *The refund on Selective Employment Tax (SET)* and the *Regional Employment Premium (REP)* both acted to reduce the labour costs of firms. However, the SET refund and REP were both designed for firms in certain assisted areas only. These measures and other measures designed to reduce regional unemployment are discussed in detail in Chapter 24.

(vi) Firms' labour costs will also be controlled by *measures which reduce real wages in the economy generally.* Measures designed to *reduce the power of trade unions* (such as the *1980 Employment Act*) should reduce workers' bargaining power, so curbing any rise in real wages. If real wages are reduced, the unemployment caused by people pricing themselves out of a job should fall.

4. Policies to reduce demand-deficient unemployment

Demand deficiency probably accounts for most of the recent rise in unemployment. Therefore, *unemployment will probably be reduced most efficiently if aggregate monetary demand (i.e. total expenditure) is increased.* Keynesian economists recommend that the government should increase government expenditure, reduce taxation or increase private consumption, investment and export expenditure (while reducing private expenditure on imports), and thereby increase aggregate monetary demand, leading to a fall in unemployment.

(i) *A reduction in income tax* (as in the 1986, 1987 and 1988 Budgets) will result in individuals having more money in their pockets and will, therefore, increase their potential consumption expenditure. However, a cut in income tax might merely lead to an increase in the private consumption of imports and not to any significant rise in employment in the UK.

(ii) *Private expenditure upon imports might be reduced* by the imposition of tariffs or import restrictions, but such action is open to retaliatory tactics from other countries. An alternative course of action open to the government is to subsidize the price of British goods which have to compete in the domestic market with foreign imports. Policies which reduce the exchange rate will make imports more expensive and might, therefore, tend to reduce expenditure on imports.

(iii) *Expenditure on British exports* will be increased by making British goods and services more competitive. The price to overseas consumers of British exports may be reduced by the use of subsidies from the government. British exports may also be made more competitive by policies which reduce the exchange rate: a fall in the exchange rate reduces the price of British goods to overseas consumers and should, therefore, lead to an increase in demand for British exports.

(iv) *An increase in private investment* might be induced by reducing interest rates. However, Keynes argued that private investment is most likely to be increased if entrepreneurs expect economic conditions in the future to be more conducive to profit. Business expectations are likely to improve if prices of factors of production are kept under control; taxation on profits and on consumers' expenditure is reduced; conditions conducive to exporting are improved; imports are controlled; and government expenditure is increased (assuming that government expenditure 'crowds in' private expenditure rather than 'crowds out' private expenditure). If private investment is increased, employment will rise. However, private investment might be directed towards capital-intensive projects.

(v) The government can best reduce demand-deficient unemployment by *increasing government expenditure*. Increased government expenditure on council housing, hospitals and education has been advocated not only because such sectors are very labour-intensive (so that increased expenditure will greatly increase employment), but also because greater expenditure in such sectors will improve the economy's stock of social capital.

It is easier for the government to increase its own expenditure counter-cyclically (in an attempt to reduce demand-deficient unemployment) than it is for it to encourage private firms to increase their investment expenditure counter-cyclically, because during a recession expectations are usually low. An increase in government expenditure might well encourage an increase in private investment (i.e. an increase in government expenditure will 'crowd in' rather than 'crowd out' private investment). Increased government expenditure upon state schools, for example, is likely to increase the demand for stationery and text-books produced by private firms.

Increasing government expenditure counter-cyclically might, however, be *de-stabilizing*: by the time a policy of increased government expenditure begins to have an effect the economy might be on the upturn, and policy could then prove very inflationary.

It seems reasonable to assume that, at least in the short term, a rise in total expenditure (as a result of a rise in government expenditure) will lower unemployment, but at a cost of higher inflation. This 'trade-off' is discussed in greater detail later in this chapter.

It may be possible to avoid the inflationary trap by the use of incomes policies, as described in Chapter 19.

5. Policies to reduce youth unemployment

In the UK and in many other countries in recent years, there has been a tendency for unemployment to be particularly prevalent amongst young people. This applies partly because many firms, faced with redundancies, have used a method known as '*natural wastage*' to reduce the workforce. That is to say, they have not recruited new workers when existing workers have left or retired and so have not recruited young people.

Youth unemployment was not really a major concern of governments until the mid-1970s, when declining international competitiveness and recession began to make apparent the need for policies especially designed for young people. Young people in the UK are the most likely members of the population to be unemployed.

Policies designed specifically to reduce youth unemployment have concentrated mainly upon increasing and improving the training young people receive.

(i) Employment and training policies designed specifically for young people were introduced in the mid-1970s. These policies took the form of a *youth training programme* run by the *Manpower Services Commission* (*MSC*) from 1973 to 1981. As part of the programme, the *Youth Opportunities Programme* (*YOP*) was introduced in 1978. YOP was designed for people aged nineteen or under, unemployed for six weeks or more. It was designed to provide work preparation and work experience. Employers who took on unemployed young people under YOP paid them nothing: the MSC funded the programme, paying the trainees a weekly allowance. However, employers were expected to give genuine training to the people they used in the scheme. One problem with the programme was the tendency for firms to employ people on YOP as an alternative to employing other workers. Furthermore, in 1980 only one third of YOP entrants were still in employment once their YOP place had ended.

(ii) In 1981 the *New Training Initiative* was formulated. It aimed to deal with youth unemployment by improving work preparation in schools and colleges. As part of this initiative, the *Youth Training Scheme (YTS)*, which absorbed YOP, was begun in 1983. YTS is a more training-intensive scheme than YOP, but it does not cater for those who still cannot find a job at the end of the training period. The scheme was designed for sixteen- and seventeen-year-olds. Taxes bear most of the costs of YTS. The scheme provides participating firms with a grant and provides an allowance to trainees (£26.25 per week in 1985).

In its first year, YTS aimed to provide about 5,000 young people with a year-long place. The scheme has since been extended from a one-year to a two-year programme. The aims of YTS are to provide basic skills in numeracy and literacy. It has been pointed out that, in some cases, it might be more cost-effective to provide compulsory education in colleges, where the opportunity costs might be relatively low, especially as existing colleges are not always fully utilized. The net cost to the Exchequer of providing compulsory education within colleges instead of through the YTS might well be quite small, especially where use is made of teachers who are currently unemployed.

(iii) Attempts to encourage firms to employ more young people by *reducing their labour costs* have also been made by the government. For example, in 1975 a system of recruitment subsidies of £5 per week for school-leavers was begun. These subsidies were payable to employers for employing school-leavers who had not worked previously. This system was replaced by a youth employment subsidy of £10 per week for up to six months. This was payable to private firms and nationalized industries for full-time workers under twenty years of age who had been employed for six months or longer. This was replaced, in turn, by the Youth Opportunities Programme in 1978.

When one considers the value of training schemes, one has to take into account the fact that many of the participating firms may have taken on school-leavers anyway and the fact that some young people are taken on through these schemes at the expense of other workers, particularly part-time workers or married women.

6. Policies to reduce the supply of labour

Reducing the supply of labour means reducing the number of people looking for work (i.e. the size of the working population). The fewer people there are looking for work, the greater is the likelihood of those who are looking for a job actually finding one.

(i) One way to reduce the supply of labour is to *reduce the retirement age*. However, surveys seem to indicate that relatively few people wish to retire early if their occupational pension scheme is based on earnings; salaries in the last few years before retirement tend to be substantially above salaries earned in previous years.

If the aim is to increase the number of jobs for young people, it is important to ensure that the reduction in potential supply resulting from workers forced to retire is matched by a rise in employment opportunities for younger people and that it does not simply lead to a process of 'natural wastage'. Firms might be reluctant to replace retiring employees with younger people if the younger people are likely to have a lower productivity than those they replace.

The government has introduced *'job-release schemes'* under which, if employers agree to replace (directly or indirectly) workers – usually those within one year of retiring age – through internal promotion, government financial assistance will be given.

(ii) *A reduction in the amount of overtime* that employees are allowed to work in any one week might make firms willing to employ extra workers. Even though unemployment is very high, a considerable volume of overtime is still worked. This could, however, be due to a mis-match of skills between the potential supply of labour and the type of labour required by firms; the fact that firms generally pay a premium rate for overtime hours tends to bear this out. Overtime may be a more attractive proposition to firms than the hiring of more people, who would have to be paid irrespective of any seasonal fluctuations in demand.

(iii) Another possible way of reducing the labour supply would be to *extend holidays*, increasing a typical paid holiday period from, say four weeks to five. However, figures from the Department of Employment tend to suggest that this would not reduce unemployment by any considerable extent; not all firms hire people to fill in during the holiday periods. Firms would tend to be reluctant to increase holidays because they would have to pay more holiday allowance, increasing their costs.

(iv) *Job-sharing* might reduce the supply of labour. The assumption behind job-sharing seems to be that, at least in the short run, there is only a certain amount of work to go round and one job could be handled by more than one person. The government has given grants to some firms which encourage job-sharing. Some education authorities have tried to encourage job-sharing by having a register of people who are willing to share jobs. For many firms, however, job-sharing may be difficult, particularly in some of the service industries where it will be difficult for one person to follow another person's work. However, the difficulties should not be overstated.

(v) The supply of labour could also be reduced by a *reduction in the working week*. While some economists and others have talked about the 'leisure revolution', hours of work have not declined substantially in recent years. Firms would generally be reluctant to reduce the working week if it were to lead to lower productivity and higher average costs because of the effect of under-utilization of fixed capital. There would need to be fairly lengthy negotiations between trade unions and employers before measures designed to reduce the working week could be introduced. One would also need to consider the effects on the balance of payments. For example, less productivity in certain areas would lead to a greater degree of importing.

7. The Phillips curve

The Phillips curve shows an arithmetic relationship between unemployment and inflation (that lower unemployment can be traded off for higher inflation), but it does not indicate causality, i.e. the Phillips curve does not, of itself, show whether higher rates of unemployment cause lower rates of inflation or whether lower rates of inflation cause higher rates of unemployment.

It was derived from data relating to the period between about 1862 and 1958; for much of that period the government, in fact, had relatively little direct influence on inflation or unemployment.

The policy prescription usually concluded from the Phillips relationship is that by pursuing full-employment policies, inflation is increased: an increase in government expenditure increases the aggregate monetary demand and this leads to an increase in the demand for labour which reduces unemployment and increases wages.

The Phillips relationship seems logical when we consider that at high

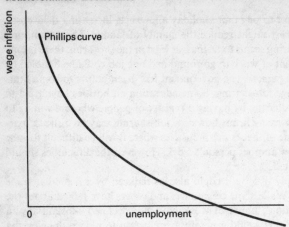

Figure 58. *The Phillips curve*

rates of unemployment, trade unionists and other workers have little scope for raising wages and salaries, unless there is an extremely efficient 'closed shop'. Yet, even in industries where there are closed shops, new firms may decide to enter and charge lower prices (assuming that potential new firms are not deterred by the factors which caused the unemployment in the first place).

The 'expectations-augmented' Phillips curve

Not all economists agree that the Phillips curve is of any great practical use. In fact, in the early 1970s the relationship seemed to break down: there was both high inflation and high unemployment. This breakdown may be partly explained by the occurrence of a number of external 'shocks', particularly the OPEC price rise.

The breakdown of the Phillips relationship led to greater interest in the *'expectations-augmented'* version of the Phillips curve, devised by *Milton Friedman. Friedman argues that policies designed to increase aggregate monetary demand are undesirable because in the long run they do not affect unemployment at all, they merely lead to higher inflation.* He does accept, though, that inflationary policies will reduce unemployment temporarily (i.e. that there is a downward-sloping short-run Phillips curve), but he argues that in the long run the level of unemployment will return to its original level (the natural rate of unemployment), with the economy suffering a higher rate of inflation than originally. The long-

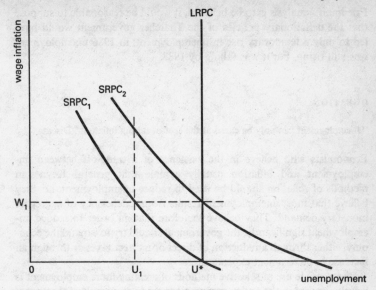

Figure 59. *The 'expectations-augmented' Phillips curve*

run Phillips curve is, therefore, vertical (according to Friedman): unemployment can only be kept below its natural rate (i.e. kept below U* in Figure 59) at the expense of higher and higher inflation, i.e. by moving on to higher and higher short-run Phillips curves.

Friedman argues that if the economy is at a level of unemployment in Figure 59 of U* (the natural rate of unemployment), any unemployment can be explained by people demanding too high a wage. If (starting from a level of unemployment of U* and zero inflation) the government increased its expenditure, this would have the effect of increasing the demand for labour, so increasing the money wage, and would be an incentive for more people to be willing to work. This increase in employment, Friedman argues, is only temporary though, because the increase in money wages pushes up prices, which results in real wages actually not rising at all. As soon as people realize that real wages have not increased at all, those people who joined the job market when the money wage went up now leave it, so that unemployment returns to U* at a higher level of wage inflation (W_1 in Figure 59).

Friedman's analysis fails to explain how countries such as Sweden have managed to achieve near full employment at very low rates of inflation. His analysis also fails to explain how long the short run is: if

Friedman's analysis is to be believed, it would be reasonable to suppose that the deflationary policies of the Thatcher government would have led to only a temporary rise in unemployment; in 1986 unemployment was still rising, but it was falling by 1988.

*

QUESTION

'Unemployment can only be cured at the cost of raising inflation.' Discuss.

Economists who believe in the existence of a trade-off between unemployment and inflation usually assume that general Keynesian methods of reflation should be used to reduce unemployment, i.e. they believe that most unemployment results from a deficiency of aggregate monetary demand. They believe therefore that, in order to reduce unemployment significantly, the government should try to expand the economy, either through a reduction of direct or indirect taxes or through an increase in government expenditure.

The possible use of selective methods of creating more employment is largely ignored in the policy prescriptions made as a result of the apparent Phillips curve relationship. However, governments in the 1960s frequently tried to avoid the unemployment–inflation dilemma through the use of regional policy. In this way governments hoped to avoid inflationary pressures in areas of near full employment (such as south-east England); they only partly cured unemployment in areas of high unemployment, such as north-west England and Northern Ireland, however.

Keynesian economists usually argue that a prices and incomes policy can be made to work if there is sufficient will to make it work. One of the aims of a prices and incomes policy is to avoid the problems of unemployment which can be caused by tight fiscal or monetary policies. For example, raising taxes and increasing HP controls will lead to unemployment in certain industries.

MULTIPLE-CHOICE QUESTIONS

1. If the government wished specifically to reduce unemployment, which of the following would not be an appropriate measure?
   (a) Reducing income-tax thresholds.
   (b) Reducing indirect taxation.
   (c) Reducing interest rates.
Answer – (a)

340

2. The government might best reduce demand-deficient unemployment by:

    (*a*) a policy to encourage firms to move to Development Areas;

    (*b*) reducing income tax;

    (*c*) encouraging work sharing;

    (*d*) increasing government expenditure.

Answer – (*d*)

3. The government might best reduce unemployment caused by people pricing themselves out of a job by:

    (*a*) introducing a direct subsidy similar to the Temporary Employment Subsidy;

    (*b*) introducing a marginal employment subsidy;

    (*c*) reducing income tax;

    (*d*) introducing a system of investment grants.

Answer – (*b*)

DATA RESPONSE

1. The first question is whether the Chancellor is right that wage changes cause job gains or losses. This 'real-wage debate' is still one of the most contentious in economics and one which is bedevilled by jargon. The second question is whether his proposed wage restraint is at all practicable without direct measures such as incomes policy.

For the first time, Mr Lawson [the Chancellor] quantified the effects of restraint on jobs, saying that each percentage point change in the average level of real earnings (gross pay before tax but after inflation) would, in time, change unemployment by $\frac{1}{2}$–1 per cent or by 150,000–200,000 jobs.

He went on to point out that this need not imply pay cuts: the beneficial effects on jobs would happen if pay merely rose in line with prices, rather than at 3 per cent or so more than prices as during the last few years. Gross pay would clearly be lower than it would otherwise be, but not lower in absolute terms. We would forgo real wage increases. On this view, three successive years of such restraint would create a cumulative $1\frac{1}{2}$ million jobs.

In one of the most interesting passages, Mr Lawson tried to reassure anyone afraid of pay cuts that keeping gross pay flat, after allowing for inflation, could still mean rising spending power for the average worker. The solution to this apparent paradox is the tax wedge: 'take-home pay should gradually increase as taxation is reduced'. This is a far cry from the simple pleas for wage cuts . . .

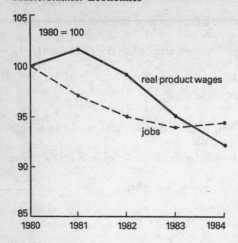

Figure 60. *The trend in real wages and job since 1980*
Unit wage costs derived from *NIESR*, no. 109; employment totals from *OECD Main Economic Indicator.*
Graph reproduced from the *Guardian*, 1 November 1984.

There is also, of course, another tax wedge between gross pay and the costs of an employee to a firm, namely National Insurance contributions. The Chancellor did not mention this, but he could cut wages, on this definition, by cutting employers' NIC. Gross pay and take-home pay would not be affected.

So the way that most economists talk about real wages (as the cost of labour to firms) is not the way most people think about their real wages (or what they have left in their pockets). There are, nevertheless, considerable problems with the simple way in which the Chancellor asserted that changes in real gross pay cause changes in jobs.

Real earnings, after all, nearly doubled between 1946 and 1970 but the unemployment rate was exactly the same in both years. The reason why people did not 'price themselves out of jobs' was because output per person (productivity) rose broadly in line with earnings, thus keeping labour costs to employers for each unit of output fairly stable . . . But . . . the link between real product wages and jobs since 1980 does not look strong . . .

This, though, is not conclusive. Monetarists can point out that, in Britain, rising pay forced companies to boost productivity. This, in turn, lowered the real product wage, which responded to the rise in wage costs in the first instance. It can merely show what happens after the event, not what caused it.

However, Keynesians can reply that it is simply incredible to argue that it was only the rise in real gross pay between 1980 and 1981 which caused the rise in unemployment. The government's anti-inflationary policies, depressing demand, were more important. Indeed, the rise in real pay costs to employers was actually aggravated by the government's pressure on demand and prices (because profits and prices were squeezed and pay, after allowing for prices, rose). So once again, another definition of real wages (real gross pay) merely responded to other developments: tight government policy.

In each case, there may indeed be a link between real wages and jobs, which can be observed using sophisticated statistical techniques, but the link alone does not imply that it is always a change in real wages which is the prime mover in a chain of events. Real-wage changes can, in turn, be caused by other factors, notably government policy.

(Taken from the article 'People are not like bananas, whatever the Chancellor says', by Christopher Huhne in the *Guardian*, 1 November 1984.)

(a) How might the government encourage wage restraint by workers?

(b) Instead of reducing labour costs to employers (reducing real wages) how might reducing tax increase employment? How might increasing government expenditure be a better way of reducing unemployment than reducing income tax?

(c) Was increasing unemployment since 1979 caused by earnings rising faster than inflation or by depressed demand? Give reasons for your answer.

2. In the United Kingdom, as well as in most Western European countries, unemployment has risen much faster amongst the younger members of society than those in their thirties, forties or early fifties. While some government ministers have urged youngsters to accept lower wages in order to gain employment, this seems to be a vast over-simplification of the problem. It is difficult to find evidence that young people's wages have increased disproportionately to those of people in the so-called 'core' of employment. It also seems unlikely that these groups cause inflationary costs. The calls by a government minister for people to moderate wage increases, since they may price themselves out of a job, also seems misguided. It is in direct contrast to the Phillips relationship,

which seems to indicate that higher wages are often correlated with higher levels of employment.

What, then, may be the underlying causes of this increase in unemployment amongst the young? One possibility is agreements between trade unions and employers for 'natural wastage'. This means that, as workers leave an industry for whatever reason (including in some cases voluntary redundancy), they will not be replaced. The young will, therefore, tend to suffer disproportionately, since in many cases the jobs which they would normally take would replace workers who are retiring. Another possibility is that the young are not being trained for the most suitable jobs. This, however, is difficult to quantify. While some employers suggest that young people are less well qualified than other people, this is not shown up in examination results, though examination results are a poor proxy variable of suitability for a particular job. Another possibility is that automation is disproportionately altering the types of jobs which can be done effectively by young people. This again is difficult to quantify. A further possibility is that employers are more willing to employ women returning to work on a part-time basis. This partly depends upon the taxation system which may encourage women to do a small number of hours, since, up to the married women's allowance, they will not be taxed. Employers may also be willing to employ part-time workers, especially women, who are not liable to pay National Insurance.

(a) What reasons does the author suggest may explain why youth unemployment has been rising disproportionately to unemployment among other age groups? What problems are involved in trying to quantify these reasons?

(b) What does traditional Keynesian analysis have to say about the suggestion from some government ministers that young people have priced themselves out of a job?

SELF-EXAMINATION QUESTIONS

1. What is meant by 'seasonal unemployment'? Which industries does this particularly affect? How, if at all, can the government or individual firms help to solve the problems of seasonal unemployment?

2. What is meant by 'cyclical unemployment'? What has happened to trade cycles in recent years? How far can governments pursue counter-cyclical policies?

3. Some economists have suggested that government policies to counter cyclical unemployment have been destabilizing. Why?

4. In most countries unemployment has risen more rapidly amongst young people than amongst other age groups. Is this a result of relatively higher earnings or failings in the young people, or is it merely that firms are not recruiting young people? If possible, test your hypothesis by comparing data from different countries.

5. How will the introduction of visual display units and computers affect the demand for typists and printers in publishing and comparable industries?

6. How far is it true and how is it possible to test the hypothesis that people have priced themselves out of jobs?

7. The Cambridge School of Applied Economics has suggested that we should increase employment because it might help to reduce inflation. How would you test the validity of such a statement?

8. Should the government use selective or general measures to tackle unemployment? Explain your answer.

9. How far have restrictive practices by trade unions and other such organizations hindered or helped the problems of unemployment?

10. How far have job-security measures helped increase or reduce unemployment?

11. [Energy] 'Conservation schemes, for example loft insulation, cavity insulation and the lagging of tanks, are labour-intensive, either save on imported fuel or make national fuel available for exports and tend to improve the environment. They should therefore be thoroughly investigated and welcomed as a helpful, non-inflationary method of overcoming unemployment.' Discuss.

12. Should the government attempt to reduce unemployment by reflating the economy (the policy prescription suggested by the Phillips relationship) or by attempting to reduce wage inflation (the policy prescription suggested by the Thatcher government)? Explain your answer.

13. Would it help, as the TUC has occasionally suggested, to insist on a reduction in the average number of hours worked, as well as on reductions in overtime, to reduce the unemployment problem? Explain your answer.

14. Some economists have suggested that a siege economy would tend to help reduce unemployment; others have suggested freer trade. How can we test such hypotheses?

15. How far has the introduction of monetarism affected unemployment?

16. Should we, as in the United States of America, have a large-scale budget deficit to try to produce more economic growth and hence reduce unemployment? Explain your answer.

21. Economic growth

1. What is economic growth?

Economic growth is conventionally defined as the process of increasing the economy's productive capacity, i.e. as the process of increasing national income.

Thus, *national income statistics or gross national product statistics are often used as indicators of economic growth and as indicators of rises in the standard of living.* However, a rise of GNP over time, as we shall see later, does not necessarily indicate a rise in the standard of living for the nation's inhabitants.

2. How might economic growth (measured as a rise in GNP) be achieved?

(a) *Productivity gains in agriculture*

Originally, economic growth in most countries (as measured by GNP) appeared as *productivity gains in the agricultural sector*, which happened as a result of the *agricultural revolution*. With the greater profits available from the agricultural sector, money was pumped into the industrial sector.

(b) *Investment in industry*

(i) At the same time as the agricultural revolution, *increases in the industrial sector* (*because of inventions, etc.*) meant that further increases in GNP could be achieved.

(ii) *Even replacement investment* (*as well as net investment*) *is likely to increase GNP,* because new machinery often incorporates built-in productivity improvements. This is particularly true in the 1980s, with the 'micro-chip revolution'. Perhaps for the first time, we see this more in the service sector than in the manufacturing sector. The growth of word-processors, electronic typewriters and micro-computers has meant that far fewer people can carry out the same volume of work as in earlier periods. This does not necessarily lead to unemployment, since

347

relative reductions in labour costs may lead to lower prices and, hence, greater demand.

(iii) *Investment in the social infrastructure* may well increase GNP. The type of social infrastructure which a country has may have an important impact upon economic growth. For example, most economic historians would suggest that the development of the railway system in the United States of America in the nineteenth century helped to develop its economic growth. Less glamorous industries, such as the water-supply industry, have often been crucial to both agricultural and industrial development.

(c) *Greater basic numeracy and literacy*

The growth, in most Western countries, of basic numeracy and literacy has led to a more educated workforce and this, in turn, has led to potentially higher economic growth. However, many people in old industries are by no means using their full potential.

(d) *Greater expectations of improved standards of living*

Expectations may well be important in maintaining a given rise in GNP. For example, whereas there was little change in the standard of living in the United Kingdom for the average labourer between the fourteenth and eighteenth centuries, the standard of living has changed greatly in the twentieth century (even within the last twenty years); partly because people nowadays expect higher incomes, they are more willing to investigate methods of increasing their own standards of living and this has a cumulative effect.

(e) *Increasing the supply and quality of labour*

(i) Since 1964 successive UK governments have introduced *Industrial Training Acts. Youth training schemes and the provision of further and higher education* at universities, polytechnics, technical colleges, etc., are all intended to improve the quality of the labour force in terms of productivity.

(ii) It was hoped that *the raising of the school-leaving age* in 1973 to sixteen would lead to improved quality of the labour force. There was, anyway, a growing tendency to remain in full-time education beyond the age of sixteen (a tendency which has continued), partly because of the lack of suitable jobs available. It should be noted, of course, that the educational system is not entirely geared to industrial training.

(iii) *Retirement conventions* also affect the size and quality of the labour force. The substitution of school-leavers for workers over the age of, say, fifty-five might tend to increase productivity, especially in the long run (given that young people's productivity increases once they have learnt the nature of the job).

(iv) *The number of married women joining the labour force* has risen over recent years. This trend has affected economic growth because the more workers there are, the higher GNP will be, because incomes are higher. However, the rise in GNP as a result of this trend may have been smaller than if there had been a similar rise in the number of men entering the labour market, because many of these women work part-time rather than full-time.

(v) *Emigration and immigration* affect the size and maybe even the quality of the labour force. Despite much publicity, emigration and immigration have not been important factors affecting productivity in the UK in recent years.

(vi) Of course, if the supply of labour is raised so much that there are considerable *unemployed resources*, this will adversely affect economic growth, since any economy with unemployment is operating below full capacity. In the UK, the number of people unemployed had risen to well over 3 million by 1986, but has fallen since.

(f) *Increases in efficiency*

(i) Some economists suggest that if the economy had *more competitive industries and fewer monopolies* (not only in the public sector, but also in the private sector) and fewer monopolistic organizations such as trade unions (and fewer restrictive practices), then many of the problems of inertia would be overcome and productivity would rise.

It was hoped that entry into the European Economic Community would make Britain more competitive.

(ii) On the other hand, a few economists (particularly from the Cambridge School) have suggested that *a more closed economy, free from imports*, would enable industry to plan more effectively and would, in turn, lead to higher productivity.

(iii) Efficiency would probably be improved if firms devoted more resources to *research and development*. It is difficult to compare the amount spent on research and development by the UK with the amount spent by other countries, since the original data from firms is not

349

necessarily homogeneous: items which one firm considers as research and development, another might not. There has been considerable controversy as to whether firms with a high degree of monopoly power or those in a more competitive market are the most likely to invest in research and development. Monopolistic firms are the most likely to have the resources available for research and development, but more competitive firms are more likely to have an incentive to invest in research and development, in an attempt to improve their market position, if only in the short run.

(iv) Within firms, the type of *wage structure* may influence total productivity. Wage systems need to be seen to be reasonably fair if good industrial relations are to be maintained. This has been a failing of industrial relations in many sectors in the UK: many disputes occur because of widening or narrowing differentials. It would, therefore, seem reasonable to suggest that productivity (and GNP) would rise if industrial relations were improved.

(v) Some economists have suggested that *prevailing class attitudes* (more apparent in the UK than in, say, the Scandinavian countries) have impeded progress towards greater economic growth. Prevailing class attitudes are evident within industrial relations in the UK.

(g) *Government policies*

(i) The government may be able to raise GNP by raising productivity through *policies designed to improve the quality of the labour force*, through the use of Training Acts, etc. (see subsection (e) and Chapter 4).

(ii) *Prices and incomes policies* have sometimes affected differentials and thus the potential productivity of workers (and, hence, GNP) for the reasons mentioned in subsection (d).

(iii) *Regional policy* could be used to raise economic growth. Regional policy has often focused on propping up ailing industries. If similar help was given to newer industries, rather than to ailing industries, economic growth might be higher. It has been argued that leaving ailing industry to market forces would lead to a natural progression towards private investment in newer industries and lead to greater economic growth this way. However, the existence, as a result, of any structural unemployment might mean that economic growth is lower than it would have been had the government not intervened.

(iv) Economists have often used the phrase '*constrained maximization*' to suggest that *one policy objective cannot be achieved except at the expense of other objectives*. Thus, policies designed to achieve balance of payments stability and/or declining inflation tend to be pursued at the expense of economic growth. *The National Plan, 1965,* for example, would, it was hoped, lead to greater economic growth, but failed to do so partly because of the increase in sterling prices. Similarly, the *1973 'run for economic growth'* under the Heath government failed partly because of increasing balance of payments problems, which were compounded by the increase in oil prices. These BOP problems led to the government concentrating on the balance of payments rather than on economic growth.

(v) On the other hand, *policies designed to reduce unemployment* (particularly demand-deficient unemployment), by raising effective demand, should raise GNP.

(vi) In purely free-enterprise economies and in mixed economies there might be bottlenecks in certain parts of production and surpluses in others. Some economists have, therefore, suggested that economic growth (as measured by GNP) could be raised through *indicative planning,* whereby bottlenecks are identified and information disseminated. This information should enable the efficiency of both public- and private-sector firms to be improved. Indicative planning takes account of the views of industry, trade unionists and others about where bottlenecks and surpluses might occur.

(vii) *The National Board for Prices and Incomes (NBPI)* in the 1960s aimed to improve the overall efficiency of firms. It was an independent body set up by the government in 1965 to examine productivity within firms and industries. While many firms objected to the expense of providing suitable information for the Board, the Board may have helped improve productivity in those industries it examined, since its findings revealed much evidence of waste in firms' total costs. There is considerable evidence, for example, to suggest that most people who work in offices spend little time productively.

(viii) We have said that research and development may lead to a rise in GNP. In the UK, as in many other countries, a great deal of *research and development is funded by the government,* mainly for strategic reasons. This type of research and development may have some spin-off effects (beneficial externalities) but is likely to raise GNP less than the same amount of research and development geared to more commercial purposes. For example, a given amount of research and development spent on defence equipment is likely to increase GNP less than the same amount of research and development spent on, say, office equipment. This aspect, often overlooked, would seem to some extent to explain the resurgence of Japan and West Germany in post-war years, since only a small proportion of their investment has tended to go on defence. There is, however, no general agreement on this matter.

(ix) GNP may be raised if *expenditure on health* is increased, since the health of the working population affects productivity. Economic growth might, therefore, be increased if the government increases expenditure on the National Health Service.

(x) The government also influences health through *other aspects of the social infrastructure*, for example by ensuring that *housing conditions* are not unhealthy. Conditions at work may affect the health and, hence, quality of workers. Generally, strikes lead to fewer work days lost than do accidents. *The Health and Safety at Work Act 1974* has helped to reduce the number of accidents and has, therefore, reduced the time lost in some industries.

(xi) We have already suggested, in subsection (f), that trade unions' restrictive practices impede economic growth by adversely affecting productivity. For example, within the newspaper printing industry productivity was much lower than it needed to be because of unions' refusal to allow computers to be used to set the type. *Legislation which aims to improve industrial relations and which aims to prohibit restrictive practices* might, therefore, be successful in raising productivity. Recent legislation has included the *Industrial Relations Act 1971* and the *Employment Acts* of the 1980s, which have all aimed to reduce strikes and improve the mobility of labour. While legislation relating to trade-union membership has been controversial, the industrial-relations codes of practices may well have been beneficial to industrial relations and may, therefore, have led to some increase in economic growth.

3. Limits to economic growth

The MIT survey *Limits to Growth* suggested that we cannot have economic growth at the same rate in the future as in the past, partly because of differences in the availability of resources and because of increasing social costs, including pollution. The MIT survey reasoned that fossil fuels and land space may well impose constraints. However, the survey did not fully appreciate the possibility that in the future renewable resources, such as the wind and waves, might become increasingly important sources of energy, enabling economic growth to be maintained at a reasonable level.

Other economists, noticeably *E. J. Mishan*, have queried the value of economic growth. In particular, attention has been drawn to the problems of harmful externalities which might result from economic growth. For example, the project to develop London's third airport will add to GNP, but the resultant increase in noise and pollution might mean that the standard of living is reduced rather than increased.

4. Gross national product as a measure of welfare

(a) *What adjustments might be made to the GNP as a measure of welfare?*

(i) While *gross national product* over time is often used as a measure of welfare over time, it is not necessarily satisfactory.

(ii) Since population size alters over time, *gross national product per head* is often a more useful measure of welfare than total gross national product.

(iii) Gross national product also ignores inflation; we therefore need to use a deflator, such as the Retail Prices Index, to give *GNP at constant prices*, in order to make reasonable comparisons of welfare over time.

(iv) Gross national product does not have capital consumption deducted from it and therefore tends to overestimate the value of investment to welfare. The economist defines investment as additions to the capital stock. Since, however, part of gross investment is replacement investment (investment which is used to replace capital as it wears out or, possibly, as it becomes obsolete), *GNP minus replacement investment* (i.e. capital consumption) gives a better measure of welfare than GNP.

It should be noted that replacement investment includes that investment which replaces old capital with newer, more productive capital. Thus, there is an element of increased productivity in replacement investment. None the less, it is still clear that GNP tends to overstate the level of productive investment. This is particularly true in wartime when capital consumption (and hence the level of gross investment) tends to be very high, while the level of productive investment is not necessarily very high. In many ways, therefore, *net national product*, which equals GNP minus replacement investment, is a more useful measure of welfare. It is net national product (i.e. *national income*) which is often used by economists as a measure of economic growth.

(b) *Deficiencies of both GNP and net national product as measures of welfare?*

(i) *Both GNP and net national product omit the value of services, such as housewives' services, which are provided within the home for no cash.* The Legal and General Assurance Group has estimated that inclusion of the value of women's unpaid domestic work in GNP would increase GNP by about 25 per cent. If the value of women's unpaid work is estimated to be a fairly steady proportion of GNP over time, its exclusion will not affect GNP's reliability as a measure of economic growth very much. However, the value of women's unpaid work has probably declined slightly with the increased mechanization of housework.

(ii) *Both GNP and net national product ignore the extent to which the distribution of income is unequal.* It is possible to get GNP to rise with one group getting richer while most other people are getting poorer. In this way economic growth will appear to have taken place, but welfare for many people will have deteriorated. Conversely, it would be possible for GNP to be reduced, but for the majority of people to become better off.

(iii) *Many elements which we might assume add to the nation's welfare, such as improvements in health, improvements in working conditions, reductions in the existence of unfavourable externalities (such as noise and air pollution) and increases in leisure time do not necessarily have elements which directly raise GNP or net national product.* In fact, air pollution might only be reduced at the expense of GNP. For example, if a factory is closed, air pollution may be reduced, but output (and incomes) will also be reduced. Whether or not welfare is increased as a result of this action is very much a matter of conjecture and depends upon *value judgements.*

(iv) *There are problems in using GNP and net national product as measures to compare welfare between countries because exchange rates do not always indicate purchasing power.* A sudden devaluation, such as the devaluation of the pound in 1967, will tend to suggest that one country has suddenly experienced a great loss in welfare, although this is, in fact, unlikely to be the case. Furthermore, the slump in the pound from $2.40 in 1981 to $1.10 in 1985 did not result in personal incomes being halved. If, for example, an American received an annual income in 1981 of $10,560 he would have earned the equivalent of someone in the UK receiving £4,400. If in 1985 the American still earned $10,560, the equivalent income for someone in the UK, according to the exchange rate, would have been £9,600. Therefore a person earning £4,400 in 1985 would appear to be worse off than someone on the same salary in 1981. However, assuming zero inflation, his purchasing power in 1985 would be the same as in 1981.

5. The OECD's measure of welfare

Traditionally, differences in welfare or economic growth over time or between countries are calculated using easily quantifiable measures, such as GNP. However, the *Organization for Economic Cooperation and Development* or *OECD* (which was established in 1961 to promote policies designed to achieve the highest sustainable economic growth in employment and rising living standards, while maintaining financial stability, in its member countries and to contribute to world development) set out a new *qualitative approach to measuring welfare* in June 1973.

The OECD's approach attempts to measure changes in, for example, health, working conditions and the physical environment, since changes in such indicators are likely to affect the quality of life just as changes in real national income per head do. *The OECD attempts to measure the objectives of economic growth.*

(a) Health

In the area of health, for example, a rise in expenditure on cigarettes is likely to lead to a greater incidence of lung cancer and to greater health expenditure. This raises GNP in two ways: firstly, as a result of the rise in cigarette expenditure; secondly, as a result of the rise in health expenditure. In this case, the rise in health expenditure recorded by GNP is not an indicator of any improvement in health. In fact, ideally we should aim to have a perfectly healthy population, which would require little health expenditure.

The OECD attempts to compare health over time and between countries by considering, for example, *the probability of a healthy life*, which might be gauged by studying *life-expectancy figures* and *figures which show the recorded incidence of various diseases*.

(b) Employment and the quality of working life

While a high level of unemployment will affect GNP, even if there is full employment, there may be '*hidden unemployment*' which will not directly affect GNP.

The OECD attempts to measure the availability of suitable employment: if a person unwillingly moves from Newcastle to London in order to find work, any work he finds will add to GNP, but it may not add to welfare as measured by the OECD because there is *an absence of choice of employment.* An individual who transfers from one job to another and as a result enjoys *better working conditions* but receives a lower income will, according to GNP, suffer a decline in welfare, but the OECD's measure of welfare may indicate a rise in welfare.

Any improvements in working conditions over time might be gauged by the OECD from, for example, *downward trends in working hours* or from *the OECD's own surveys.*

(c) *Time and leisure*

If people have to spend a lot of money on travel in order to get to the countryside and open spaces, any expenditure on this travel will increase GNP. However, *a greater provision of parks and open spaces will increase welfare as measured by the OECD,* but will reduce the amount of money spent travelling to open spaces and will reduce GNP.

Also, if the amount of money commuters have to spend travelling to work falls (if, for example, the price of petrol falls) and this money is spent on leisure activities, GNP will be unaffected, but *welfare, as measured, by the OECD will rise, since there will be a greater availability of effective choices between consumption of goods and services necessary for work and consumption of leisure goods and services.*

(d) *The physical environment*

The existence of pollutants and of poor housing conditions, etc., will reduce welfare as measured by the OECD. If the output of a factory is increased, so that air pollution is also increased, welfare (as measured by OECD) may fall, but GNP will rise. Similarly, if a house is pulled down and replaced by a worse house, GNP will rise, but welfare (as measured by OECD) will fall.

(e) *The command over goods and services*

We have already illustrated that the OECD sees the existence of effective choices as very important in increasing welfare. In terms of the personal command over goods and services, *if the range of choice of goods and services is increased as a result of the control of monopolies and the en-*

couragement of greater competition, this may or may not raise GNP, but it will raise welfare, according to the OECD.

(f) *Education*

Improvements in literacy and numeracy and in the acquisition of basic knowledge, values and skills may not increase GNP directly, but are considered as improvements in welfare by the OECD.

Improvements in education may be measured by *increases in education facilities* (which will increase GNP), but are, perhaps, best measured by looking at *examination results* or by *surveys carried out by the OECD.*

(g) *Deprivation*

GNP does not measure levels of overcrowding and does not measure whether houses constructed are of a good quality or of a poor quality. Yet *overcrowding and poor housing reduce welfare.* The OECD attempts to measure the extent to which overcrowding and poor housing exist, by looking at *housing figures* (which might show how many people live in each house and whether or not a house has running water) and by carrying out *its own surveys.*

*

QUESTION

How effective is GNP as a measure of economic welfare?

It has often been assumed that GNP is synonymous with the standard of living, but it is not necessarily so. At the very least, when using GNP to compare economic welfare over time, allowance has to be made for changes in the population size and for inflation. It is difficult to allow for inflation over long periods of time: new products come on to the market; old products disappear; the quality of products varies.

GNP, as a measure of economic welfare, is also defective in that it only takes into account goods and services which are sold on the market: do-it-yourself and women's unpaid work at home are not taken into account. Also, GNP does not take into account hours of work or working conditions.

Furthermore, incomes (and hence GNP) might tend to fall as leisure time (which is assumed to add to welfare) rises.

GNP does not take into account how well goods and services are utilized. In the energy sector, better insulation may reduce the demand for energy, but will hardly have reduced welfare. Similarly, GNP ignores the externalities aspect: as GNP rises air pollution (the existence of which, one imagines, reduces welfare) may well rise.

The value of collective goods, such as parks, are only measured by GNP at factor cost, but the utility gained as a result of their existence may well be a lot higher.

Also, GNP ignores the way income is distributed.

Finally, if our main obsession is to become better off than our neighbours, then the quest for growth becomes a zero-sum game: one country's GNP rises at the expense of another's.

MULTIPLE-CHOICE QUESTIONS

1. Which of the following lead to an increase in GNP:
(A) an agreement by trade unions to end some restrictive practices;
(B) an increase in research and development;
(C) a lowering of the rate of inflation?
   (*a*) A only.
   (*b*) A and B only.
   (*c*) A and C only.
   (*d*) B and C only.
   (*e*) All.
Answer – (*b*)

2. Which of the following make GNP in real terms an unsatisfactory measure of welfare:
(A) a change in the quality of goods;
(B) an increase in inflation;
(C) an increase in pollution;
(D) a change in working conditions?
   (*a*) A and C only.
   (*b*) B only.
   (*c*) B and D only.
   (*d*) A, C and D only.
   (*e*) All.
Answer – (*d*)

3. If in 1980 the price index was taken as 100 and in 1985 was 140, and GNP has risen from £120bn to £168bn, which of the following is correct:
   (*a*) GNP has grown in real terms;

(*b*) GNP has remained unchanged in real terms;

(*c*) GNP has fallen in real terms?

Answer – (*b*)

4. Which of the following is the best measure of economic welfare:

(*a*) Gross National Product;

(*b*) Net National Product?

Answer – (*b*)

5–7. What will be the outcome of each of the situations illustrated in questions 5–7?

(*a*) There will be no change in GNP and no change in economic welfare as measured by the OECD.

(*b*) There will be no change in GNP, but there will be a change in economic welfare as measured by the OECD.

(*c*) There will be a change in GNP, but no change in economic welfare as measured by the OECD.

(*d*) There will be a change in GNP and a change in economic welfare as measured by the OECD in the same direction.

(*e*) There will be a change in GNP and a change in economic welfare as measured by the OECD, but in opposite directions.

5. A person decides to leave a job which pays £10,000 per annum to work in a more pleasant job which pays £8,000 per annum.

Answer – (*e*)

6. Workers produce the same output this year as they did last year, but work shorter hours.

Answer – (*b*)

7. An oil spillage occurs and is not cleared up.

Answer – (*b*)

DATA RESPONSE

In recent years there has been considerable controversy regarding whether or not economic growth can continue at the rates customary in the post-war period. One of the best-known books dealing with this controversy was the MIT survey, *Limits of Growth*. This survey, given certain assumptions, seemed to indicate that either the scarcity of resources or pollution and other social costs would increasingly limit potential growth. It is difficult to test the reliability of such models, although we can see whether we arrive at sensible results when we run such models backwards. There are a number of limitations to any such models. For example, research and development into alternative energy may mean that the unavailability of fossil fuels will not necessarily affect economic growth in the future. However, at the present time, there is little evidence to suggest that the government is looking seriously into such areas. Furthermore, we are often using fuels inefficiently. Such use is irrational. If one estimate (from the late 1970s) is to be believed, by improving insulation at a cost of between £5,000m and £6,000m, about £30,000m in fuel costs would be saved. However, it is often difficult to quantify figures and much official data is probably over-aggregated. One might be able to find figures for the mechanical- or electrical-engineering aspects, but we need finer details in order to be able to predict accurately the likely scarcity of resources in the real world in the future.

(a) Since the supply of many fossil fuels is running out, how might recent levels of economic growth (as measured by real national income) be maintained in the future?

(b) While you would expect the measures you have outlined in your answer to (a) to maintain recent levels of economic growth (as measured by real national income), into the future, what effect might these measures have upon future welfare (as measured by the OECD)?

SELF-EXAMINATION QUESTIONS

1. How, if at all, can the government increase economic growth?

2. 'Economic growth in the United Kingdom has often been slow because it has conflicted with other objectives of government.' Discuss.

3. 'Greater economic growth in the future can only be achieved if people are willing to consume less at the present time.' Evaluate this statement.

4. 'There are obvious limits to economic growth in the world as a whole because of the problems of scarce resources.' Evaluate this statement.

5. How far do restrictive practices by (a) trade unions and (b) professional associations affect economic growth?

6. How far do poor industrial relations and outdated class attitudes affect economic growth in the United Kingdom?

7. How far do job-security measures increase or decrease economic growth?

8. The government has sometimes given investment grants or depreciation allowances towards investment in the private sector. How does this affect economic growth?

9. What effect might the 'chip revolution' have on economic growth?

22. Cost Benefit Analysis

1. Introduction

Cost benefit analysis is, in essence, an accounting procedure for invest-ment appraisal whereby the costs of a particular project are weighed against its benefits. *The costs and benefits are not just the private costs and benefits*, i.e. the costs and benefits which the firm takes into account. *Externalities (both harmful and favourable) are also evaluated in cost benefit analysis. Cost benefit analysis attempts to weigh the social costs of a project against its social benefits.* Thus, in cost benefit analysis the private costs plus harmful externalities of a project are weighed against the private benefits plus favourable externalities.

2. Private costs and benefits

A private firm, when evaluating the likely costs and benefits of a project, will tend only to weigh the private costs against the private benefits.

(i) We can say that the *private costs are mainly the costs of production* (i.e. factor payments). However, there may be other costs which the firm will tend to take into account, such as employers' National Insurance contributions.

(ii) We can call the *private benefits revenue. If expected revenue exceeds the expected private costs, the firm expects to make a net profit if it goes ahead with the project.* If this proposed project gives a higher expected net profit than any alternatives which have been considered, we can expect that a profit-maximizing firm will wish to go ahead with the project.

3. Social costs and benefits

Governments, on the other hand, tend to be interested in the likely social costs and benefits of a proposed project. Therefore, if the government concludes that the likely harmful externalities (such as noise and air pollution) are likely to outweigh the likely net private benefits plus favourable externalities of a project, it might dissuade the firm concerned from going ahead with its proposed project.

Governments take account of all costs because they are interested in increasing welfare.

4. Public goods

Consideration of any likely externalities is particularly important when deciding whether or not to produce public goods (i.e. collective goods). This is because there tends to be *little scope for excluding people from using a public good or service if they do not pay for it.* Such goods include street lighting and roads in the absence of an effective road pricing system. The revenue to be gained by a firm which provides public goods is likely to be very low, even zero. Thus, the private costs are likely to outweigh the private benefits. This implies that, generally, *profit-maximizing firms are unwilling to produce public goods unless they receive some form of subsidy.*

Public goods such as roads, open spaces and defence may be considered as goods which add to the welfare of the population. Thus, *the provision of public goods can be said to have certain favourable externalities*. If the expected favourable externalities plus private benefits of the proposed production of a public good exceed the expected harmful externalities plus private costs, the government is likely to be keen that the public good be produced. However, since the private costs are likely to exceed the private benefits, we can assume that the government will have to meet the costs of production, i.e. the government may hire a private firm to produce the public good in question and pay for all the costs of production, such as the cost of materials and the cost of capital and wages.

5. The importance of consumer surplus in cost benefit analysis

Consumer surplus is defined as the amount a consumer is prepared to pay for a good over and above the amount he actually pays for it. Where there is no direct price charged, as is usually the case with roads, the area of consumer surplus (as represented in Figure 61) covers the whole area

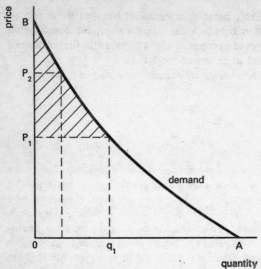

Figure 61. *Consumer surplus*

If the price charged is P_1, the amount of consumer surplus is represented by the shaded area. Consumer surplus derives from the fact that if the price were higher than P_1 (for example, P_2) there would still be some people willing to buy the good.

AOB. In such cases, the concept of consumer surplus is extremely important. Where there are direct financial returns, the private producer will merely take into account how much revenue he will derive from charging a certain price. However, the government, when deciding what price to charge for a particular good or service it provides, will consider how much consumer surplus will be derived. Clearly, the lower the price, the greater the consumer surplus.

6. The costs and benefits of the building of a new motorway

We can consider the sort of costs and benefits which cost benefit analysis attempts to evaluate by taking a public good as an example: we can consider the likely costs and benefits that the building of a motorway will have.

One of the best known instances when cost benefit analysis was used was in the case of the M 1 motorway. This, however, was a rather odd use of cost benefit analysis because it took place after the motorway had been built. None the less, it is helpful in suggesting what sort of externalities a government might consider in the context of deciding whether or not to build a motorway.

(a) Benefits

If we assume that there is no road pricing scheme, then there are no direct financial returns resulting from the building of a new motorway; revenue will be zero, i.e. there will be *no private benefits*. However, we might expect there to be some favourable externalities, otherwise the government would not wish a new motorway to be built.

(i) One of the favourable aspects justifying the building of the M 1 was the apparent *saving of time to users*. The higher speed limits on motorways compared to most other roads, the existence of three of four lanes on motorways and the absence of traffic lights and roundabouts makes journeys by motorway quicker, generally, than journeys on other roads, kilometre for kilometre.

(ii) Another favourable externality which a new motorway might have is that of a *reduction in road accidents*: motorways tend to be safer than other roads (there tend to be fewer accidents per passenger kilometre) because of the absence of pedestrians, the separation of oncoming traffic by barriers and the absence of roundabouts, etc. Thus, the building of a motorway might save on the costs of medical attention, days at work lost and personal inconvenience and suffering.

(iii) The use by motorists of *a new motorway will tend to reduce the traffic on other roads in nearby areas. The reduction of air pollution and noise in these areas can be considered as a favourable externality.*

(iv) The most important favourable external effect will probably be the *reduction of unemployment*. The implementation of public works schemes, such as the building of roads, is usually advocated in times of high unemployment. Thus, it seems reasonable to suppose that a government will be particularly keen to build a new motorway in times of high unemployment because it will create new jobs. Wages will be received by those people employed to build the motorway. If these people would have been otherwise unemployed, it would seem reasonable to suppose that their welfare is increased by the government's decision to build a new motorway. Furthermore, although the government has to pay the wages to those employed to build the motorway, it will *save on social security payments* made to the unemployed and may *receive some revenue from taxation on incomes.*

(v) We might expect there to be *multiplier effects* of government expenditure on a new motorway, further reducing unemployment. Policemen will be required to patrol the motorway and jobs will probably be created at service stations. If the people employed to patrol the motorway and the people employed at the service stations would otherwise have been unemployed, it is clear that the government makes further savings in social security payments.

(b) *Costs*

The various social benefits which are likely to arise as a result of the building of a new motorway (which as we have said, are likely to be merely favourable externalities with there being no private benefits) have to be weighed against the social costs.

(i) Firstly there will be *private costs: the costs of production.*

(ii) Other costs will be harmful externalities. The harmful externalities resulting from the building of a new motorway are likely to include *an increase in the level of noise in surrounding areas,* reducing the welfare of people who live or work in these areas. There is also likely to be a lot of noise caused during the construction of the motorway.

(iii) Since a new motorway is likely to lead to an increase in traffic in the affected area, there will not only be an increase in noise, but also *an increase in air pollution.*

(iv) The building of a new motorway might lead to the *destruction of areas of natural beauty,* reducing the welfare of those people who live and work in these areas. The destruction of areas of natural beauty is also likely to have an adverse effect upon tourism.

7. The evaluation of externalities

At the present time, a large number of externalities are not paid for directly. Thus, beneficial externalities are not paid for by consumers of the good or service concerned and the producers do not have to pay for any harmful externalities.

If the pricing system adequately measured social costs and social benefits rather than just private costs and private benefits, there would be less need for cost benefit analysis. The EEC has suggested that roads, for example, should have a *marginal-social-cost pricing* system. However, since in the UK there is not even an effective road pricing system to take account of private costs, an effective pricing system for roads to take account of all social costs and social benefits would be very difficult indeed to implement.

It is not just for public goods that an effective marginal-social-cost pricing system would be very difficult to implement: it would be very difficult to implement for virtually all goods and services, even where there are effective private-cost pricing systems. This is largely because there is a great deal of difficulty involved in evaluating the benefits derived from favourable externalities and the costs incurred by individuals as a result of harmful externalities. For example, if a factory increases production with the result that a harmful waste product is produced which kills someone, how do we evaluate the loss of this life? We could look at the number of days' work lost: if the person was young and productive, the loss to the economy's workforce could be calculated as very significant. We could also measure fairly accurately the cost of any medical attention that the person received before he or she finally died. However, it is very difficult to measure the degree of personal loss felt by the person's family and friends.

The cost of road accidents in the UK in the mid-1980s has been valued at about £2,000,000,000, but this figure cannot measure accurately the degree of personal loss which results from fatal accidents. The evaluation of externalities is very much a matter of *value judgement*. In its decision to build a new motorway, the government might value the social costs of unemplyment much more highly than the cost of increased noise and air pollution which might result from a new motorway.

The Channel Tunnel Group, in their literature about the proposed Channel Tunnel, 1985, emphasized that employment would rise significantly as a result of such a major construction. It might be felt that an increase in employment at a time of recession is a good thing, even though in the longer term the Channel Tunnel might lead to a fall in employment as a result of a fall in demand for ferry services. Thus, a fall in unemployment now might be more highly valued than a maintained level of employment in the future.

In principle, there are two main methods of trying to measure external costs and benefits.

(i) The first of these is *the willingness to pay principle* (i.e. to *ask people how much they would be prepared to pay to receive a particular benefit* or how much they would be prepared to pay to avoid receiving a particular harmful externality). While the use of questionnaires would be one way of trying to obtain such information, it may be difficult to obtain reliable answers, since most people are not used to thinking of such ideas and would probably regard it as hypothetical in any case. Other people would almost certainly regard the absence of noise as a right for which they should not have to pay in the first place.

Sometimes it might be better not to use the questionnaire approach, but to obtain values in other ways. For example, estate agents might be able to quote the prices of two houses, identical in almost every way apart from the amount of noise or air pollution in the neighbourhood. The difference in price between the two properties might be said to reflect the difference in the incidence of externalities and, in this way, provide some evaluation of externalities.

(ii) The alternative method of evaluating externalities is *the compensation principle (i.e. to ask people how much compensation they would require to feel as well off living with harmful externalities as without them or without beneficial externalities as with them).*

The two methods do not necessarily give the same results. The first method may well give lower values for the effect of externalities than the second method since the evaluations are based partly upon people's present and likely future incomes: under the first method there is an upper limit to the evaluation. For example, if we asked people how much they would be willing to pay to avoid a fatal accident, they would place an upper limit upon the figure. If, however, we tried to measure the cost of fatal accidents through the compensation principle, it would be seen that most people would require an infinite or a very high amount of money as compensation for their families.

Adopting the second method might lead to a more realistic view of accidents than that gained by adopting the first method. The first method, we can assume, will show that rich people are willing to pay more than poorer people to avoid a new road being built in their neighbourhood. Such a method of evaluation might, therefore, suggest that the building of a new road in a poor neighbourhood entails less social cost than the building of a new road in a richer neighbourhood, even though rich people do not necessarily suffer more from the effects of noise and air pollution and so on than poorer people do.

Some economists have suggested that it is difficult to make '*interpersonal comparisons*, even though the price mechanism, as usually applied, does this.

The importance of making interpersonal comparisons is that many measures help some people, but harm others. For example, a new airport would benefit customers, but would be a nuisance to nearby residents. If the potential customers have a greater ability to pay for the benefits gained from a new airport than have the residents to avoid the harmful externalities of a new airport, the first method of evaluation might suggest that a new airport should be built. However, the compensation principle might suggest that a new airport should not be built, since the second method, using the compensation principle, values the views of poor people as much as the views of richer people.

Perhaps the main problem of using the compensation principle is that people might require so much compensation, if given the opportunity, that all proposed public works schemes would appear to reduce the welfare of the country as a whole.

Problems involved in evaluating externalities are not just a matter of knowing whether to use the willingness to pay principle or the compensation principle: there is also the problem of knowing what should be measured. For example, when looking at the social cost of road accidents, there are various ways of calculating the value: the number of working days lost; the cost of medical attention; personal discomfort, etc.

There are likely to be various biases involved in evaluating the effect of externalities, caused by other factors as well as the ability to pay. We can consider some of the problems of evaluating externalities by looking at some of the more obvious externalities.

(a) *The evaluation of time savings*

Time savings are usually divided by economists into *savings in working time* and *savings in non-working time*. Observation suggests that most people value savings in working time more highly than savings in non-working time. Thus, people might use a taxi for business purposes to save working time, but would not necessarily use a taxi to save leisure time. Even taking into account the fact that people will be more willing to take a taxi if their firm is paying than if they have to pay themselves, it is still observed that people are more concerned about saving working time than leisure time from a purely time-saving aspect, even though there does not seem to be much logic in this behaviour. (It should be noted that working time does not include time spent commuting.)

When calculating the social benefit gained as a result of time saved from a new motorway being built, it is important, therefore, to take account of the *bias derived if the time saved is working time rather than non-working time*.

Using the example of transport, we can show that *the willingness to pay for time saved depends very much upon the mode of transport being considered.* For example, the time-savings of air passengers who use Concorde rather than a Boeing 747 might be valued at the difference between the price of a ticket for a seat on Concorde and the price of a ticket for a seat on a Boeing 747. If Concorde cuts the journey time by one hour compared to a Boeing 747 but costs £50 more, we might say that passengers on Concorde value one hour's journey time saved at £50. However, it would seem unreasonable to use this valuation to measure the benefit that the building of a new bus lane, which is expected to reduce a bus journey time by one hour, would have.

From what we have said, it should be clear that *time is not homogeneous*.

(b) *The evaluation of accidents*

The number of deaths on the roads is far greater than the number of deaths caused by other modes of transport. The number of deaths per passenger kilometre is generally less on motorways than on other roads. While it is probably impossible to put a realistic monetary value on the benefits that a new motorway would have if it reduced the number of road deaths, it may still be possible to make a honest, though non-monetary, judgement about the benefit gained.

If time lost at work is used to evaluate the cost of accidents, the effect of accidents upon the unemployed and elderly is likely to be underestimated.

It should be clear that evaluation of the likely benefits derived from the reduction in the number of road accidents because of the building of a new motorway, varies depending upon what is being measured: the saving in medical costs, the saving in vehicle-repair costs, the reduction in days at work lost or the saving in state compensation payments (such as widow's pensions), etc.

If the building of a new motorway is justified because it is likely to lead to a reduction in the number of road accidents, it is important to consider the concept of *cost effectiveness*. While many road lobbyists have suggested that motorways are the most cost effective way of reducing road accidents, the introduction of compulsory seat-belt wearing in 1983 was in fact much more cost effective. The introduction of compulsory seat-belt wearing in back seats would probably further reduce the cost of road accidents more effectively than the building of a new motorway.

It should be noted that what we mean by cost effectiveness is cost effectiveness not just in terms of private costs but in terms of social costs in general.

(c) *The evaluation of noise*

Before trying to put a monetary value on noise, it is important that we should be able to measure noise. One method of measuring noise is the '*L10*' *method*, which measures the maximum amount of noise for 10 per cent of a particular period. However, this method is likely to overstate the annoyance caused to the residents of nearby areas by the building of a new motorway, because most of the noise would occur during the day. If most of the noise were to occur during the night rather than during the day, the level of discomfort would be greater.

There is evidence to suggest that intermittent noise may have different effects on individuals from continuous noise.

The evaluation of the effect of noise is further complicated by virtue of the fact that different people may evaluate the effects of noise differently. For example, some people like to listen to the noise made by steam engines, while others do not. Thus, noise may be a benefit to some people, but a disbenefit to others.

Monetary values may be obtained by looking at the prices of two houses which are identical apart from the level of noise suffered in the two neighbourhoods. Also, it may be possible to measure the distracting effect noise can have upon productivity at the workplace.

(d) *The evaluation of pollution*

We might estimate the cost of pollution by measuring the cost of cleaning-up operations. For example, the Torrey Canyon accident in the 1960s, which involved an oil spillage, led to the UK and France spending about £6m on cleaning up. However, the costs to tourism, the effects upon the fishing industry, etc., are not taken into account when using the cost of cleaning up as the measure of the cost of pollution. Furthermore, if oil spillages, etc., are not cleaned up, as is often the case, the costs of pollution may be ignored altogether.

(e) *The evaluation of unemployment*

The cost to an unemployed individual of being unemployed might be estimated as the next best wage forgone minus any social security he would lose if employed. However, someone who is unemployed might lose self-respect and suffer from boredom; these psychological factors are difficult to measure and it is thus difficult to attach monetary values to them.

371

8. Why is cost benefit analysis used?

Cost benefit analysis is widely used in areas where there is likely to be a *significant divergence between private costs and benefits and social costs and benefits*. If there were an effective marginal social-cost pricing system for all goods and services, firms could take into account all costs, not just private costs, when deciding whether or not to go ahead with a particular project. However, because, generally, firms only have to pay for the private costs, if the government wished to increase the welfare of the population, it should ensure that there is some way of measuring social costs and benefits and some way of making sure that those who receive the benefits which result from the production of goods and services pay for them, and that those who suffer as a result of production are compensated. To some extent, the price mechanism takes account of externalities. For example, as we have suggested, the price of houses may be partially determined by the existence of externalities. However, *it is rare that the producer of the good or service which produces these externalities has to pay the cost or receives the benefit*. For example, if the price of houses falls in the areas near a new motorway, it is the sellers of these houses and estate agents who have to pay the costs resulting from these externalities rather than the road builders.

The lack of an effective marginal-social-cost pricing system leads to the emergence of the problem of *free riding*. Even if users of a new motorway had to pay a toll which reflected the social costs involved in building and maintaining the motorway, the system may be considered to be unfair if users of other roads are able to enjoy the benefits of reduced congestion without having to pay tolls on these roads. A truly effective marginal-social-cost pricing scheme for public goods, and for most other goods as well, is unlikely, because of the difficulty of preventing free riding. For example, a car manufacturer might produce a car which produces less air pollution than other models. If this car is priced more highly than those models which produce more air pollution, buyers of this car might be said to pay for the social benefit of the reduction in air pollution; the population as a whole might benefit from the reduction of air pollution, but most of the population would not be having to pay for it.

9. Conclusion

We can say that cost benefit analysis is a method of investment appraisal which compares the likely effects of a project with the next best alternative. If the next best alternative to the building of a new motorway is considered to be not to invest at all, *the opportunity cost* of building a new motorway can be said to be the difference in net social cost or benefit between the situation before the building of the motorway and the situation after the building of the motorway. Thus, any revenue gained by the firm and any reduction in unemployment, congestion and accidents, etc., which result from the building of the new motorway can be considered to be benefits resulting from the decision to invest rather than to do nothing. *Increases in noise, air pollution, etc., which result from the building of a new motorway can be considered to be part of the opportunity cost of a new motorway to society as a whole.* Any costs of production are seen as part of the opportunity costs to the firm.

It is difficult to determine what is the next best alternative forgone when we are considering social costs and benefits rather than just private costs and benefits. If the reduction in the number of road accidents is evaluated as the most important reason for the building of a new motorway, the next best alternative may well be to spend this same money on increasing the police patrolling of existing roads. While increasing the policing of roads might not reduce the number of road accidents as much as the building of a new motorway, it would, perhaps, be more cost effective in terms of the level of noise and the level of air pollution. If a reduction in unemployment is seen as the most important reason for building a new motorway, the next best alternative use for the given amount of money available for investment purposes might be to invest in nuclear weapons. However, some measures of welfare might suggest that increasing investment in nuclear weapons is not the next best alternative.

It should be clear that the methods used to evaluate externalities are important in determining what is the best use for a given amount of money. One evaluation might suggest that investment in hospitals will increase welfare the most. If, however, evaluation is biased towards the reduction of unemployment, a road-building scheme might be seen as increasing welfare more than a scheme to increase investment in hospitals. Biased evaluation might not be the result of carelessness in method adopted, but rather a deliberate matter of value judgements by the government. For example, the government might decide that the social benefit to be gained from investing in a project which reduces unemployment is far greater than just the reduction in unemployment benefit which has to be paid: it might value the increase in self-respect that the people who gain employment experience as increasing the welfare of the country far more than an investment programme which does not increase employment but does reduce the amount of air pollution emitted by nationalized industries.

*

QUESTIONS

Why has cost benefit analysis been increasingly used in the public sector?

One of the reasons for the increasing importance of cost benefit analysis has been that, in many countries, at least until recently, there has been a growth in the public sector. In order to determine priorities between and within the sectors, governments need some criteria for investment appraisal.

Since many of the goods or services produced by the public sector are collective or semi-collective goods, there is no alternative to cost benefit analysis for appraising investment, i.e. the price mechanism will tend to give no incentive to investment.

Investment in many transport projects would not take place were it not done by a public-sector firm or with some government assistance (for example, the government might pay the costs of production of a new road for a private firm). In the area of transport, there are often very few direct private benefits to be gained from investment, but there are likely to be many externalities, affecting both consumers and non-consumers alike. For example, British Rail might consider electrification of the railways worthwhile on a cost-benefit-analysis basis: electrification reduces harmful externalities, but it may not increase revenue sufficiently to cover costs (in which case, a private railway company would not be willing to invest in electrification without subsidy).

Cost benefit analysis is particularly important in the non-commercial area of the public sector, such as education and health. It may not be worth while for an individual with an infectious disease to pay to be cured because the costs to him of having the disease are not very high. However, it may be worthwhile for the government to invest in curing the individual in order to prevent an epidemic which would greatly increase the number of working days lost.

MULTIPLE-CHOICE QUESTIONS

1. Cost benefit analysis takes into account which of the following:
(A) the reduction in journey time for drivers after the construction of a new motorway;
(B) the increase in noise and pollution in an area as a result of a new airport having been built;
(C) the increase in employment in the local economy as a result of the opening of a new main railway line?
 (*a*) A and B only.
 (*b*) C only.
 (*c*) All.
 (*d*) None.
 Answer – (*c*)

2. Private-sector activity, such as motoring, generates large external costs. These would be reduced if which of the following happened:
(A) the government taxed motoring activity more heavily;
(B) the government subsidized alternative modes of transport;
(C) the government imposed constraints upon motoring, such as banning it in town centres?
 (*a*) A and B only.
 (*b*) C only.
 (*c*) All.
 (*d*) None.
Answer – (*c*)

3. The willingness-to-pay principle of measuring externalities is likely to suggest that the social costs of building a motorway through an area where rich people live rather through an area where poorer people live are:
 (*a*) higher;
 (*b*) the same;
 (*c*) lower.
Answer – (*a*)

4. Which of the following are free-riders?
(A) People who use a new motorway instead of an older road, because of the saving in journey time, without incurring any increased expenses.
(B) Residents who find that noise in their neighbourhood is reduced as more motorists travel along a new motorway in another neighbourhood instead of along roads in the neighbourhood in question, other things being equal.

(C) Residents who suffer from an increase in noise because of the building of a new road in their neighbourhood, for which they receive no compensation.

(*a*) A only.

(*b*) B only.

(*c*) A and B only.

(*d*) All.

Answer – (*d*)

Explanation. People who suffer the effects of harmful externalities for which they receive no compensation are free-riders, although they are defined as 'unwilling free-riders'.

DATA RESPONSE

The original idea for Concorde was conceived in the 1960s. It was, perhaps, a product of the so-called 'technological revolution', when it was felt that technical improvements would solve most of the existing economic problems.

Some people have tried to justify the vast expense of Concorde on a number of different grounds, such as the time-savings for individuals, the 'technological spin-offs', employment, prestige and the balance of payments.

Most economists, I would suggest, wish to see which of these could be covered by the normal price mechanism and which would require some other form of investment appraisal. We might expect the difference in fares between Concorde and other aircraft to reflect to some extent the differences in travel time. However, fares might be subject to control by national or international bodies. Therefore, differences in fares might not accurately reflect differences in travel time.

It is difficult to justify Concorde on the grounds of time-saving, since time-savings can be made, perhaps more cost effectively, if measures are taken to reduce the accessibility time to airports or the waiting time at airports.

The Plowden Committee suggested that, in practice, the technological spin-offs from Concorde were not important. A supersonic transport committee in the United States of America came to the same conclusions.

Since most of the Concorde workers were highly skilled and were working, at that time, in an area of fairly high employment, the employment concept seems somewhat dubious.

Prestige is more difficult to quantify, but it seems difficult to see why the taxpayers should regard Concorde as necessarily more prestigious than other forms of transport and why they should want to pay for this prestige.

When we consider the balance of payments, we need to consider the likely import savings if people travel on Concorde rather than on other countries' aircraft. Would it have been better to have put the money into other forms of air transport, for example jumbo jets, which might have had better sales prospects?

How much oil does Concorde in fact use? For example, one forecast stated that if Concorde, as originally planned, operated fourteen hours a day, it would use about 100,000 metric tonnes of kerosene per year. If there were a fleet of, for example, three hundred, the number required to make the production of Concorde profitable, a vast fuel resource would be used.

Concorde has also been criticized for other unfavourable externalities, particularly noise pollution, but this has latterly been rectified by the plane's travelling more slowly over land.

(*a*) Why might some of the benefits of Concorde be covered by the normal price mechanism?
What are the defects of relying on the price mechanism for measuring such benefits?

(*b*) How can we evaluate time-savings resulting from the building of Concorde?

(*c*) Would the above analysis have been altered if, for example, Concorde workers were mainly unskilled? Explain your answer.

(*d*) How does the author suggest that Concorde affects the balance of payments? What further criteria would you need before deciding whether or not Concorde assists the British balance of payments?

SELF-EXAMINATION QUESTIONS

1. Why has cost benefit analysis often been used for road investment appraisal?

2. What is meant by the term 'consumer surplus'? Why might it be important in cost benefit analysis?

3. What is meant by the 'compensation' and 'willingness-to-pay' principles? Which is the more appropriate for cost benefit analysis, and why?

4. Cost benefit analysis takes no account of income distribution nor of who pays for and who receives the benefits. Discuss.

5. 'Rather than having the spurious accuracy of putting time-savings, the effects of noise pollution, congestion and safety in monetary terms, it would be much better to have a balance-sheet summarizing the main data.' Critically discuss.

6. Why might cost benefit analysis be appropriate in the health and education sectors?

7. 'Railway closures should be considered solely on commercial criteria.' Discuss.

8. Railway closures in the United Kingdom have often been considered only in terms of costs to users. Some economists have criticized this approach because non-users of a railway system often benefit from it. Explain why.

23. The distribution of income

1. Determining the distribution of income

(i) One of the problems involved in determining the distribution of income is knowing *which sources of income are to be measured*. Do we only look at *earned income* (such as wages and salaries) or do we look at *both earned and unearned* income and so include state benefits? Unearned income is forming an increasing proportion of some people's income because of the large number of people unemployed and receiving social security benefits, and because an increasing number of people are receiving pensions. There are also benefits such as family allowance (now called child benefit) to consider.

(ii) In addition, we need to know whether we are concerned with *individuals' incomes or with households' incomes*. A measure of households' incomes is probably the most useful because most families pool their money for use by the whole family. However, when using such a measure we need to take account of the size of each household.

(iii) We must decide, too, whether we should consider *incomes before tax or after tax*. We should note that there are many *fringe benefits* (many of which escape taxation), especially, one suspects, for the richer members of society. In 1984, for example, payments in kind, subsidized services and training (i.e. fringe benefits) accounted for 3 per cent of total labour costs in manufacturing. So should we include fringe benefits as part of income? If so, we should be aware that it can be difficult to measure just what fringe benefits people actually receive.

(iv) There are also problems in *comparing different age groups*. For example, young people will tend to earn less than people in their forties in comparable jobs because they have less experience and are, usually, less productive. It is also somewhat misleading to compare old people's incomes with those of other people because old people generally receive a fixed income in the form of a pension and they will tend to have a lower mortgage than other people or no mortgage at all.

(v) It can be shown, from data from the Department of Employment, that *men, generally, receive higher wages than women*. *Discrimination* may explain part of the difference, but, in order to make fair comparisons, we might need to look at *the degree of training, the number of hours worked* and so on. *Differences in education* might, similarly, help

379

explain *differences in wages between different ethnic groups.*

(vi) We need to look at *the government's influence upon the distribution of income,* not only in terms of its *taxation policy* but also in terms of its *expenditure and subsidies.* There is evidence to suggest that rich families benefit more than poorer families from some state benefits and from state spending on education.

2. Which members of society are likely to have the lowest incomes?

i. *The unemployed*
ii. *The elderly,* especially those receiving only state pensions
iii. *Young workers* rather than older workers
iv. *Residents of development areas and inner city areas* (see Chapter 24)
v. *The unskilled and semi-skilled*
vi. *Non-unionized workers* rather than unionized workers
vii. *Those people able to work only part-time*
viii. *Those people unable to work,* such as the disabled.

3. The effect of trade unions on the distribution of income

(a) *The effect of unions' policies to raise their members' earnings*

Trade unions have a particularly important effect on the distribution of income. Most trade unions are interested in obtaining the highest possible wages for their members. Those trade unions whose members are skilled workers will want to maintain or widen the wage differential between their members and unskilled workers. However, general trade unions tend to want to close differentials. General trade unions, such as the Transport and General Workers' Union, include in their membership skilled and semi-skilled workers, but also unskilled workers. These unions usually desire equal pay for all their members doing the same task, regardless of skill, and they successfully reduced many wage differentials in the 1970s. Many such unions have attempted to gain more equality of pay between the sexes and between different races *within the context of the firm,* but they have been relatively ineffective in this area; trade unions seem to have been more successful at gaining more equality of wages *between firms* for similar tasks.

(b) *The effect of unions pursuing other objectives*

Trade unions are also interested in getting *improved working conditions* for their members and in times of recession, such as the 1980s, they may be more concerned about *protecting the jobs* of their members than about gaining higher wages. The workers most at risk of losing their jobs are the unskilled workers. Thus, skilled workers might be thought to be in a relatively stronger bargaining position and better able to raise their wage differential. However, the presence of general unions tends to dampen down this effect.

(c) *The effect of the existence of trade unions on the incomes of non-unionized workers*

The extent to which trade unions are able to increase the wages of their members relative to non-unionized workers is not necessarily very significant. It is difficult for an employer to give a pay rise to the unionized workers in an industry without giving the rise to the non-unionized workers also. Similarly, it is difficult, when a union manages to get an employer to improve working conditions, to exclude non-union members from gaining the benefits of these improved conditions. However, it does seem that the wages of workers who are in unionized sectors of industry (whether they are members of unions or not) have gained relatively to those workers who are in sectors not covered by unions. Sectors not covered tend to be small private firms, whose workers are perhaps most likely to receive lower wages, have worse working conditions and have less job security than workers in larger firms anyway. The workers in these sectors are likely to be unskilled, women or from racial minorities.

4. The effect of the government on the distribution of income

(a) *Taxation policy*

The government can, of course, redistribute income through taxation policy. Empirical data may not be entirely accurate in revealing just how far taxation reduces income inequality because of tax evasion and tax avoidance through the use of fringe benefits, for example. None the less, by changing its taxation policy, the government can have some effect upon the distribution of income. For example, it is known that the incidence of indirect tax tends to rise, but less than proportionately, with income. Therefore increases such as the rise in VAT to 15 per cent in 1979 will tend to affect the poor more than the rich. The government also knows that direct taxation tends to rise more than proportionately with income. Using this knowledge, the government can make the appropriate cuts and increases in taxation to influence the distribution of income. *Negative income tax* for low-wage earners has often been advocated, but it is unlikely that negative income tax would apply for part-time workers and so it would not help the many one-parent families where the only worker in the household works part-time. Neither would a negative income tax solve the problem of poverty amongst old-age pensioners.

(b) Benefits

Social security is perhaps the best-known method which the government uses to alleviate poverty.

(i) The *family income supplement* was originally introduced to try to help people on low incomes. However, the problem of *low take-up* of benefits has often been neglected and family income supplement is a conspicuous example of a benefit which has a low take-up.

(ii) *Family allowances* (i.e. child benefit) have been introduced to help, in particular, large families. These allowances replaced children's tax allowances and are usually paid directly to the mother, to avoid the problems which occur when the father keeps the money for himself.

(iii) *State pensions.* In 1979 there was considerable discussion about whether state pensions should be related to earnings or to the cost of living. If related to earnings, pensioners would gain more if general living standards rose.

(iv) From time to time, governments have introduced *subsidies* on milk, bread, cheese, and other basic commodities. These have sometimes been criticized on the basis that they benefit all consumers rather than just those in need.

Some people have argued that the provision of state benefits might lead to 'scrounging'. However, perhaps a more serious problem is that not everyone receives all the benefits to which they are entitled. For example, it has been estimated that there were 600,000 non-claiming unemployed actively seeking work in the second quarter of 1983. The source of these figures is the *OECD Economic Survey for the United Kingdom*, January 1985.

It has sometimes been claimed that *means-tested benefits* are desirable, but there are objections to means testing, partly as a hangover from the 1920s and 1930s (when there was considerable snooping by officials) and partly because of the costs of supervising such benefits.

Some state benefits, such as educational benefits, tend to benefit people from families with high incomes more than people from families with low incomes. Examples of this can be found in the Newsom Report on Education, 1963. It has been argued that the government could make educational benefits more progressive by offering grants to people from families on low incomes to stay in education after sixteen, in which case more people from the working classes might progress to universities or polytechnics.

(c) *Legislation*

The government could try to deal with some of the causes of low pay. For example, it could try to deal with the problem of racial and sexual discrimination, since differences in earnings between men and women and between different ethnic groups may reflect prejudice. (Some people still think that a married woman does not need a living wage if she is supported by a working husband.) But such prejudices help cause poverty, particularly for single women and women who are sole wage-earners in charge of one-parent families.

Legislation such as the *Sex Discrimination Act 1975* and the *Race Relations Act 1976* was intended have two effects: first, *to reduce the incidence of unemployment falling upon women and racial minorities*; second, within employment, *to produce an equality of prospects and an equality of wages*.

Available data seems to suggest that there has not been a significant narrowing of the gap between men's and women's wages since the 1975 Act. Table 27, overleaf, shows that the gap between men's and women's wages did narrow between 1970 and 1976, but that there has been little (if any) narrowing since.

It has been claimed that anti-discrimination legislation (and especially the Equal Pay Act 1975) actually leads to an increased likelihood of unemployment for women, because some employers prefer to employ men if women's labour is no cheaper.

If the government believes that certain groups, such as women and racial minorities, have low aspirations and that this is a major cause of poverty for them, effective anti-discrimination legislation should help increase their prospects and boost their aspirations.

383

Table 27. The differential between men's and women's earnings.

	Average gross weekly earnings*					
	1970	1976	1981	1982	1983	1984
Men	£29.3	£70.2	£137	£150.5	£164.7	£178.8
Women	£16.3	£46.2	£91.4	£99	£109.5	£117.2

Women's gross weekly earnings as a percentage of men's gross weekly earnings					
1970	1976	1981	1982	1983	1984
55.6	65.8	66.7	65.8	66.5	65.5

* The figures are for men and women over 18 years of age for the years 1970–82; the 1983 and 1984 figures relate to males and females on adult rates.
Source: Department of Employment, *New Earnings Survey*, HMSO.

(d) *Education policy*

Research shows that middle-class families are more likely to be aware of the value of education for future prospects than working-class families are. Thus, *the educational system seems geared towards the middle-classes* and the educational system has a strong influence upon wages received at work. By raising the school-leaving age, as it did in 1972, the government increased the number of people from working-class families in education. Retraining schemes, like the *Training Opportunities Scheme* (*TOPS*), and the setting up of *Industrial Training Boards*, are methods by which the government can help reduce the inequality of income distribution, especially where these schemes mainly attract people from the working classes.

If it is believed that low productivity contributes to low wages, policies to improve education and training might improve the distribution of income. However, it is often difficult to define productivity and to raise it in sectors such as agriculture, postal services and, to some extent, the transport sector.

(e) *Regional policy*

There is something of an inequality of income distribution between different regions. This is partly borne out in the figures showing higher unemployment in some regions than in others (see Chapter 24). A *regional policy* should help to reduce income-distribution inequality.

(f) *Measures to reduce unemployment*

If a major cause of the inequality of income distribution is unemployment, selective measures (whether on a national or regional basis), such as *job-creation programmes* and *youth-opportunity schemes*, should help reduce income inequality (see Chapter 20).

(g) *Minimum-wage policy*

It has sometimes been suggested that there should be a *national minimum wage* to help reduce income inequality, but such a policy would ignore the problem of regional variations in the cost of living and a national minimum wage might result in lower employment (with the least-skilled and lowest-paid being most vulnerable to unemployment), since firms might not wish to employ the people the policy is supposed to help if they had to pay them more. It has also been suggested that a national minimum-wage policy would not be successful because of the existence of wage differentials, which skilled, highly paid workers want to maintain. The powerful general trade unions might be able to solve this problem, but, as already mentioned, not all low-paid workers are covered by a trade union, particularly part-time workers.

(h) *Housing policy*

(i) *Subsidies to council-house tenants.* There has been a great deal of controversy about the role of council houses in the redistribution of income. The subsidy the government gives to council-house tenants tends not to be significantly greater than the income-tax relief given to owner-occupiers. Also, the weekly rent council-house tenants have to pay may not be vastly different from the weekly mortgage payments a private house-owner has to pay. This situation has largely arisen because of inflation. If a private house-owner bought his house in 1960, his mortgage would have been decided then. His weekly mortgage payment may have been fixed at £10 per week. Thus, by 1985 his weekly mortgage payment is still £10 per week. A council-house tenant may similarly have moved into a new council house in 1960. His weekly rent may have been £5 in 1960. However, the effects of inflation would have pushed his weekly rent up and up; by 1985 it might be £30. In this case council housing has no beneficial effects upon current income inequality. However, a council-house tenant living in a council house built in 1985 may find that his weekly rent is £30, whereas a private house-owner may find that the weekly mortgage payments for a house built in 1985 are £70. In this case, at the current time, income may be redistributed from the private house-owner living in a house built in 1985 to the council-house tenant, whether his house was built in 1985 or 1960, but the effects of inflation are shown to reduce this redistribution process over time.

(ii) *The sale of council houses.* The effect of the sale of council houses to their tenants upon the redistribution of income is also controversial. We can best explain the controversy by an example. We can assume that a council house has a market value of £30,000 and that the government will allow the tenant to buy the house for £15,000. This £15,000 subsidy can be seen as having a beneficial redistributing effect for the tenant. However, when the owner dies or moves away, this house is not passed on to someone on the council-house waiting list and the house represents a reduction in the stock of council housing. The buying and selling of council houses may therefore be seen to have a negative effect upon the redistribution of income. If, however, the £15,000 the government receives from the sale of the council house is used to build another council house, the sale of council houses may be said to have a beneficial effect upon the redistribution of income. The Thatcher government, which favours the sale of council housing, actually believes that the money received from the sale of council housing should not be used to build more council houses.

(iii) An alternative to providing council housing is perhaps to *encourage the private sector to provide adequate housing for the poor.* There has been reluctance by the building societies to lend to people in 'redline' districts, i.e. inner-city areas. The government could improve the situation by acting as some sort of guarantor to the building societies. Often local authorities have made the situation worse because of the many cases of planning blight.

(i) *Rating policy*

It has sometimes been suggested that *local-authority rates are not linked to the ability to pay.* However, this suggestion is only partly correct because richer families tend to have larger houses and will therefore have to pay higher rates.

The rating system provides a disincentive for owners to improve their housing. This disincentive has been one of the reasons for un-employment in the building industry despite the fact that there is still a large amount of inadequate housing. By replacing the rating system by a form of revenue which does not have this disincentive, the government could redistribute income and create more employment, and thereby reduce income inequality even further. The community charge does not have this disincentive.

(j) *Inner-city policy*

The problem of poverty is particularly evident in inner-city areas. Inner-city poverty might be reduced through government housing policy. The seven *Inner City Partnerships* (see Chapter 24) were designed to ease the problems of poverty in inner-city areas: decisions about which sectors (for example, education or housing) should receive most help were left to the local authorities rather than to the central government, because it was felt that the local authorities have a better idea of what the priorities are. It is, however, difficult to assess the success of the Inner City Part-nerships scheme.

(k) *Inflation policy*

Since inflation tends to hit the poor, pensioners and students particularly badly, *inflation tends to redistribute income towards the richer members of society*. Inflation has a particularly bad relative effect on the poor when it hits commodities such as food and fuel the hardest, because poor people tend to spend a greater proportion of their incomes upon these commodities than do richer people.

(i) The government could make sure that the poor do not lose out in terms of income distribution to the richer members of society in times of inflation by *index-linking state benefits* such as unemployment benefit and student grants. The only state benefit at the current time (1988) which is index-linked is pensions.

(ii) Some *prices and incomes policies* in the past were partly designed to help the poor by setting fixed limits for wage increases for the period the policies ran. For example, the July 1975 policy allowed a maximum increase in weekly wages of £6 for the year until July 1976, which meant that people on lower incomes would catch up, in percentage terms, with people on higher incomes; other policies have not allowed people on high incomes any wage increase at all.

5. Measures of inequality

The government needs to know whether the poor are a *constant group* or a *changing group* and to initiate policies accordingly. A changing group pattern might occur if the source of the problem is mainly low incomes at the bottom of an incremental scale, i.e. people who are at the bottom of the occupational ladder, but will gain higher incomes as their experience grows. This problem is not as serious in the long run as the problem of people who are on low incomes indefinitely.

The government therefore requires data on the extent of inequality and on who are the most likely to suffer from inequality, so that it can maximize the effectiveness of policies designed to eliminate inequality.

(a) *Figures of total wealth*

There is more data on incomes than wealth, although wealth inequality is perhaps a more useful measure of social inequality than income inequality. Wealth has a much more skewed distribution that income (see Tables 28 and 29).

An individual's wealth is defined as including all of his possessions (whether tangible or intangible) which have a market value.

Tables 28 and 29 give some idea of inequality. It is evident that wealth is much more unequally distributed at the top than income. It is also shown that income tax has some redistributing effect, but *both income and wealth are still highly unequally distributed.*

Table 28. The distribution of income before and after income tax

	Income before tax (%)	Income after tax (%)
1975–6		
Top 1% of population	5.7	3.9
Bottom 50%	23.8	26.6
1981–2		
Top 1%	6	4.6
Bottom 50%	22.7	25.2

Source: Central Statistical Office, *Social Trends*, HMSO, 1985.

Table 29. The distribution of wealth

	Marketable wealth plus occupational and state pension rights (%)		
	1976	1979	1982
Most wealthy 1% of population over 18 years old	14	13	11
Least wealthy 50%*	15–20	17–21	18–22

* Figures for the distribution of wealth of the least wealthy 50% of the population vary according to data used.
Source: Central Statistical Office, *Social Trends*, HMSO, 1985.

(b) *Figures relating to pensions*

The number of people receiving pensions is considerable: 8,999,000 in March 1984, according to the Department of Employment's *Monthly Digest of Statistics*, September 1985. Figures such as those in Table 30 suggest that *old age is a major cause of poverty*. Furthermore, of the families at or below the supplementary-benefit level of income, 42 per cent were single pensioners in 1983, according to the Department of Employment.

(c) *Family-income-supplement figures*

In January 1980 82,000 families received the family income supplement, of which 46,000 were one-parent families. The coverage has increased in recent years with, in April 1985, 202,000 families receiving the supple-

Table 30. The connection between old age and poverty

	Average gross normal weekly household income 1983
One man and one woman, retired and dependent mainly on state pensions	£70.74
One man and one woman, non-retired	£224.32

Source: Department of Employment, *Family Expenditure Survey*, HMSO, 1983.

ment, 82,000 of which were one-parent families. The source of these figures is the *Monthly Digest of Statistics*, September 1985.

(d) *Figures relating to regional differences in income levels*

There are quite strong regional variations in income. For example, the gross normal average weekly household income in the UK for 1982/3 was £182.09. Regional differences are shown as follows: in the south-east of England the gross normal average weekly household income was £210.51; in northern England it was £158.54; in Northern Ireland it was £144.71. (Source: Department of Employment, *Family Expenditure Survey*, HMSO, 1983).

(e) *Figures relating to inequality in health*

A person's state of health affects his or her ability to earn. Ill-health is one factor involved in creating income inequality. The incidence of ill-health tends to rise with age, as the figures in Table 31 show.

(f) *Inequality in housing conditions*

Many people who have low incomes can only afford to live in bad housing, for example in inner-city areas, and cannot afford private housing (relying instead on council housing).

Growing waiting lists for council housing may be used as a measure of a rise in the number of people with low incomes. Yet a number of houses (in both the private and public sectors) stand empty. In the private sector houses have often stood empty so that owners may accrue capital, as houses rise in market value in times of inflation; the owners are unwilling to let these houses because this might tie up the houses when they wish to sell. On the other hand, many council houses stand empty because they are unsuitable for letting.

Table 31. Annual medical costs per person according to age and sex

	NHS: annual costs per person, 1982	
Aged 25–44	£131 per male	£136 per female
Aged 75 and over	£803 per male	£984 per female

Source: Central Statistical Office, *Social Trends*, HMSO, 1985.

Inequality in housing conditions might be measured by looking at house prices, whether or not houses have running water or how many occupants there are per room.

(g) *Inequality in the ability to buy particular goods and services*

Inequality may be measured by the ability to purchase certain commodities. For example, people with very little wealth are unable to afford to purchase luxury housing or Rolls-Royce cars. Similarly, people with little wealth are unlikely to be able to afford private medical attention. Especially since 1979, there has been a lot of controversy about the role of the National Health Service. The Conservative government has tended to suggest that private medicine helps to improve the quality of life because it gives freedom of choice. However, not everyone can afford private medicine. Thus we get situations where the same doctor treats both private patients and NHS patients, with private patients tending to face shorter waiting lists for operations than NHS patients and, possibly, receiving more favourable treatment. Therefore, we can probably say that *the quality of medical attention is largely affected by a willingness and ability to pay for private medicine.*

(h) *Other measures of inequality*

Measures of income or wealth inequality are not necessarily the best measures of inequality within society. When considering the extent of differences in the quality of life it is important to consider aspects other than the amount of income or wealth people have. The quality of *education* and of *medical attention* received, the existence of *social amenities* and the incidence of *unfavourable externalities* suffered and of *favourable externalities* enjoyed may all affect the quality of life (as suggested in Chapter 21) and may or may not be related to individuals' level of income or wealth.

*

QUESTION

What influence does the government have on the distribution of income? How might this influence be improved?

There is a strong correlation between education and income: the more education one has the more one's income is likely to be over one's

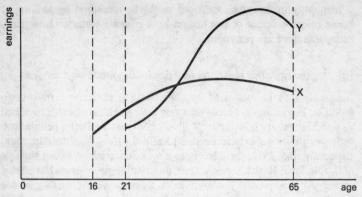

Figure 62. *Earnings during a life cycle according to education*

lifetime. Figure 62 shows that someone who joins the workforce at sixteen (person X) will have a fairly steady income path, with his income rising as his experience earns him promotion and pay rises.

A person who joins the workforce at twenty-one (person Y) after A-levels and college, will have not been earning for the five years between sixteen and twenty-one. When he joins the workforce he will be earning less than person X at the same age because he lacks experience. However, because of his greater qualifications, Y will receive greater pay rises than X and his lifetime's income will exceed that of X, so that Y is compensated for his lack of earnings between sixteen and twenty-one. The peak in Y's earnings and productivity might well come at a different age than for X because of the difference in education.

It seems unlikely that this income pattern and the decision of how much education to take is merely linked to 'intelligence'. It seems that people from middle-class families will earn more over their lifetimes than people from the working classes. Furthermore, people from middle-class families are more likely to receive education after sixteen than people from working-class families.

Many families cannot afford to keep their children in full-time education beyond the age of sixteen, and the government should, perhaps, provide grants to keep 'bright' children at school until they are eighteen. The argument is that, by encouraging more people from poorer families to stay longer in full-time education, the differential between incomes will be reduced because of the greater productivity that should result from the extra education. As is shown in Figure 62, wages rise as productivity rises, since it is usually assumed that productivity tends to rise with age up to a point.

The government may be thought to be able to influence income distribution by legislation. For example, anti-discrimination legislation, such as the Equal Pay Act 1975, may be expected to reduce income inequality eventually. However, in general women still do not receive as much pay as men, even when they are doing similar work.

The government may also try to influence income distribution by attempting to control trade unions, perhaps through the use of legislation such as the Employment Acts. While some unions are interested in narrowing wage differentials, those unions whose membership consists of skilled workers tend to be interested in maintaining or widening differentials. Control of the latter may help reduce income inequality but is, in practice, very difficult.

Taxation and spending policy can be used by the government to alter the distribution of income. Negative income tax has often been suggested (though never implemented in the United Kingdom) as a way of improving the distribution of income. A system of family income supplements for people on low wages does exist, and its application is presumably similar to that of any future system of negative income tax.

The family income supplement makes up part of the difference between the wage paid and the assumed needs according to the size of family, but does not avoid the 'poverty trap': as households receive a slightly higher income, they lose means-tested benefits such as the family income supplement and have to pay a higher marginal rate of income tax and make higher National Insurance contributions and, consequently, are made worse off.

Many means-tested benefits are based on a 'cut-off point': people below a certain wage will receive a certain benefit, but people slightly above that wage do not receive the benefit. In terms of school meals, the children of a wage-earner will either receive free meals or will have to pay the standard price. There is no system whereby only half the full price has to be paid. If there were a system (such as a system of negative income tax) whereby the amount of money received from a benefit was slowly phased out as more was earned, low-paid workers might be encouraged to search for higher wages.

A system of negative income tax would tend to assist only people with low earnings, while many other low-income groups, such as one-parent families (where it is difficult to obtain full-time employment) and old-age pensioners, will receive no benefit from such a system.

Furthermore, some economists and some trade unionists, especially, dislike the idea of negative income tax because they feel it would put less pressure upon employers to pay reasonable wages, since they would know that if they were to pay lower wages, the state would make up part of the deficiency.

1. General trade unions are more likely to reduce differentials than are craft unions.
   (*a*) True.
   (*b*) False.
Answer – (*a*)

2. In 1988, women's gross earnings as a percentage of those of men were approximately:
   (*a*) 55;
   (*b*) 65;
   (*c*) 75;
   (*d*) 85.
Answer – (*b*)

3. Subsidies on basic foodstuffs are likely to be:
   (*a*) progressive;
   (*b*) regressive;
   (*c*) proportional.
Answer – (*a*)

4. Imposing 15 per cent VAT on take-away food is:
   (*a*) progressive;
   (*b*) regressive;
   (*c*) proportional.
Answer – (*b*)

5. The family income supplement is calculated as part of the difference between the assumed minimum wage and the actual wage payable.
   (*a*) True.
   (*b*) False.
Answer – (*a*)

6. The index-linking of pensions to average earnings instead of to prices will increase pensioners' incomes if:
   (*a*) earnings are rising faster than prices;
   (*b*) prices are rising faster than earnings;
   (*c*) prices and earnings are rising at exactly the same rate.
Answer – (*a*)

7. At the present time, pensions paid by the state are earnings-related.
   (*a*) True.
   (*b*) False.

Answer – (a)

8. The average subsidy to council-house tenants in 1988 was greater than the tax relief on mortgages to the average owner-occupier.
   (*a*) True.
   (*b*) False.

Answer – (b)

9. If the income-tax threshold for a married man is £4,000 (below which there is a marginal negative income tax of 25 per cent), how much will a married man receive in the form of negative income tax if he is earning £3,000?
   (*a*) £100.
   (*b*) About £133.
   (*c*) £250.
   (*d*) £400.

Answer – (c)

10. The distribution of income in the UK is more highly skewed than the distribution of wealth.
   (*a*) True.
   (*b*) False.

Answer – (b)

DATA RESPONSE

The distribution of income is still highly skewed, in spite of the number of years of alleged moves towards greater equality. By 1980 the top 10 per cent of households had just over one quarter of the total income in the United Kingdom before tax and just slightly less than one quarter after tax. Conversely, the lower half of the population had just less than one quarter of the UK's total income before tax and just over one quarter after tax.

However, the differences are even greater when we look at the distribution of wealth. For example, by 1980 the top 1 per cent of the population had about one eighth of the total marketable wealth, which included pension rights as well as housing assets. At the other end of the income spectrum, the bottom 50 per cent had about one fifth of the total marketable wealth. Ignoring state pension rights, the bottom 50 per cent of the population had only about one twentieth of the total marketable wealth. This, perhaps, indicates the importance of any possible changes which might be introduced as a result of the far-ranging review of pensions ordered by the government in 1985.

(a) Why is the distribution of wealth likely to be highly skewed than the distribution of income?

(b) What is meant by the term 'marketable wealth'? How far does government intervention affect this?

(c) Why might changes in the *Financial Times* Index affect the marketable wealth of the most wealthy much more than those in the bottom section of the community?

SELF-EXAMINATION QUESTIONS

1. What do we mean by 'distribution of income'? Are we concerned with individuals' or householders' incomes?

2. What problems do we find when we try to look at the distribution of income? Why should we also try to take wealth into account when measuring inequality?

3. Why was the family income supplement introduced? Why was the take-up so low?

4. Why has a negative income tax been suggested? How would it help one-parent families and old-age pensioners?

5. In which ways is income-tax relief to house-buyers progressive?

6. Why has a minimum national wage sometimes been suggested? What effects would it have?

7. Why do women earn less than men?

8. What do you think are the problems with the Equal Pay Act 1975? Why was the Race Relations Act 1976 introduced?

9. Which people are paid low wages?

10. How far is family allowance progressive? What is meant by 'clawback'?

11. Why was a different system of child allowances brought in?

12. How are pensions progressive? Should they be related to earnings or to the cost of living? Explain your answer.

13. How are subsidies on milk, bread, cheese or beef progressive?

14. Who gets the benefits of education?

15. How would you define 'inadequate housing'?

16. Is the provision of council houses progressive? Do sales of council houses hinder or help poor people?

17. Should prices and incomes policies be directed at helping the poor? Explain your answer.

18. What do we mean by 'selective subsidies'?

19. Is the National Health Service progressive? How do private beds help or hinder the NHS's progressiveness? (See the report of the TUC 1979 debate on this subject for help with your answer.)

20. Are means-tested benefits desirable? Explain your answer.

24. Regional policy

1. The factors which have traditionally influenced the location of industry

Microeconomic theory predicts that a profit-maximizing firm will choose areas where its total costs are at a minimum, other things being equal. These costs are production and transport costs.

The factors which have traditionally influenced firms in their location decisions include those listed below.

i. *Access to sources of power and fuel*, particularly coal. (This was one of the main reasons why much of the original textile industry was located in the north of England.)

ii. *Access to raw materials*

iii. *Access to the market*

iv. *Access to a supply of labour*

v. *Access to an adequate transport network*

vi. *Access to adequate and cheap land space*. (The Ford Motor Company established a factory at Dagenham, Essex, on cheap, readily available marshland.)

vii. *External economies of scale*. (Some firms choose areas where similar firms are already located, in order to take advantage of any specialist services which have developed in these areas. For example, local colleges in the Midlands may have held courses on mechanical engineering because of the large number of motor-car factories which were traditionally located in the Midlands. Because of the heavy concentration of the number of financial institutions in central London, people wishing to work in finance are likely to begin looking for work there, and so new financial institutions also set up their headquarters in central London.)

2. Changes in factors influencing location

Industry in recent years has tended to become more 'footloose', that is to say many industries can be located in almost any part of the country without additions to costs. This has arisen partly because electricity is available almost anywhere in the United Kingdom and partly because oil has replaced coal as the main fuel: the use of coal tied many firms to locations near pits or railways. The comparative decline of the railways' and inland waterways' share of freight, coupled with the growth of the road haulage industry and the development of a comprehensive network of roads means that firms can now locate in many more areas.

One estimate is that about two thirds of manufacturing industries are footloose. There are, of course, a number of exceptions, for example shipbuilding. The growth of light engineering and of many service industries has meant that the influence of raw materials on location is appreciably less than in the past.

3. The theory behind government intervention in firms' location decisions

It could be argued that, without state intervention, profit-maximizing firms will locate in areas where their costs are lowest. If state location policy involves the development of industry in areas other than the least-cost locations, there will be adverse effects upon the economy's real income. However, there are a number of reasons why the government intervenes in location.

(i) There may be *costs of congestion* which are not borne by the firm. This, however, is as much an *intra-regional* problem as an *inter-regional* problem.

(ii) Government intervention in the location of industry has often been advocated as a means of *reducing unemployment in particularly badly depressed areas of the country*, i.e. it has often been advocated that the government should have a *regional policy*. Traditional Keynesian measures to reduce unemployment (i.e. the lowering of interest rates, the removal of HP restrictions, etc.) may be inflationary in areas, such as south-east England, where unemployment tends to be comparatively low. After all, why should workers in the South-East reduce their wage claims just because unemployment in, say, the North-West is high? A good regional policy should be able to avoid such an *inflationary trap*.

(iii) Since industry has become more footloose, *many firms can function efficiently in a variety of locations*. Thus, government intervention in the location decisions of firms will not necessarily affect the efficiency of firms a great deal.

(iv) *Are most firms, in fact, profit-maximizers in their location decisions?* *Luttrell's* studies in the early 1960s, and some subsequent studies, seem to indicate that few firms are profit-maximizing in choosing their location. If these studies are reliable, it would seem reasonable to assume that government intervention is unlikely to affect the profitability of firms very significantly. If, however, most firms are profit-maximizers in their location decisions, the government could perhaps sensibly intervene in the location of industry by altering the prices of factors of production (through taxes or subsidies) *until marginal social costs equal marginal social revenue* (see Chapter 22). In this way, government intervention will increase the efficiency of the price mechanism.

4. Why might firms not profit-maximize in their location decisions?

(i) *Small firms, especially, are unlikely to be aware of the costs and benefits of all possible locations.* The government has tried to improve information about different locations. For example, the Department of Trade and Industry gives wide publicity to many of its relocation schemes. The former *Location of Offices Bureau,* which tried to persuade firms to move from the London area, helped to improve information about other areas.

(ii) However, *firms may deliberately pursue objectives other than profit-maximization in their location decisions.* Small firms, in particular, may be influenced by factors other than profit. For example, their managers may want *social facilities* near their firms or they may have social ties in particular areas. If this is the case, the government might be able to persuade firms to move by improving the social environment of depressed areas. The Conservative government in 1972 used *'Operation Eyesore'* to clear up derelict land, in conjunction with schemes such as *The North Midlands Clearance Scheme.*

5. Is there a regional problem?

Where government intervention in the location of industry is advocated as a means of reducing disparities between regions, it is important to

Table 32. Regional differences in household income

	Gross average normal weekly household income, 1983–4
UK	£191.88
North England	£163.79
Yorks and Humberside	£167.87
East Midlands	£188.27
East Anglia	£181.02
South-east England	£230.68
South-west England	£190.97
West Midlands	£180.08
North-west England	£177.71
Wales	£164.75
Scotland	£176.01
Northern Ireland	£152.97

Source: Department of Employment, *Family Expenditure Survey*, HMSO, 1984.

have measures of regional disparities in order to be able to tell if there really is a regional problem.

Regional disparities can be measured fairly satisfactorily in terms of *unemployment*. In January 1986 unemployment rates were as follows: Northern Ireland 21.6 per cent; Scotland 16.4 per cent; Wales 17.9 per cent; northern England 19.5 per cent; the UK as a whole 14.1 per cent – indicating that there is a regional problem. Such disparities are by no means new: in the inter-war years unemployment averaged 14 per cent, but was 50 per cent in some areas.

Differences in employment rates per thousand and *differences in average income levels* between regions also indicate that there is a regional problem. Figures such as those shown in Table 32 suggest that the government should intervene in the location of industry, since firms' location decisions affect regional differences in unemployment. However, each of these measures of regional disparities has some limitations. For example, differences in activity rates may represent cultural differences; differences in incomes do not take account of regional differences in prices, especially of transport and housing. The 1965 National Plan suggested that the increase in manpower that would result from reducing unemployment rates in depressed areas to the national average would increase GNP by about 2 per cent. Such action now would increase GNP by even more.

401

6. Causes of regional disparities

(i) The main cause of regional imbalances is *structural decline*: there has been over-reliance in certain regions of the country on one or two staple industries, for example textiles and shipbuilding, the demand for whose products has been declining since the mid-1950s. Thus, many of the regions with below-average levels of income, output and employment have high levels of *structural unemployment*.

(ii) Some regions have below-average levels of income, output and employment because they suffer from *remoteness*: they are too far away from major markets and major supplies of labour to attract firms to locate there. Such regions include the Scottish Highlands.

(iii) Since the 1970s governments have begun to pay more attention to the problems of *inner-city areas*. These problems have tended to arise because *many families have moved from the inner cities to suburban areas*. This movement has meant that the demand for, for example, schools and the services of local shops in the inner cities has fallen, and many local shops and firms have been forced either to close or to move. Thus, many inner-city areas are faced with the under-utilization and decay of social capital. The people left in those areas tend to be fairly old and with outdated skills. New firms are unlikely to be attracted to these areas, unless there are government-provided incentives, given that there is an ageing population and an environment less attractive than that of most provincial towns.

Most regional policies, in practice, have concentrated on encouraging firms to locate in such depressed areas rather than in areas of lower-than-average unemployment, where there may be the possibility of congestion, i.e. the over-utilization of social capital.

7. Government intervention in practice

The government can either encourage firms to expand to depressed areas or discourage expansion in other areas. The government might encourage expansion to depressed areas by offering financial assistance. Some financial inducements have been in the form of *discretionary grants and loans*, conditional upon the creation of sufficient employment. There have also been systems of *tax allowances*.

(a) *Regional policy up until the 1960s*

Up until the 1960s the main features of governments' regional policy were the *Distribution of Industry Acts* (the first of which was in 1945) and the *Town and Country Planning Acts* (the first being in 1947), under which firms wishing to build premises of more than 5,000 sq ft had to have *Industrial Development Certificates* (*IDCs*). This policy appears to have been a form of negative persuasion, which could have led to firms refusing to expand instead of to firms moving into the areas of the greatest unemployment. It was probably still more profitable for a firm to stay where it was rather than move elsewhere.

(b) *Assisted areas*

Regional policies have usually distinguished four types of areas requiring special treatment. These *assisted areas* are:

(i) *Development Areas*, which cover broad regions, such as north-east England and north Wales, and have existed in their present form since 1966;

(ii) *Special Development Areas*, which are smaller areas within Development Areas and include the industrial area of the North-East and Greater Merseyside; they were originally created to deal with problems caused by the closure of collieries;

(iii) *Intermediate Areas*, which are areas lying outside Development Areas but suffering from similar problems, if not as severe. Development and Intermediate Areas together cover: north-west, central and south-west Scotland; north-east England; parts of Lancashire; north Wales; most of south Wales; much of south-west England.

(iv) There are also *Enterprise Zones*, which are generally zones in depressed, inner-urban areas; firms are given tax concessions to locate there and are faced by fewer restrictions than elsewhere; there are eleven Enterprise Zones, established in 1981; such zones include the Isle of Dogs and the lower Swansea Valley. The identification, in such a way, of depressed regions should help governments in their regional policies, i.e. in deciding whether to encourage firms to move to areas of high unemployment (i.e. *take work to the workers*; encourage the mobility of industry) or to encourage unemployed workers in areas of higher-than-average unemployment to move to areas of lower-than-average unemployment (i.e. *move workers to the work*; encourage the mobility of labour).

We will look at schemes designed to encourage firms to move to areas of high unemployment and then at schemes designed to encourage unemployed workers to move to areas where work is available. We will then attempt to compare the logic of the two different types of approach. Before we do this, however, we will look at how governments have attempted to coordinate their regional policies.

(c) *The coordination of regional policy*

(i) *Regional Economic Planning Boards* and *Regional Economic Councils* were established in 1964 to develop and coordinate economic policy for the economic regions of England, Scotland and Wales.

Regional Economic Planning Boards were responsible for coordinating the work of different government departments in their regions and for preparing economic plans for their own regions. They were staffed by civil servants. In theory, the Boards helped the Regional Economic Councils elaborate plans for their own regions.

Regional Economic Councils consisted of non-elected, part-time members who were local people (such as academics, businessmen, trade unionists and local government officials). They were intended to provide local views and experience for the regional planners. They were purely advisory. In practice, a lot of each Council's so-called 'advice' consisted of little more than cries for help. The northern region's Council was well-known for having little regard for other regions' problems. The aims of the different regions would often clash.

(ii) *The Industry Act 1972* reorganized the way in which the development of the economic planning regions is administered by the Department of Industry. An *Industrial Development Executive* was established within the Department and was responsible for giving advice about how financial assistance might be given to encourage industry to locate in areas of high unemployment.

(d) *Schemes designed to take work to the workers*

Regional policy has often taken the form of the government of the day encouraging firms to locate in assisted areas or in Enterprise Zones (or discouraging firms from locating in other areas). This has been done by offering firms tax concessions, cash grants for investment, tax-free tenancy, training allowances or ready-built factories, etc. (i.e. *investment incentives*). Industrial Development Certificates, on the other hand, act as a *disincentive* to firms to locate in areas other than assisted areas: a firm which wishes to build a new factory over a certain size in any area of the country other than a Development Area or a Special Development Area must have an IDC. However, IDC controls are not being strictly enforced.

Some of the schemes designed to encourage firms to locate in areas of high unemployment are described below.

(i) *Manufacturers in Development Areas (and in no other areas) received a 37p refund per week on Selective Employment Tax (SET) for each worker employed.* The SET refund may have acted as an *economic rent* to manufacturers in Development Areas, helping them increase their profits rather than attracting new firms or preventing the closure of existing firms. SET was introduced in 1966 and abolished with the introduction of value added tax in 1973.

(ii) *The Regional Employment Premium (REP)* was introduced as an addition to the SET refund. It was payable to manufacturing firms in assisted areas to encourage manufacturers to move to such areas. It was introduced in September 1967: £1.50 per week per man was paid originally; it was later raised to £3. *The REP was designed as a means by which the government might influence the price of factors of production* (the REP reduced labour costs) and as a means of raising employment since: (1) it lowered labour costs in assisted areas (i.e. areas of particularly high unemployment); (2) it reduced the cost of labour relative to capital, encouraging the substitution of capital by labour. One criticism of the Regional Employment Premium is that it may well have acted as an economic rent. Instead of the differential in unemployment rates between Development Areas and other areas narrowing, it widened; this was perhaps one reason why the REP was abolished.

(iii) The Industry Act 1972 introduced *Regional Development Grants (RDGs)*, which are investment grants covering 22 per cent of the cost of new buildings and machinery in Special Development Areas and 15 per cent in Development Areas. These grants are given not only to new firms, but also to existing firms investing in new plant and equipment for modernization.

One problem, however, with investment grants is that they may merely bring in highly capital-intensive industries, such as the north Highlands hydroelectricity scheme, where more labour-intensive industries would be better. However, capital-intensive industries do have multiplier effects.

(iv) *Regional Selective Assistance (RSA)* is also available and usually takes the form of a further, discretionary (i.e. conditional) grant towards capital and training costs for job-creating projects.

Firms may not like the idea of conditional schemes (which might, for example, offer a period of rent-free tenancy or ready-built factories) because of fears of bureaucracy.

(v) Other measures which governments *might* use to encourage firms to move to depressed areas include *government-provided subsidies to key workers* (those workers who are vital members of a particular firm's workforce) to encourage them to move to an area of high unemployment, so that their firm is attracted to re-locate in that area. Alternatively, governments could *pay sums of money to firms which have already created new jobs*.

(vi) *Measures to discourage the expansion of firms into areas with lower-than-average unemployment rates include IDCs and a congestion tax on new firms.* For a government, such as the Thatcher government, which believes in the free working of the price mechanism, the imposition of a congestion tax would seem to be a sensible means of intervention. However, in practice governments have tended to impose planning controls, rather than use the price mechanism, to discourage the expansion of firms into certain areas.

Of all the measures used to encourage firms to move to depressed areas, the provision of cheap or ready-built factories and of cheap rents appear to have been the most effective measures.

(e) *Schemes to take workers to the work*

Policies designed to encourage unemployed workers to move to areas where there is work available attempt to make workers more *geographically mobile*. Some labour is not very mobile at all. For example, some people are tied to tenancies and will only be made geographically mobile if the housing market is reformed. The Thatcher government's policy of encouraging council-house tenants to buy their homes may help improve the geographical mobility of labour.

However, *retraining schemes* are, perhaps, the most efficient way of encouraging workers to move to areas where work is available. Re-training schemes attempt to enlarge people's range of skills and, as a result, improve their *occupational mobility*. Assisted areas tend to be dependent on declining, traditional industries, while regions such as the South-East with lower-than-average unemployment rates tend to have newer, relatively buoyant industries; retraining people living in depressed regions so that they acquire skills in, for instance, computer programming, may mean that they can more easily move to a more prosperous area.

Regional policies tend to concentrate more on encouraging work to move to the workers than on encouraging workers to move to the work, for reasons which are discussed in subsection (f). However, some policies designed to improve the mobility of labour have been formulated. Generally, these policies have taken the form of *selective retraining schemes*.

(i) *The 1964 Industrial Training Act* created *Industrial Training Boards* (*ITBs*). The ITBs gave grants to firms which provided approved training. However, each ITB only covered one industry and was not concerned with retraining labour from a declining industry for an expanding one.

(ii) *The Manpower Services Commission (MSC)* was created in 1973 to initiate employment and training policies on a national basis and to administer the *Training Opportunities Scheme (TOPS)*, an adult retraining scheme.

(iii) The MSC funded a *youth training programme*, which ran from 1973 to 1981. These *Special Training Measures* were allocated through the ITBs and other training organizations. In 1976 an experimental *Unified Vocational Preparation* programme was introduced for young people who, although employed, had skills below craft level. Finally, in 1978 the MSC introduced the *Youth Opportunities Programme (YOP)*. YOP was designed for people aged nineteen or under, unemployed for six weeks or more. It provided work preparation and work experience.

(iv) The MSC programme was replaced in 1981 by the *New Training Initiative*, which aimed to improve work preparation in schools and colleges, to modernize training in occupational skills and to provide wider opportunities for adults to improve their skills.

(v) *The Youth Training Scheme (YTS)* absorbed the YOP scheme in 1983 and is the central part of the Thatcher government's youth training policy. The aim of YTS is to provide general skills, so that those on the scheme are made more adaptable. The scheme is designed for sixteen- and seventeen-year-olds.

Training policies were discussed in greater detail in Chapter 20.

(vi) Occupational, and (as a result) possibly geographical, mobility might also be increased through *legislation (such as the 1980 Employment Act) which reduces the effectiveness of the closed shop*.

(f) Should work be taken to the workers or workers taken to the work?

Governments' regional policies have tended to concentrate on encouraging industry to move to depressed areas rather than on encouraging labour to move from depressed areas to areas with lower-than-average unemployment rates.

(i) *Policies designed to encourage workers to move to the work are likely to be unpopular since social ties are liable to be broken.*

(ii) *Policies to encourage the geographical mobility of labour are unlikely to be successful unless there is a shortage of workers in other areas of the country.* During the recession of the 1980s, there has been a shortage of labour in no area of the country; even in south-east England unemployment has averaged about 10 per cent of the total labour force.

(iii) *Taking workers to the work might lead to congestion* in those areas to which they are moved: the social capital (schools, hospitals, etc.) in the depressed areas will become under-utilized and the social capital in other areas will become congested (over-utilized). However, it has been argued that the problem of under- and over-utilization of social capital is not just an inter-regional problem, but an intra-regional one as well. That is, not only may certain schools in Newcastle become underpopulated while schools in London become overpopulated, but schools in the inner-city area of Newcastle may become under-populated while schools in Newcastle's more suburban areas become overpopulated.

(iv) A more valid argument in favour of taking work to the workers rather than moving workers to the work is that in the relatively poor areas, such as Wales, the activity rate of women tends to be relatively low. *If greater participation of married women is to be encouraged, the only course of action open involves taking work to the workers,* since married women are unlikely to move if their husbands have work in these areas.

(v) *A policy of encouraging workers to move will usually result in skilled workers moving from depressed areas, making the long-term situation for these areas worse.* Skilled workers should not be encouraged to leave depressed areas because they are more likely to attract industry to move to such areas than are the unskilled, even if their skills are not completely compatible with any industry that does move to such areas.

(vi) *There are problems associated with policies which encourage firms to relocate in assisted areas.* For example, if new firms or new branches of firms from other parts of the country are relocated in assisted areas, *workers in these areas may have to be retrained. For key workers, special arrangements may have to be made,* such as giving them travel allowances, so that they may be encouraged to remain in such areas.

Table 33. The effectiveness of regional policy, as measured by disparities between regional unemployment rates and the UK average in 1967 and January 1986

	1967		January 1986	
	Unemploy-ment rate (%)	Index (UK = 100)	Unemploy-ment rate (%)	Index (UK = 100)
United Kingdom	2.3	100	14.1	100
North	3.9	170	19.5	138
Yorks and Humberside	1.9	87	16.0	113
East Midlands	1.6	70	13.1	93
East Anglia	2.0	87	11.5	82
South-East	1.6	70	10.3	73
South-West	2.5	109	12.9	91
West Midlands	1.8	78	15.8	112
North-West	2.3	100	16.7	118
Wales	4.0	174	17.9	127
Scotland	3.7	161	16.4	116
Northern Ireland	7.3	317	21.6	153

Sources: Central Statistical Office, *Regional Trends*, HMSO, 1982, and *Monthly Digest of Statistics*, February 1986.

(g) *The effectiveness of regional policy*

Since the major objective of regional policy is, presumably, to reduce regional disparities in output, incomes and unemployment, the effectiveness of regional policy would seem to be best assessed by looking at trends in regional variations in output, incomes and employment.

Table 33 shows how much the unemployment rate in each region of the UK differed from the national average rate (in index form) in both 1967 and January 1986. These figures show that, generally, *those regions with the highest unemployment rates in 1967 continued to be the regions with the highest unemployment rates in January 1986*. However, in those regions in which there was higher-than-average unemployment in 1967, the differential (as measured by the index) between their own rates of unemployment and the national average had been reduced by January 1986.

Yet we can conclude that *regional policy does not seem to have been very effective*, since more regions had higher-than-average rates of unemployment in January 1986 than in 1967 and because unemployment in regions identified, for example, as Development or Intermediate Areas rose dramatically between 1967 and January 1986. Furthermore, we can see from the figures in Table 33 that regional imbalances have widened. For example, the difference between the unemployment rate in the North and the unemployment rate in the South-East in 1967 was 2.3 per cent and in January 1986 was 9.2 per cent.

In recent years the government, faced with a dramatic rise in unemployment in every region of the country, has tended to concentrate less on regional policy; any policies designed to reduce unemployment, such as the New Training Initiative discussed earlier, tend to aim to reduce unemployment generally.

Regional policies are unlikely to be successful during times of recession because firms are less inclined to risk moving and unemployed workers are unlikely to be willing to move from one area to another in search of work when unemployment is high everywhere.

It has sometimes been stated that, while the government in its official unemployment policies has been pursuing regional policies, in other aspects it has not: the effects of the *Beeching Report* in 1962 for example, were that Development Areas were deprived of their transport facilities; furthermore, the building of the Channel Tunnel will reinforce the attractions of the South-East from a transport point of view.

Perhaps the main criticism of regional policy in general is that, in spite of all the emphasis since the war on a regional policy, regional unemployment rates seem to have varied more proportionately compared with the national average. We cannot of course be sure that without such policies the position would not have been worse. None the less, one of the aims, i.e. that of increasing productivity without increasing inflation, does not seem to have been achieved. We can perhaps best blame the lack of effectiveness of regional policies in general upon the nonexistence of any overall planning.

*

QUESTION

What are the arguments for allowing market forces to solve regional problems?

There is a strong case for allowing market forces to solve the regional problems, as far as possible allowing both workers and firms to make their own decisions rather than having central or local government impose its decisions on them. Regional policy, in any case, has been described as 'empiricism run mad', i.e. no sooner has one set of regional policies come in than another takes over. For example, at one stage the government encouraged firms to move out from the London area and at a later stage it encouraged firms to move to the inner-city areas of London.

If there is a divergence between social and private costs, this, where possible, should be corrected through the pricing mechanism rather than through an administrative mechanism. For example, if there is an argument against greater use of office space in the centre of London because of the likely increase in congestion, a road-pricing system, reflecting the higher social costs of motoring in peak periods, should be initiated rather than a policy of direct government intervention to encourage firms to move. Alternatively, those who favour market-orientated policies might recommend that, if congestion costs are high, firms should pay more for Industrial Development Certificates: the price of IDCs should be pitched at the point at which marginal social costs equal marginal social revenue. In any case, it is argued that the costs of congestion will cause some firms to leave the area, so that the problems of congestion are largely self-correcting.

Furthermore, those who advocate market-orientated policies may argue that workers will see where the job opportunities lie. Therefore, they argue that there is little point in helping 'lame duck' firms in Development Areas. Workers in such areas will, as economic models show, look for the highest wages or at least the best jobs which are available to them and will, therefore, migrate to them, with or without government help. Thus, if there are surpluses of labour in some areas, people will move away, while if there are shortages, people will move in from other areas, even from overseas.

MULTIPLE-CHOICE QUESTIONS

1. For which of the following reasons might the government intervene in the location of industry:
(A) over-utilization of social capital in some regions;
(B) the existence of significantly lower-than-average earnings in some areas;
(C) over-reliance on one or two industries in certain regions?
   (*a*) A only
   (*b*) A and C only.

    (*c*) B and C only.

    (*d*) All.

Answer – (*d*)

2. The Selective Employment Tax refund may have acted as a rent to manufacturers in Development Areas because:

    (*a*) it attracted new manufacturers to move to Development Areas;

    (*b*) it encouraged them to expand;

    (*c*) it helped prevent them closing down;

    (*d*) it raised the profits of firms which did not need assistance.

Answer – (*d*)

3. The Regional Employment Premium was designed to encourage manufacturers in assisted areas to:

    (*a*) reduce the wage they pay to their workers;

    (*b*) become more labour-intensive;

    (*c*) become more capital-intensive;

    (*d*) obtain an economic rent.

Answer – (*b*)

4. Which of the following is most likely to be 'footloose':

    (*a*) a microcomputer manufacturer;

    (*b*) a shipbuilding firm;

    (*c*) a textile manufacturer;

    (*d*) a manufacturer of cars?

Answer – (*a*)

DATA RESPONSE

1. A House of Commons Expenditure Committee, looking in 1964 at the decisions of firms to move from one location to another, showed that expansion of output was a major reason for relocation for over 80 per cent of firms that had moved and the primary reason for 20 per cent. Inadequate premises was one of the major reasons for 50 per cent, while unsatisfactory labour supply was a major reason for 40 per cent and for 15 per cent the single outstanding reason.

    Unless we know why firms move it seems almost impossible to formulate a rational regional policy or even to formulate a more general policy for dealing with unemployment. Yet many moves by successive governments since the war seem to have been '*empiricism run mad*'.

(a) Explain what is meant by the term in *italic* type.

(b) The article explains data for 1964. For what reasons might the decision-making process have altered since then?

(c) Why is it important to know the reasons why firms move when formulating a regional policy?

2. In the post-war years many new towns have been developed. These can be divided into two groups. Firstly, some new towns – including Basildon, Crawley, Stevenage and Milton Keynes – were located around the London area, partly to relieve the housing problems in central London. These towns were also developed to relieve the congestion in the London area, and because it was easier to build purpose-built factories of the right size for prospective owners in the new towns than in the already developed areas. Firms moving to new towns such as Basildon and Crawley would be able to find a workforce located near by, but in residential areas situated far enough away from industry to avoid the problems of noise and pollution from factories. It was intended that such new towns should be relatively self-contained. Basildon, for example, originally had a town centre near the main railway line from Fenchurch Street to Southend, but did not have a station. The citizens of such towns are able to find work locally, but in practice many commute; hence the eventual development of rail links both at Basildon and Milton Keynes Central.

Secondly, new towns such as Cwmbran, Washington and Cumbernauld were built in assisted areas partly to relieve the problem of congestion in nearby major towns, but mainly to try to stimulate employment: it was hoped that these new towns would be able to attract new industry to focal points. Firms were encouraged to move out of the London area, particularly, as a result of fairly effective advertising from the Location of Offices Bureau, which showed, for example, typical rents in the central London area and compared them with rents elsewhere. The Location of Offices Bureau also provided a great deal of information, including case studies about firms which had relocated.

In the late 1970s government policies towards new towns altered slightly, as governments became increasingly aware of problems in the inner-city areas. While the firms and possibly the households who had moved to the new towns were gaining from the emphasis upon new towns, the inner cities were suffering because they contained a great deal of old housing, because rates were often high (because of the problems of providing social services) and because the general nature of the inner-city areas (with problems such as congestion and unattractive buildings, etc.) was such that they were unlikely to attract new firms. The Toxteth Riots in 1981 reinforced the belief that the problems of inner cities need to be considered seriously.

- (*a*) Why does the author suggest that new towns were developed in and around the London region? Are the original reasons still valid? Explain your answer.
- (*b*) Why does the author suggest that new towns were built in the so-called 'assisted areas'? Are these reasons still valid? Explain your answer.
- (*c*) Governments, in recent years, have paid more attention to the problems of inner cities. How might governments attempt to attract firms to locate in inner-city areas?

3. *Inner City Partnerships.* During the 1970s successive governments became more concerned about the problems of the inner cities. Many inner-city areas suffered from old housing and, in many cases, derelict buildings. Many residents were moving out to the suburbs; the shop-keepers tended to follow them out. While some social infrastructure remained, compared with the infrastructure of the suburbs the facilities were often poor and likely to deteriorate, since there was little incentive to re-invest.

Seven Inner City Partnerships were established in the late 1970s; each one was designed to research into the problems of one inner-city area, and was a partnership between central government and the relevant local authority. The logic behind them was that the local authority knows the problems of its own inner city better than the civil servants in Whitehall do.

The aim of the Inner City Partnerships was for central government and local authorities to have a plan of action for up to ten years to improve the inner-city areas. Inner City Partnerships looked at the potential for commercial land use and, in particular, tried to encourage small firms, which might wish to be reasonably near the city centres, to locate in inner-city areas. While there was high unemployment, some inner-city firms still had shortages of skilled labour. There was, therefore, a need for local government and central government to try to improve training.

The inner-city areas often suffered from relatively poor transport. Many inner-city railway stations had been closed and there was a considerable degree of congestion in many areas, though most of this consisted of 'through' traffic rather than traffic terminating in the area itself. Therefore, in many cases, improved transport schemes were required.

Housing was (and still is) a major problem. In some cases, building societies have not invested (i.e. 'given mortgages to people') in the inner-city areas, though they tend to deny this. Because housing is geared, to some extent, to expectations, many people are reluctant to improve their houses unless other people around are carrying out such improvements too.

Inner City Partnerships also aimed to improve the physical environment, in order to encourage both firms and people to enter the areas: open spaces were developed, existing parks improved and the more unsightly areas were cleared up.

(a) Why might the price mechanism not solve the problems of the inner-city areas?

(b) What factors does the author suggest might encourage new firms to move into the areas? What other factors might also be involved?

(c) Why might small firms be more likely to enter the inner-city areas than other firms?

(d) Why might health facilities be poorer in the inner-city areas than elsewhere?

4. The London Docklands Area. The Docklands have suffered, as have many other inner-city areas, from a general decline. Additionally, Dockland activity has declined as the majority of the Port of London services have moved down river to Tilbury, about twenty-five miles from the centre of London.

One of the aims of the London Dockland Development Corporation, which was set up under the Local Government Planning and Land Act 1980, was to regenerate land and buildings and create a more attractive environment.

The problems of the area can be dramatically illustrated looking at the unemployment figures, which, according to the Corporation, were 30 per cent for men and 15 per cent for women, which was far higher than the average unemployment figures of 9.6 per cent for Greater London and 12.4 per cent for the UK as a whole (in the mid-1980s).

The Corporation decided to try to make the area more attractive to tourists. This is perhaps easier in London than in many other cities, since a great many people are already visiting London. There were developments such as the World Trade Centre and the establishment of museums, such as at St Katherine's by the Tower of London. Jobs were consequently created. One criticism which has been made is that the Corporation did not seem to be too perturbed if the jobs were created at the expense of jobs elsewhere, rather than providing jobs for the unemployed locally.

The Corporation also tried to encourage small firms, in particular, to enter the area; firms might be attracted to the area by concessions such as rate-free premises for ten years.

In an attempt to encourage people to move to the area, a great deal of money was spent on infrastructure, including roads. The Corporation also tried to improve transport by encouraging the building of a new light railway, which was opened in 1987; it was thought that it would be an attraction in itself, but the cost of it was estimated to be about £77m for a relatively short length of track. In 1988 the LDDC began a £150m extension to the Bank and also announced a possible extension to the east.

The Corporation also aimed to build a large number of houses, for which priority would be given to council tenants. However, there was also a desire to build some private housing in order to avoid some of the problems faced by inner-city areas elsewhere.

A controversial feature was the desire to build a Docklands airport. While it was suggested by some that this would improve tourist facilities, others suggested that the amount of space which it would occupy would be better utilized by more labour-intensive firms.

(a) What problems are there in attracting large firms to the London Dockland Area? How, if at all, might the incentives need to be different for smaller firms?

(b) What are the advantages and disadvantages of tourism as a method of generating jobs?

(c) £77m has been spent on the light railways system. What are the advantages of this?

(d) Why did the Corporation wish to have a balanced mix of private and public housing? What longer-term effects might this have on the area?

SELF-EXAMINATION QUESTIONS

1. Why in the early 1960s were there few examples of firms which profit-maximized in location policy?

2. 'Only firms know the best ways in which they can locate their industry. The government should, therefore, not intervene in the location of industry.' Discuss.

3. The following factors might influence industrial locations: access to raw materials; access to the market; the availability of cheap fuel; the

availability of cheap land; the availability of water; the availability of skilled labour. Which are likely to be the most important factors in the location of: (a) a computer firm; (b) a brewery; (c) a furniture firm; (d) a newspaper firm; (e) a retailer's; (f) a steel works? Explain your reasoning.

4. Because of the changing nature of many of governments' regional policies in the last twenty years, how, if at all, is it possible to evaluate the success or otherwise of regional policy?

5. How can we determine whether a region has a major problem? What are the comparative merits of looking at each of these determinants and what, if any, are the disadvantages of using these measures?

6. At many times in the post-war era, IDCs had to be obtained in the central London area and some other areas. What were the purposes of such certificates?

7. Would it be possible to use IDCs through a pricing policy rather than through administrative action? Explain your answer.

8. Would the failure of Keynesian measures to remove unemployment in development areas suggest a fault in the usual Phillips curve analysis? Explain your answer.

9. What is meant by the term 'activity rates'? Why, for example, might they be lower in south Wales than in some other regions?

10. Which age groups and which socio-economic groups are most likely to move from a declining area? Does your answer suggest that the regional problem is a self-correcting one?

11. The 1980 Budget introduced the concept of Enterprise Zones, in which there would be fewer planning restrictions and rates would not be charged for considerable periods to industries moving to such areas. Why were these introduced and what are the advantages and disadvantages of the Enterprise Zones?

12. Why do you think that the Fatstock Marketing Corporation (which was set up to sell meat directly from the farmer to the butcher) was located in Shaftesbury Avenue? When looking through the former Location of Offices Bureau's case-studies of other firms, which firms can you find which would seem not to be ideally located?

13. How far are transport costs a deterrent to new firms locating in a particular area? Contrast car firms with the major users of clerical labour in this respect.

14. If firms are run for the benefits of managers rather than shareholders, what inducements might persuade firms to move and what inducements might dissuade them from moving?

15. What do we mean by the term 'key workers'? What inducements might be required to get them to move?

16. What was the Regional Employment Premium? Did this merely act as an economic rent? Explain your answer.

17. How, if at all, can the government get over the problem of a lack of training of workers in the depressed areas?

18. Why do you think that in 1972 the government launched 'Operation Eyesore'? What does your answer suggest about the aspirations of managers?

19. Even students who have lived in new towns tend to overlook the fact that they are one of the major items of regional policy. We can broadly subdivide them into two categories – those (such as Basildon and Stevenage) which seem to be overflows for the London area, and those (such as Cwmbran, Cumbernauld and Washington) which are meant as focal points for new industry. What are the advantages of both types of new town from potential employers' points of view? What are the advantages from the employee's point of view?

20. Why were investment grants introduced?

21. Is capital-intensive industry what is required for depressed areas? Explain your answer.

22. Does the remission of taxes on profits help firms to move? Explain your answer.

23. What do we mean by 'the multiplier aspects' of firm's activities? What sort of projects might have a fairly large multiplier aspect?

24. Why do you think that the provision of factories at low rates seems to have been one of the greatest inducements to firms to move?

25. What effects might the building of the Channel Tunnel have on the location of industry?

26. Should work be moved to the workers or workers to the work? Explain your answer.

25. International trade

1. What are the reasons for international trade?

Trade, whether international or within a nation, will take place if both parties believe that trade is *mutually beneficial*, i.e. if it is believed that *it will increase the welfare of both parties concerned*. The ability to trade internationally allows *international division of labour*, i.e. it allows countries to specialize in the production of particular goods or services.

If a certain country is able to produce more units of a particular commodity than another country (because it has greater deposits of the necessary raw materials, because capital has been developed specifically to produce the commodity in question and because labour has been trained specifically to produce the commodity), it may wish to specialize in producing this commodity in order to benefit from the *economies of scale*. A country which specializes in the production of a particular commodity will wish to trade any surpluses for other commodities. We have already said that two parties will trade if it is mutually beneficial to do so. Thus, if a country specializes in the production of steel and wishes to trade some steel for wheat, another country which produces wheat will only wish to trade some wheat for steel if it has a surplus of wheat and insufficient supplies of steel to satisfy its demand.

From what we have said so far it might seem that a country will only specialize in the production of a certain commodity if it is more efficient than another country at producing the commodity (i.e. if it has an *absolute advantage* over another country) and, therefore, that international trade will only be mutually beneficial if one country has an absolute advantage in the production of one commodity and another country has an absolute advantage in the production of another commodity.

However, economists have often stressed that *it is not the principle of absolute advantage which explains why foreign trade takes place; rather, it is the principle of comparative advantage that is important*. This can be shown by assuming a world consisting of just two countries (a developed country and a developing country) and just two outputs (wheat and steel) and by assuming that the developed country can produce both more wheat and more steel with its resources than the developing country. Thus, the developed country might be able to produce 1,000

419

tonnes of steel or 100 tonnes of wheat, while the developing country can only produce 200 tonnes of steel or 50 tonnes of wheat in a given period.

If the demand for wheat in the period in question is 50 tonnes in the developed country and 25 tonnes in the developing country, it might well be that each country will devote half of its resources to the production of wheat and half to the production of steel and that no trade will take place. The resulting situation will be as follows:

	Developed country	Developing country	Total
Output of steel (tonnes)	500	100	600
Output of wheat (tonnes)	50	25	75

If there is some specialization and international trade, the demand for wheat in both countries could still be met and the output of steel increased. In this way, international trade will be beneficial to both the developed country and the developing country even though the developing country has an absolute advantage in neither the production of wheat nor the production of steel. However, the developing country does have a *comparative advantage* in the production of wheat.

It is clear that the developed country can produce five times as much steel as the developing country when both countries devote the same proportion of their resources to the production of steel. Given the same conditions for the production of wheat, it is clear that the developed country can only produce twice as much wheat as the developing country. If specialization takes place on the basis of comparative advantage (whereby the developed country devotes more of its resources to the production of steel than to the production of wheat), trade is beneficial to both countries.

If the developed country allocates its resources in such a way that it produces 750 tonnes of steel, it can only produce 25 tonnes of wheat. If, however, the developing country allocates all its resources to the production of wheat, it produces 50 tonnes of wheat and no steel. In this way, the total output of steel is greater than previously while the total output of wheat is the same:

	Developed country	Developing country	Total
Output of steel (tonnes)	750	0	750
Output of wheat (tonnes)	25	50	75

If we assume that the developed country still requires 50 tonnes of wheat, while the developing country only requires 25 tonnes, it will be mutually beneficial to trade. Further assuming that the developing country requires 100 tonnes of steel while the developed country requires 500 tonnes, it will be beneficial for the developing country to trade wheat for steel and for the developed country to trade steel for wheat. Given that there will be an excess output of 150 tonnes of steel, it may well be that the price of wheat in terms of steel will be said to be such that in return for the 25 tonnes of wheat exported to the developed country, the developing country will receive 175 tonnes of steel, leaving the developed country with 575 tonnes of steel and 50 tonnes of wheat, as shown below:

	Developed country	Developing country	Total
Consumption of steel (tonnes)	575	175	750
Consumption of wheat (tonnes)	50	25	75

This example shows how a degree of specialization in areas of comparative advantage and foreign trade based on the principle of comparative advantage are beneficial to all parties involved.

However, it is difficult to see how the principle of comparative advantage applies in the modern pattern of trade. For example, a great number of cars are imported by the UK, while similar cars are exported. Many other manufactured goods which the UK exports are similar to those it imports. Here the principle for trade does not appear to be one of comparative advantage, but rather one of product differentiation.

2. Possible disadvantages of international specialization

(i) A country which specializes in the production of a particular commodity may suffer *dis-economies of scale* (see Chapter 9).

(ii) A country which over-specializes in a particular commodity may well find itself *very susceptible to changes in demand, which could lead to large-scale unemployment*, at least in the short term. This, for example, could apply particularly to countries growing cotton, the demand for which is susceptible to a rising demand for synthetic fibres.

(iii) *Specialization puts the specializing country in a very vulnerable*

421

position if other countries take economic action, such as imposing quotas.

3. Obstacles to international trade

(i) Obstacles include *quotas*, which restrict the amount of goods countries allow to be imported.

(ii) There may be *tariffs*, which are import duties.

(iii) Governments may give '*hidden*' subsidies to home industries. For. example, governments have often allowed firms in the shipbuilding industry to obtain cheap loans. The products of firms which receive 'hidden' subsidies can be produced relatively cheaply, making them more competitive than the products of rival foreign firms which do not receive such subsidies. Thus, importing is discouraged.

(iv) *Governments might purchase domestic goods only*; for example, the British government might give subsidies to schools to buy British computers.

(v) Countries might impose *non-tariff barriers* (*NTBs*). Such barriers might include the imposition of regulations which tend to favour the home market rather than the overseas market. It has often been alleged that Japan uses such regulations to keep out imports.

(vi) A government might impose *higher taxes upon those goods its country is likely to import than on those goods it is likely to produce itself*. For example, the case of the UK having much higher taxation on wines and spirits (which it tends to import) than on beer (which is generally home-produced) was brought up within the EEC, and led to the duties on wines being cut in the 1984 Budget.

(vii) *Where information is more inadequate in one country than in another*, there may be a reluctance to trade. In the UK, the *Export Services Branch*, the *Export Credits Guarantee Department* and commercial banks are able to provide a great deal of information.

(viii) *Differences in currency* can make international trade difficult. While sterling is acceptable within the United Kingdom, an exporter from the United States will generally want payment to be made in dollars.

Similarly, if the Rover Group are exporting Metros which sell for £3,000 on the home market, they will require payment in pounds from whoever they sell their cars to, so that they can ensure that they receive at least £3,000 per car.

4. Exchange rates

As we have already said, if the Rover Group exports Metro cars, it will wish to receive payment in sterling. If Metros are exported to the United States, the US importer purchases a cheque to pay the Rover Group. Assuming that each car is priced at £3,000 and that the rate of exchange is $1.80 to £1, the cheque must be worth $5,400 per car for Rover to receive at least £3,000 per car. This cheque may take the form of a bill of exchange.

The exchange rate is the price at which transactions take place. Since 1972, British exchange rates have not been fixed but have floated, i.e. they respond, in theory, to changes in supply and demand.

(a) *Fixed exchange rates; the gold standard*

Under a fixed-exchange-rate system the price at which one currency is exchanged for another is stable despite any short-term fluctuations in the demand for or supply of a currency.

All the currencies in a fixed-exchange-rate system need to be fixed in terms of a standard unit. From the nineteenth century until 1914 and from 1925 until 1935 the pound was fixed in terms of gold. Under this *gold standard* one pound was said to be worth 0.257 ounces of gold. In 1914 the US dollar was worth 0.053 ounces of gold. Therefore, the exchange rate between the pound and the dollar was £1 = $4.86.

This system required all currencies within it to be readily *convertible* into gold. In other words, it had to be possible to convert £1 into 0.257 oz gold. This required each country's central bank to have adequate reserves of gold in order to meet any run on its currency. That is to say, if speculators felt that the pound's exchange rate (or price) was higher than it would have been had the forces of supply and demand been allowed to determine it, they would wish to convert any pounds they held into gold, which would reduce the Bank of England's reserves; if this pessimism about the pound continued, it would be necessary for the pound to be devalued, otherwise the demand for sterling would continue to fall, leading to a fall in demand for British exports (because their price would be too high), bearing in mind that if other countries were reluctant to convert their own currency into sterling (via gold), they would be reluctant to hold the sterling which they would need to buy British goods.

The gold standard worked well until the First World War, but in the 1920s most countries on the gold standard suffered severe inflation.

Some countries, notably the UK, returned to the gold standard after the First World War at its pre-war rate (the pound was, therefore, overrated) for prestige purposes. The countries with the most severe inflation had the most over-valued currencies and, as a result, suffered the largest balance of payments deficits.

(b) *The abandonment of the gold standard*

The gold standard was abandoned in the early 1930s. What followed was a period of *competitive devaluations* whereby countries devalued their currencies in an attempt to increase their exports and reduce their imports (since the price of exports is reduced and the price of imports increased by devaluation) and in an attempt to reduce their unemployment, which in the 1930s was very high in most Western countries. If, as a result of devaluation, a country was able to reduce its imports and reduce its unemployment, the problem was merely pushed on to other countries, since their exports would be reduced and their unemployment increased. These competitive devaluations were '*beggar my neighbour*' *policies*.

(c) *The Bretton Woods system*

Many of the countries participating in the *Bretton Woods Conference* in 1944 agreed that the Depression had been deepened by countries pursuing 'beggar-my-neighbour' policies of competitive devaluation and import controls. The Bretton Woods agreement aimed at a system of *managed exchange rates*, which, it was hoped, would lead to more stable trading conditions and, thus, contribute to fuller employment.

The Bretton Woods agreement allowed market forces to determine the price of currencies within an agreed band. Exchange rates were allowed to fluctuate to 1 per cent either side of a par. If a country had a balance of payments deficit, it would be expected to reduce its prices. A country with a balance of payments surplus was expected to raise its prices, so that the demand for its exports would fall. Only where countries suffered persistent balance of payments deficits would they be allowed to resort to devaluation. Countries were only supposed to devalue as a measure of last resort.

One of the weaknesses of the Bretton Woods system was that *countries with persistent balance of payments surpluses were often reluctant to inflate their prices: there was little onus on countries in surplus to adjust; most of the onus was on deficit countries to adjust.*

The United Kingdom suffered balance of payments problems for much of the period of the Bretton Woods system. The UK devalued in both 1949 and 1967. It was felt for a long while prior to 1967 that the pound was over-valued and that it was this over-valuation which was the main cause of the UK's payments problems. However, not all economists agreed with this diagnosis and they quoted other factors, such as the quality of products and the type of products (it was argued that the UK was not supplying the products which were in most demand) as being perhaps more important.

(d) *Features of a floating-exchange-rate system*

(i) Since 1972 the pound has 'floated'. In a freely floating exchange-rate system, *the determination of equilibrium will be made through supply and demand.* The point of equilibrium is where the value of a particular currency neither appreciates nor depreciates. If at a given exchange rate, say £1 = \$2, the demand for dollars exceeds the supply, the value of dollars will appreciate. As the price of dollars rises, the price of US exports rises. Thus, the demand for US exports falls and the demand for dollars falls towards the equilibrium level. As the value of dollars appreci-

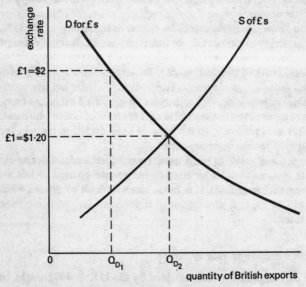

Figure 63. *The equilibrium exchange rate*

425

ates, the relative value of the pound depreciates. Thus, one pound becomes worth fewer and fewer dollars. The exchange rate, from the British point of view, falls until the equilibrium point is reached, which might be, say, £1 = \$1.20. As the value of the pound falls, British exports become more and more cheap relative to US exports. Thus, more and more UK exports will be demanded until the equilibrium exchange rate is reached.

(ii) A freely floating exchange-rate system is *easily operated: exchange rates under such a system fluctuate freely without the need to deflate or inflate through monetary or fiscal policy.* In the UK, for example, deflationary policies are likely to be politically unpopular and cause resistance from trade unions.

(iii) Furthermore, under a floating regime, *there is little need for large reserves,* assuming that currencies really are allowed to find their own level, i.e. there is no intervention by the government. It is assumed that under a freely floating exchange-rate system, *the central bank is free to look after domestic price stability, without having to be concerned about the effects that a change in interest rates would have on reserves.*

(iv) Many economists argue that it is better to have a system of freely floating exchange rates than to have *a system of direct controls which may adversely affect investment and, therefore, employment.* However, the Cambridge School, for example, favours direct controls to limit imports.

(v) Many economists argue that *full employment and flexible exchange rates tend to be incompatible,* especially where, as in the case of the UK, many raw materials are imported; for these the price elasticity of demand is likely to be between zero and one, implying that as the price of imports rises, costs of production rise, leading to firms reducing production and reducing employment. However, since there are few countries, whether with floating exchange rates or with fixed exchange rates, with levels of unemployment anywhere near the level of full employment, it is not clear that returning to a regime of fixed exchange rates in the UK would help reduce unemployment.

(vi) *International trade is much more complicated* under floating-exchange-rate systems than under fixed-exchange-rate systems. When we have floating exchange rates, it is much more difficult to predict what the rates will be in, say, three months' time than when we have fixed exchange rates.

(e) *The UK's exchange-rate system*

While the exchange-rate system adopted by the UK in 1972 might be thought to lead to the pound's exchange rate being determined by supply and demand, many commentators feel that the British government has tended to push up the price of sterling above that which purchasing-power-parity theory might suggest to be reasonable. However, it seems that the exchange rate in the mid-1980s has been below the level that supply and demand would suggest to be reasonable.

Reluctance to allow the exchange rate to be determined solely by supply and demand might be partly due to the historical role of sterling as a reserve currency. More important, though, seems to be the fact that *the government is reluctant to let the exchange rate fall, since this lowers the price at which North Sea oil can be exported.* A fall in the price of North Sea oil is unfavourable, since the demand for North Sea oil tends to be inelastic: a fall in its price reduces revenue.

(f) *The European Monetary System*

All the members of the EEC, except Spain, Portugal and the UK are also members of the *European Monetary System (EMS)*. The exchange rates of the member countries are bound within a narrow band, which is, however, wider than the band which existed under the Bretton Woods system.

The EMS is regarded by some commentators as a prelude to full economic and monetary union. It is helpful to the European Economic Community, partly because it creates a greater stability for traders and partly because it enables Common Agricultural Policy decisions to be made without having recourse to artificial features, such as the so-called 'green pound'. The United Kingdom, however, still retains the reserve role of sterling, which might be difficult to reconcile in the European Monetary System.

5. Foreign exchange

Foreign exchange consists of the claims on another country held in the form of that country's currency or in interest-bearing bonds.

Factors affecting the supply of and demand for foreign exchange

(i) Changes in *tastes and income* may alter countries' supply of and demand for foreign exchange. As countries get richer, their tastes might change, partly because of the *demonstration effect*. We might expect that as UK residents become richer, they will want more consumer durables. The consumption of more consumer durables might lead to the UK trading with different countries and so alter the supply of and demand for foreign exchange.

(ii) Changes in *tariff barriers* may alter the supply of and demand for foreign exchange. If the EEC's Common External Tariff were abolished, the price of British exports to and imports from countries outside the EEC would both fall. Therefore, the UK's demand for the currencies of these countries would be expected to rise.

(iii) A reduction in *non-tariff barriers* (for example, a harmonization of regulations relating to vehicles) might be expected to have a similar effect.

(iv) A relative change in the price of one country's export prices, perhaps because of *general inflation*, can affect the demand for foreign exchange. If British prices rise relative to US prices, the demand for British goods will tend to fall and, therefore, the demand for sterling will fall. The effect would be shown diagrammatically as a movement along the demand curve (see Figure 64).

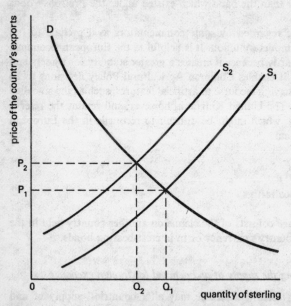

Figure 64. *The effect of general inflation on the supply of and demand for foreign exchange*

Table 34. The UK's imports by commodity, 1985 (£m)

Food, drink, tobacco	Basic materials	Fuels	Semi-manu-factures	Finished manu-factures	Other imports	Total imports
9,274	5,389	10,517	19,619	35,334	4,637	84,790

Source: Department of Trade and Industry (CSO).

6. Balance of payments accounting

A country's balance of payments compares its overseas expenditure with the income it gains from overseas. Economists usually refer to a situation where overseas expenditure exceeds overseas income as a balance of payments deficit. If overseas income exceeds overseas expenditure, there is a balance of payments surplus.

(a) *The current account*

The UK's current account shows the value of its trading in non-capital items. This trading consists of either *visible trade* or *invisible trade*.

(i) *Visible trade*

Visible trade consists of the exporting and importing of tangible goods. A high proportion of the UK's imports consists of food and raw materials. However, the value of food imports has been growing less rapidly than the value of total imports, partly because of the large-scale subsidies paid to British farmers both under the former *deficiency-payments system* and the current *Common Agricultural Policy*.

The importing of raw materials is also becoming proportionately less, while the importing of manufactured and semi-manufactured goods is becoming proportionately more important for the UK.

Oil imports to the UK have become less significant, compared to oil exports, since the exploitation of North Sea oil. In 1974 imports of oil exceeded exports by £3,357m; in 1984 exports exceeded imports by £7,136m.

Table 35. The UK's exports by commodity, 1985 (£m)

Food, drink, tobacco	Basic materials	Fuels	Semi-manu-factures	Finished manu-factures	Other exports	Total exports
4,970	2,145	16,712	18,449	30,033	5,922	78,331

Source: Department of Trade and Industry (CSO).

The composition of the UK's exports is shown in Table 35. Since the UK joined the EEC, a growing proportion of its exports has gone to EEC members and a declining proportion to Commonwealth countries.

The difference between the value of visible exports and the value of visible imports is the value of the *visible balance* or *balance of trade* (see Table 36).

There have been considerable changes in the pattern of British export trade over the years. The UK was once an important exporter of textiles and machinery; in more recent years the UK has tended to suffer visible trade deficits, but generally these have been more than compensated for by invisible trade surpluses. In 1980, 1981 and 1982, though, the UK had visible and invisible surpluses.

(ii) *Invisible trade*

Invisible trade consists of trading in services (such as banking, insurance, shipping, tourism and education and consultancy) plus profits earned overseas, dividends and interest payments.

Tourism has become an increasingly important item in invisible trade. Tourism to the UK has increased rapidly, with more and more visitors from Europe and the US. The number of British people touring overseas has also tended to increase.

Another significant trend has been the decline in the number of overseas students entering the UK for education since 1979.

The balance on current account is the sum of the visible balance and invisible balance (see Table 36). The balance of payments is usually measured as the balance on current account.

The current account is often used as a measure of a country's ability to pay. But it may not be the best measure, since, for example, a country might have an unfavourable current account, but have significant reserves.

Table 36. Summary of the UK's balance of payments, 1974-84 (£m)

	1974	1975	1976	1977	1978	1979	1980	1981	1982	1983	1984
Current account											
Visible balance	-5,351	-3,333	-3,929	-2,284	-1,542	-3,449	1,361	3,360	2,331	-835	-4,101
Invisibles											
services balance	949	1,336	2,245	3,038	3,478	3,804	4,036	4,170	3,215	3,701	3,985
interest, profits and dividends balance	1,507	890	1,557	246	827	1,188	-219	950	1,115	2,440	3,304
transfers balance	-422	-475	-786	-1,128	-1,791	-2,279	-2,078	-1,952	-1,998	-2,138	-2,253
Invisibles balance	2,034	1,751	3,016	2,156	2,514	2,713	1,739	3,168	2,332	4,003	5,036
Current balance	-3,317	-1,582	-913	-128	972	-736	3,100	6,528	4,663	3,168	935
Capital transfers	-75	—	—	—	—	—	—	—	—	—	—
Investment and other capital transactions	1,602	154	-2,977	4,169	-4,137	1,865	-1,503	-6,972	-3,199	-4,865	-3,291
Allocation of Special Drawing Rights	—	—	—	—	—	195	180	158	—	—	—
Official financing	1,646	1,465	3,629	-7,361	1,126	-1,905	-1,372	687	1,284	820	1,316
Balancing item	144	-37	261	3,320	2,039	581	-405	-401	-2,748	877	1,040

Source: The United Kingdom's Balance of Payments (The CSO Pink Book), HMSO, 1985.

(b) *The capital account*

The UK's capital account is made up of the flow of money for investment purposes between the UK and other countries, and of the flow of international grants.

The flow of investments between the UK and other EEC members should increase as the mobility of capital within the EEC improves.

(c) *Official financing and currency flow*

The currency flow represents both the outflow of currency from and the inflow of currency to the United Kingdom. An increase in the flow of currency to the UK increases the UK's foreign-currency reserves. Having a positive supply of reserves tends to be helpful to the country in question because it gives it an ability to pay for its imports. However, an increase in investment overseas (which, other things being equal, will reduce the country's reserves), while leading to a worsening of the capital account, might lead to an increase in the current account in the future.

Official financing shows how currency flow is financed.

7. Balance of payments disequilibrium

A balance of payments disequilibrium may take the form of a deficit or the form of a surplus. A payments deficit leads to a loss of reserves, while a payments surplus leads to a build-up of reserves.

(a) *How might a government attempt to correct a balance of payments deficit?*

(i) If a deficit is expected to be temporary, *borrowing from another country or from an international organization such as the IMF* may be possible. The conditions for borrowing from the IMF become more stringent when more money is borrowed.

Borrowing to finance long-term deficits is inadvisable because it can lead to debt problems.

(ii) A government might try to correct a payments deficit which is expected to be of a more long-term nature by trying to *restrict imports*, either through a series of *quotas* or through higher *tariffs*. This would, however, contravene the General Agreement on Tariffs and Trade and EEC policy. It might also limit consumer choice.

Such a policy might be successful if there were no retaliation, but is liable to be unsuccessful if higher tariffs are imposed on products with elastic demand.

(iii) Alternatively, a government might try to restrict imports through the use of *foreign-exchange controls*. In the 1960s there were limitations on the amount of sterling British tourists going abroad could take out of the country. Similar limitations have applied in other countries. Foreign-exchange controls have frequently been used by many developing countries. There is the possibility, though, of a 'black market' developing.

(iv) If a government imposes *restrictions on the flow of investments abroad*, the balance of payments may improve, but these restrictions may prove unpopular with industrialists. There might be payments problems in the future as a result of restricting investment abroad, because more investment abroad now often leads to a better balance of payments in the future.

(v) *Restrictive fiscal and/or restrictive monetary policy* might be used by the government to try to control the balance of payments by controlling the level of aggregate demand at home.

During the 1960s, '*stop-go*' *policies* were used in the UK in an attempt to control aggregate demand during boom periods and thereby reduce imports: the higher the level of aggregate demand, the higher the demand for imports is likely to be.

Attempts to control the balance of payments in this way tend to conflict with other policy objectives, particularly the attainment of full employment.

Another disadvantage of 'stop-go' policies was that they led to uncertainty, so adversely affecting investment, which, in turn, adversely affected the balance of payments in the long run.

(vi) '*Back-door*' *methods* may lead to the exclusion of some imports. For example, regulations specifically designed to curb imports may be introduced. Japan has been accused, on a number of occasions, of using such regulations. Indirect subsidies, such as 'soft' loans, may be given to help gain export orders.

(vii) Another method of trying to restrict imports might be through the use of *higher interest rates*. These will tend to attract, in particular, more 'hot' money and will therefore lead to some inflow of currency. American interest rates were high in 1985, partly for the purpose of attracting hot money. However, high interest rates discourage firms from investing (borrowing) and so may prove to be self-defeating.

(viii) A government, rather than trying to discourage imports, might try to *stimulate exports* in an attempt to improve the balance of payments. Exports might be encouraged if the government provides improved information. The provision of information in the UK might be improved through the *Export Services Branch* and the *Export Credits Guarantee Department*.

(ix) A policy of *devaluation* (in the case of a fixed exchange-rate regime), or of *allowing the exchange rate to move downwards*, will make exports cheaper and imports more expensive, other things being equal. When the demand for exports and imports is elastic, a devaluation will improve the balance of payments. This is the *Marshall–Lerner condition*.

(b) *The importance of adjusting a payments surplus*

(i) A persistent balance of payments surplus for one particular country is undesirable in the context of the world economy since *one country's surplus is another country's deficit*. A country which maintains a surplus at the expense of a trading partner might find that this partner is reluctant to import commodities from the surplus country because of its own payments difficulties.

(ii) It is possible that, in the case of the UK, for example, *a persistent surplus in the balance of oil trade in the early 1980s forced up the exchange rate and so made the UK uncompetitive in other fields.*

*

QUESTION

What were the main consequences for the UK's balance of payments of the drastic fall in the value of the pound against the dollar in late 1984?

The fall in the value of the pound meant that British firms, particularly in the car industry (which had complained bitterly during the earlier part of the 1980s about the high cost of sterling), found it easier to sell their goods abroad. On the other hand, firms which import, particularly from the USA, had to pay a much higher price in the short run. The overall effect upon the UK's balance of payments depended upon the trade taking place between the UK and the US, and the relative price elasticities of exports and imports. Figures for the UK's balance of payments for 1984 compared to 1983 show a sharp rise in the UK's visible deficit, which may be partly due to the pound's decline (see Table 36).

The British government was eager to halt the slide of the pound and get the value of the pound to rise to something like its former value against the dollar. The government therefore raised interest rates in an attempt to attract money into the UK.

This rise in interest rates was intended to reduce the likelihood of the pound declining further, but a rise in interest rates also tends to discourage investment, and this might make the balance of payments worse, leading to a further decline in the exchange rate (assuming that the exchange rate is determined by supply and demand).

MULTIPLE-CHOICE QUESTIONS

1. Devaluation is most likely to improve the balance of payments if:
   (a) the price elasticity for both imports and exports is greater than one;
   (b) the price elasticity of demand for exports is greater than one and for imports less than one;
   (c) the price elasticity of demand for exports is less than one and for imports greater than one;
   (d) the price elasticity of demand for both imports and exports is less than one.

Answer – (*a*)

2. If, as a result of negotiations, the common external tariff is reduced from 10 per cent to $7\frac{1}{2}$ per cent and the price elasticity of demand for imports is 0.5, there will be:
   (a) an increase in demand of $1\frac{1}{4}$ per cent;
   (b) an increase in demand of 15 per cent;
   (c) a decrease in demand of $1\frac{1}{4}$ per cent;
   (d) a decrease in demand of 15 per cent.

Answer – (*a*)

3. If a country has a favourable balance of trade:
   (a) the volume of goods exported is greater than the volume of goods imported;
   (b) the value of goods exported is greater than the value of goods imported;
   (c) the value of services exported is greater than the value of services imported;
   (d) there is deficit on the capital account.

Answer – (*b*)

4. The term 'dumping', when used in relation to international trade, refers to:

    (*a*) the divergence between social and private costs of pollution;

    (*b*) countries which wish to sell items below their cost of production;

    (*c*) countries which impose bureaucratic controls in order to reduce imports;

    (*d*) the imposition of tariff barriers.

Answer – (*b*)

5. If the value of the pound fell against the dollar, but maintained its value against the French franc, other things being equal:

    (*a*) more American tourists would visit Britain, but the number of French tourists would remain unchanged;

    (*b*) the number of French and American tourists visiting Britain would both increase;

    (*c*) the number of French and American tourists visiting Britain would both decrease;

    (*d*) the number of American tourists visiting Britain would decrease, but the number of French tourists would remain the same.

Answer – (*a*)

6. Which of the following measures would be least likely to reduce a UK balance of payments deficit in the short run:

    (*a*) increasing, temporarily, the minimum lending rate;

    (*b*) using back-door methods to subsidize exports;

    (*c*) encouraging British firms to invest overseas;

    (*d*) reducing the value of the pound against other currencies?

Answer – (*c*)

DATA RESPONSE

1. In 1984 there continued to be high unemployment in most Western countries. A slight growth in world trade suggested that unemployment had not grown at such a rapid level as in previous years during the 1980s. The United States' budget deficit accounted for a large part of the total increase in world exports. However, concern was expressed that, as a result of the re-election of President Reagan, the United States government might take an *orthodox, pre-Keynesian view of budget deficits*. If such a view were to be taken, this might lead to the President trying to restrict imports by, for example, increasing the price of the dollar or reducing public expenditure. The result of such action would probably be the limitation of world trade.

World trade would also be limited if protectionism increased. In recent times, European countries, in an effort to protect their own industry, have persuaded Japanese manufacturers to agree 'voluntarily' not to export more than a certain volume of goods.

Individual countries' involvement in world trade may be affected by exchange rates. The UK, for example, experienced a large increase in imports in 1984, but the declining value of the pound led to suggestions that exports would increase and imports would fall in 1985.

(a) Explain the term in *italic* type.
(b) Explain the relationship between America's budget deficit and the increase in world trade.
(c) Explain the effects of quotas imposed upon Japanese manufacturers. Illustrate your answer with supply and demand diagrams.

2. During 1984 the pound fell against the dollar. By late 1984 the value of the pound against the dollar was only about half of what it was in 1980. One might have expected the falling value of the pound to lead to increases in the flow of British exports and a fall in imports. However, US prime rates and middle rates were considerably higher than the London clearing banks' base rates. Therefore, '*hot*' *money* tended to flow to the US from the UK.

During 1981, when the exchange rate was high (the pound was worth about $2.40), many British manufacturers complained bitterly about the problems of exporting with high exchange rates. However, the same firms did not seem very much more able to export at much lower exchange rates. While some economists have suggested that exchange rates are basically self-stabilizing, this seems to be unlikely since, for the speculator, there is no one level for a currency which would be seen to be correct. This contrasts sharply with prices of many goods or services. For example, an increase in house prices would eventually be seen to lead to more houses being built and, thus, to some extent, a self-correcting mechanism might be said to exist.

It becomes difficult for importers and exporters to make decisions if the price of sterling cannot be predicted. Instability of the value of sterling, some economists believe, undermines international trade and, hence, indirectly reduces prospects for employment.

Some politicians, notably Sir Geoffrey Howe in 1981, believe that North Sea oil should be used to raise the exchange rate gently. Such a policy would help to reduce inflation and help to increase the living standard. However, the Thatcher government has not pursued such a policy.

(*a*) Explain the term in *italic* type.

(*b*) Why might exchange rates not be self-stabilizing?

(*c*) Why might the abolition of exchange controls in 1979 have led to large fluctuations in the exchange rate?

(*d*) How are exchange rates and inflation linked?

SELF-EXAMINATION QUESTIONS

1. 'Investment by British firms overseas should be discouraged as it leads to short-term losses on the capital account.' Critically discuss this statement.

2. 'Investment by Japanese companies in the United Kingdom should be encouraged as it will improve the British balance of payments.' Discuss.

3. 'The government should try to increase the number of tourists coming into the United Kingdom, since this will improve the invisible trade of the United Kingdom.' Discuss.

4. What are the arguments for and against freely floating exchange rates?

5. Does the theory of comparative advantage offer any explanation as to why the proportion of the UK's imports and exports to the EEC has grown substantially since British entry into the EEC in 1973? Explain your answer. See also Chapter 26.

6. Britain's share of world trade has fallen substantially since 1949. What are the reasons for this fall and is a further decline inevitable?

7. What is meant by the term 'comparative advantage'? How far does it explain modern international trade patterns?

8. Under what circumstances would free trade lead to the optimal allocation of resources? Why are there so many obstacles to free trade?

9. What is meant by the 'terms of trade'? How do the changing terms of trade affect countries' imports, exports and balance of payments?

10. 'For a long while during the 1960s, the pound was over-valued.' What is meant by this statement? Explain the effects of such an over-valuation.

11. What is meant by 'exchange control'? What disadvantages, if any, arose from the abolition of exchange controls by the United Kingdom in 1979?

26. International cooperation

1. The International Monetary Fund

The International Monetary Fund was set up after the *Bretton Woods Agreement* in 1944. The main aim was to avoid the problems of protectionism and competitive devaluations which had occurred during the 1930s and had contributed to the world recession.

The International Monetary Fund aimed originally at having a system of *stable exchange rates*, under which each member country had to keep the parity of its currency within relatively small bounds. However, because of problems during the 1960s this system of stable exchange rates has been virtually abandoned. Most currencies are now floating, although within the E E C the *European Monetary System* applies, whereby most E E C member states keep parity with each other. Under the original concept of stable exchange rates, devaluations or revaluations in excess of 10 per cent had to be notified to the International Monetary Fund in advance.

The Fund obtains money from its member countries partly according to each member's gross national product. If countries have difficulties with their balance of payments, they can withdraw some foreign currency in exchange for their own. The more money they borrow, the more stringent are the conditions applied. Interest payments are made on any loans from the International Monetary Fund.

Unlike national trade, where the domestic currency is accepted throughout the country, there is no international currency for use among members. However *Special Drawing Rights*, which can sometimes be obtained from the International Monetary Fund, help to overcome this difficulty of there being no single international unit of account.

2. Customs unions

Features of a customs union are that (i) there are *no restrictions on trade between member countries* and (ii) there is a *common external tariff*, i.e. duties on imports from non-members are the same, irrespective of which country they enter.

One of the earliest customs unions was the Zollverein, which was a customs union involving most of the German states when it was formed in 1933. A customs union differs from a free trade area in that members of a free trade area retain the right to fix their own, separate tariffs on imports from the rest of the world.

3. The European Economic Community

The EEC consists of twelve member states: the six original members are West Germany, France, Belgium, Luxembourg, the Netherlands and Italy; Britain, Eire and Denmark joined in 1973; Greece joined in 1981; Spain and Portugal joined on 1 January 1986. The EEC is a customs union, but it is more than just a customs union because *its aims go beyond mere liberalization of trade.* The Single European Act, 1985, commits the member countries to create an 'area without frontiers' by 1992, with free movement of goods, persons, services and capital.

(a) *Aims and policies of the EEC*

(i) *Competition policy*

The EEC does not rule out the possibility of giving state aid to companies, but will only allow it if market conditions hinder progress towards certain economic or social objectives, or if market conditions only allow these objectives to be attained with unacceptable repercussions. The EEC would also allow state aid if intensified competition would be self-destructing. Therefore, aid for production should not be permitted except if it is part of a reorganization programme or of a rescue measure permitting a breathing space. In general, state aid should not expand capacity.

The EEC has sometimes been concerned that research and development costs are borne entirely by the domestic consumers of the nationalized industries, with the result that goods or services should be sold overseas at artificially reduced prices.

The EEC policy towards restrictive practices was laid down by Article 85 of the *Treaty of Rome.* This states, 'Agreements between undertakings or decisions by associations of undertakings and concerted practices which may affect trade between member states and which have as their object prevention, restriction or distortion of competition within the Common Market shall be regarded as incompatible with EEC rules.'

The EEC is eager to limit price-fixing by firms seeking competitive advantages. There have also been moves towards uniform regulations regarding competition in an attempt to make sure that firms do not impose their own restrictions to prevent imports.

(ii) *The mobility of labour*

The EEC aims to achieve the mobility of labour, i.e. it wants people to be able to take a job in any other member state without needing a work permit. There are, however, some barriers to complete mobility of labour. For example, some jobs in public administration may be confined to nationals. There are also obstacles such as language and national prejudices. If complete mobility of labour is to become a reality for professional people in the long run, there must be some harmonization of professional qualifications.

(iii) *The mobility of capital*

The EEC aims to remove all real obstacles to medium-term and long-term movements of funds between member states. The UK has abolished the majority of its foreign-exchange controls since joining the EEC.

In the longer term, we might expect British financial institutions, such as building societies, to wish to enter other members' national markets. Similarly, we might soon find that other members' commercial banks wish to expand their lending into the UK. Such moves could well pose problems for any country which is trying to impose a unilateral restrictive monetary policy.

(iv) *Regional policy*

The EEC's *Common Regional Policy* aims to help regions of high unemployment. However, relatively little has been done about regional policy, partly because of budgetary constraints. Yet a number of grants have been given to firms to set up in regions which have been affected by the closure of steel plants and coal pits, etc.

(v) *Transport policy*

The EEC also has a *Common Transport Policy*, without which some firms might gain hidden advantages over others. While progress towards harmonization of transport systems has been slow, there has been harmonization of restrictions on drivers' hours throughout the EEC for all road haulage vehicles over three and a half tons. Tachographs have also been introduced, mainly for reasons of safety. (Tachographs record speed, distance and time of driving.)

At the present time, road haulage companies cannot carry goods solely within a foreign country. For example, while British firms can transport goods from France to the United Kingdom they cannot transport goods solely within France. There are a number of bilateral agreements between countries about the number of overseas vehicles which can carry goods within their countries. In the longer term we would expect to see a system of multilateral agreements, so that road haulage firms can compete on the same basis as other firms.

During the 1980s, the EEC has been discussing the possibility of cheaper air fares, since that would encourage more trade between EEC member states.

(vi) *The harmonization of taxation*

Unless there is some harmonization of taxation, particularly value added tax, there might be a number of hidden barriers to trade. For example, Britain has, in the past, imposed a much higher rate of taxation upon wine, which is generally imported, than upon beer, which is generally home-produced. This has been held to distort trade between the member states. In the long term there should be harmonization of tax rates, at least upon fuel and alcohol. There are currently no proposals for harmonizing income tax.

(vii) *The Common Agricultural Policy*

One of the most controversial aspects of the EEC has been the *Common Agricultural Policy* (*CAP*). Although one of the most important aims of the EEC is the liberalization of trade between the member states, CAP provides a system of protection for EEC agriculture, in order to prevent the closure of uneconomic farms. Originally, the Common Agricultural Policy was expected to restrict trade less than the individual national protection schemes had done, but in fact it has led to more, rather than less, protection.

It is felt that some degree of protection for agriculture will:

1. *increase efficiency by providing a better flow of agricultural products and by increasing specialization*;
2. *eliminate price variability*;
3. *encourage self-sufficiency and protect members' balance of payments*.

CAP uses a system of setting *bureaucratic prices* for various agricultural products in an attempt to keep the price of, say, grain fairly stable. The equilibrium price of EEC-produced grain tends to be well above the world price, mainly because of higher costs of production. This means that, in the absence of a very high tariff on imports of grain from non-member countries, consumers within the EEC would buy foreign grain rather than EEC-produced grain.

Using Figure 65, we assume that the EEC aims to keep the price of EEC grain at P_2, the bureaucratic or *intervention price*. If the world price is P_1, at this price EEC producers would only supply an output Q_{S1} while consumers in the EEC would demand Q_{D1}. For this demand

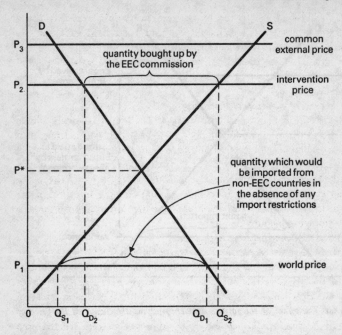

Figure 65. *The effect of the CAP on the price of grain*

to be satisfied there must be some imports of non-EEC grain. However, a common external tariff which pushes the price of non-EEC grain to P_3 (above the intervention price) discourages any consumption of non-EEC grain. This makes it possible for the EEC to force the price of its grain up to P_2. This is the price consumers in the EEC must pay, since there are no imports flooding the market to force the price down.

Since the intervention price is P_2, this encourages EEC farmers to produce an output Q_{S2}. Given that this price is above the equilibrium price (P^*), this leads to excess supply. The EEC, though, buys up any excess stocks at price P_2. These stocks are released at times when the equilibrium price is higher than the intervention price (P_2). Since, in the case of grain, the intervention price tends to be way above the equilibrium price, it is unlikely that any shifts in demand and/or supply will be sufficient to force the EEC to release any stocks. The prices of many agricultural products tend to be kept artificially high nearly all the time, so that a great deal of produce is wasted. This aspect of CAP has been criticized on moral grounds.

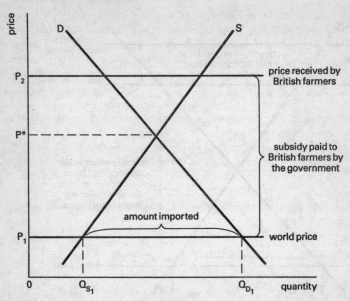

Figure 66. *The effect of the former deficiency-payments scheme on the price of grain*

The effect of CAP differs from the effect of the former British *deficiency payments system*, which made up the gap between the price the government was willing to pay to farmers for an agricultural product such as grain and the world price. Unlike CAP, the deficiency payments system was a cheap food policy.

Working from Figure 66, if the government wished farmers to receive price P_2 for each unit of grain supplied, while the world price was P_1, under the deficiency-payments system consumers only paid price P_1. British farmers received price P_2, while supplying an output of only Q_{S1}. Since the price paid by consumers was P_1, they demanded an output of Q_{D1}, which meant that grain had to be imported in order to satisfy this demand.

(vii) *European monetary union*

In the long term, the EEC aims to provide an economic and monetary union. Such a union might involve the use of a common currency circulating throughout the EEC. However, the introduction of a common currency seems an unlikely development. A more likely concept is that currencies will be linked very strongly with each other.

To some extent, the *European Monetary System*, to which most member states (although, most significantly, not the UK at the time of writing) belong, reduces fluctuations in exchange rates between members. This, in turn, helps to increase the volume of trade.

(b) *The European Parliament*

Members of the European Parliament are elected by the electorate of member countries.

A large part (about 70 per cent in 1984) of the *European Parliament's Budget* is devoted to agriculture. Expenditure is limited by the fact that the main source of revenue is from a fixed percentage of value added tax. The majority of countries within the EEC would like to see the European Budget expanded, but so far the UK has been against such a development.

4. Cooperation with the Third World

(a) *Identifying the Third World countries*

The term '*Third World*' is often used to denote underdeveloped or poor countries. It is difficult to give an exact definition of an underdeveloped country. To some extent, the level of development may be gauged by looking at the *gross national product* of a country and dividing the figure by the figure for the country's population. *The degree of literacy* and *the percentage of the population living below a particular income level* may also be regarded as giving some idea as to the degree of development a particular country has experienced (see Chapter 21).

In many developing countries, the subsistence sector is the most common sector. Therefore, accurate figures for GNP may be difficult to obtain. Changes in exchange rates and the fact that the exchange rate often does not reflect purchasing power accurately further reduce the reliability of statistics. Nevertheless, it is easy to recognize many of the poorest countries of the world. India, Pakistan, Bangladesh and Ethiopia are obvious examples of countries experiencing very acute problems of poverty. Awareness of the problems of underdeveloped countries tended to increase after the vast majority of those countries obtained their independence from former colonial powers such as the UK, France and the Netherlands.

(b) *Problems for Third World countries*

(i) *The rapid growth in population* in many of the Third World countries has caused alarm. Rapid population growth is not totally due to a rising birth rate; improved hygiene and medical care mean that people are now tending to live longer in these countries. However, life expectancy of many people within the Third World is still very low compared to life expectancy in the developed world.

The high birth rate in the Third World may be regarded, to some extent, as a symptom of the problems of poverty rather than the cause. Given the absence of a welfare state and fairly high mortality rates, many people wish to have large families to guarantee that they will be maintained in their old age. A decline in the birth rate would probably be helpful to nearly all Third World countries. Some countries, notably India and China, have adopted fairly ruthless measures to reduce their birth rates.

(ii) Britain's Industrial Revolution was made possible largely because vast increases in agricultural productivity meant that surpluses were produced which could be invested in industry. It is less easy for Third World countries to 'take off' in this way because, in many cases, industry is in the hands of a few multinational companies and there are often widespread barriers hindering these countries from exporting. Thus, *any agricultural surpluses produced in Third World countries will not necessarily go to industries over which they have control.*

(iii) While theories of comparative advantage might indicate that most Third World countries should specialize in labour-intensive industries, such as agriculture, there are many problems. For example, the supply of agricultural products is very erratic, leading to violent price fluctuations. Thus, *it is very difficult for countries specializing in agriculture to plan for development with any degree of confidence.* Furthermore, since the demand for these products tends to be very price inelastic, when the price is very low, total revenue will be very low, because a fall in price does not lead to a particularly large rise in demand. As productivity in agriculture increases, real income falls because fewer people are required to work in the sector, leading to increased unemployment.

(iv) Some developing countries, for example Zambia, *rely heavily on a few minerals.* Minerals are susceptible to wide price fluctuations. The price of copper, for example, has fluctuated widely in recent years.

The price of oil was for a long time very low. However, the formation of O P E C by the main oil-producing countries increased their bargaining power, and they were able to raise prices substantially in 1973. This raised the revenue from oil for these countries significantly, because the demand for oil is relatively price inelastic.

(v) Another common characteristic of Third World countries is *rapidly increasing urbanization*, partly caused by *urban drift*. While *unemployment is rife in most urban areas of the Third World*, job prospects nevertheless tend to be slightly higher there than in the rural areas.

(vi) Developing countries also suffer *inadequate social infrastructures*. Many underdeveloped countries are disadvantaged because *the workforce is poorly educated*. The standard of education is not assisted by the fact that teaching is often regarded as a low-status job, and so teachers' incomes are often low. Many Third World countries, particularly in Africa, also have *poor transport sectors*. The relatively low density of population makes it very difficult to build up adequate transport sectors in many countries. An illustration of the sort of problem which results from an inadequate transport sector is the fact that in some African countries the second milk yield of the day is wasted because it cannot be transported.

(c) *How can the developed countries help?*

(i) *Loans* from developed countries do not necessarily help the plight of Third World countries, largely because of the very high interest payments demanded. Many Third World countries, particularly in South America, are experiencing very severe debt problems, which threaten banking crises.

(ii) Perhaps the best way developed countries can help the Third World is by providing *aid*. However, there may be political and economic motives behind any aid given, rather than just moral motives. Often the aid is tied, directed towards projects which the recipient country does not necessarily require. One of the failures of aid in the past has been that governments of developed countries have often been enthusiastic about massive, prestigious aid projects which require skilled labour from developed countries but do little to reduce unemployment in the developing countries. Aid may be given on condition that it is used for a specific purpose which benefits the country providing the aid. The developed country in question might, for example, direct aid to building a road whereby one of its own construction firms, which would otherwise be inactive, is contracted to build the road and so given a financial lifeline. In particular, aid directed towards capital-intensive projects are often inappropriate for the Third World, since they tend not to ease the problem of unemployment very much.

Especially in the case of famines (such as the famine in Ethiopia which received so much mass media coverage in late 1984), the need is often for food. Many politicians suggest that the surpluses generated by the Common Agricultural Policy should be given to help ease the problem of starvation. If the stocks would otherwise be destroyed, the opportunity costs to the EEC of the food would be very small, though transport costs might be high.

The problems faced by the Third World would be eased if there were less selfishness on the part of the developed countries. So often the level of aid given by governments from developed countries is determined by their own fiscal and monetary policies.

Aid is required to deal with crises and to prevent the recurrence of crises like the African famine.

Cooperation between developing countries as a means of improving their economic prospects is discussed in Question 2, pp. 450–52.

5. The Brandt Report

The *Brandt Report* was published in the late 1970s. It looked at the record of development in the Third World and tried to understand the reasons for the widening gap between 'the North' and 'the South'. It also examined the prospects for the world economy, looking at likely population growth, resource allocation, expenditure on armaments and the role of economic institutions such as the International Monetary Fund, the World Bank and regional banks.

The Brandt Commission was chaired by the former German Chancellor, Willy Brandt, and included Edward Heath, the former British Prime Minister, among its members.

(a) *Findings of the Brandt Report*

(i) The Report highlighted *the effects and opportunity costs of military expenditure*, pointing out, for example, that the world's military expenditure for half a day could finance a whole malaria eradication programme for the World Health Organization.

(ii) The Report also suggested that *it was in the interest of developed countries to help the developing countries to become more wealthy*, in that it has been recognized within most countries that higher wages for the workers increase purchasing power and increase the developing countries' demand for commodities produced by the developed countries.

However, the Report, while acknowledging the mutual interest of increasing trade between developed and developing countries, said that conflicts did exist and that there was a great deal of protectionism.

(iii) *Developed countries tend to have generated systems of preferences* which allow duty-free imports of manufactures from some developing countries (a trend noted by the Report).

(iv) According to the Report, *we should be moving away from aid and towards independence*, i.e. trying to help developing countries pay their own way.

(v) There is a need, according to the Report, to look at the problem of unemployment in both 'the South' and 'the North'. It pointed out that *unemployment was a great scourge in both developed and developing countries*. Unemployment was blamed partly upon the failure of the world economy to grow substantially in the 1970s. *Slow growth in Europe meant that European countries had little desire to trade with developing countries, leading to a slowing down of growth in the Third World.*

(vi) *The need for elementary provisions, such as clean water*, was made clear by the Report. It pointed out that in developing countries, between about 20 and 25 million children per year die before the age of five, with a third of the deaths attributable to polluted water. A need for *basic housing* and *education* was also pointed out.

(vii) The Report noted *the development of NICs* (*newly industrialized countries*). It said that those in south-east Asia, such as Korea, Hong Kong, Malaysia, Singapore and Thailand, had had particularly high growth rates.

*

QUESTIONS

1. Discuss the economic arguments for and against British withdrawal from membership of the European Economic Community.

One needs to consider the effect upon the balance of payments that British withdrawal from the EEC would probably have. If tariffs were not imposed upon British goods entering the EEC, we might expect there to be relatively little impact upon the balance of payments. If, however, tariffs were imposed, the UK might retaliate. The resulting effect upon the balance of payments would depend upon the price elasticity of both imports and exports. Since the UK exports to the EEC goods and services which are fairly similar to those it imports from other members, we might expect relatively little change, except the imposition of a common external tariff of about 5 per cent.

We need to consider the effect that CAP has upon the UK. If the UK withdrew from the EEC, would we return to a deficiency payments scheme? If we did, there might be relatively little effect upon the agricultural prices received by farmers. (Consumers would experience greater fluctuations in prices.)

If the UK has benefited from greater economies of scale as a result of membership of the EEC, these benefits may well be lost by withdrawing from the EEC. There might be less project coordination between the UK and other European countries. However, the harmonization of regulations in some cases may have been a hindrance to the UK rather than an advantage. There has been relatively little harmonization of taxes. British withdrawal would mean the UK losing some regional project aid and the mobility of capital and labour being restricted.

The control of multinationals would be more difficult for a British government without the cooperation of other European governments, but the control of national monopolies would probably be little affected by any decision to withdraw from the EEC.

Policies such as the Common Fisheries Policy would have to be re-negotiated if the UK were to withdraw.

There would seem to be little point to the UK withdrawing from the EEC unless it were to embark on a radically different policy. One alternative to the UK being in the EEC would be to form some sort of trade agreement either with the Commonwealth or with the USA, which would involve higher transport costs and, therefore, probably higher prices. Prior to the UK joining the EEC, the UK was in EFTA; it would be difficult to reform such a trade agreement since many of the original members of EFTA are now in the EEC.

The UK might decide to withdraw from the EEC in order to become a 'siege economy' and impose high tariffs on various imports in an attempt to reduce unemployment. It is unlikely that such action would be successful if there was retaliation.

It is difficult to assess the economic advantages and disadvantages of the UK withdrawing from the EEC, because the policy which the UK would pursue instead would very much depend upon politics. What we can say is that it would be virtually impossible for the UK to return to the patterns of trading which existed prior to its entry into the EEC.

2. In what ways might developing countries cooperate in order to improve their economic prospects? Evaluate the likely success of such methods.

One possible method of cooperation is through the formation of a cartel, particularly for primary products. Producers could then adopt the traditional methods of restricting output in order to be able to increase price. This was done fairly successfully by OPEC in 1973. If the price of agricultural products was pushed up as the result of the formation of a cartel, countries not at present specializing in such items might decide to do so.

The formation of a cartel is likely to cause problems. For example, there would need to be agreement on quotas. However, some countries, particularly those with large-scale balance of payments or other problems might be tempted to produce beyond their quotas, either openly or secretly. Low-cost producers would have very strong incentives to go beyond their quotas.

Cartels would tend to be more successful if the demand for the products concerned were price inelastic rather than price elastic. The demand for oil has tended to be price inelastic, but the demand for many agricultural products from developing countries has tended to be less price inelastic as the price moves upwards.

Cooperation can exist in manufacturing. For example, in the textile industry there are multi-fibre agreements. However, many developed countries have their own textile industries and are reluctant to import textiles from developing countries, especially where importing is likely to increase unemployment in the developed country.

Developing countries might be able to reduce their balance of payments problems through collective agreements. For example, UNCTAD suggested a 40:40:20 role for liner conferences (scheduled shipping), whereby 40 per cent of the trade between two countries could take place in the importing country, 40 per cent in the exporting country and 20 per cent of trade would be left to so-called 'cross-traders'. This action was suggested partly because developed countries, in both Western and Eastern Europe, tended to have a large part of the total shipping market. Such a move would, however, be against the principles of free trade and specialization, and would possibly lead to higher charges. Such a move, therefore, would not be in the interest of potential individual importers and exporters, though it could be beneficial to developing countries as a whole. However, some of the poorest landlocked countries might have to pay higher charges without any offsetting benefits.

Developing countries could try to develop joint projects. The 'Tan-Zam' railway was the result of a joint project, built partly to reduce the cost of transportation of exports from and imports to the the landlocked country of Zambia. The problem with such projects is that capital supplies tend to be very limited. In some cases, the instability of regimes means that there is little likelihood of the creation of an integrated social infrastructure between countries. The East African Federation split up in the 1970s partly because of political instability.

Cooperation would tend to be improved by the creation of institutions comparable to the EEC. The West African states belong to ECOWAS, for example. Such cooperation might lead to economies of scale, particularly for small countries. However, such institutions take a long time to develop and political differences may hinder progress.

There may be benefits to developing countries from forming collective agreements with existing large-scale markets in the developed world. They might try, for example, to become associate members of the EEC.

MULTIPLE-CHOICE QUESTIONS

1–4. The following questions refer to Figure 67.
1. If EEC farmers produce an output of 8 units of grain, what price would they expect to receive for each unit of grain?
(a) £2.
(b) £4.

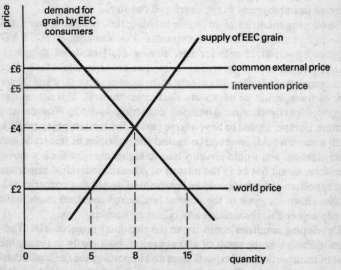

Figure 67. *The CAP and the price and quantity of grain*

(c) £5.

(d) £6.

Answer – (c)

2. Given this same output (i.e. 8 units) how much do EEC consumers pay for EEC grain?

(a) £2.

(b) £4.

(c) £5.

(d) £6.

Answer – (c)

3. If the EEC imposed no intervention price and no common external tariff on imports of non-EEC grain, how much non-EEC grain would be imported?

(a) 3 units.

(b) 7 units.

(c) 10 units.

(d) 15 units.

Answer – (c)

4. In Figure 67 what is the value of the tariff placed upon non-EEC imports of grain?

(a) £2.

(b) £3.

(c) £4.

(d) £5.

(e) £6.

Answer – (c)

DATA RESPONSE

1. The EEC Commission believes that there should be efforts to harmonize national taxation and domestic energy prices, since otherwise there will be distortions of trade between member states and of energy consumption within states. Therefore, consumer oil prices, which are largely dominated by taxation, should reflect increases in world prices.

Changes in coal prices have reflected market conditions, but EEC production costs are well above world costs and, therefore, subsidies have often been introduced to keep the price to consumers, and particularly to industry, down. For gas, conditions vary between a free market in Germany and a nationalized system in France. Electricity prices are generally either directly or informally controlled by governments. The Commission has argued that the question of harmonization of oil prices requires separate consideration. It has been suggested that the taxation burden, regarding taxation of oil, should be shifted from light to heavier products. The harmonization of energy prices is important if there is to be a genuine common market among the EEC members because expenditure on oil represented, in 1980, about 10 per cent of EEC members' gross domestic product and a quarter of total imports.

(a) Why might energy prices have fallen below their 'true' levels? What does the Commission mean by the 'true' level?

(b) Why does the EEC have different policies towards coal and agriculture?

(c) How, if at all, has the privatization of British Gas affected possible harmonization of energy policy in the EEC?

2. In 1984, as in previous years, the British Prime Minister was very concerned that Britain, which had an income which was about 7 per cent less than that of the EEC as a whole, was a net contributor to rather than a net benefactor from EEC funds. Some economists suggested that on equity grounds this should not be allowed. There would seem to be a need, if Britain and the rest of the EEC are to develop full-scale economic and monetary union, for there to be some distributive process whereby funds would flow from the rich to the poor rather than from the poor to the rich. One way of redistributing income might be to have policies benefiting the poorer members rather than the richer members. In order that policies should benefit the poorer members rather than the richer members, a strengthening of the EEC's regional policy may be required. Several studies have shown that most regions of the UK have incomes below the level of income for the EEC as a whole. A stronger regional policy would have the effect of redistributing income, but would seem not to be in line with general Conservative thinking, which has tended to regard regional policy with disfavour.

The Common Agricultural Policy has, somewhat paradoxically, helped the richer members, notably France, more than the poorer members. Thus, reducing the proportion of money spent on CAP would tend to lead to a more favourable redistribution of income. However, Italy, also one of the EEC's poorer members, does benefit from CAP.

The effects of the Common Agricultural Policy may be greater than is generally realized since, apart from the foreign-exchange costs of paying subsidies, the British consumer has sometimes paid more through paying the CAP prices than through paying the free-market prices. This, however, is not necessarily true in the longer run since there have been periods when EEC prices have been lower than free-market prices. The Thatcher government wishes to see freer trade in goods and services than is allowed by CAP, on the premise that free competition leads to the optimal allocation of resources. Some of the other governments, notably the French government, want, on the other hand, more interventionist measures to increase economic growth by reflating all member economies. With such disagreement, there is the possibility of '*beggar-my-neighbour*' policies. It is difficult to separate the political and economic aspects when looking at the EEC. It might well have helped if Britain had joined the European Monetary System, as Italy did, in the late 1970s.

(*a*) Explain the term in *italics*.
(*b*) What problems are involved in defining which regions within the EEC have a lower than average income?
(*c*) What would be the advantage of freer trade in goods and services to the EEC members? What would be the disadvantages?
(*d*) Explain how a free-trade policy in agriculture might be more beneficial to EEC members than the Common Agricultural Policy?

3. Unlike national budgets, where deficits or surpluses can occur, the EEC's budget must balance, i.e. revenue must equal expenditure. Another odd feature of the EEC's budget is that most of the revenue comes from a percentage of VAT. A further odd feature is that as much as 70 per cent of the EEC's budget is spent on agriculture, and relatively little is spent on regional and social aid.

While there has been a lot of controversy about the various contributions of members to the budget in the early 1980s, most countries' contributions amount to only about $\frac{1}{2}$ per cent of their gross national product.

(*a*) What is the effect of having a budget where expenditure always equals revenue? What are the advantages and disadvantages of such a system?
(*b*) Explain what one would normally expect a government to do about high unemployment. How far is this possible with the EEC system of budgeting?
(*c*) In late 1984 and early 1985 there was a debate in Britain and elsewhere about whether some money should be spent on regional policy, possibly at the expense of money spent on the Common Agricultural Policy. What would be the benefits and disbenefits of such a move?

1. In the EEC, most migration has taken place from Italy to West Germany. What might be the underlying reasons for this?

2. Many people suggested that when Britain joined the EEC there might be the problem of the so-called 'Golden Triangle' of northern France, south-east England and West Germany forming attractive areas for industry at the centre of the market at the expense of other areas. How far have these worries been proved to be justified?

3. What factors might deter British firms from trying to locate in other parts of the EEC?

4. Why might harmonization of regulations lead to an increase in trade? What disadvantages might there be as a result of the harmonization of regulations?

5. The EEC has often aimed at self-sufficiency in agriculture. What are the economic consequences of this to (a) EEC members; (b) non-members?

6. It has sometimes been suggested that membership of the EEC will lead to greater economies of scale in certain products, such as in aircraft and computers. How far is this suggestion correct?

7. In May 1985 the British government, among others, tried to persuade the Japanese government to remove some of its non-tariff barriers to imports. What is meant by the term 'non-tariff barriers' and why are they so important?

8. Most of the members of the EEC belong to the European Monetary System, which means that exchange rates can only fluctuate between member states within a relatively narrow band. What are the advantages and disadvantages of such a system for (a) intra-EEC trade; (b) trade between members and non-members?

9. Why have some companies manufactured cars under licence in other countries? What are the economic consequences of such practices?

10. Why was the International Monetary Fund set up? What were its original aims and how far has it been successful in achieving them?

Index

457

FOR THE BEST IN PAPERBACKS, LOOK FOR THE 🐧

In every corner of the world, on every subject under the sun, Penguin represents quality and variety – the very best in publishing today.

For complete information about books available from Penguin – including Pelicans, Puffins, Peregrines and Penguin Classics – and how to order them, write to us at the appropriate address below. Please note that for copyright reasons the selection of books varies from country to country.

In the United Kingdom: Please write to *Dept E.P., Penguin Books Ltd, Harmondsworth, Middlesex, UB7 0DA*

In the United States: Please write to *Dept BA, Penguin, 299 Murray Hill Parkway, East Rutherford, New Jersey 07073*

In Canada: Please write to *Penguin Books Canada Ltd, 2801 John Street, Markham, Ontario L3R 1B4*

In Australia: Please write to the *Marketing Department, Penguin Books Australia Ltd, P.O. Box 257, Ringwood, Victoria 3134*

In New Zealand: Please write to the *Marketing Department, Penguin Books (NZ) Ltd, Private Bag, Takapuna, Auckland 9*

In India: Please write to *Penguin Overseas Ltd, 706 Eros Apartments, 56 Nehru Place, New Delhi, 110019*

In Holland: Please write to *Penguin Books Nederland B.V., Postbus 195, NL–1380AD Weesp, Netherlands*

In Germany: Please write to *Penguin Books Ltd, Friedrichstrasse 10–12, D–6000 Frankfurt Main 1, Federal Republic of Germany*

In Spain: Please write to *Longman Penguin España, Calle San Nicolas 15, E–28013 Madrid, Spain*

In France: Please write to *Penguin Books Ltd, 39 Rue de Montmorency, F-75003, Paris, France*

In Japan: Please write to *Longman Penguin Japan Co Ltd, Yamaguchi Building, 2-12-9 Kanda Jimbocho, Chiyoda-Ku, Tokyo 101, Japan*

FOR THE BEST IN PAPERBACKS, LOOK FOR THE 🐧

PENGUIN MASTERSTUDIES

This comprehensive list, designed for advanced level and first-year under-graduate studies, includes:

SUBJECTS
Applied Mathematics
Biology
Drama: Text into Performance
Geography
Pure Mathematics

LITERATURE
Absalom and Achitophel
Barchester Towers
Dr Faustus
Eugenie Grandet
Gulliver's Travels
Joseph Andrews
The Mill on the Floss
A Passage to India
Persuasion *and* Emma
Portrait of a Lady
Tender in the Night
Vanity Fair

CHAUCER
The Knight's Tale
The Pardoner's Tale
The Prologue to the Canterbury Tales
A Chaucer Handbook

SHAKESPEARE
Hamlet
Measure for Measure
Much Ado About Nothing
A Shakespeare Handbook

FOR THE BEST IN PAPERBACKS, LOOK FOR THE

PENGUIN CRITICAL STUDIES

Described by *The Times Educational Supplement* as 'admirable' and 'superb', Penguin Critical Studies is a specially developed series of critical essays on the major works of literature for use by students in universities, colleges and schools.

Titles published or in preparation:

Antony and Cleopatra	Kenneth Muir
As You Like It	Peter Reynolds
The Great Gatsby	Kathleen Parkinson
Jane Eyre	Susie Campbell
Mansfield Park	Isobel Armstrong
Return of the Native	J. Garver
Rosenkrantz and Guildenstern are Dead	Roger Sales
Shakespeare's History Plays	C. W. R. D. Moseley
The Tempest	Sandra Clark
Tennyson	Roger Ebbatson
A Winter's Tale	Christopher Hardman
The Miller's Tale	John Cunningham
The Waste Land	Stephen Coote
The Nun's Priest's Tale	Stephen Coote
King Lear	Kenneth Muir
Othello	Gāmini and Fenella Salgādo

FOR THE BEST IN PAPERBACKS, LOOK FOR THE 🐧

PENGUIN SELF-STARTERS

Self-Starters is a new series designed to help you develop skills and proficiency in the subject of your choice. Each book has been written by an expert and is suitable for school-leavers, students, those considering changing their career in mid-stream and all those who study at home.

Titles published or in preparation:

Accounting	Noel Trimming
Advertising	Michael Pollard
Basic Statistics	Peter Gwilliam
A Career in Banking	Sheila Black, John Brennan
Clear English	Chris Magness
French	Anne Stevens
German	Anna Nyburg
Good Business Communication	Doris Wheatley
Marketing	Marsaili Cameron, Angela Rushton, David Carson
Nursing	David White
Personnel Management	J. D. Preston
Public Relations	Sheila Black, John Brennan
Public Speaking	Vivian Summers
Retailing	David Couch
Secretarial Skills	Gale Cornish, Charlotte Coudrille, Joan Lipkin-Edwardes
Starting a Business on a Shoestring	Michel Syrett, Chris Dunn
Understanding Data	Peter Sprent

FOR THE BEST IN PAPERBACKS, LOOK FOR THE

PENGUIN DICTIONARIES

Archaeology

Architecture

Art and Artists

Biology

Botany

Building

Business

Commerce

Computers

Curious and Interesting
Words

Curious and Interesting
Numbers

Decorative Arts

Design and Designers

Economics

English and European
History

English Idioms

Fairies

French

Geography

Geology

Historical Slang

Italian

Literary Terms

Microprocessors

Modern History 1789–1945

Modern Quotations

Physical Geography

Physics

Political Quotations

Proverbs

Psychology

Quotations

Religions

Rhyming Dictionary

Saints

Sociology

Telecommunications

The Theatre

Troublesome Words

Twentieth Century History